Plate Tectonics ™

An Illustrated Memoir
Margaux Motin

Translation **Edward Gauvin**
Letters **AndWorld Design**

Published by
ARCHAIA ™
Los Angeles, California

Cover by **Margaux Motin**

ENGLISH EDITION
Designer **Scott Newman**
with **Kara Leopard** and **Chelsea Roberts**
Editor **Sierra Hahn**
Assistant Editor **Gwen Waller**

ARCHAIA™

PLATE TECTONICS, December 2019. Published by Archaia, a division of Boom Entertainment, Inc. Originally published in French under the following title: La Technique des plaques by Margaux Motin © Editions Delcourt – 2013. All rights reserved. Used under license. Archaia™ and the Archaia logo are trademarks of Boom Entertainment, Inc., registered in various countries and categories. All characters, events, and institutions depicted herein are fictional. Any similarity between any of the names, characters, persons, events, and/or institutions in this publication to actual names, characters, and persons, whether living or dead, events, and/or institutions is unintended and purely coincidental.

BOOM! Studios, 5670 Wilshire Boulevard, Suite 400, Los Angeles, CA 90036-5679.
Printed in China. First Printing.

ISBN: 978-1-68415-345-9 , eISBN: 978-1-64144-304-3

Originally published in French by Delcourt.

"Life is what happens to you while you're busy making other plans."

John Lennon

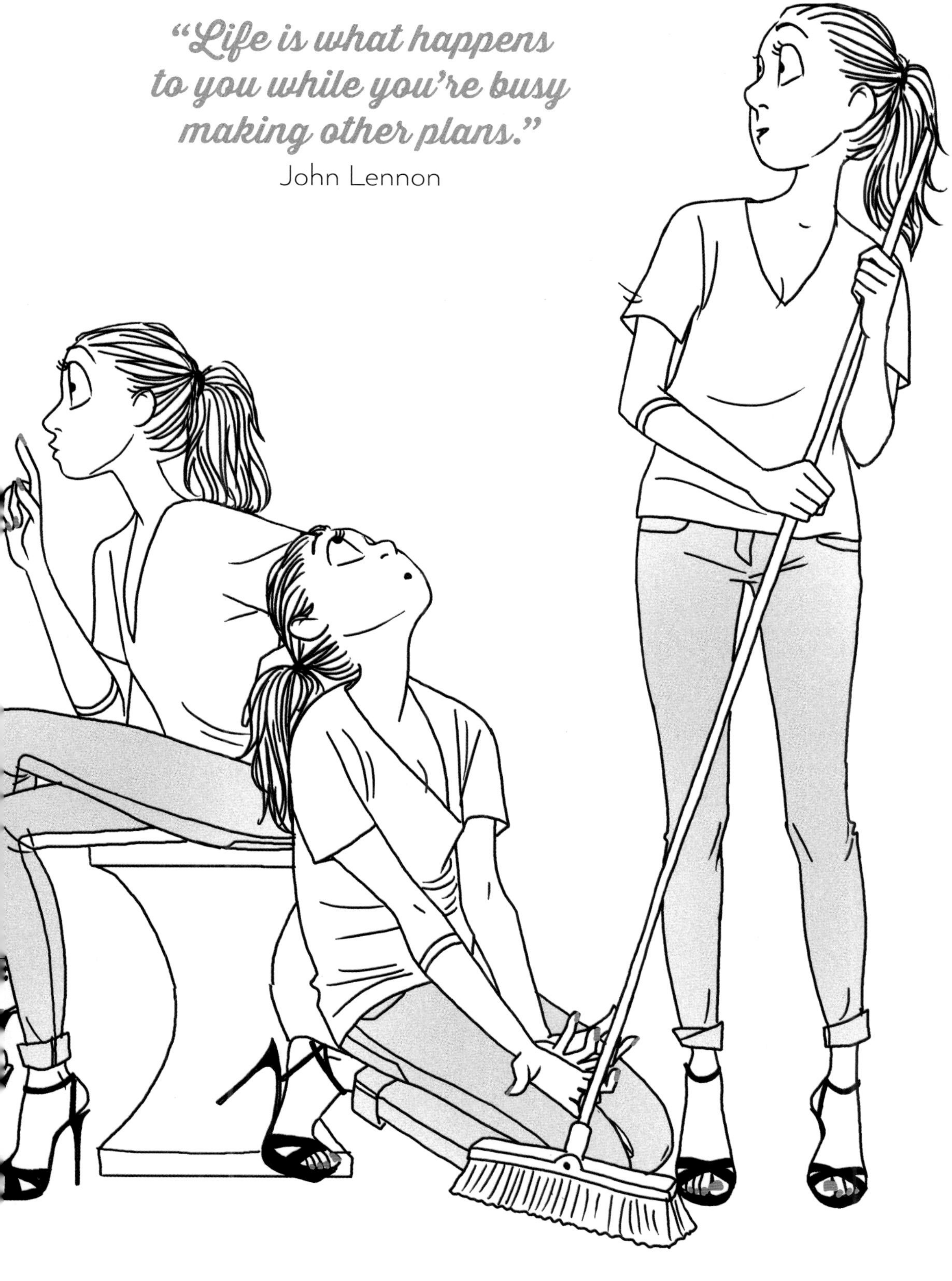

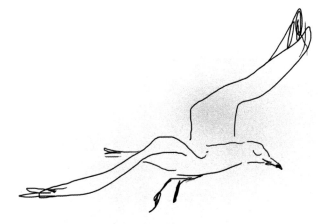

Before

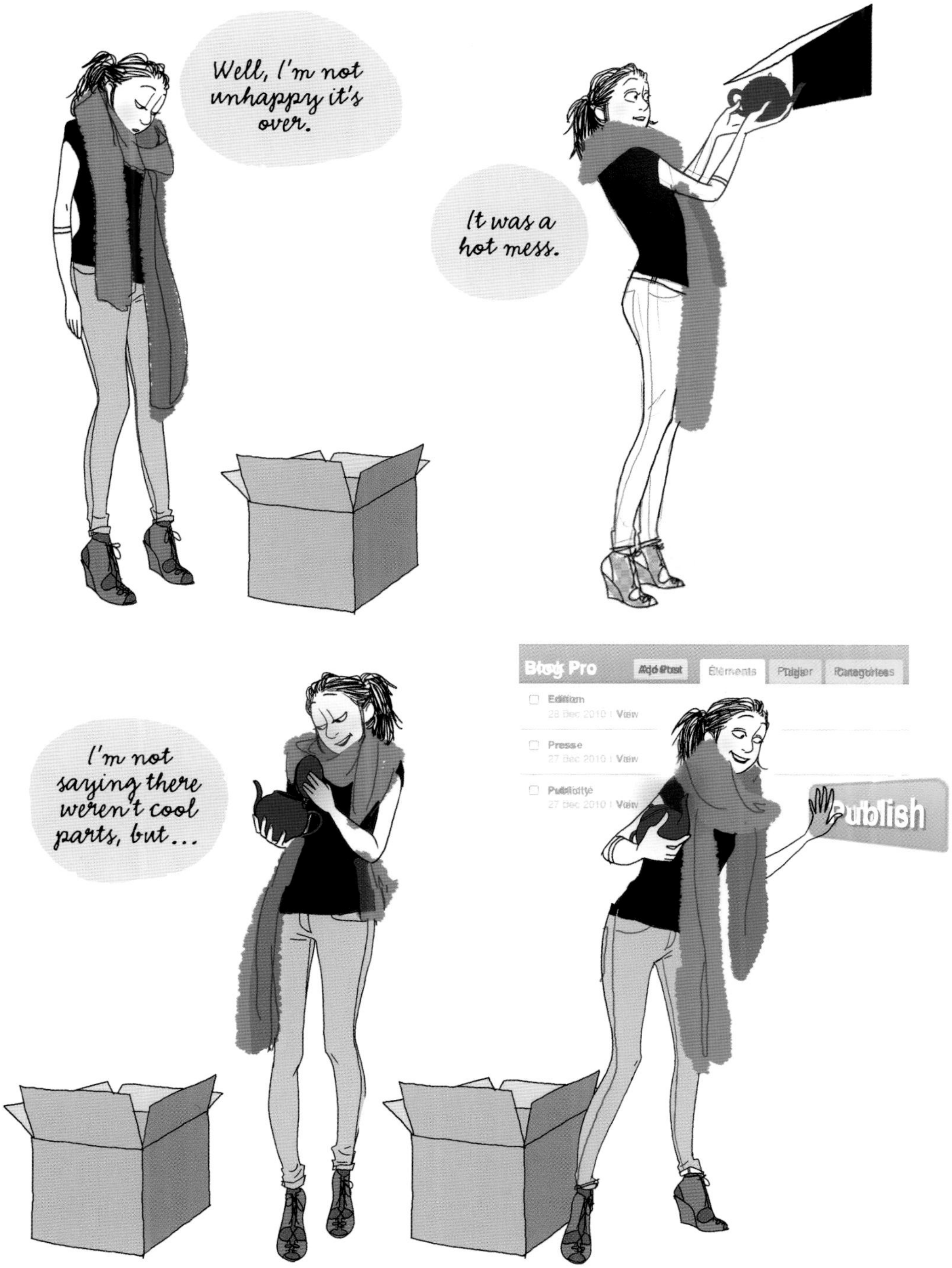
Well, I'm not unhappy it's over.
It was a hot mess.
I'm not saying there weren't cool parts, but . . .
Publish

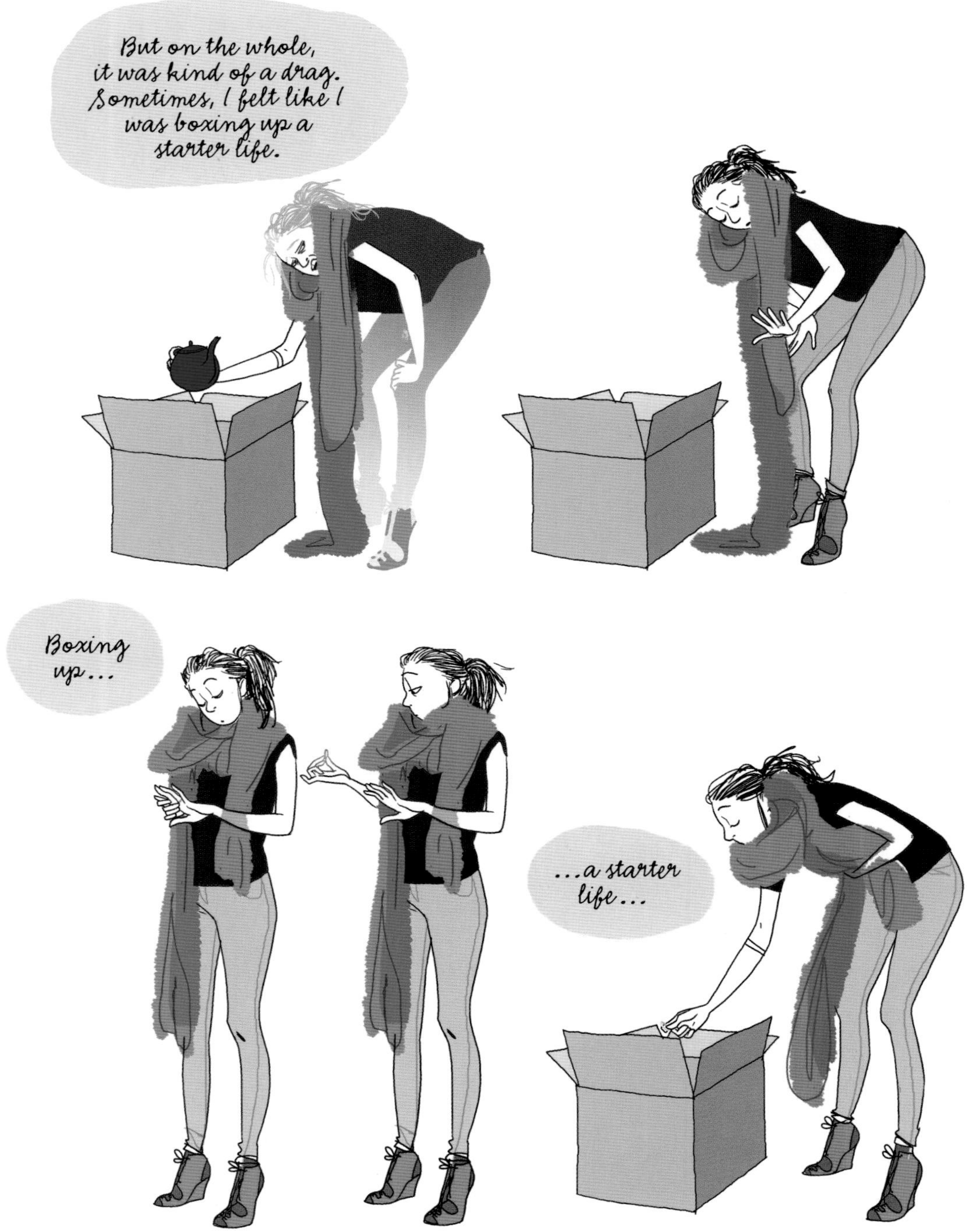
But on the whole, it was kind of a drag. Sometimes, I felt like I was boxing up a starter life.
Boxing up...
...a starter life...

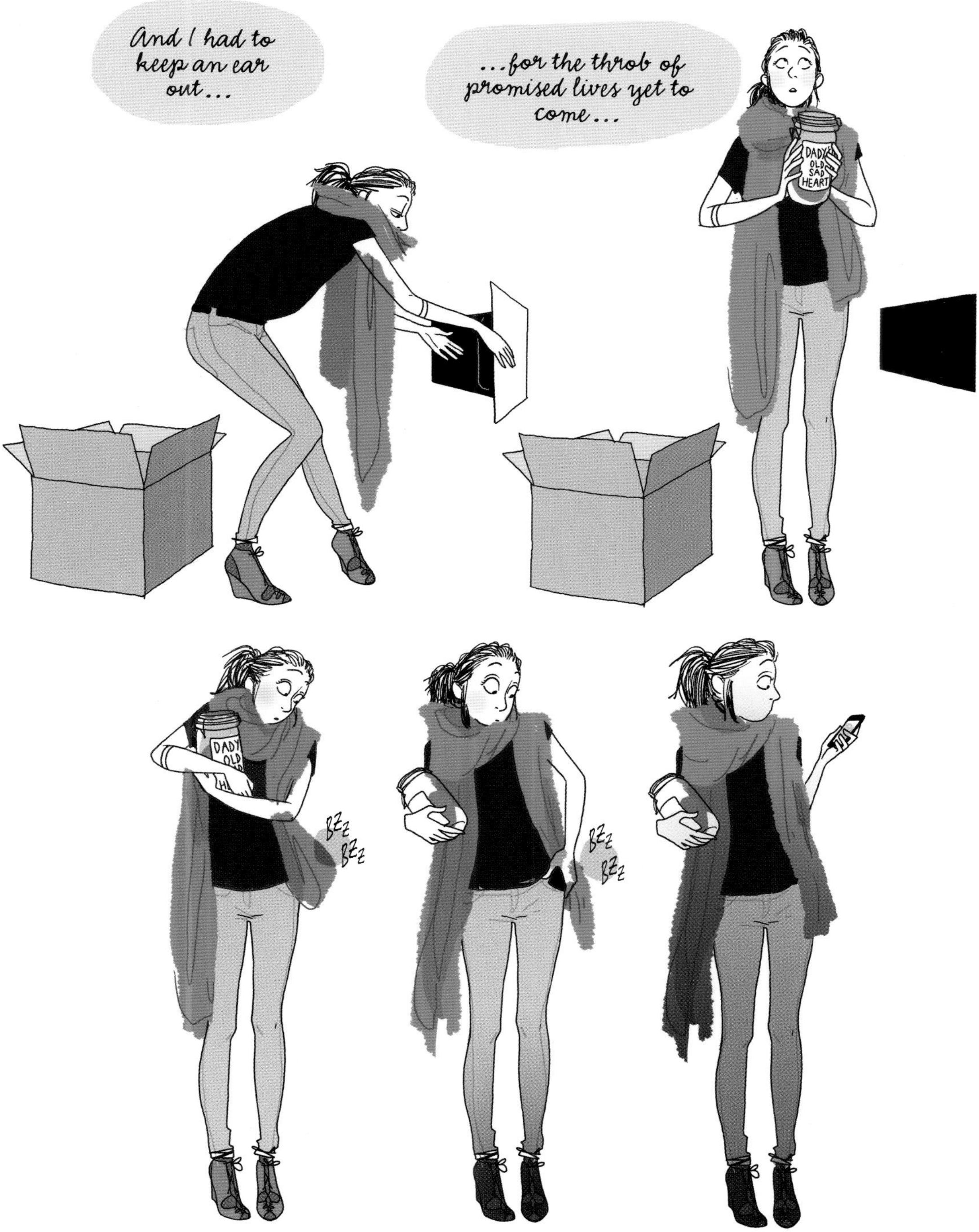
And I had to keep an ear out...
...for the throb of promised lives yet to come...
DADY'S OLD SAD HEART
BZZ BZZ
BZZ BZZ

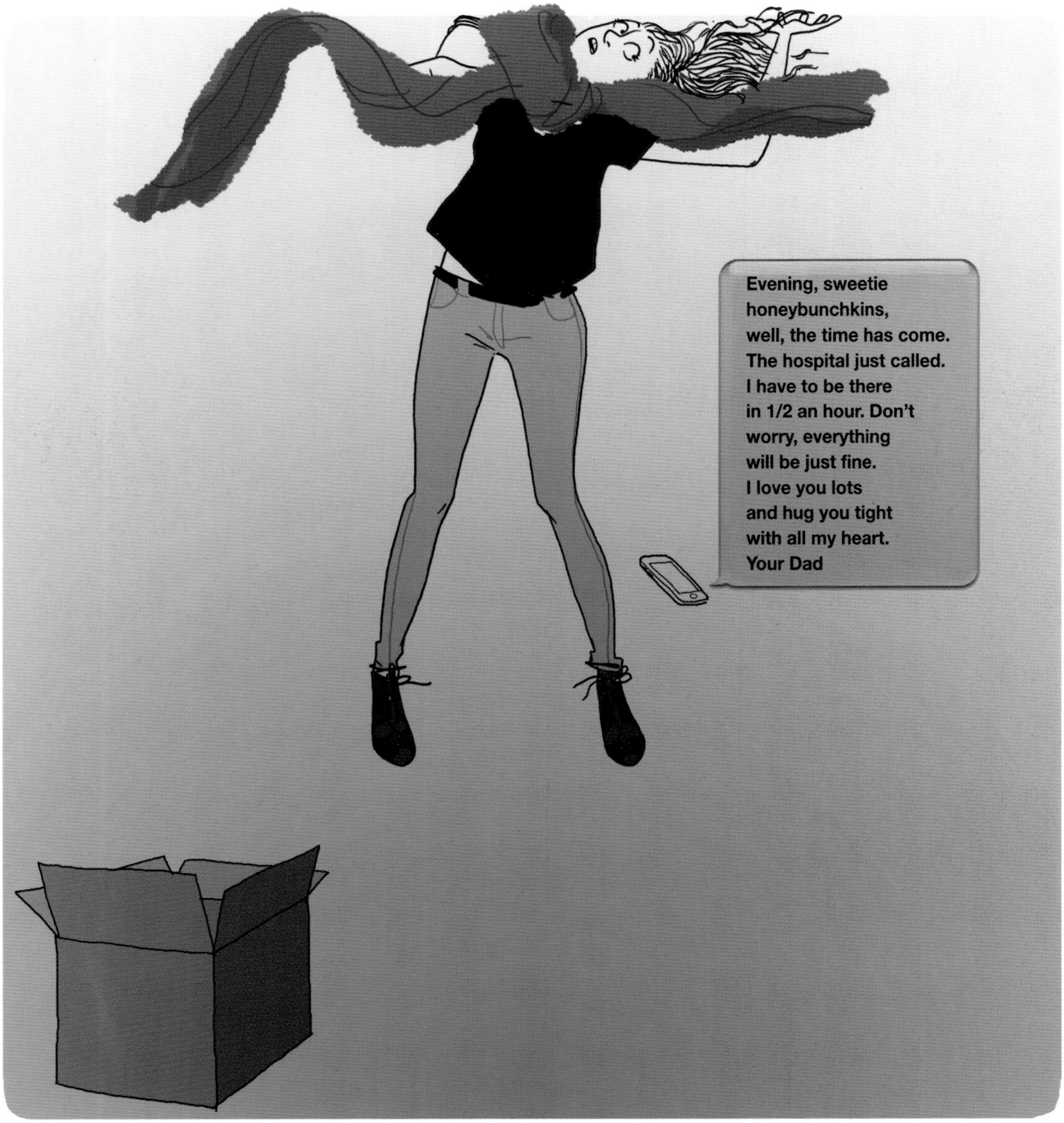
Evening, sweetie
honeybunchkins,
well, the time has come.
The hospital just called.
I have to be there
in 1/2 an hour. Don't
worry, everything
will be just fine.
I love you lots
and hug you tight
with all my heart.
Your Dad

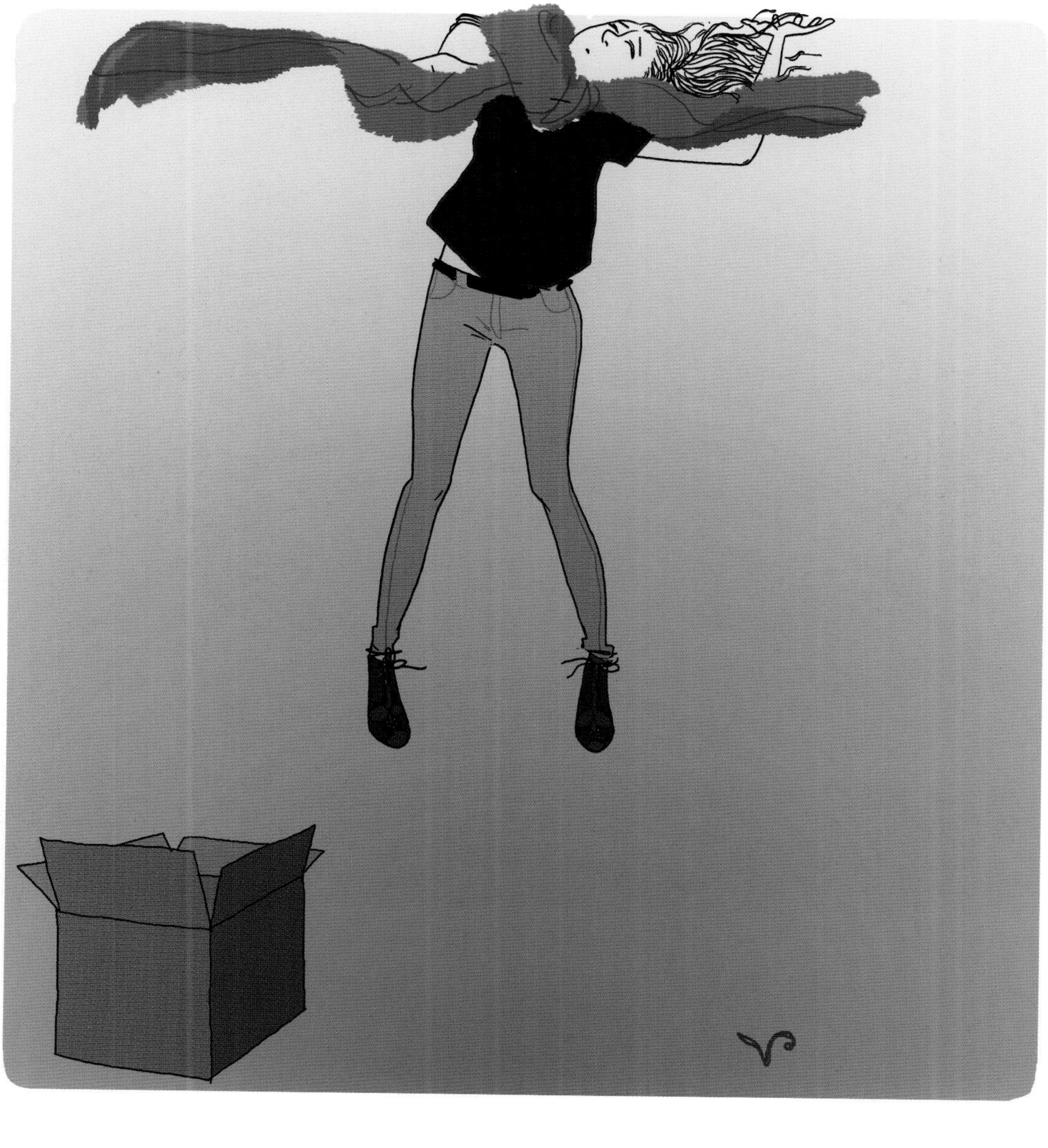

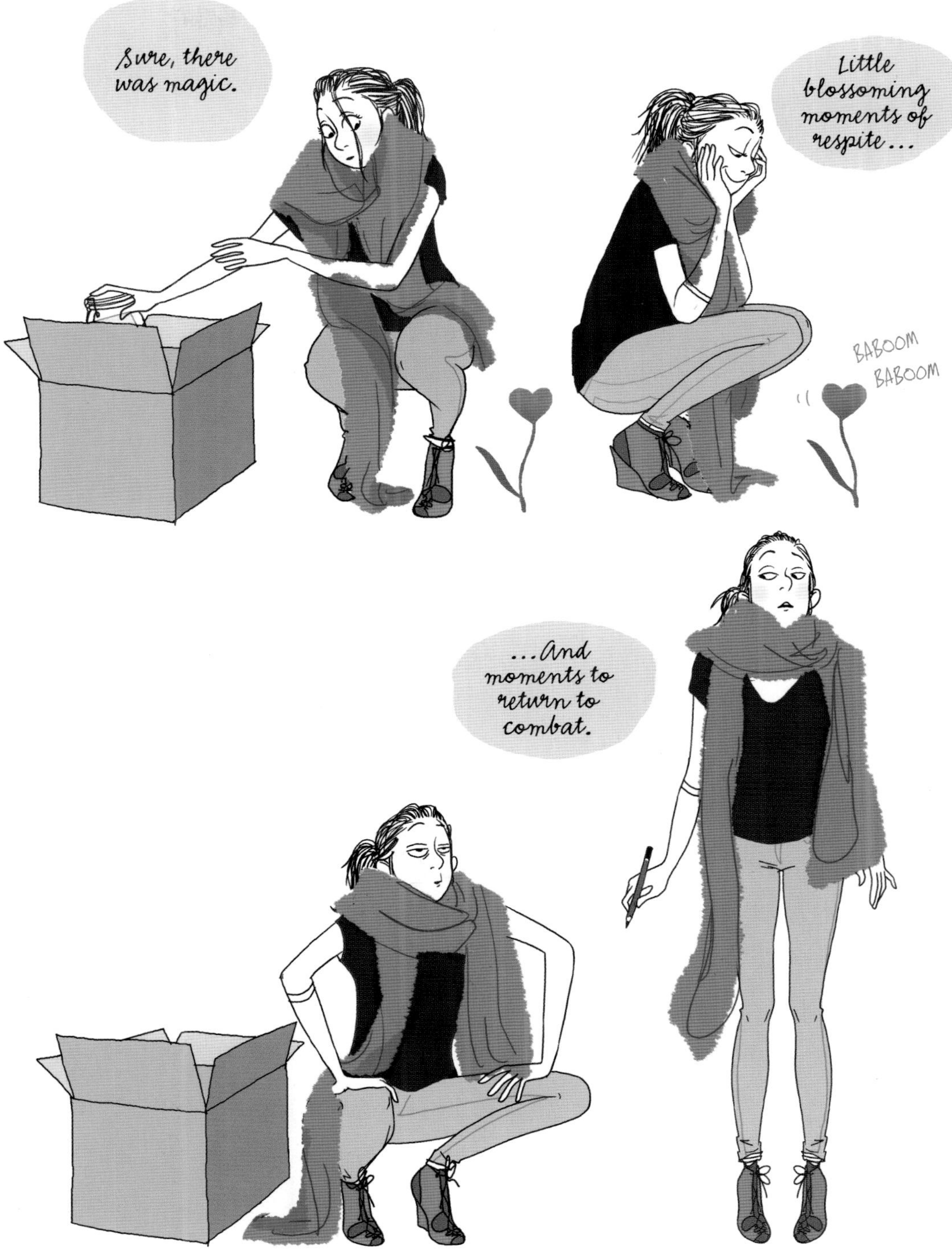
Sure, there was magic.
Little blossoming moments of respite...
BABOOM BABOOM
...And moments to return to combat.

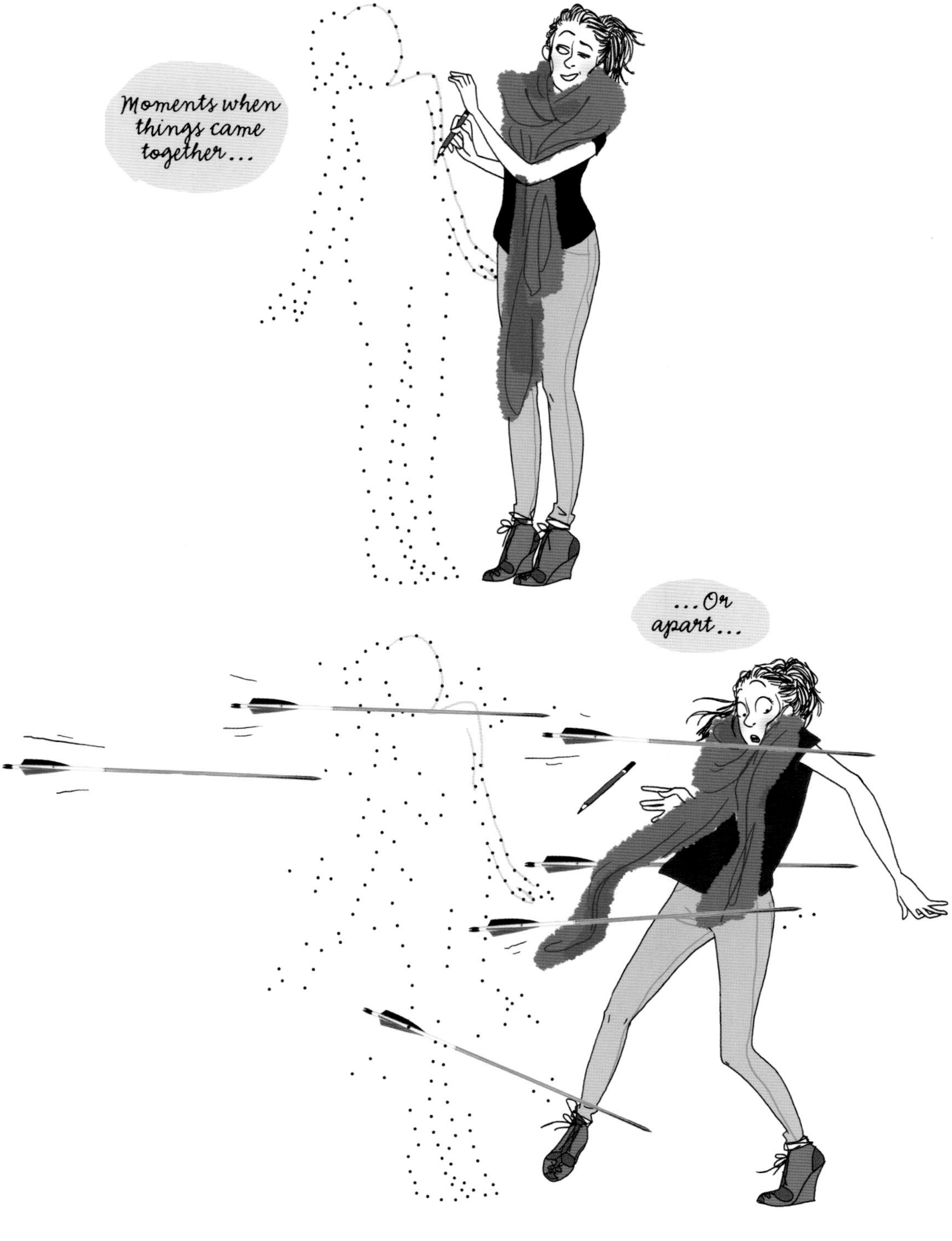
Moments when things came together...
...Or apart...

...without the serenity to accept the things I couldn't change.

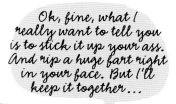

Ok, fine, what I really want to tell you is to stick it up your ass. And rip a huge fart right in your face. But I'll keep it together...

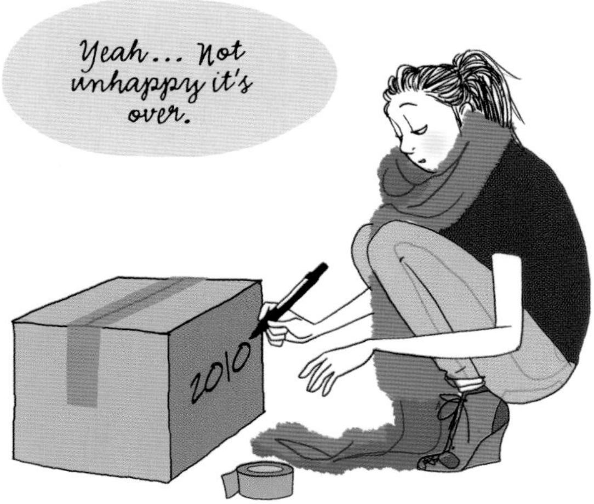
Yeah... Not unhappy it's over.
2010

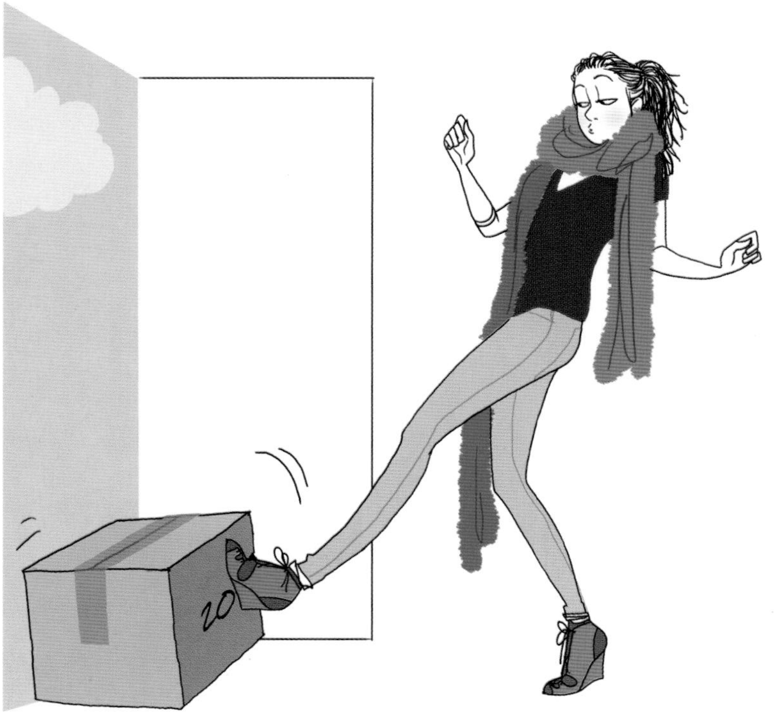
20

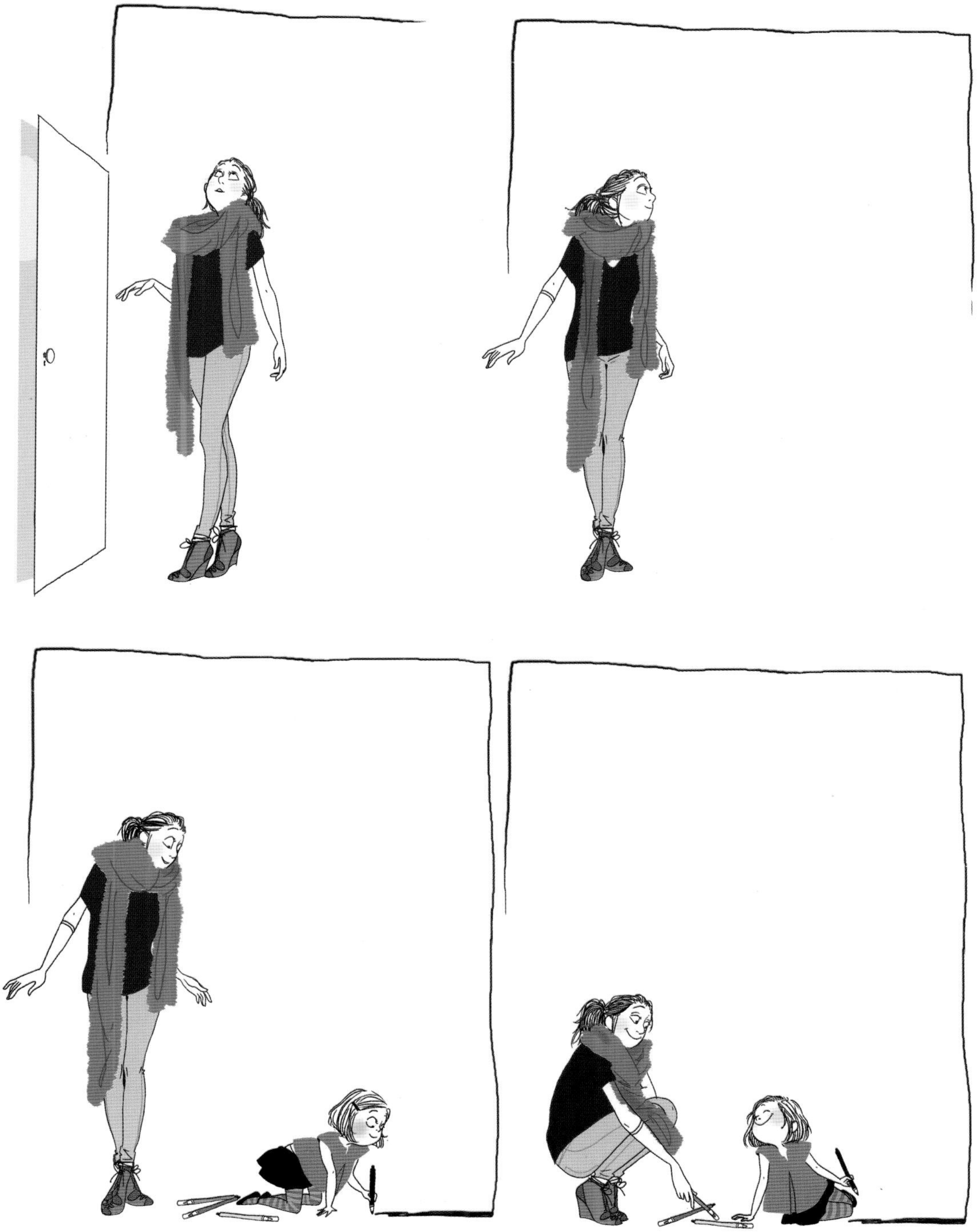

KNOCK
KNOCK

And then it was 2011.

"The difficult I'll do right now
The impossible will take a little while"

Billie Holliday, "Crazy He Calls Me"

"Fuck you, I won't do what you tell me."

After a divorce, you go through a kind of breakdown where you become a teenager again, and set out looking for all the selves you sacrificed at the altar of couple-hood: the crazy bitch, the hot mess, Ms. Impulsive, the art monster, the rebel, the Antichrist of married life. No matter how old you really are, after a divorce, you're 14.

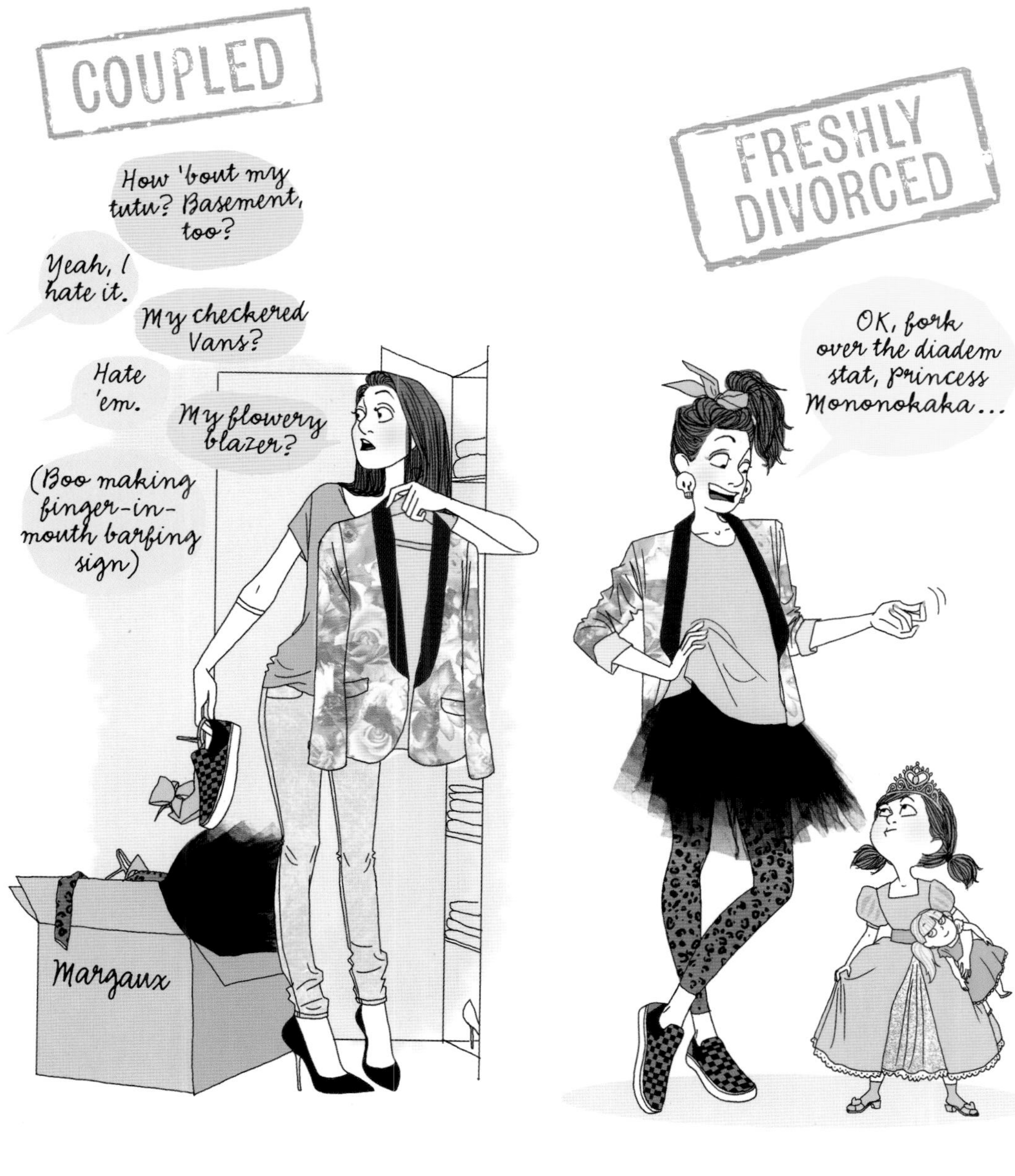
COUPLED
How 'bout my tutu? Basement, too?
Yeah, I hate it.
My checkered Vans?
Hate 'em.
My flowery blazer?
(Boo making finger-in-mouth barfing sign)
Margaux
FRESHLY DIVORCED
OK, fork over the diadem stat, Princess Mononokaka...

*Rage Against the Machine "Killing in the Name"

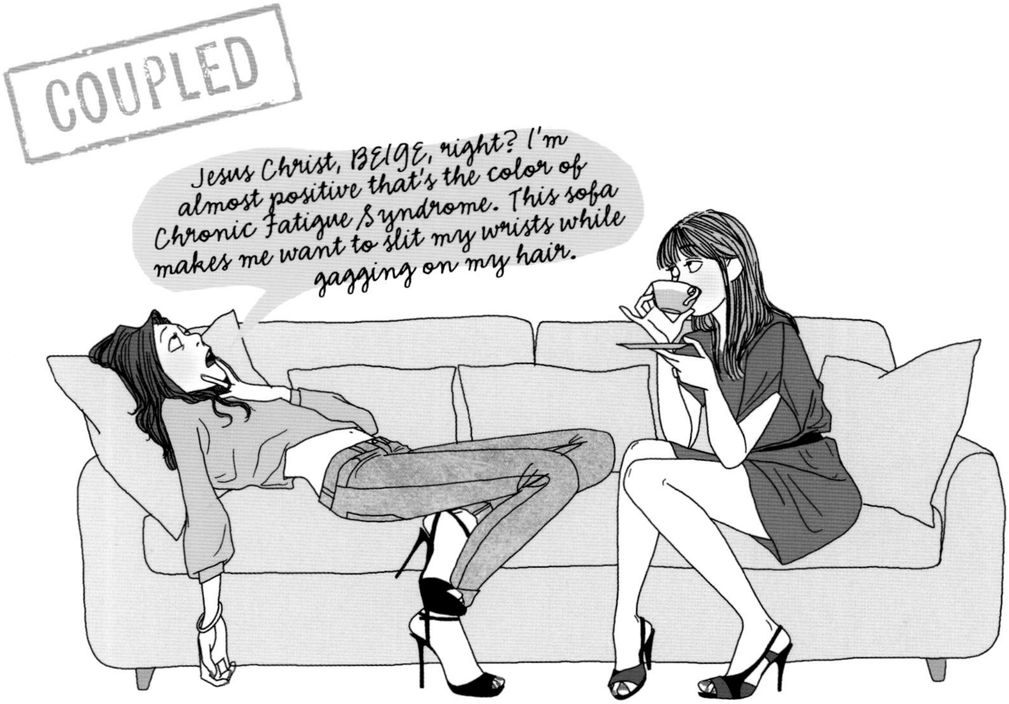
COUPLED
Jesus Christ, BEIGE, right? I'm almost positive that's the color of Chronic Fatigue Syndrome. This sofa makes me want to slit my wrists while gagging on my hair.

You have a kid. You can't just let yourself die, so you rise above.

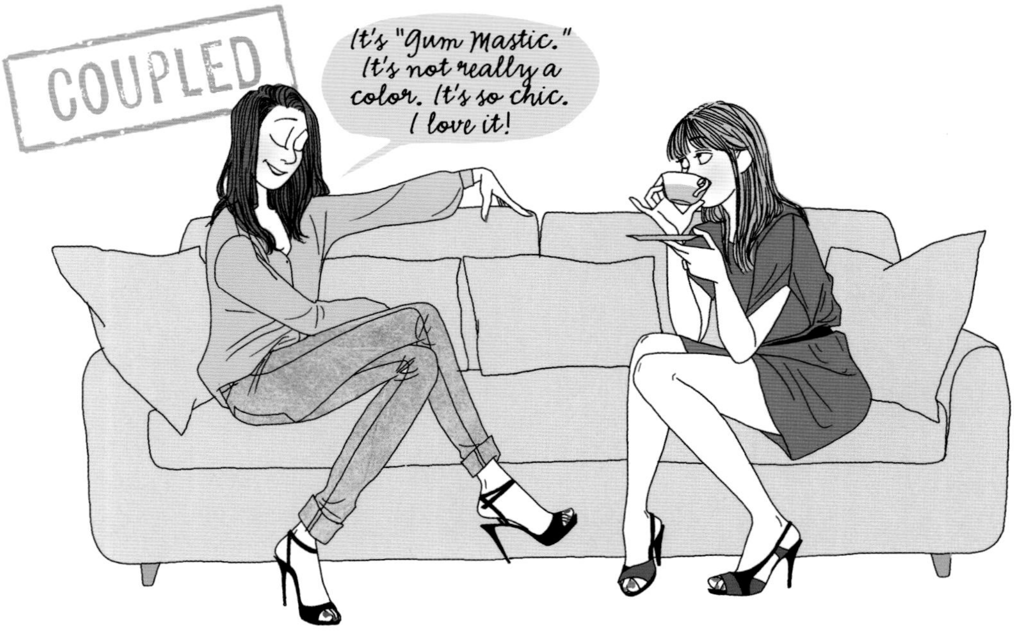
COUPLED
It's "Gum Mastic." It's not really a color. It's so chic. I love it!

FRESHLY DIVORCED

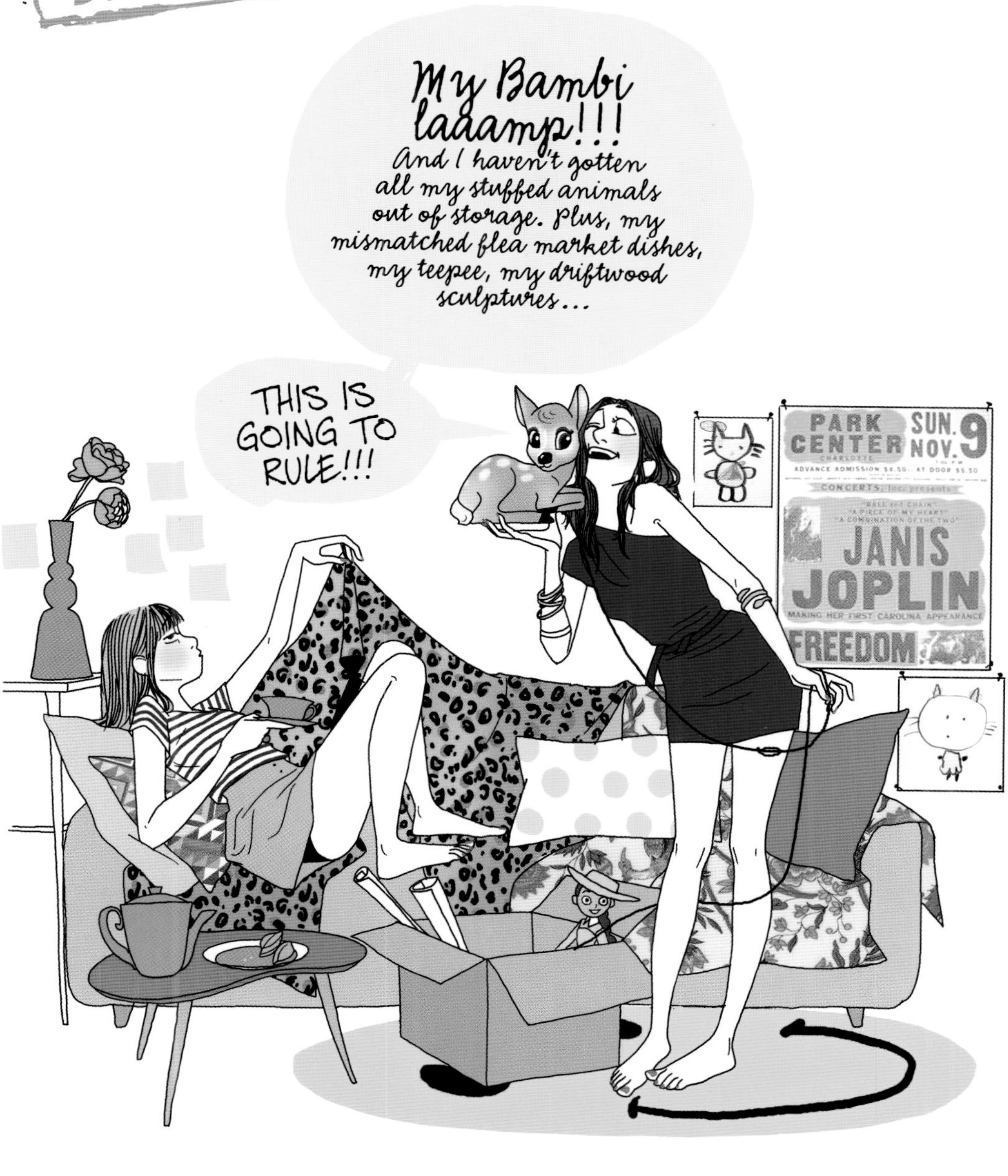

My Bambi laaamp!!! And I haven't gotten all my stuffed animals out of storage. Plus, my mismatched flea market dishes, my teepee, my driftwood sculptures...
THIS IS GOING TO RULE!!!
PARK CENTER
SUN. NOV. 9
JANIS JOPLIN
MAKING HER FIRST CAROLINA APPEARANCE
FREEDOM

YOUR RESPONSIBILITIES

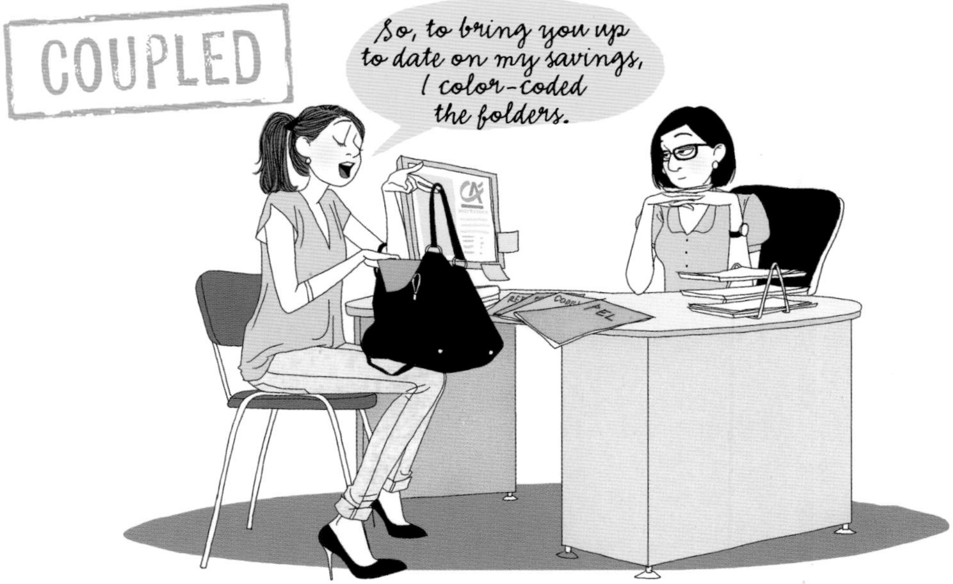
COUPLED
So, to bring you up to date on my savings, I color-coded the folders.

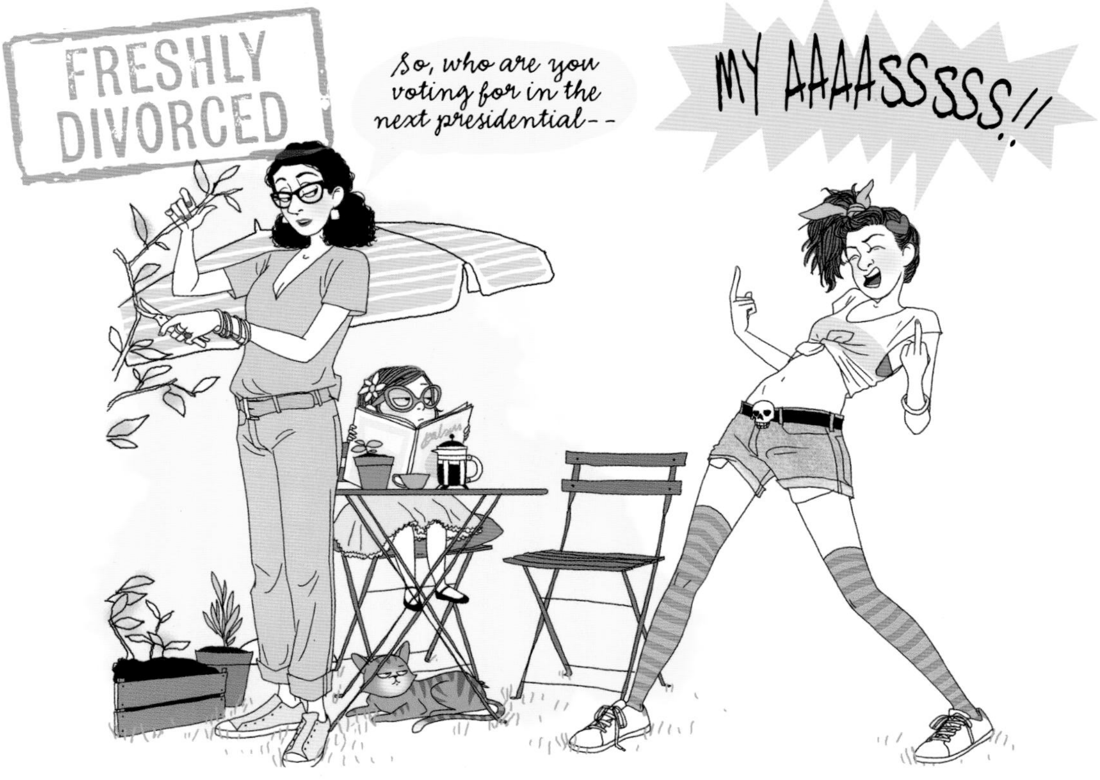
FRESHLY DIVORCED
So, who are you voting for in the next presidential--
MY AAAASSSSS!!

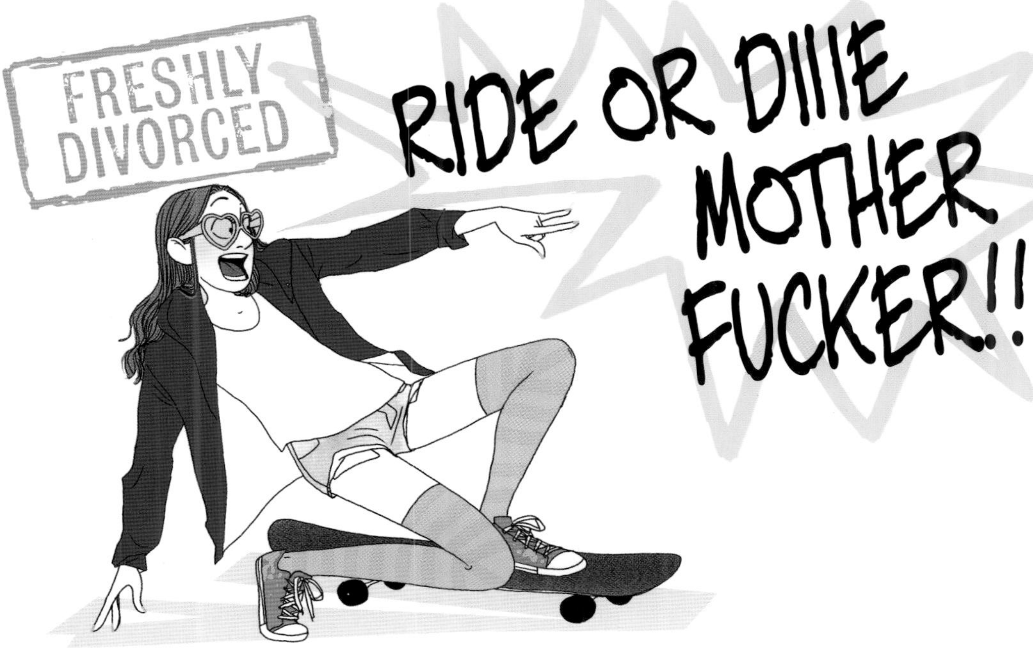
FRESHLY DIVORCED
RIDE OR DIIIE MOTHER FUCKER!!

The only turd in your Count Chocula when you think you're 14...

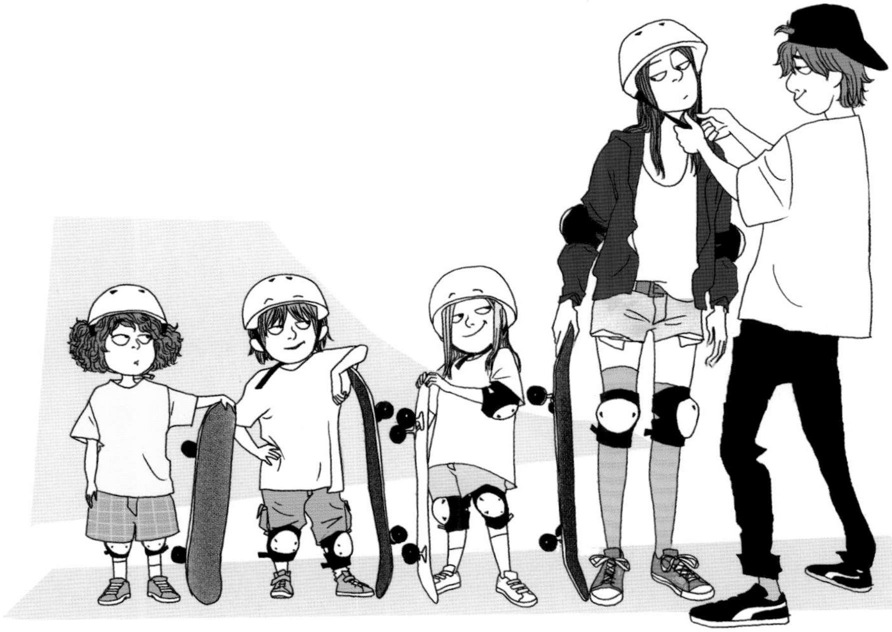

...is that the rest of the world is perfectly aware you're really 32.

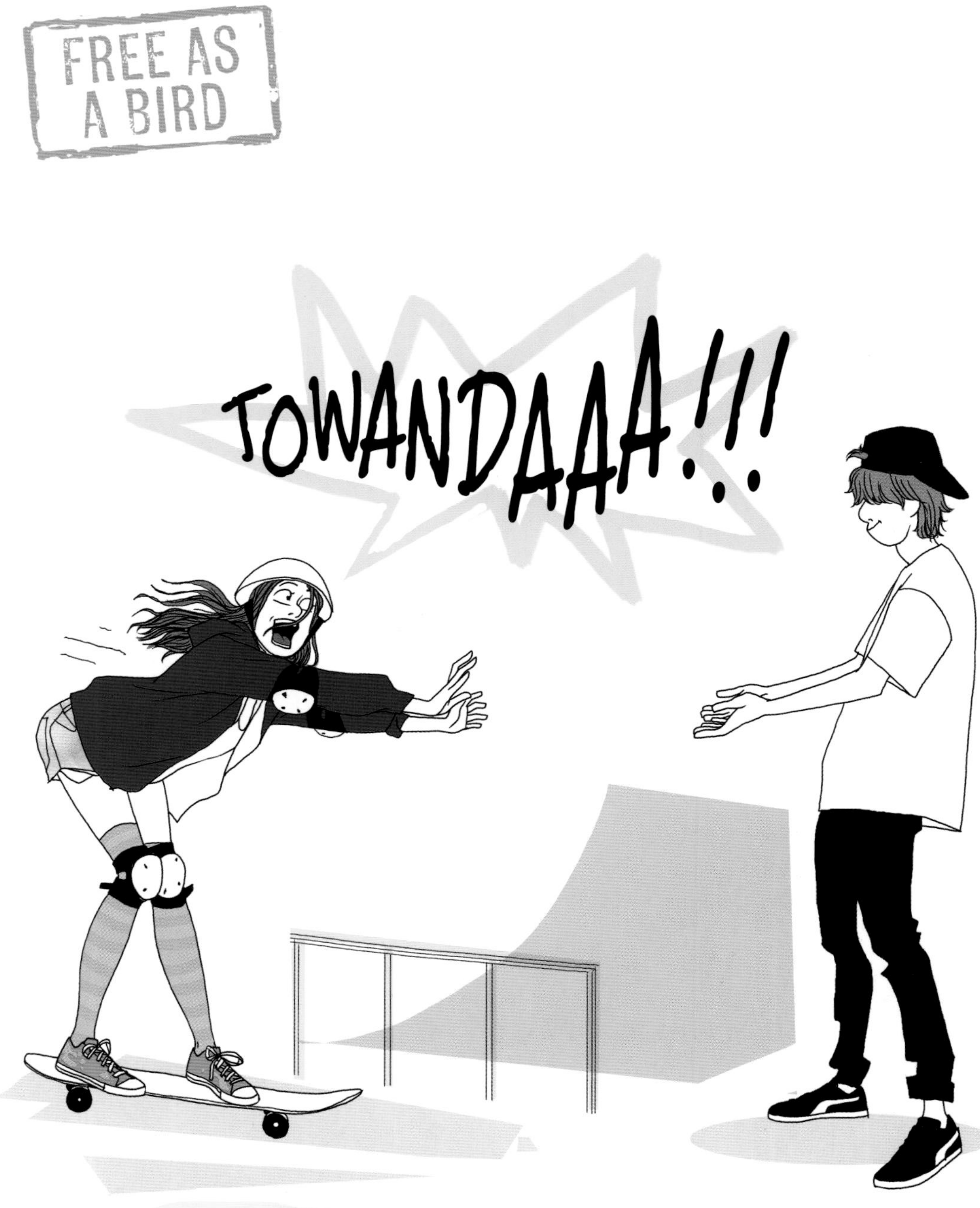
FREE AS A BIRD
TOWANDAAA!!!

But you don't give a crap, 'cause you're 14.

Mea Culpa

GAAH! WHO THE HECK'RE YOU? WHAT DO YOU WANT? HOW'D YOU GET IN HERE? YOU PANHANDLING? WHERE'S YOUR MOTHER?

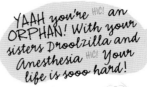

Oh, shit, I'm so sorry! You have no mom, poor thing, you're Cinderella.

YAAH you're HIC! an ORPHAN! With your sisters Droolzilla and Anesthesia! HIC! Your life is sooo hard!

Those HIC! bitches

DID YOU STEAL THAT PLATE AND RUN AWAY? DID YOU??

But you've still got your mouse friends to talk to and li'l birdies HIC! to do your hair, yes you do you cuuuutie HIC!

I want an eagle but no one'll give me one.

OH OH I GET IT! THAT PLATE! YOU'RE HUNGRY!!

Look kid, lemme tell you an inedible secret: there's Chocula in the fridge. Just grab some, I won't tell...

TRUE FACT: A DRUNK MOM IS NOT A PRETTY SIGHT.

You're sooo adoo-HIC-rable, can I adopt you?

BUT I'M FINE WITH THAT, 'CAUSE I FIGURED OUT SOMETHING REALLY BASIC ABOUT BEING A PARENT.

3 HOURS EARLIER...

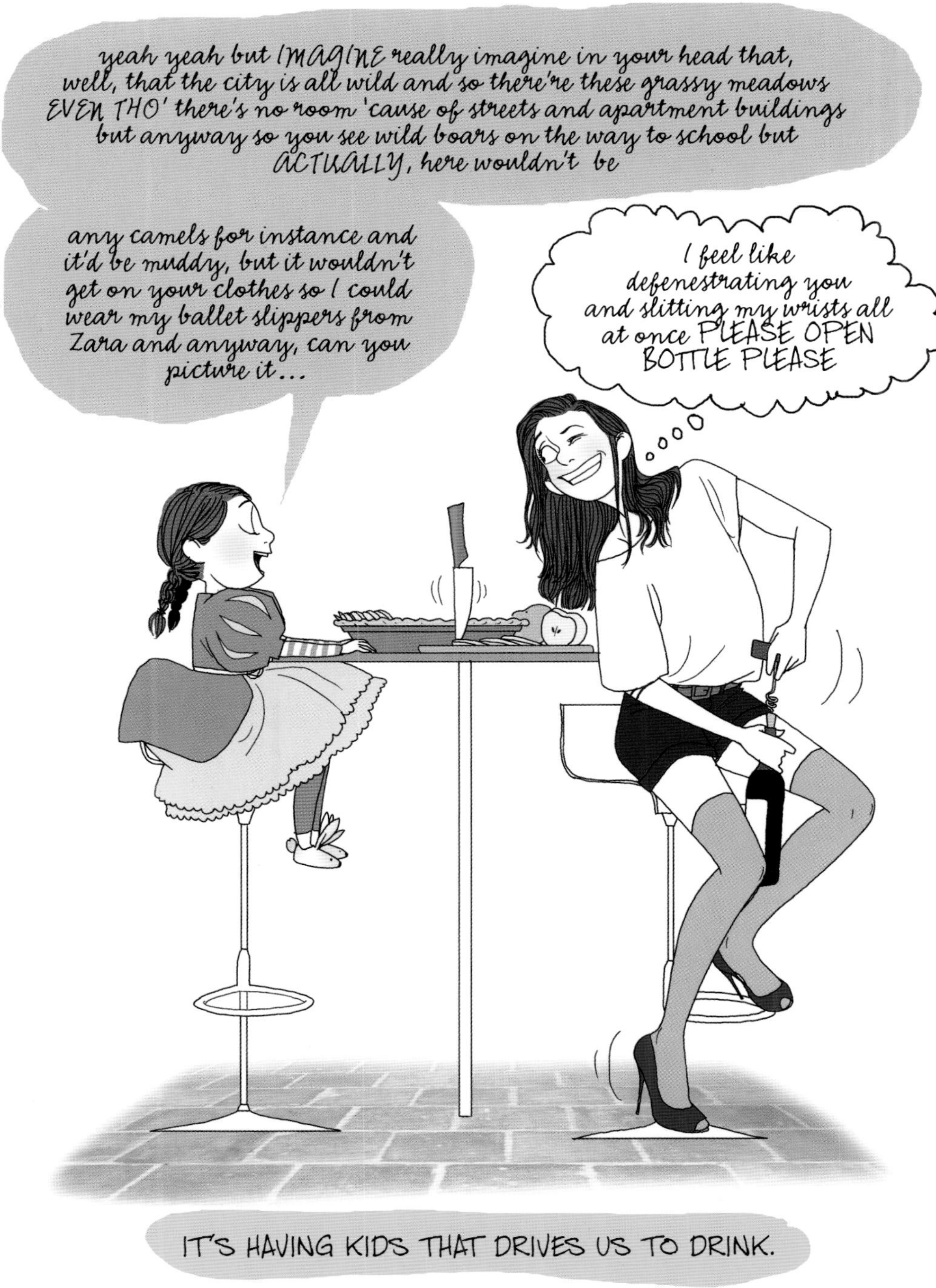
yeah yeah but IMAGINE really imagine in your head that, well, that the city is all wild and so there're these grassy meadows EVEN THO' there's no room 'cause of streets and apartment buildings but anyway so you see wild boars on the way to school but ACTUALLY, here wouldn't be
any camels for instance and it'd be muddy, but it wouldn't get on your clothes so I could wear my ballet slippers from Zara and anyway, can you picture it...
I feel like defenestrating you and slitting my wrists all at once PLEASE OPEN BOTTLE PLEASE
IT'S HAVING KIDS THAT DRIVES US TO DRINK.

Wonder Woman

ALL MOTHERS HAVE SUPERPOWERS.

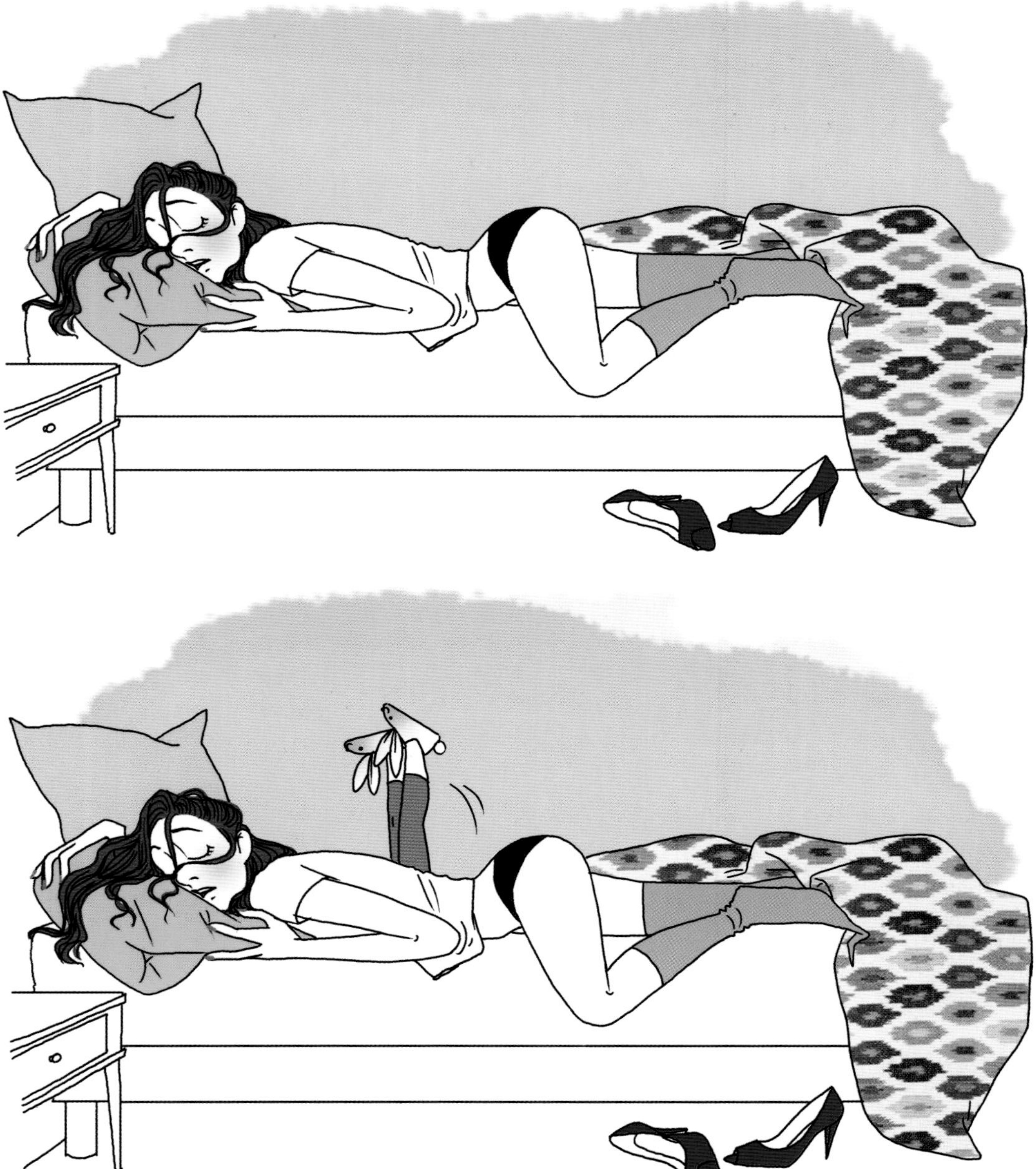

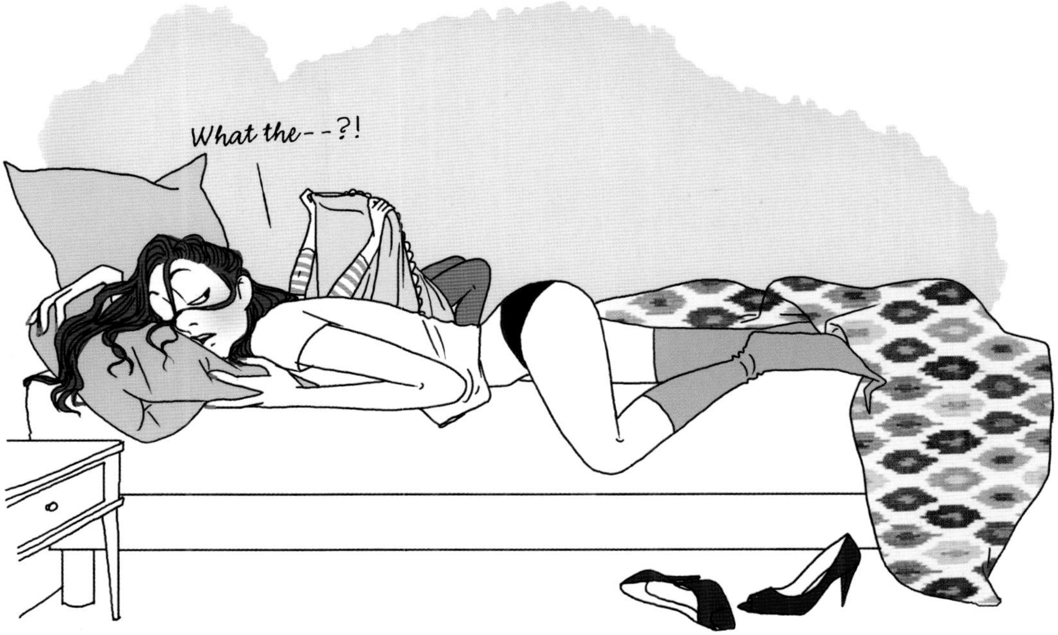
What the--?!

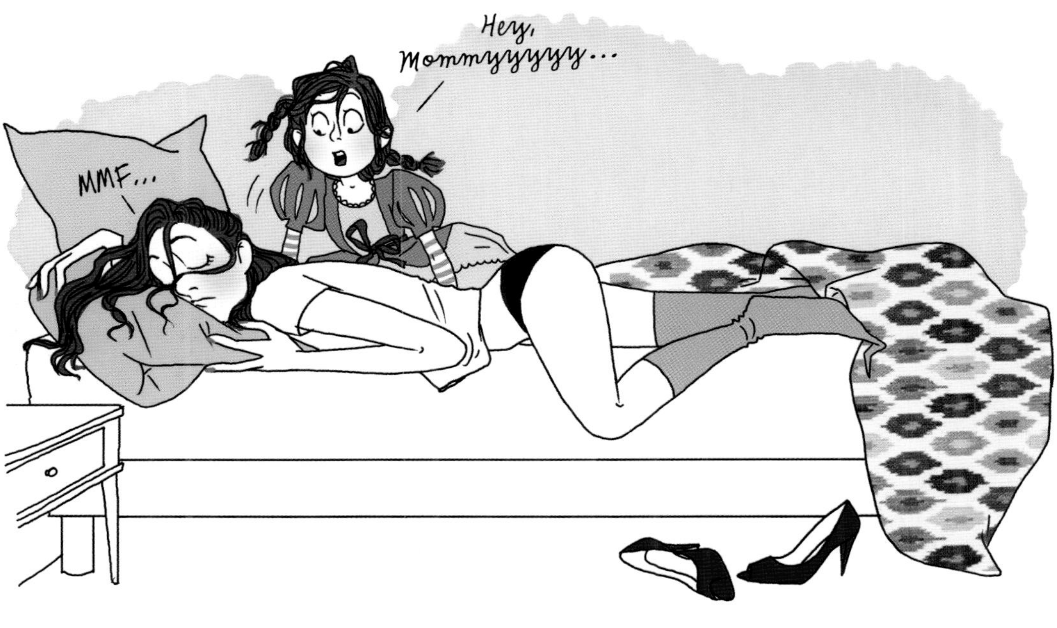
MMF...
Hey, Mommyyyyyy...

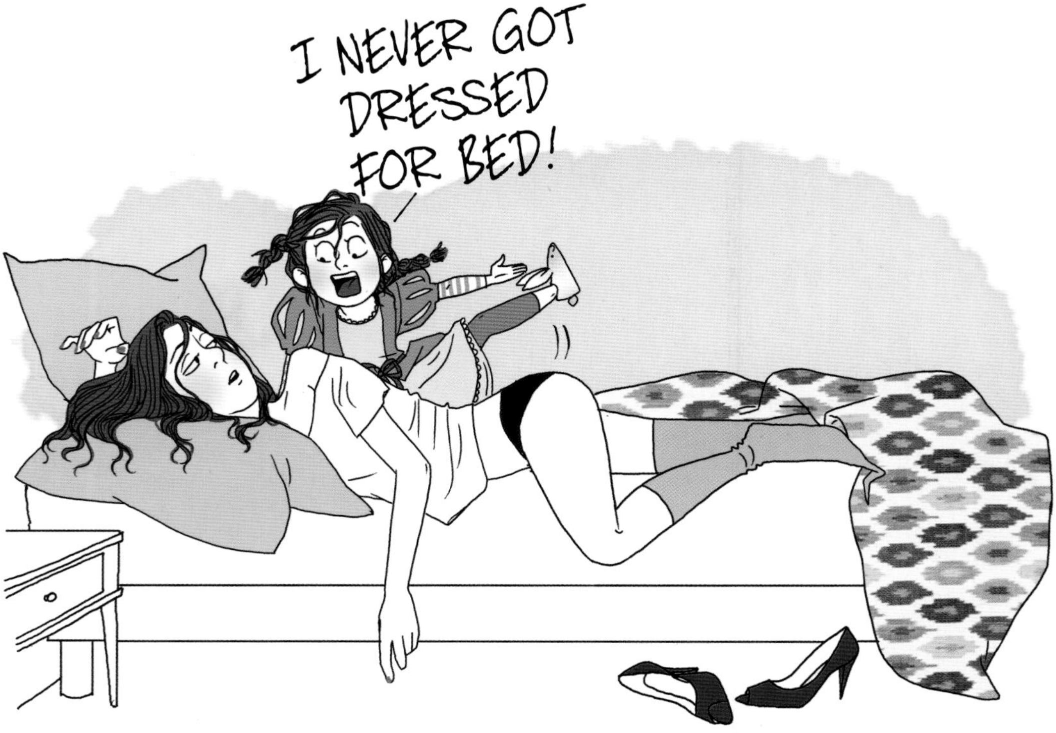
I NEVER GOT DRESSED FOR BED!

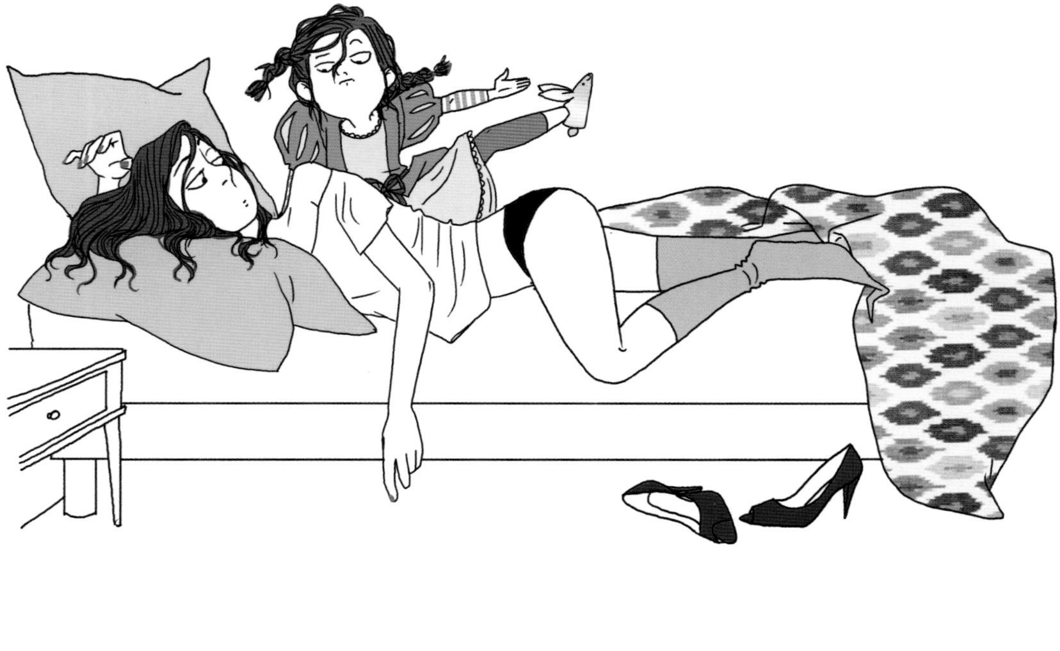

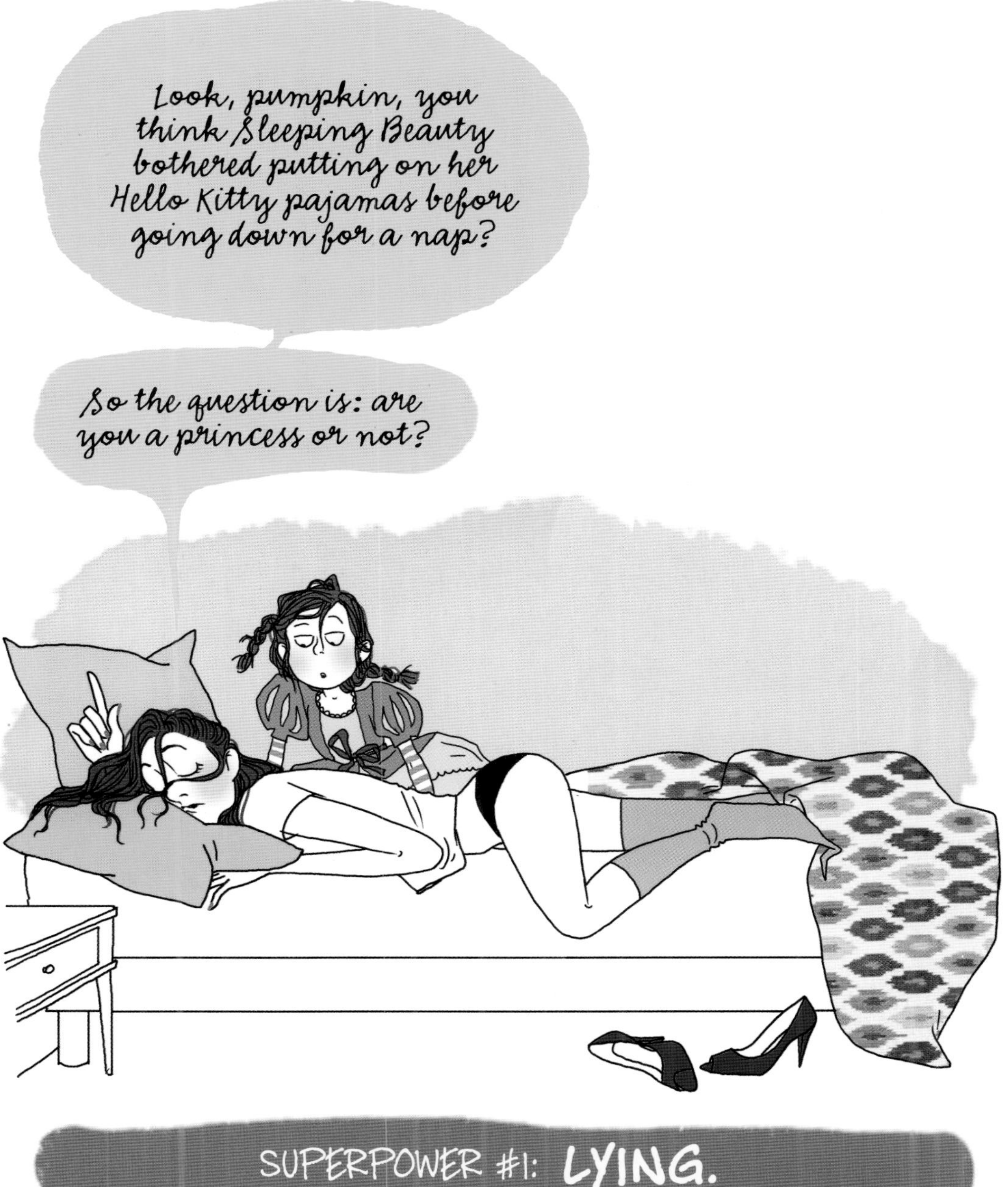
Look, pumpkin, you think Sleeping Beauty bothered putting on her Hello Kitty pajamas before going down for a nap?
So the question is: are you a princess or not?
SUPERPOWER #1: LYING.

Conventional wisdom says that "There's a right time for everything."

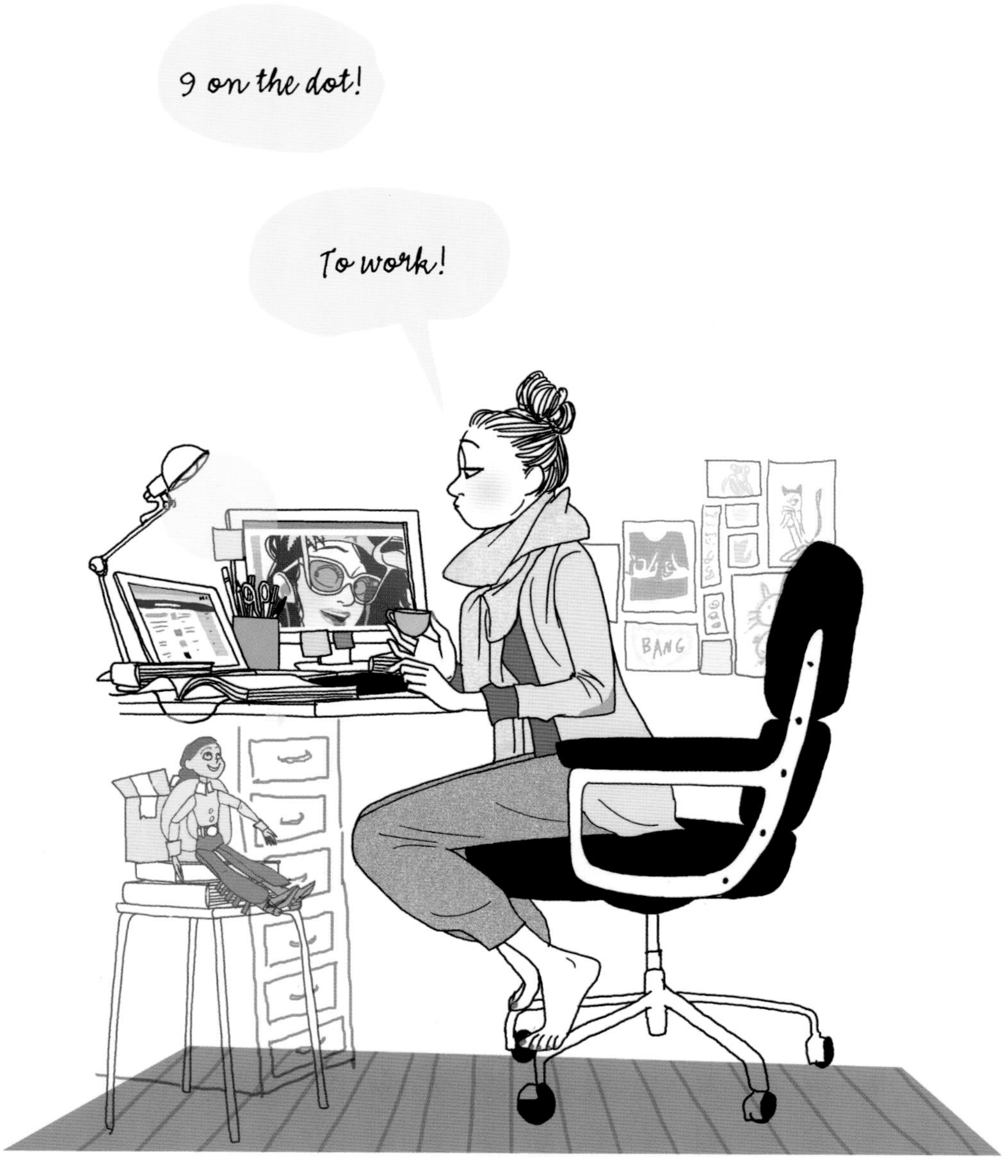
9 on the dot!
To work!
BANG

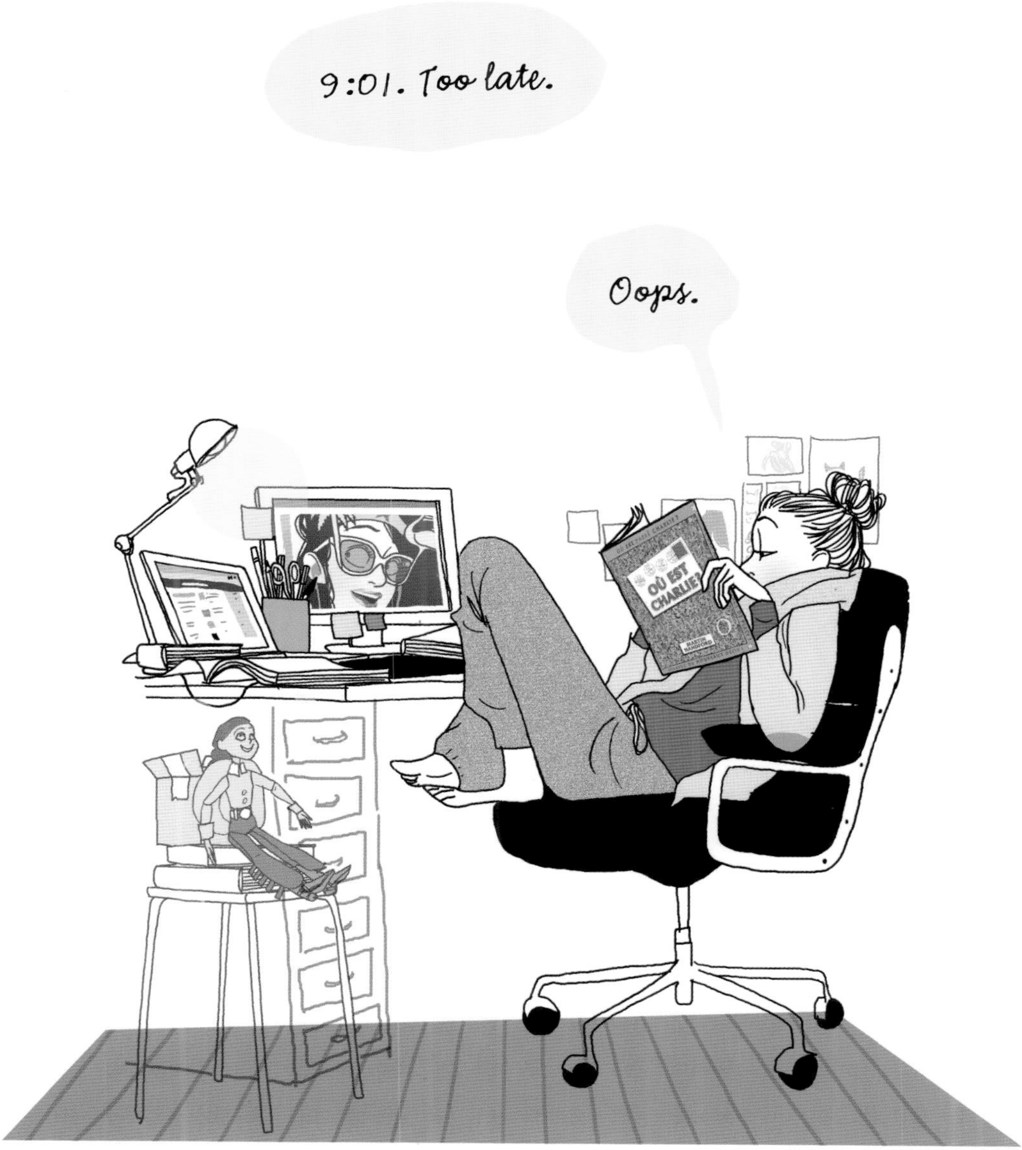
9:01. Too late.
Oops.

I'M A COUNTRY GIRL. I TAKE FOLK SAYINGS VERY SERIOUSLY.

And also

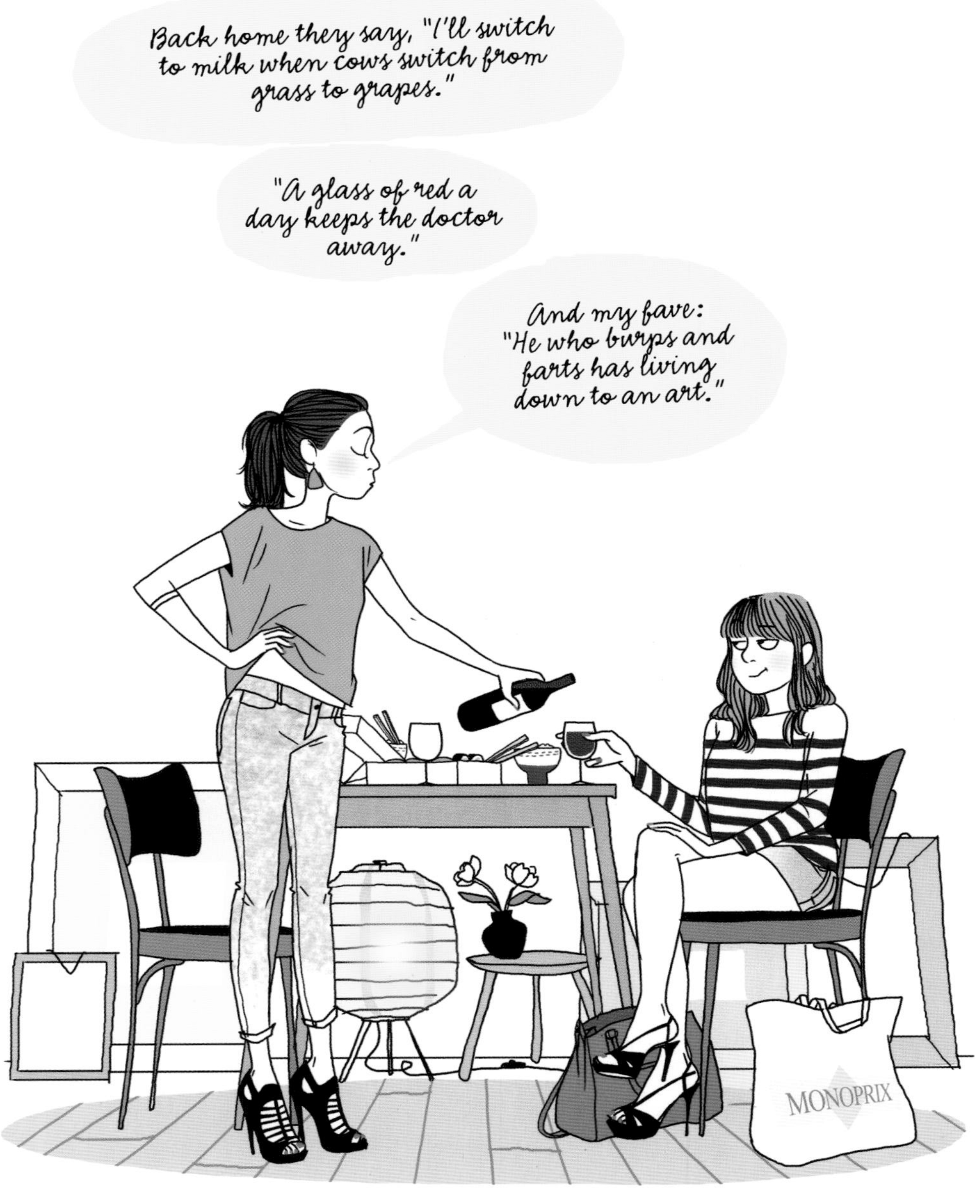
Back home they say, "I'll switch to milk when cows switch from grass to grapes."
"A glass of red a day keeps the doctor away."
And my fave: "He who burps and farts has living down to an art."
MONOPRIX

PROVERBS GIVE WONDERFUL ADVICE FOR PERSONAL DEVELOPMENT.

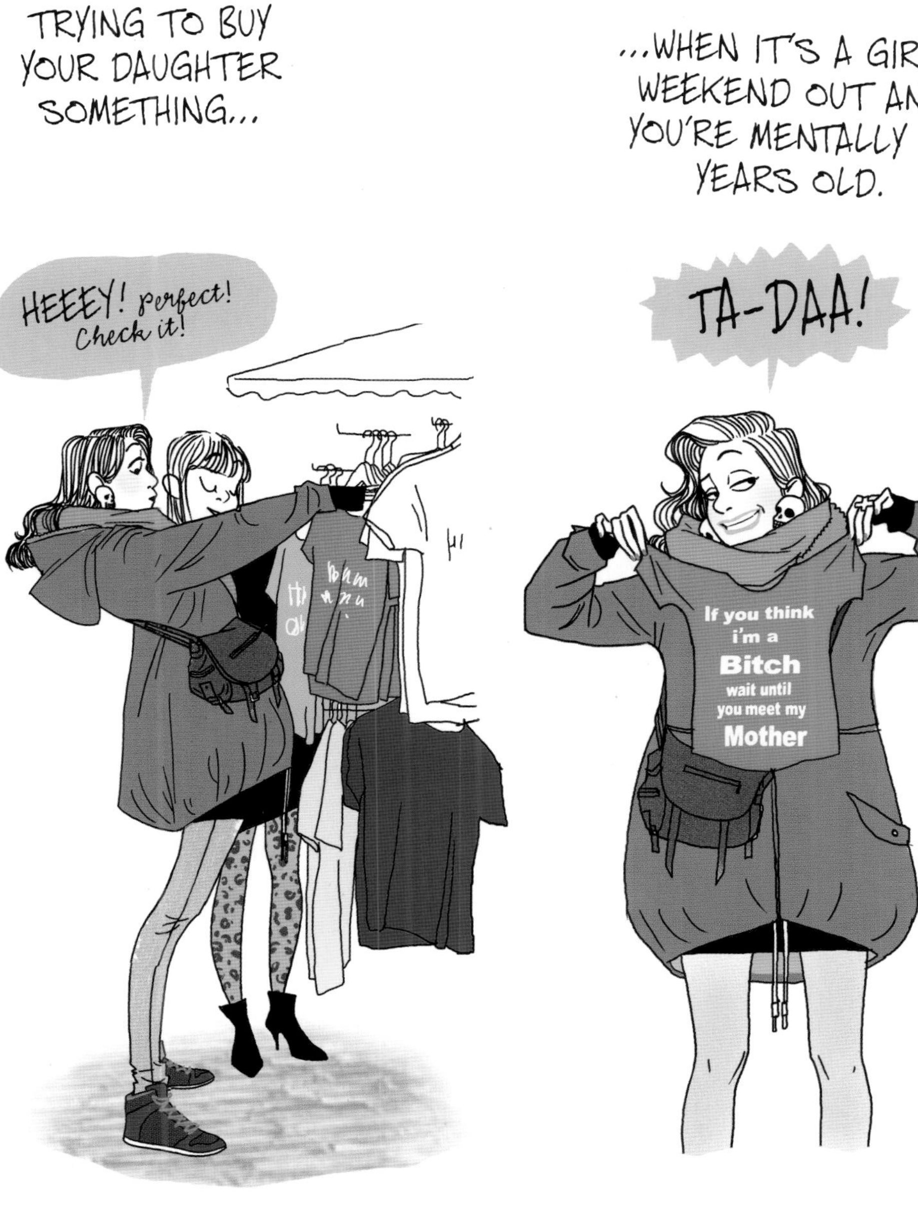
TRYING TO BUY YOUR DAUGHTER SOMETHING...
HEEEY! perfect! Check it!
...WHEN IT'S A GIRLS' WEEKEND OUT AND YOU'RE MENTALLY 15 YEARS OLD.
TA-DAA!
If you think i'm a Bitch wait until you meet my Mother

Jonesing

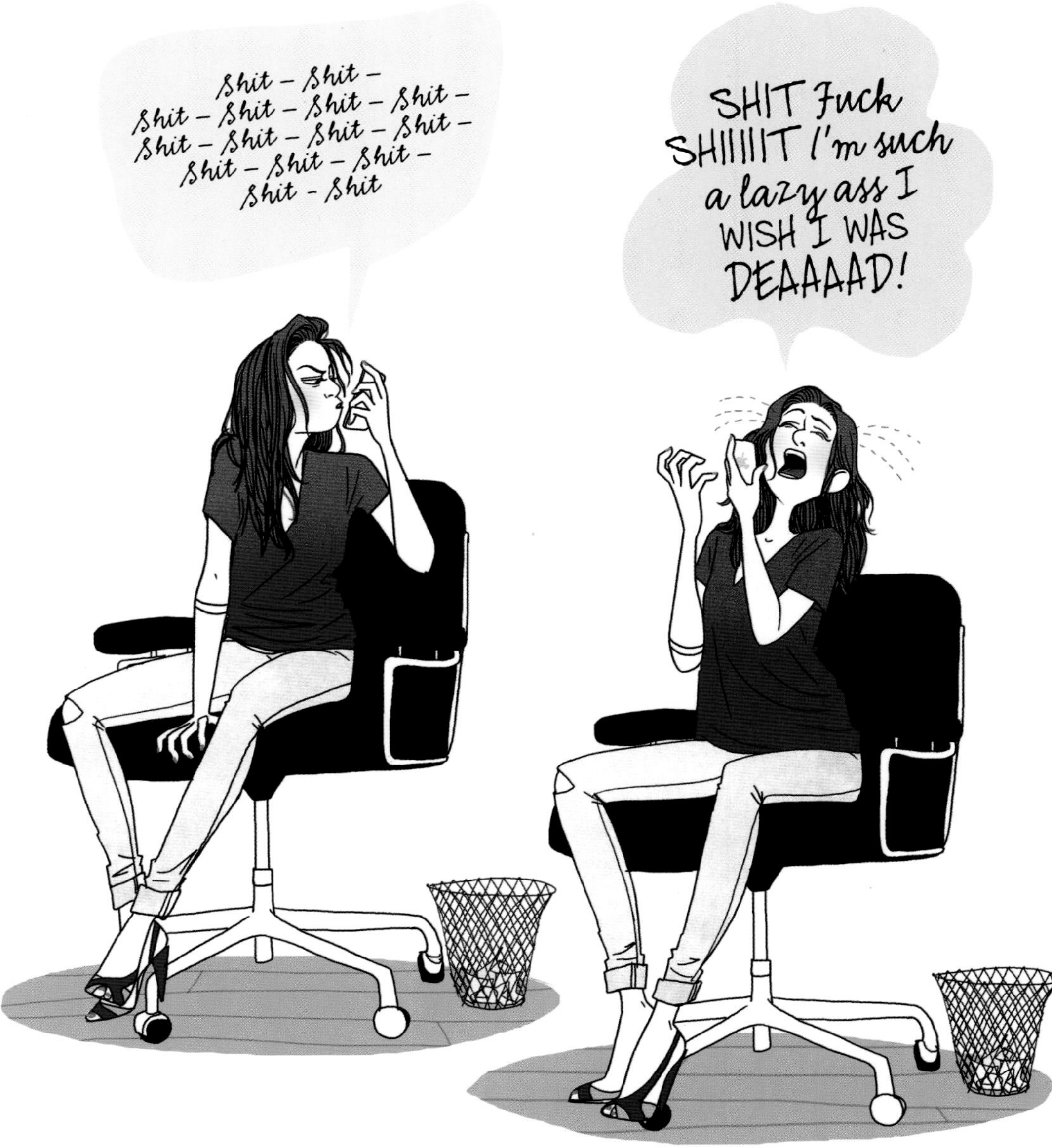
Shit – Shit – Shit – Shit – Shit – Shit – Shit – Shit – Shit – Shit – Shit – Shit – Shit – Shit – Shit
SHIT Fuck SHIIIIIIT I'm such a lazy ass I WISH I WAS DEAAAAD!

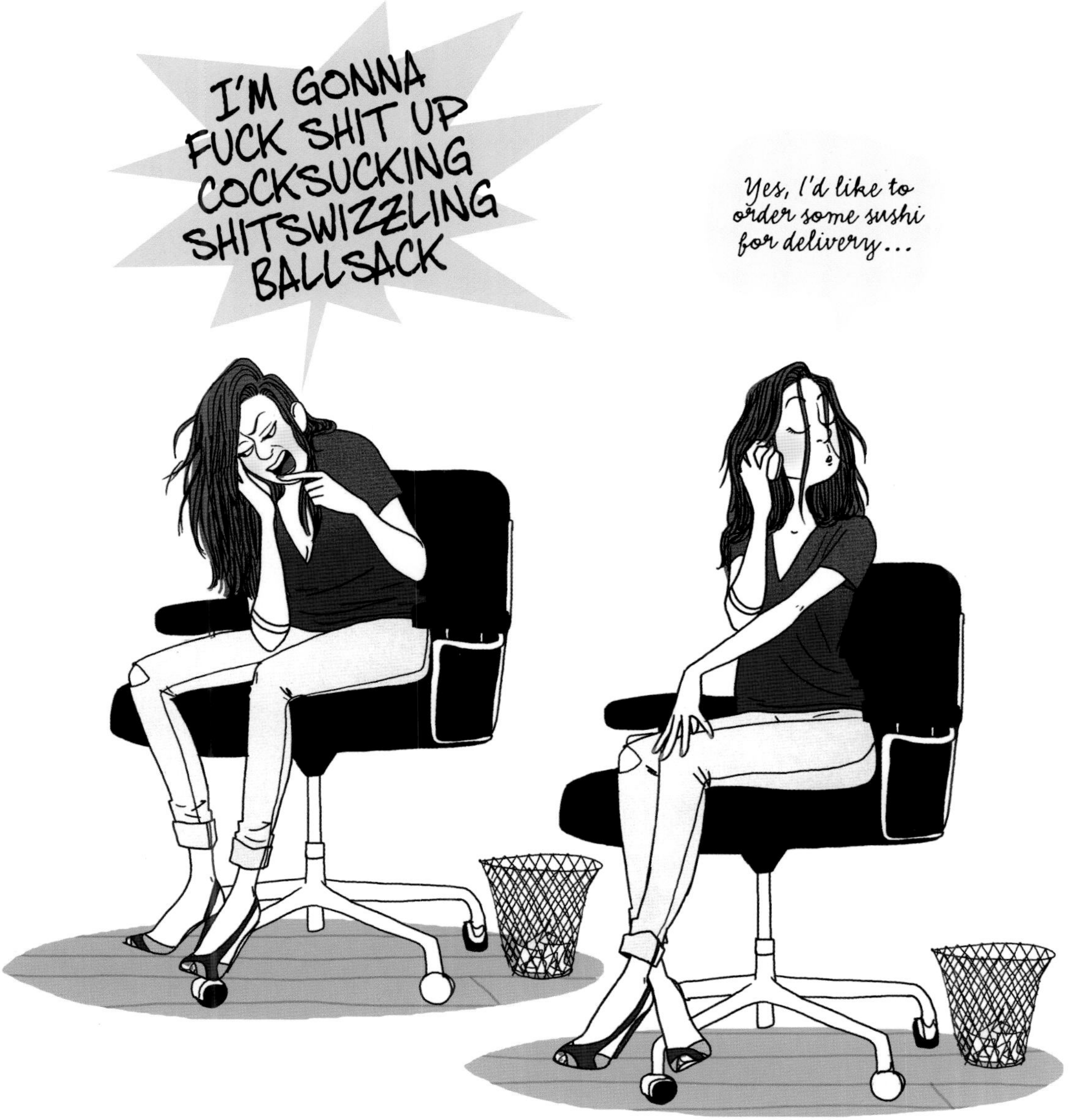
I'M GONNA FUCK SHIT UP COCKSUCKING SHITSWIZZLING BALLSACK
Yes, I'd like to order some sushi for delivery...

48 HOURS WITHOUT
A CIGARETTE

Wanna bet?

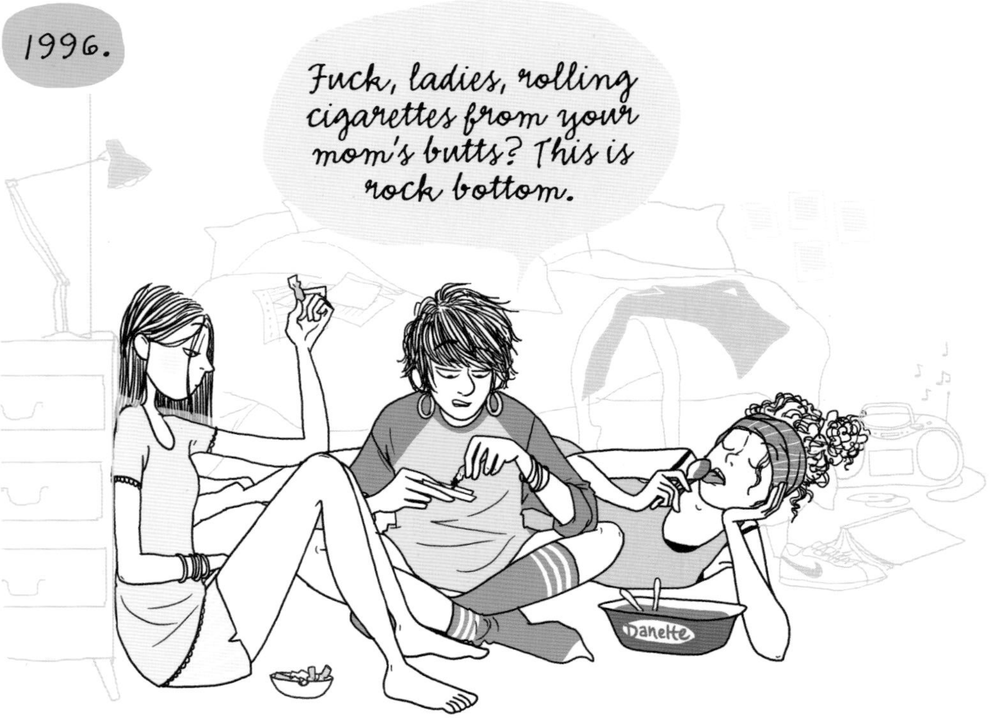
1996.
Fuck, ladies, rolling cigarettes from your mom's butts? This is rock bottom.
Danette

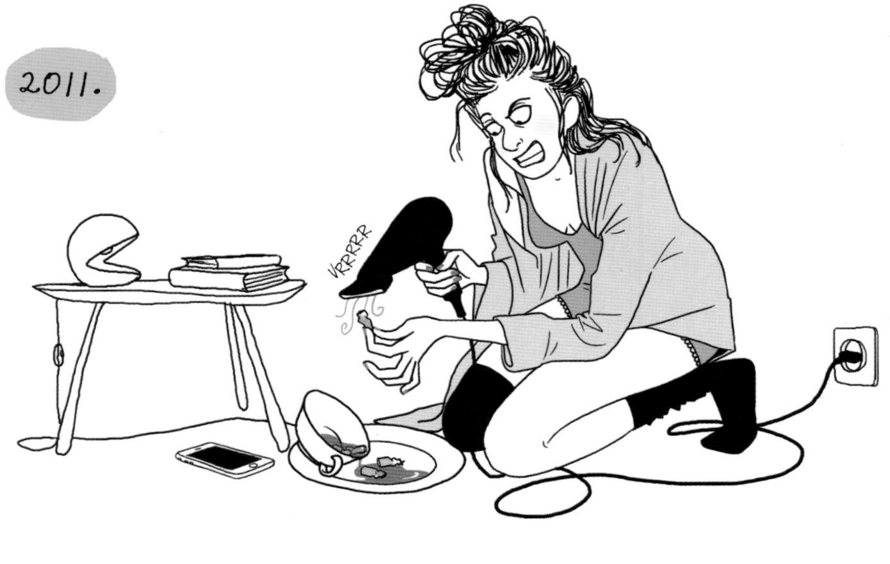
2011.
VRRRRR

Dear Monday… Fuck You

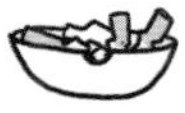

A Short primer on Hygiene

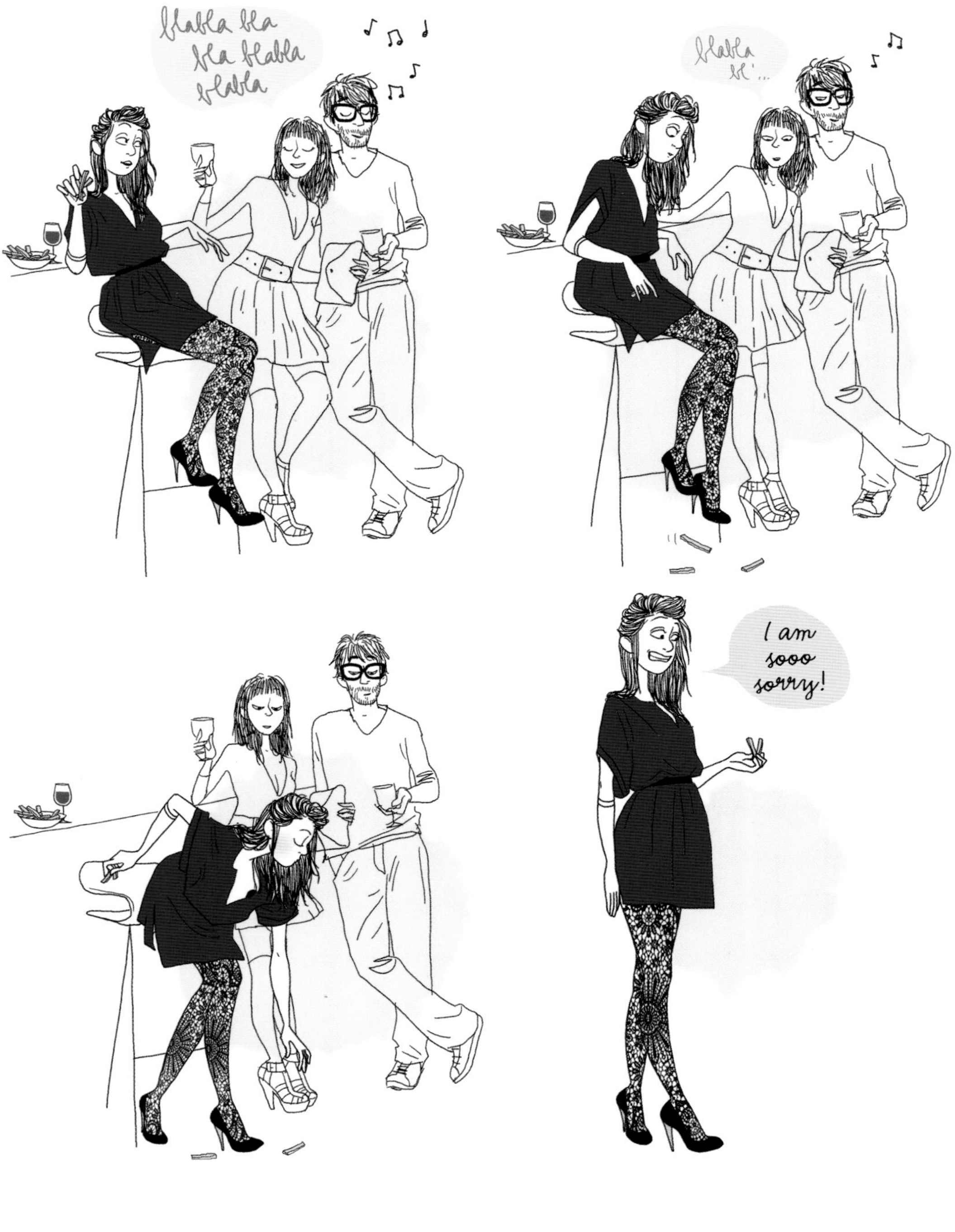
blabla bla bla blabla blabla
blabla bl'...
I am sooo sorry!

5 SECOND RULE. TOTALLY COOL.

Better Come Autocorrect

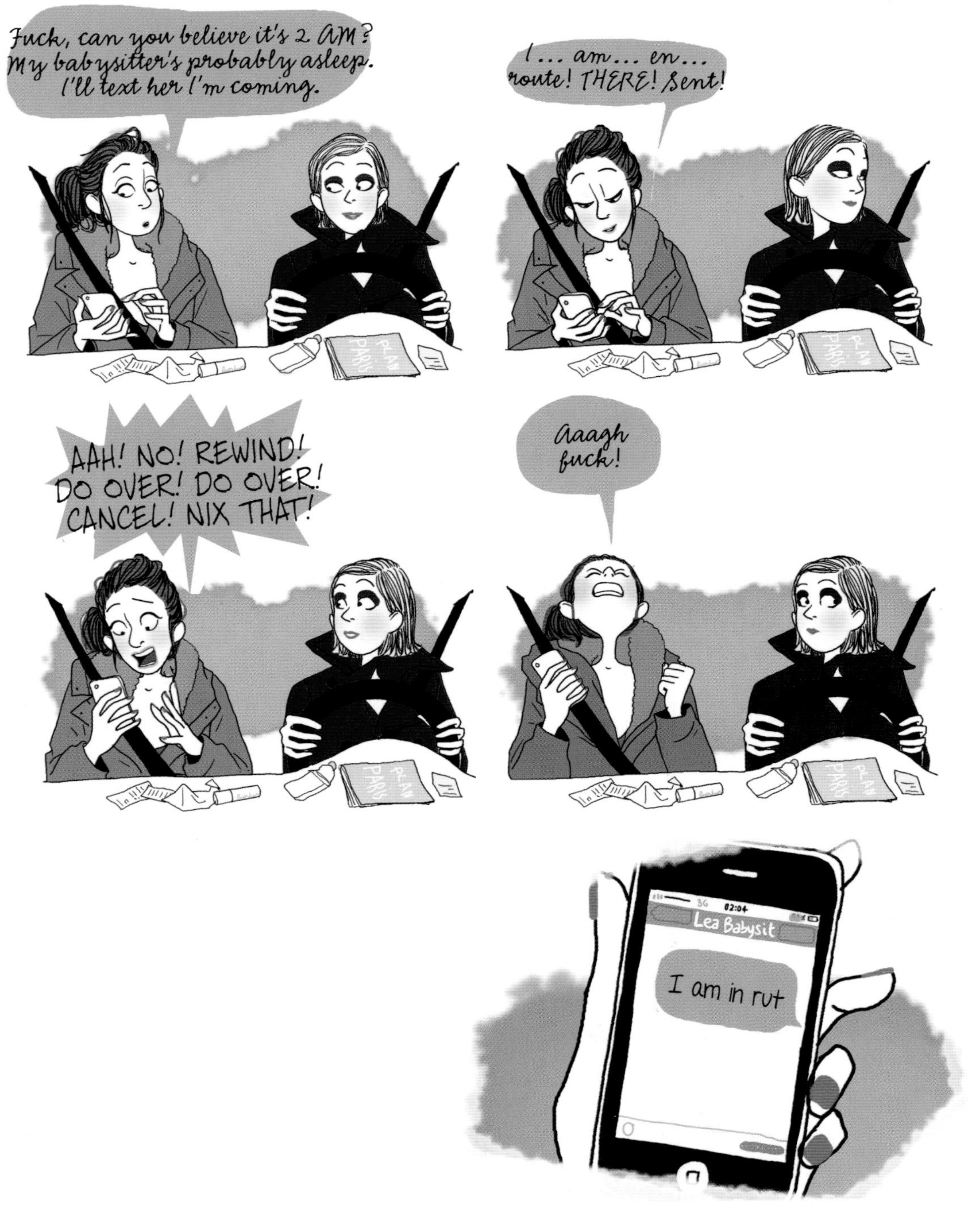
Fuck, can you believe it's 2 AM? My babysitter's probably asleep. I'll text her I'm coming.
I... am... en... route! THERE! Sent!
AAH! NO! REWIND! DO OVER! DO OVER! CANCEL! NIX THAT!
Aaagh fuck!
PLAN PARIS
02:04
Lea Babysit
I am in rut

OK, but this is strictly confidential, you can't tell anyone, OK?

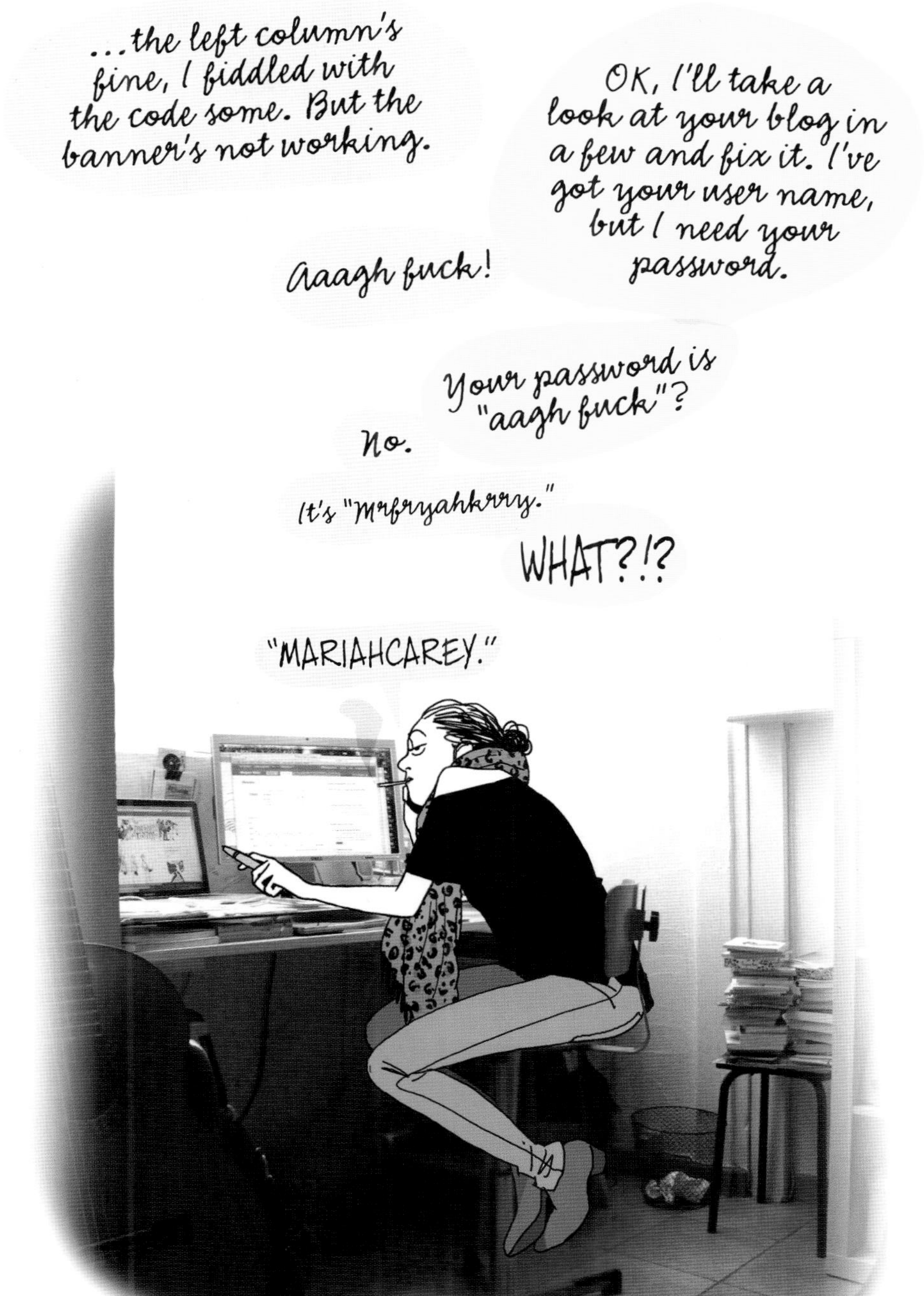
...the left column's fine, I fiddled with the code some. But the banner's not working.
OK, I'll take a look at your blog in a few and fix it. I've got your user name, but I need your password.
Aaagh fuck!
Your password is "aagh fuck"?
No.
It's "Mrfryahkrry."
WHAT?!?
"MARIAHCAREY."

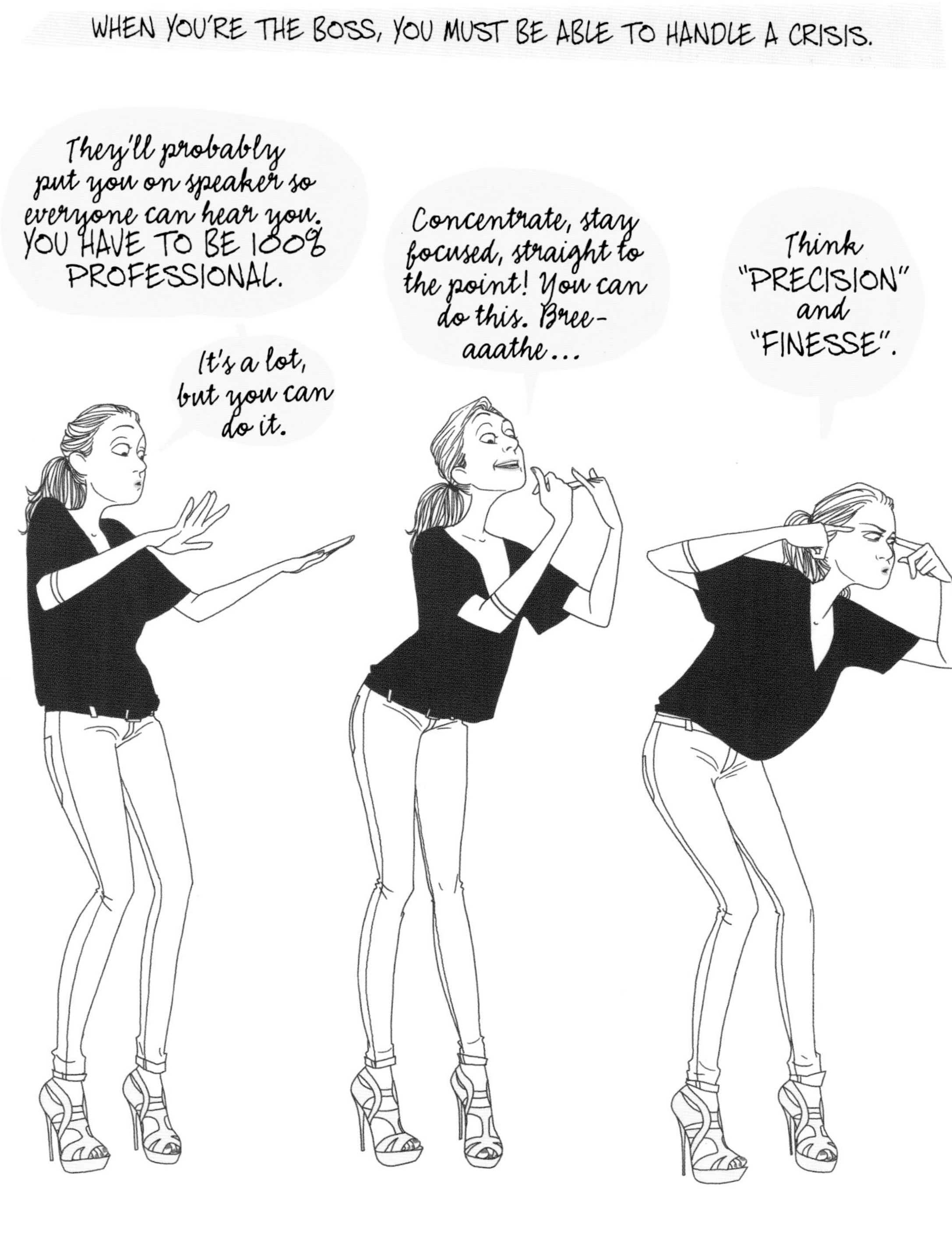
WHEN YOU'RE THE BOSS, YOU MUST BE ABLE TO HANDLE A CRISIS.
They'll probably put you on speaker so everyone can hear you. YOU HAVE TO BE 100% PROFESSIONAL.
It's a lot, but you can do it.
Concentrate, stay focused, straight to the point! You can do this. Bree-aaathe...
Think "PRECISION" and "FINESSE".

OK, so for Visual #3, we start with an establishing shot, wide angle on a woman, 40, brunette, OK? What are you thinking for the 4th image?

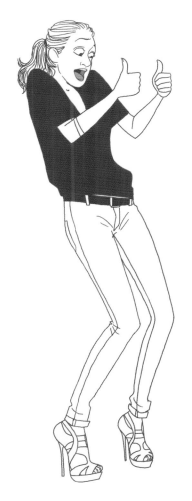

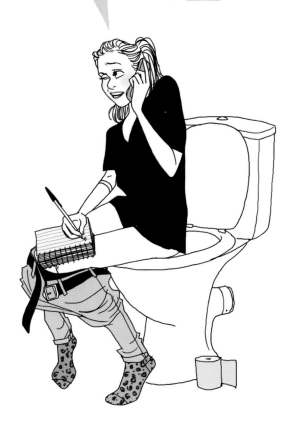

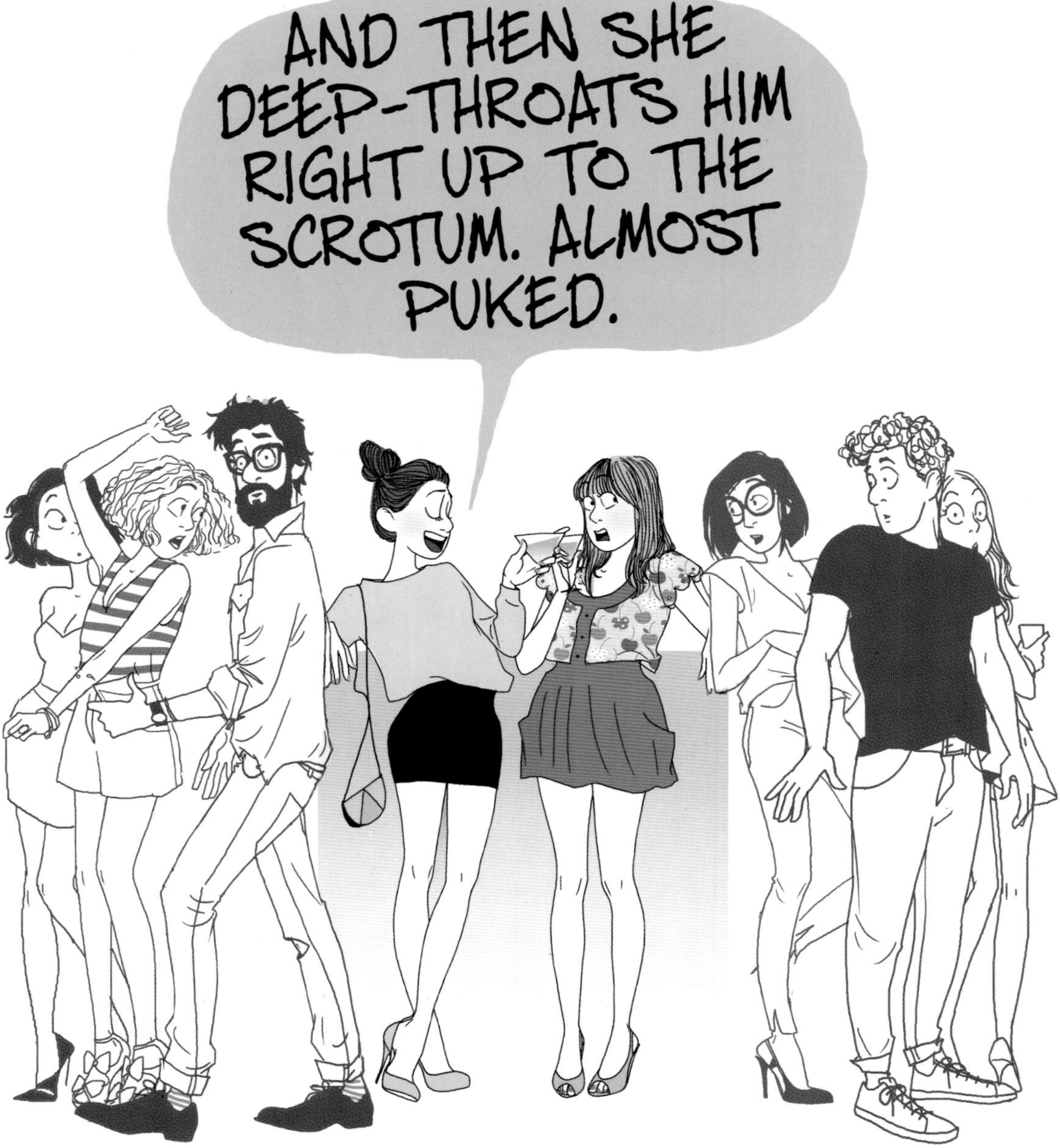
AND THEN SHE DEEP-THROATS HIM RIGHT UP TO THE SCROTUM. ALMOST PUKED.

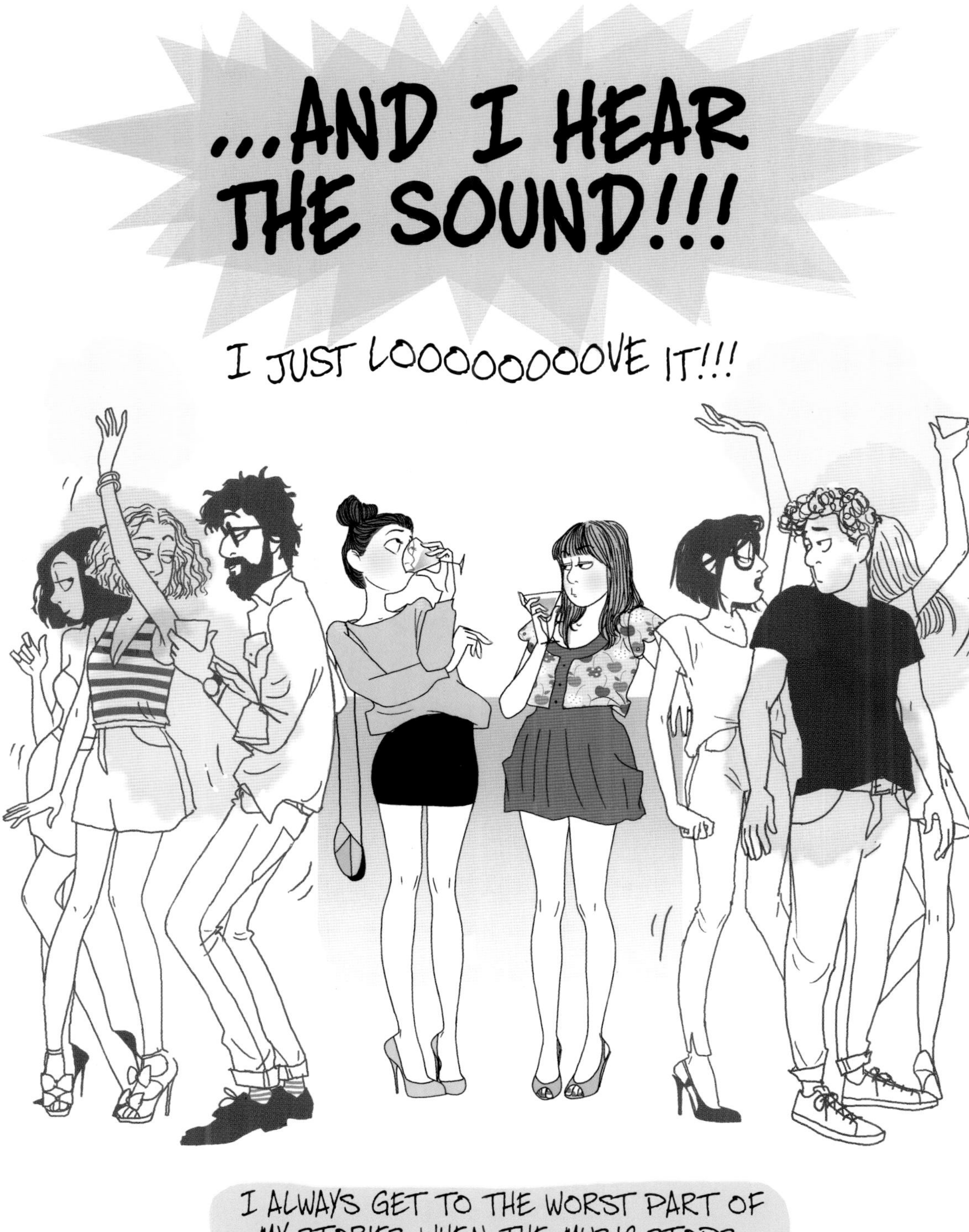
...AND I HEAR THE SOUND!!!
I JUST LOOOOOOOOOVE IT!!!
I ALWAYS GET TO THE WORST PART OF MY STORIES WHEN THE MUSIC STOPS.

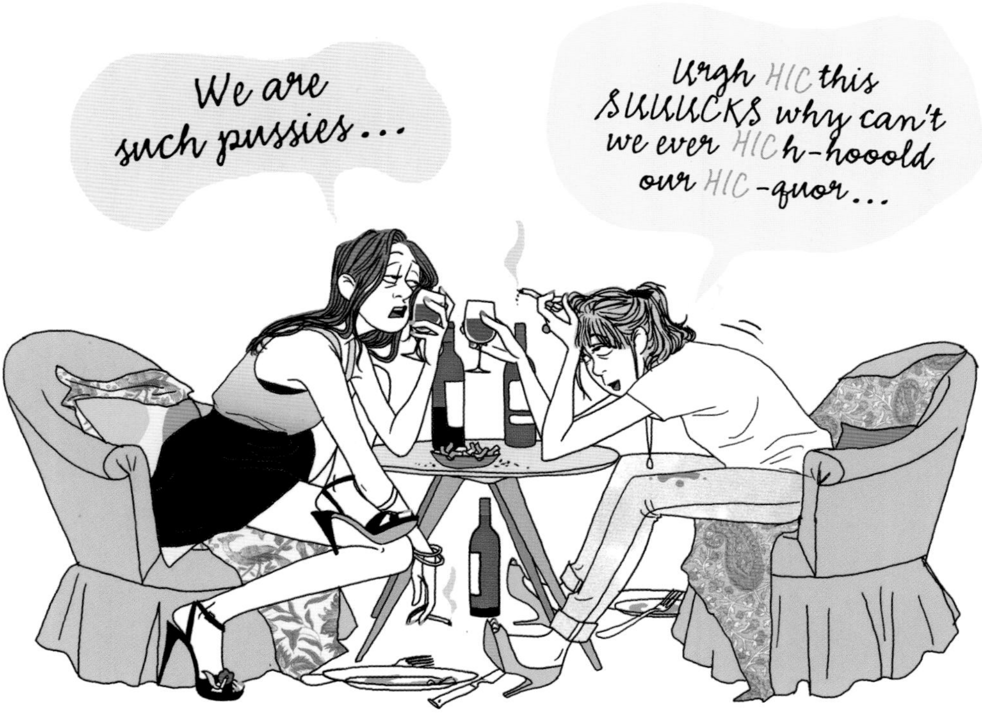
We are such pussies...
Urgh HIC this SUUUCKS why can't we ever HICh-hooold our HIC-quor...

IT'S NOT THAT WE'RE SHORT ON WILLPOWER...

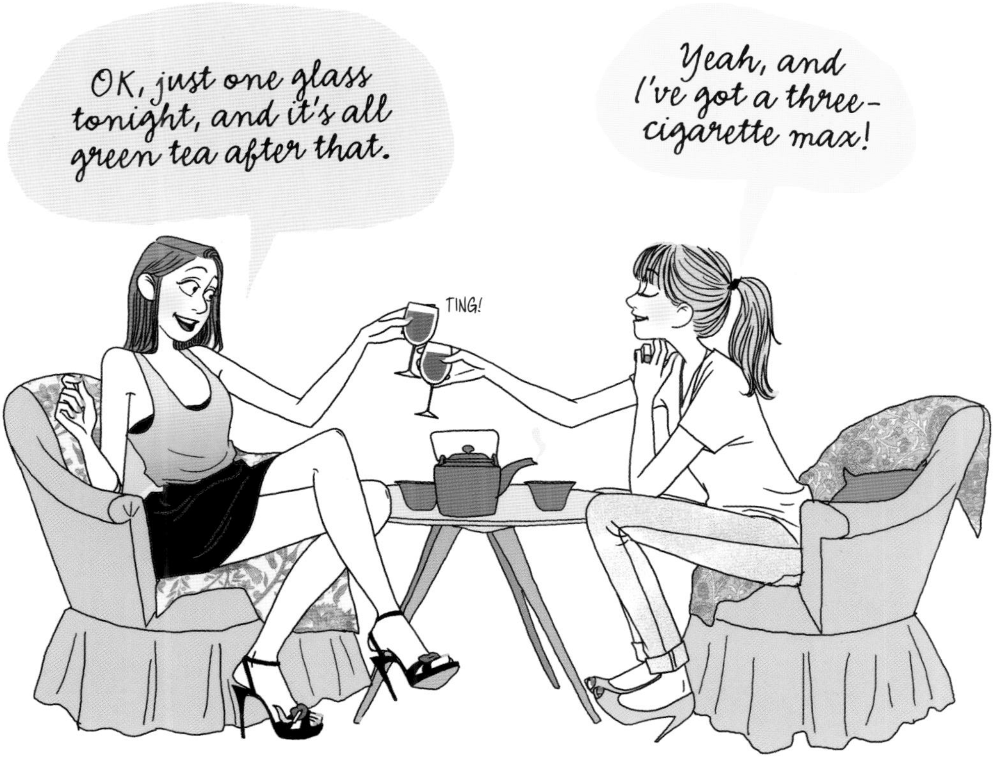
OK, just one glass tonight, and it's all green tea after that.
TING!
Yeah, and I've got a three-cigarette max!

WE'RE JUST BAD AT SETTING GOALS.

"The creative adult is the child who has survived." ~ Ursula K. LeGuin

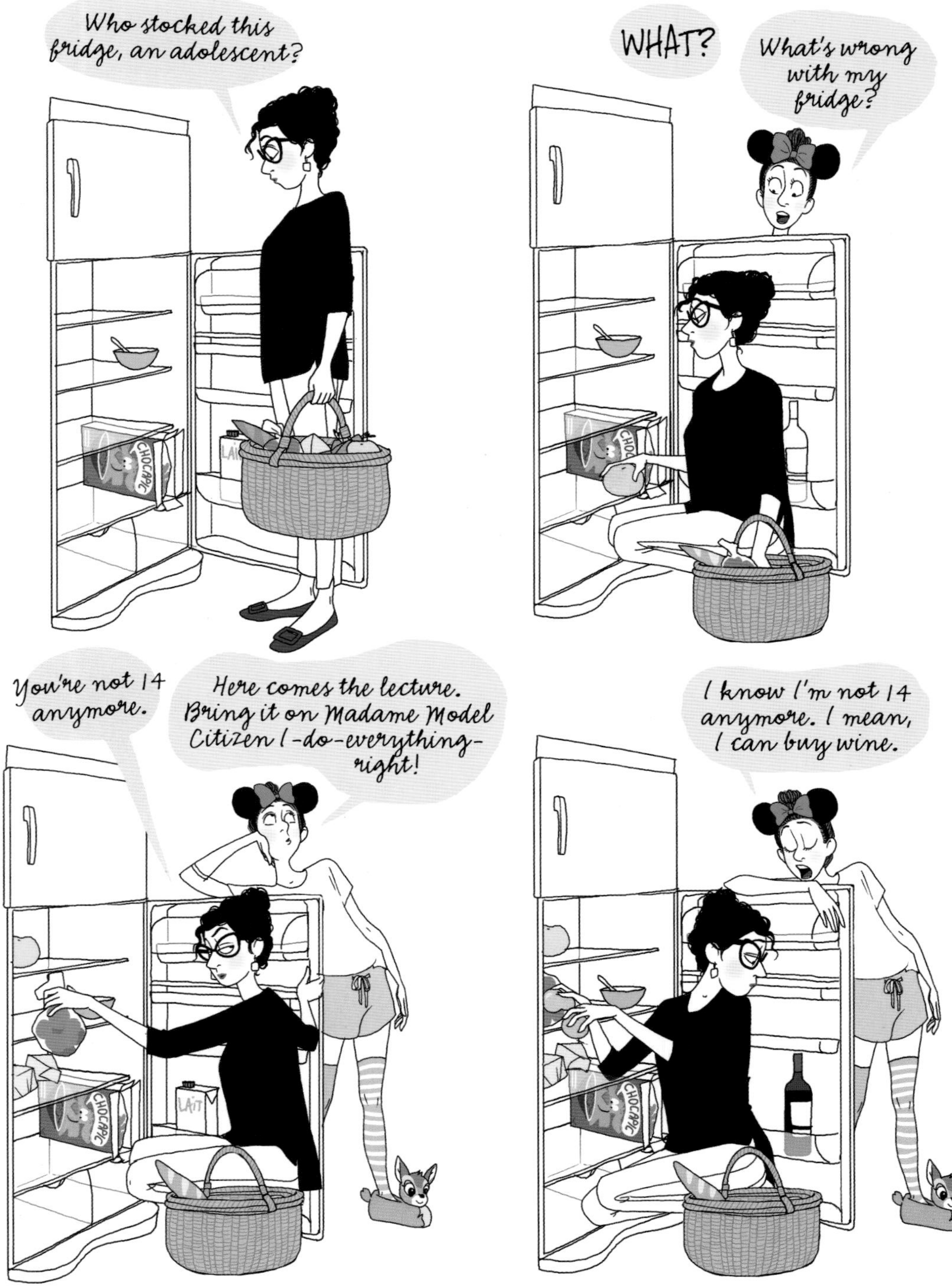
Who stocked this fridge, an adolescent?
WHAT?
What's wrong with my fridge?
CHOCAPIC
LAIT
You're not 14 anymore.
Here comes the lecture. Bring it on Madame Model Citizen I-do-everything-right!
I know I'm not 14 anymore. I mean, I can buy wine.

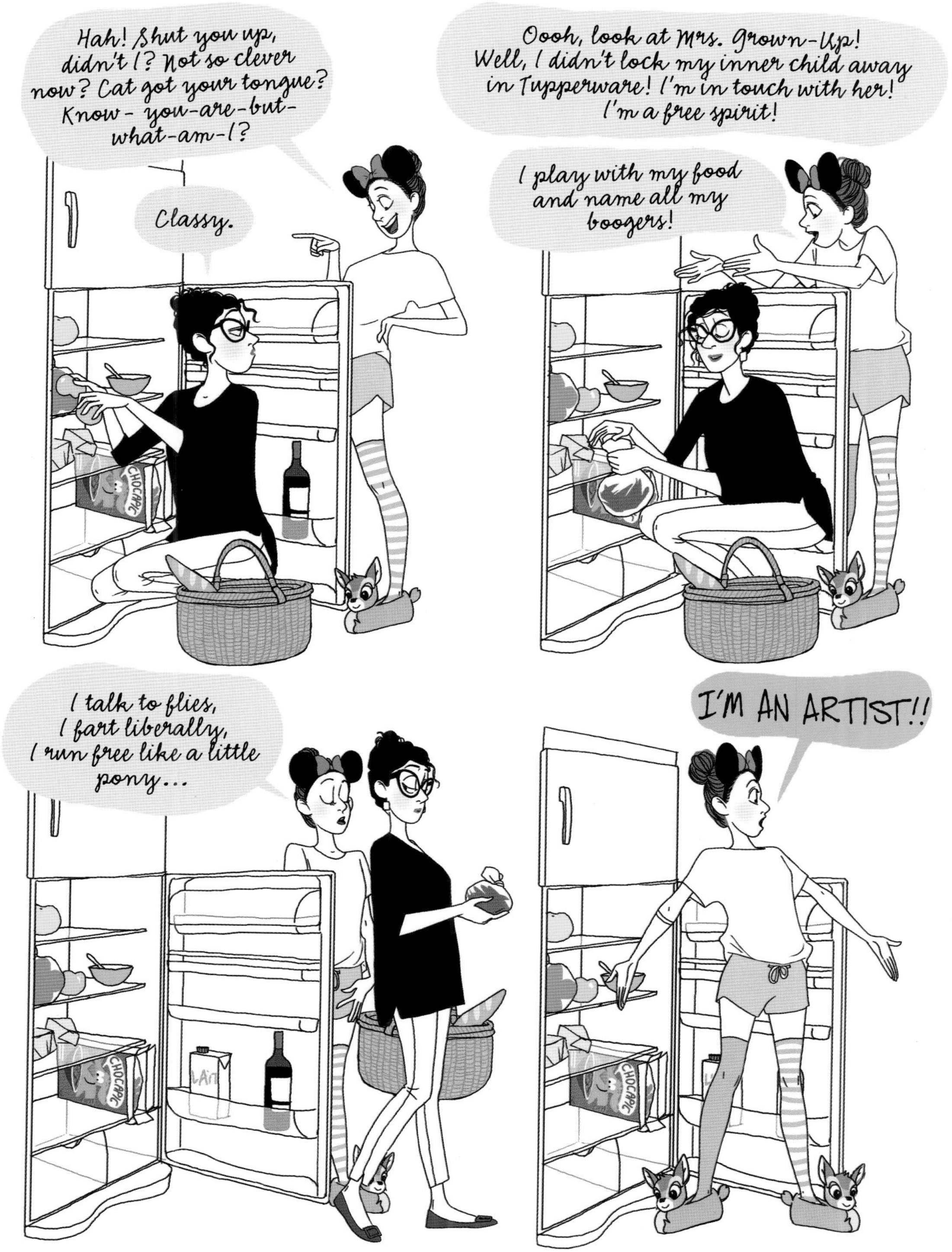
Hah! Shut you up, didn't I? Not so clever now? Cat got your tongue? Know-you-are-but-what-am-I?
Classy.
Oooh, look at Mrs. Grown-Up! Well, I didn't lock my inner child away in Tupperware! I'm in touch with her! I'm a free spirit!
I play with my food and name all my boogers!
CHOCAPIC
I talk to flies, I fart liberally, I run free like a little pony...
CHOCAPIC
LAIT
I'M AN ARTIST!!
CHOCAPIC

Yeah, that's right: an "Artist"!

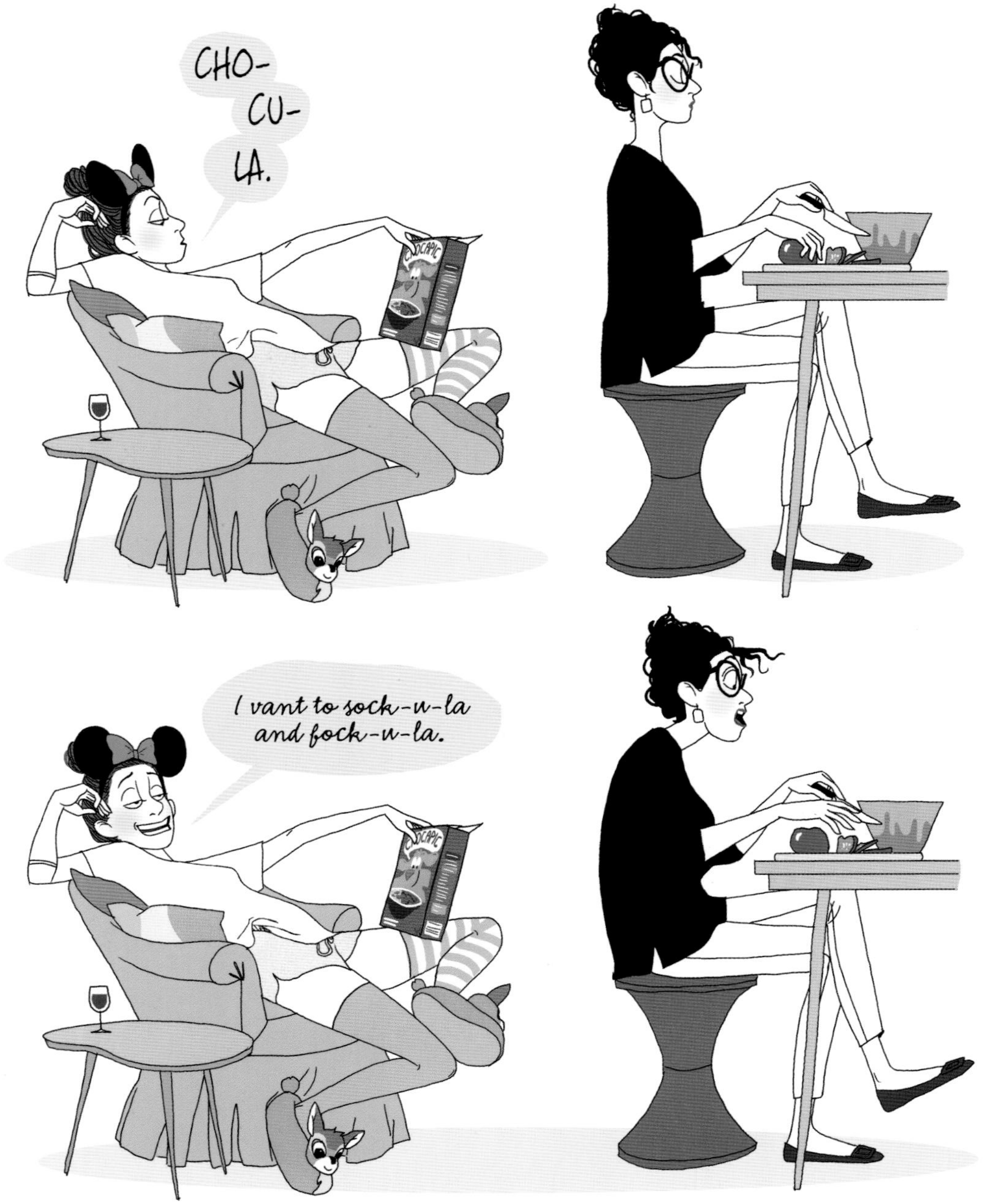

CHO-
CU-
LA.
CHOCAPIC
I vant to sock-u-la and fock-u-la.
CHOCAPIC

I'm a poet and don't even know it.

"They tried to make me go to rehab
But I said, no, no, no"

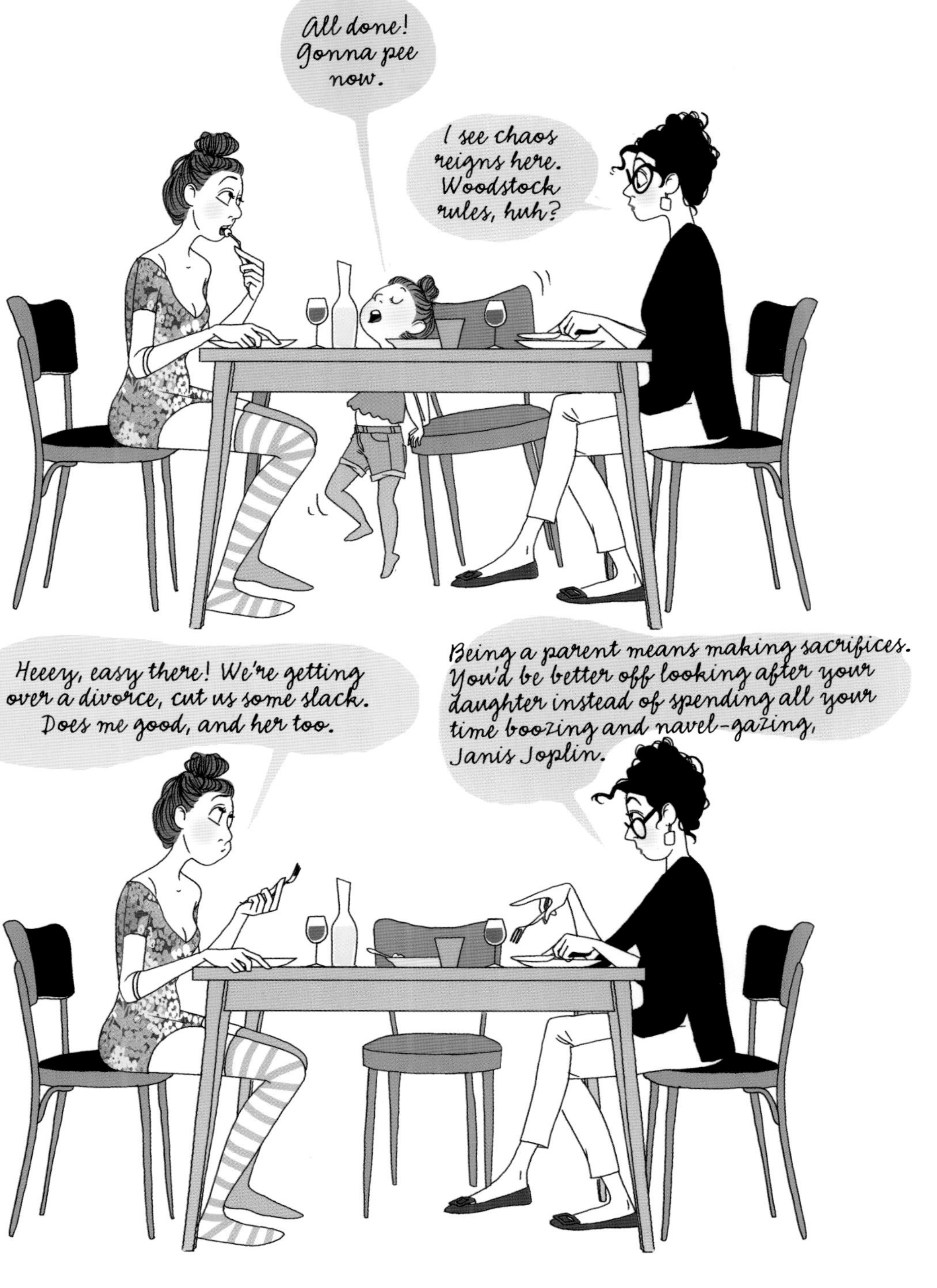
All done! Gonna pee now.
I see chaos reigns here. Woodstock rules, huh?
Heeey, easy there! We're getting over a divorce, cut us some slack. Does me good, and her too.
Being a parent means making sacrifices. You'd be better off looking after your daughter instead of spending all your time boozing and navel-gazing, Janis Joplin.

*Amy Winehouse "Rehab"

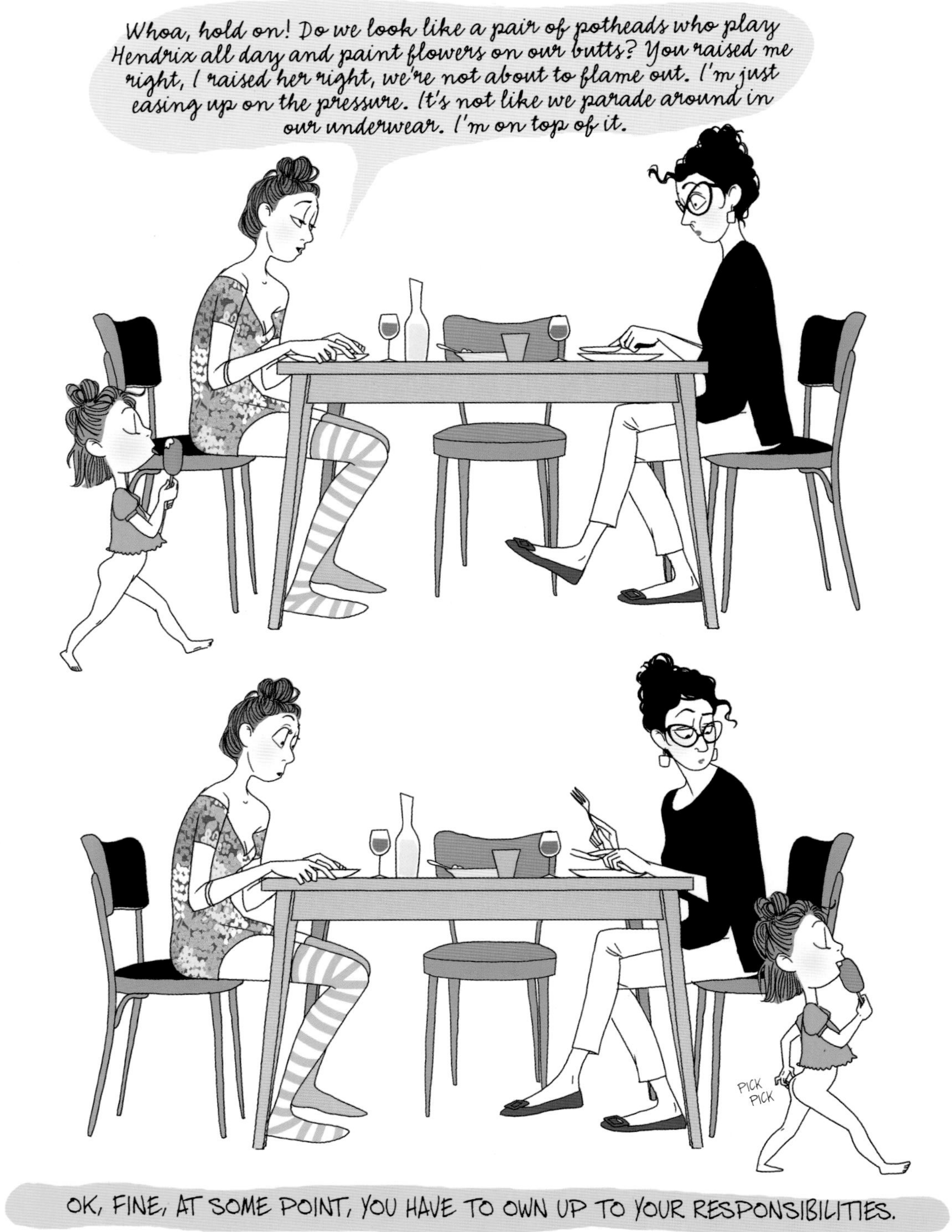
Whoa, hold on! Do we look like a pair of potheads who play Hendrix all day and paint flowers on our butts? You raised me right, I raised her right, we're not about to flame out. I'm just easing up on the pressure. It's not like we parade around in our underwear. I'm on top of it.
PICK PICK
OK, FINE, AT SOME POINT, YOU HAVE TO OWN UP TO YOUR RESPONSIBILITIES.

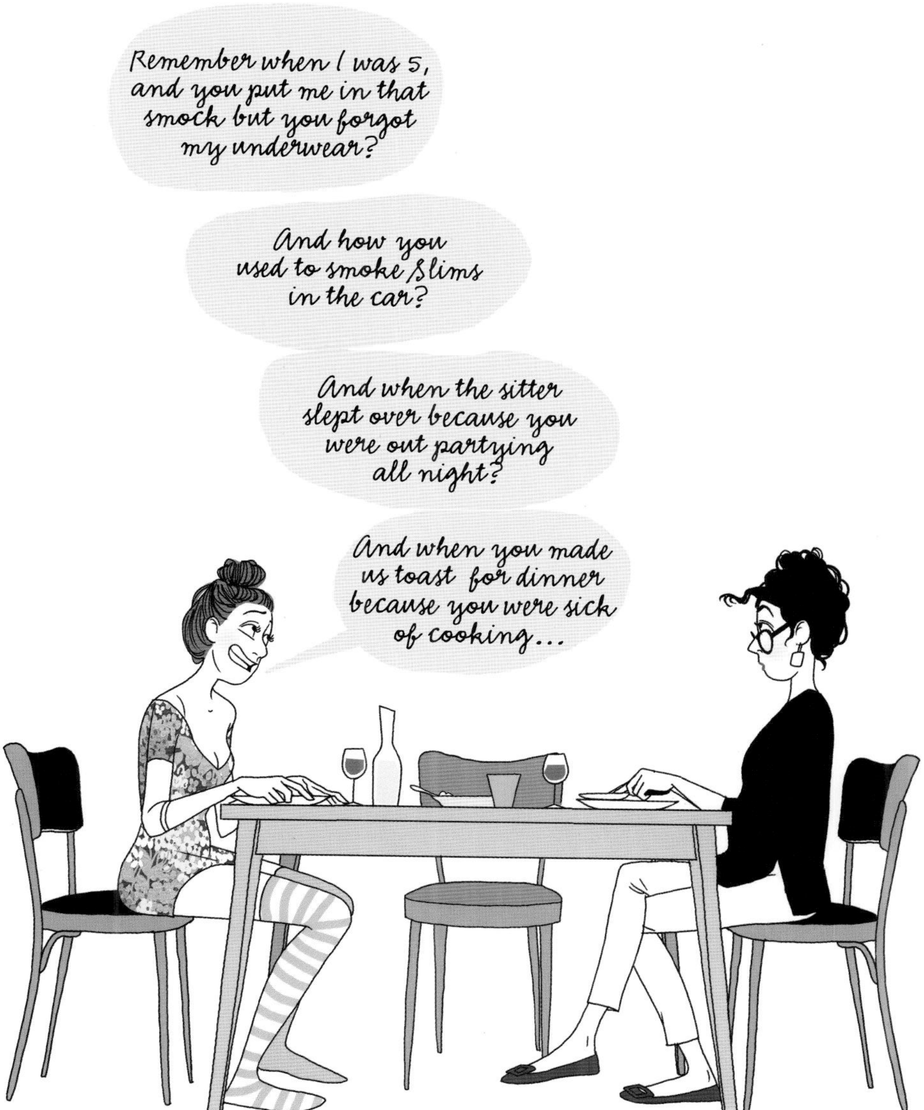
Remember when I was 5, and you put me in that smock but you forgot my underwear?
And how you used to smoke Slims in the car?
And when the sitter slept over because you were out partying all night?
And when you made us toast for dinner because you were sick of cooking...

...THAT'S HOW YOU BECOME A GROWN-UP.

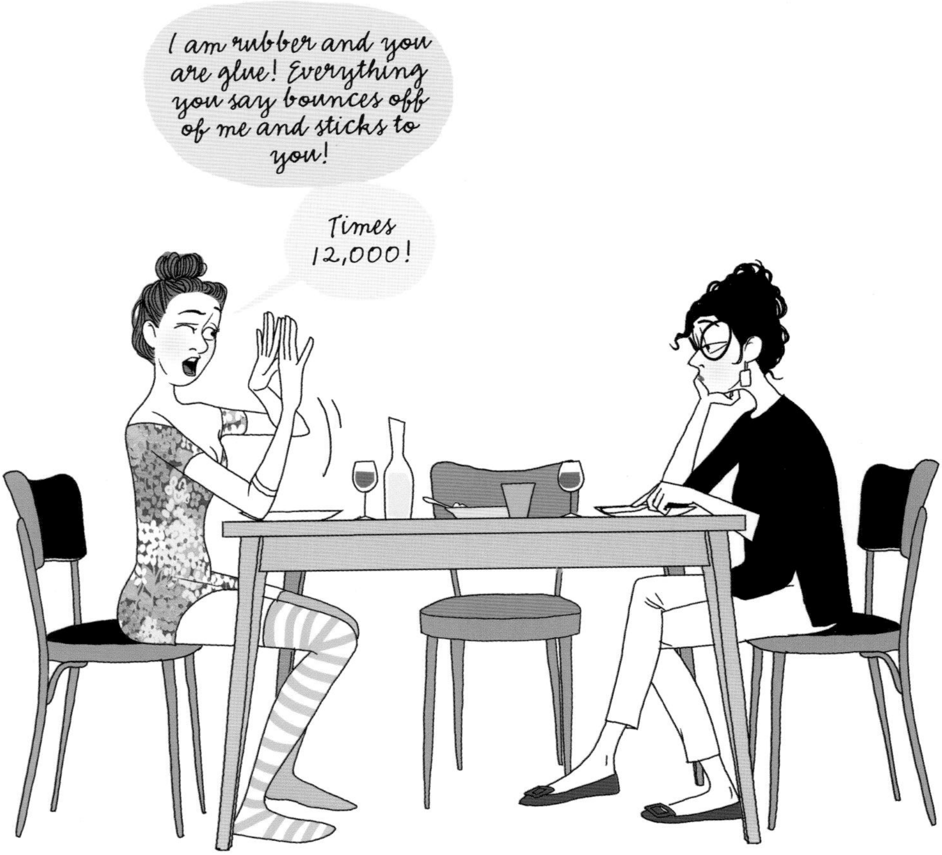
I am rubber and you are glue! Everything you say bounces off of me and sticks to you!
Times 12,000!

Just a sec, lemme slit my wrists and I'll be right back

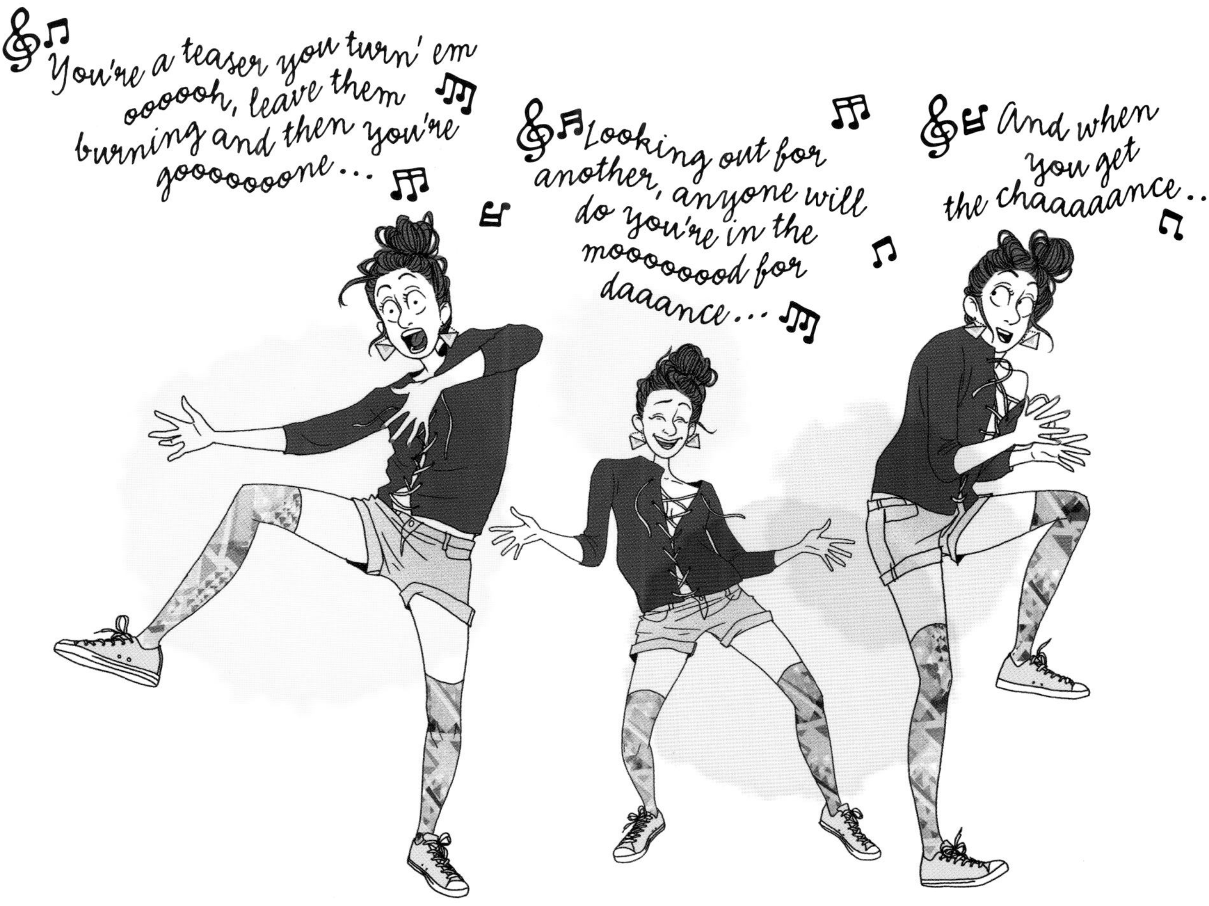
You're a teaser you turn' em oooooh, leave them burning and then you're gooooooone...
Looking out for another, anyone will do you're in the moooooood for daaance...
And when you get the chaaaaance...

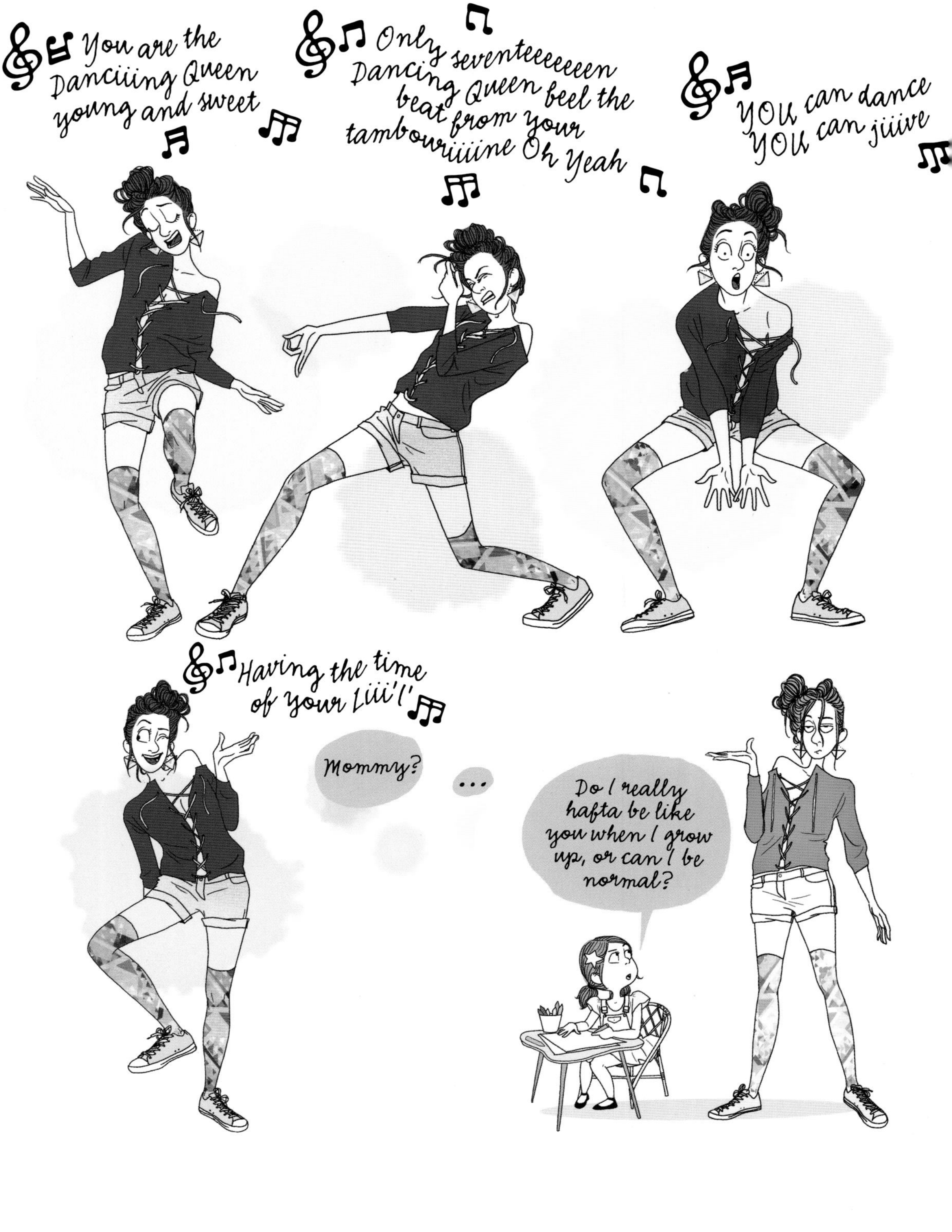
You are the Danciiing Queen young and sweet
Only seventeeeeeeen Dancing Queen feel the beat from your tambouriiiiine Oh Yeah
YOU can dance YOU can jiiive
Having the time of your Liii'l'
Mommy?
...
Do I really hafta be like you when I grow up, or can I be normal?

*Abba "Dancing Quee

Yoda

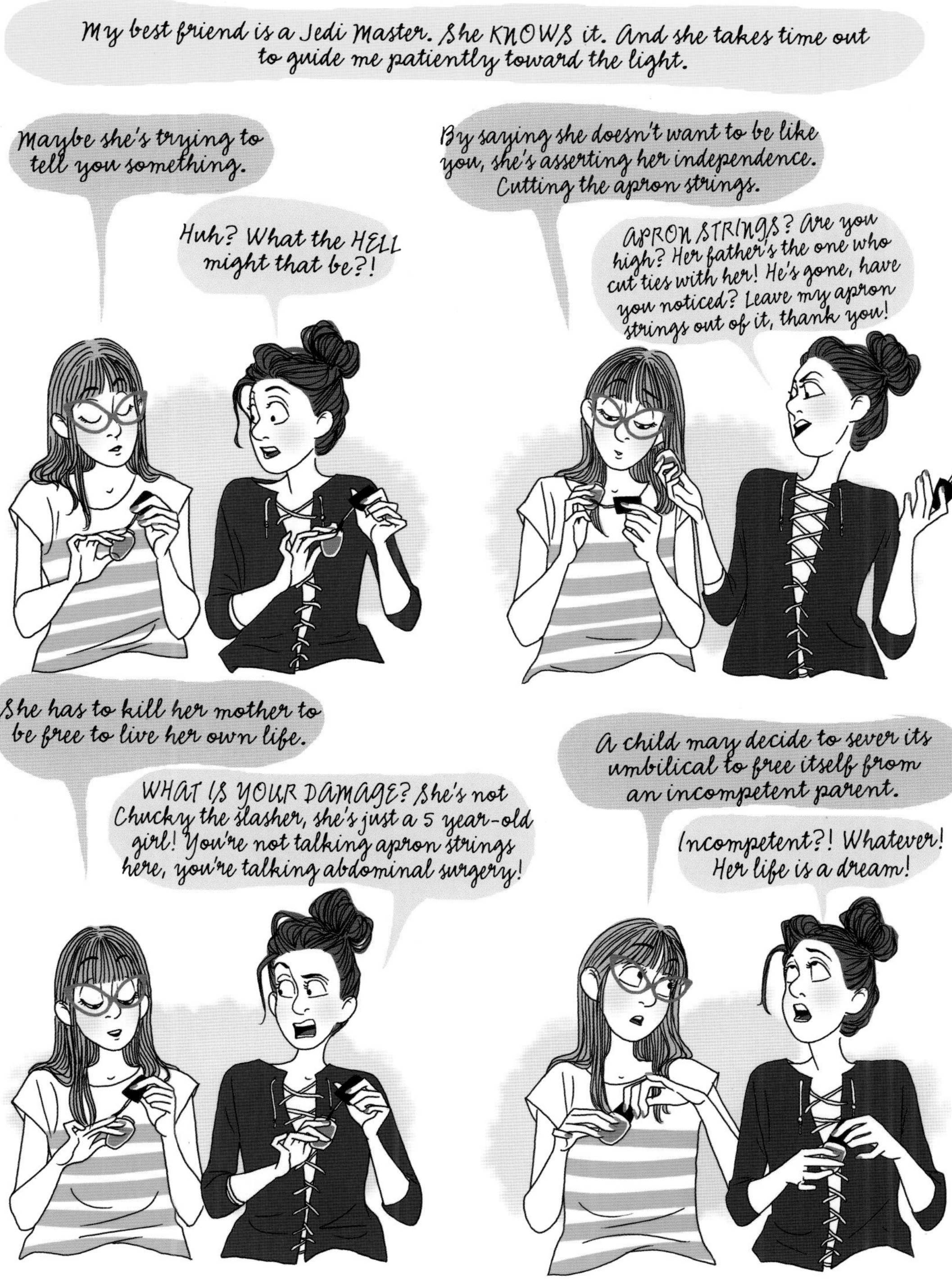

My best friend is a Jedi Master. She KNOWS it. And she takes time out to guide me patiently toward the light.
Maybe she's trying to tell you something.
Huh? What the HELL might that be?!
By saying she doesn't want to be like you, she's asserting her independence. Cutting the apron strings.
APRON STRINGS? Are you high? Her father's the one who cut ties with her! He's gone, have you noticed? Leave my apron strings out of it, thank you!
She has to kill her mother to be free to live her own life.
WHAT IS YOUR DAMAGE? She's not Chucky the slasher, she's just a 5 year-old girl! You're not talking apron strings here, you're talking abdominal surgery!
A child may decide to sever its umbilical to free itself from an incompetent parent.
Incompetent?! Whatever! Her life is a dream!

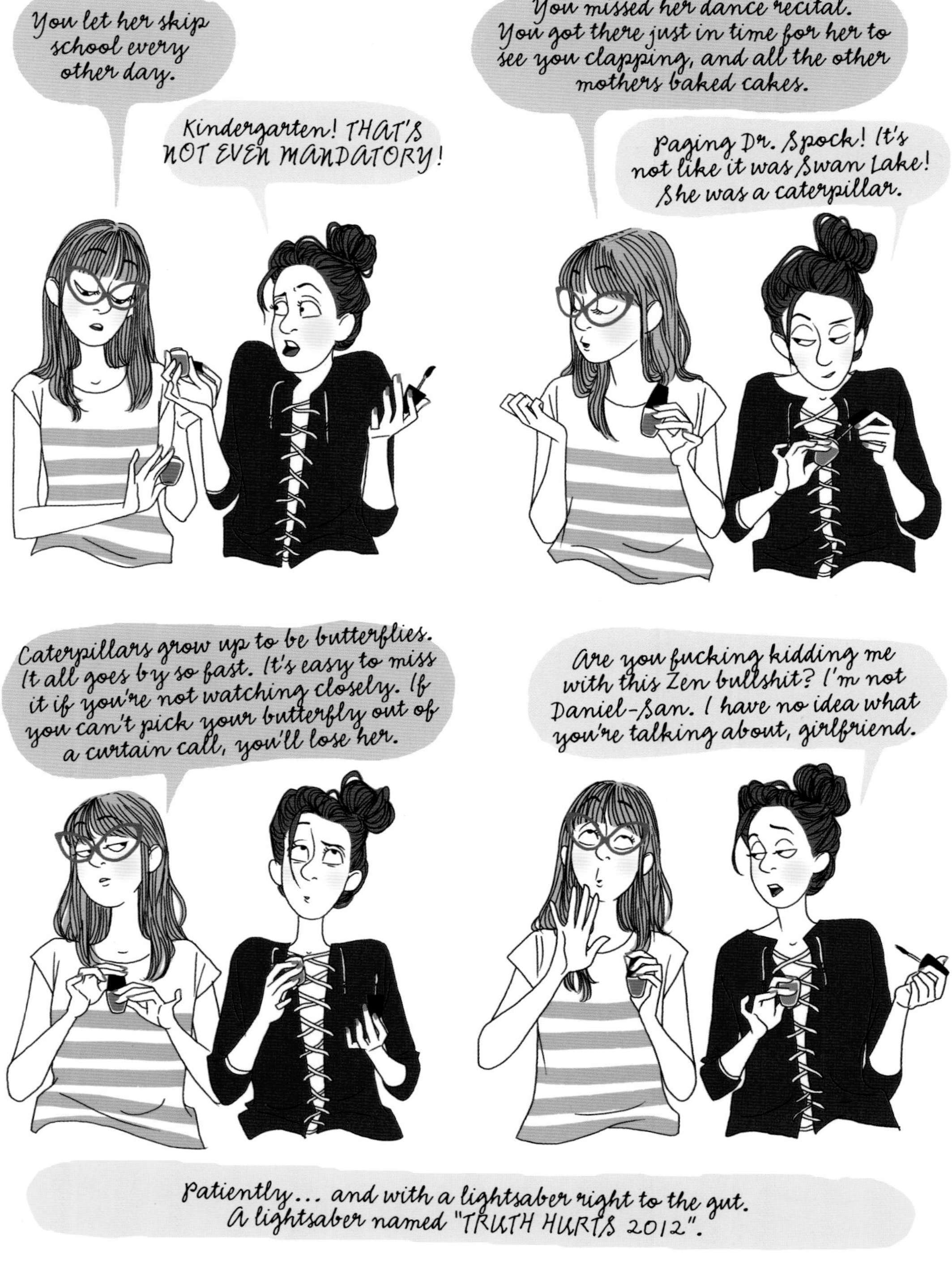
You let her skip school every other day.
Kindergarten! THAT'S NOT EVEN MANDATORY!
You missed her dance recital. You got there just in time for her to see you clapping, and all the other mothers baked cakes.
Paging Dr. Spock! It's not like it was Swan Lake! She was a caterpillar.
Caterpillars grow up to be butterflies. It all goes by so fast. It's easy to miss it if you're not watching closely. If you can't pick your butterfly out of a curtain call, you'll lose her.
Are you fucking kidding me with this Zen bullshit? I'm not Daniel-San. I have no idea what you're talking about, girlfriend.
Patiently... and with a lightsaber right to the gut. A lightsaber named "TRUTH HURTS 2012".

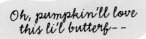 Oh, pumpkin'll love this li'l butterf--

 Oh, shit.

Oh, shit, caterpillars...

OH FUCK MY LI'L CATERPILLAR WAAAH!

And I only ever breastfed her for 3 weeks and I put rice cereal in her bottle so she'd sleep through the night at one I'M A HOOORRIBLE MOTHER!!!

...GUILT.

The Age of Reason

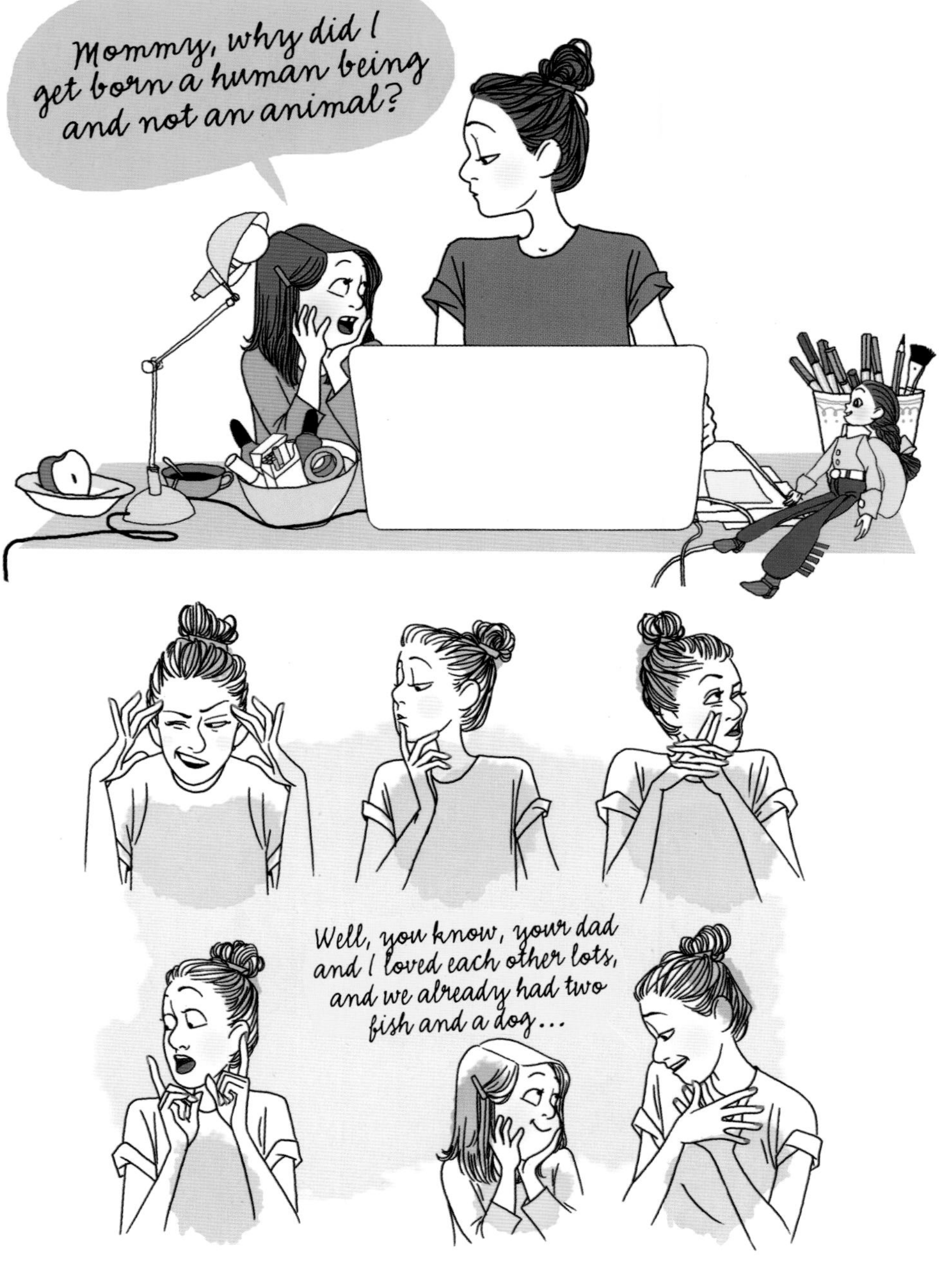
Mommy, why did I get born a human being and not an animal?
Well, you know, your dad and I loved each other lots, and we already had two fish and a dog...

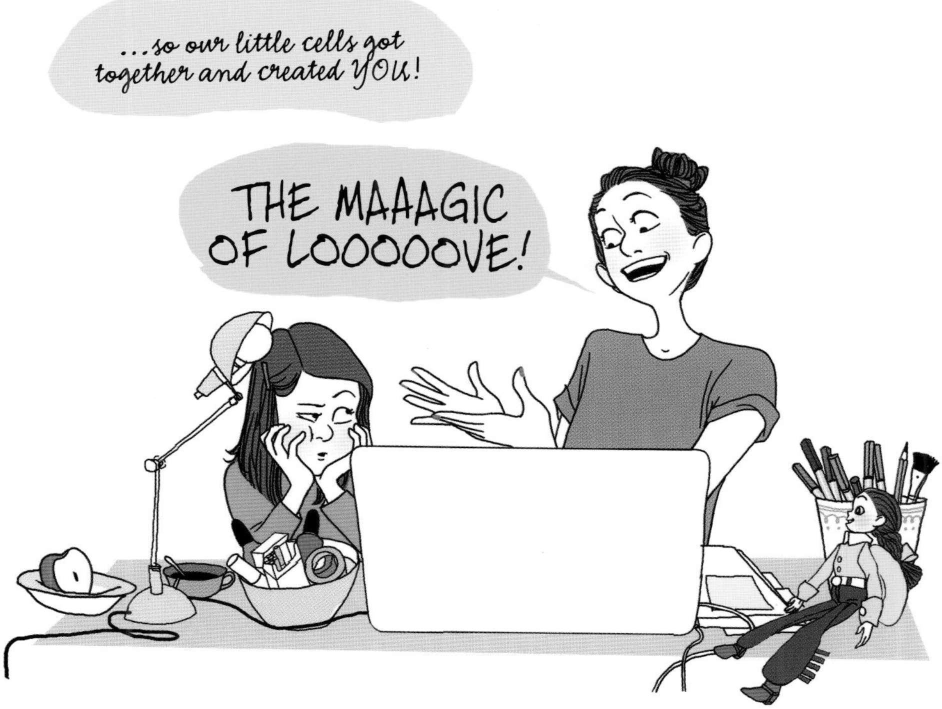
...so our little cells got together and created YOU!
THE MAAAGIC OF LOOOOOVE!

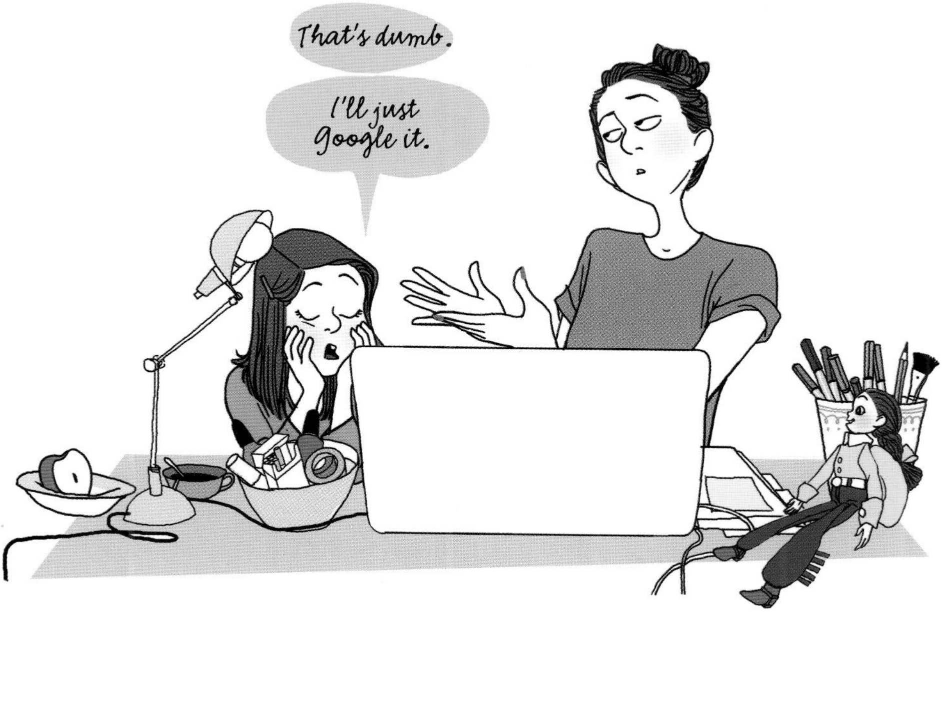
That's dumb.
I'll just Google it.

"We have to get used to the idea that at the most important crossroads in our life there are no signs." ~ Ernest Hemingway

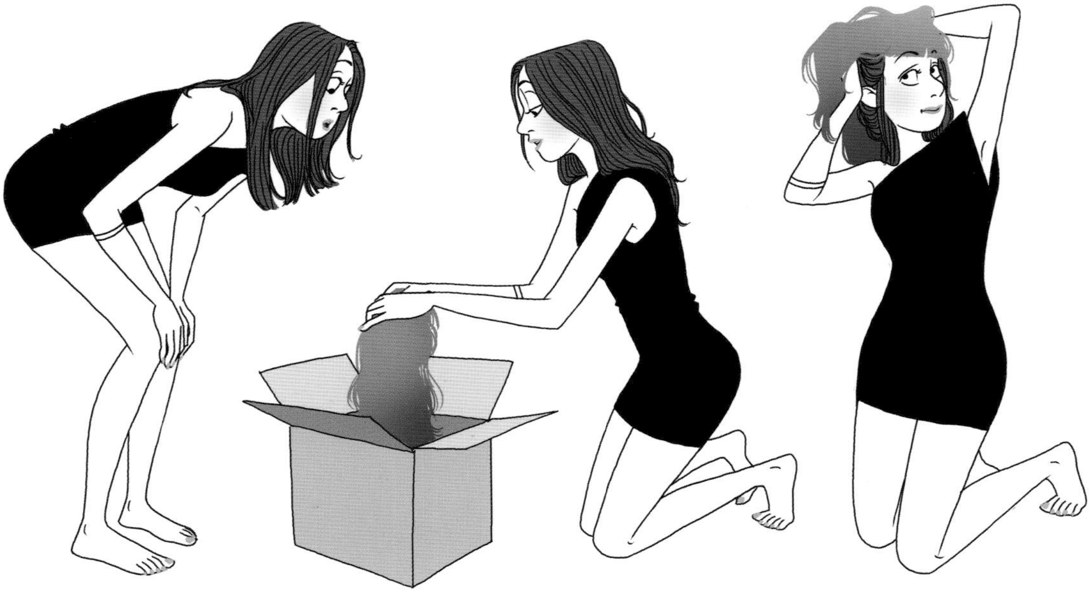

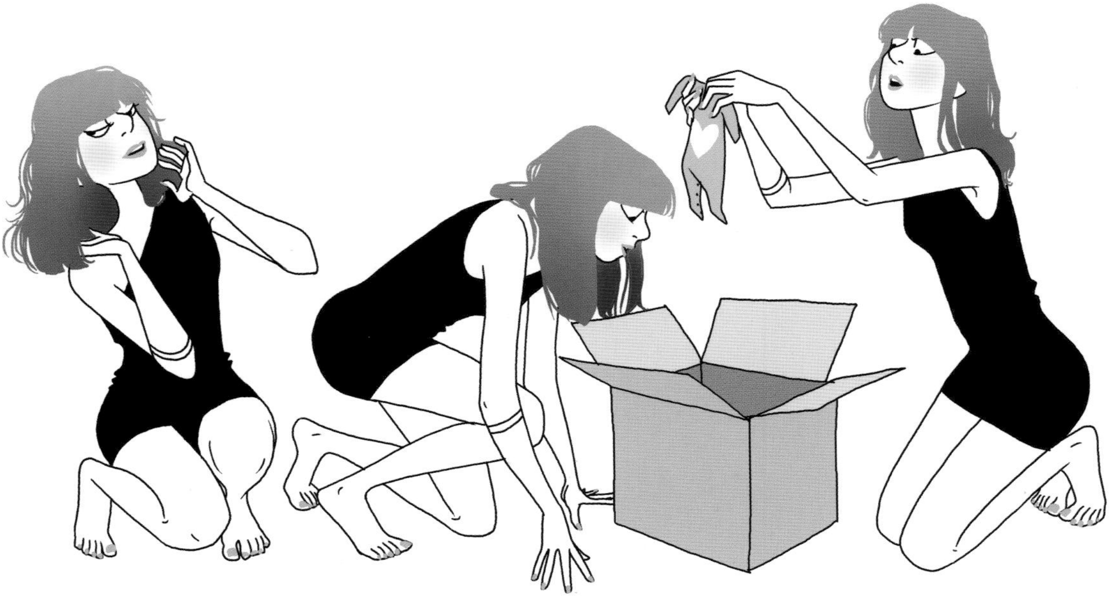

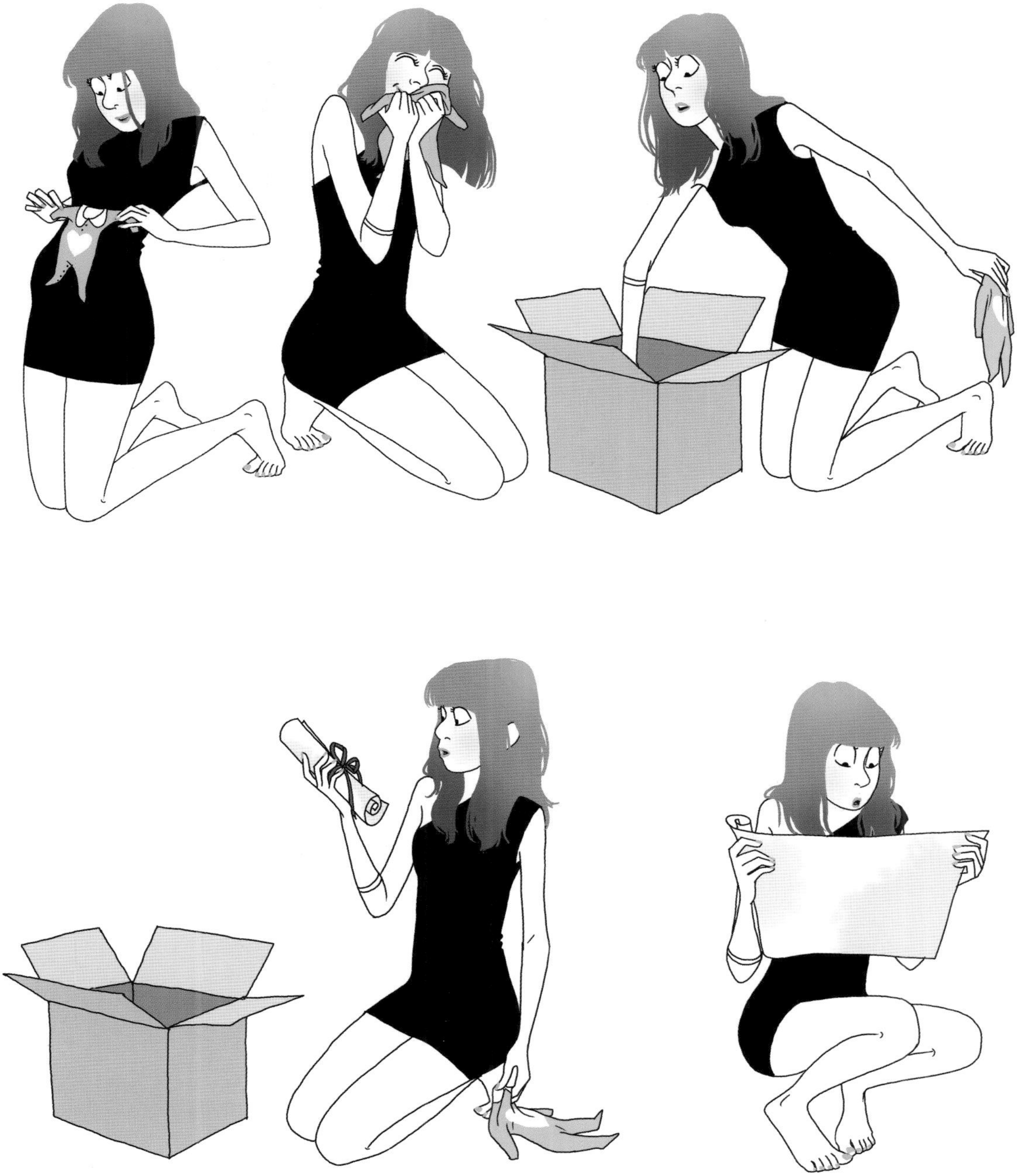

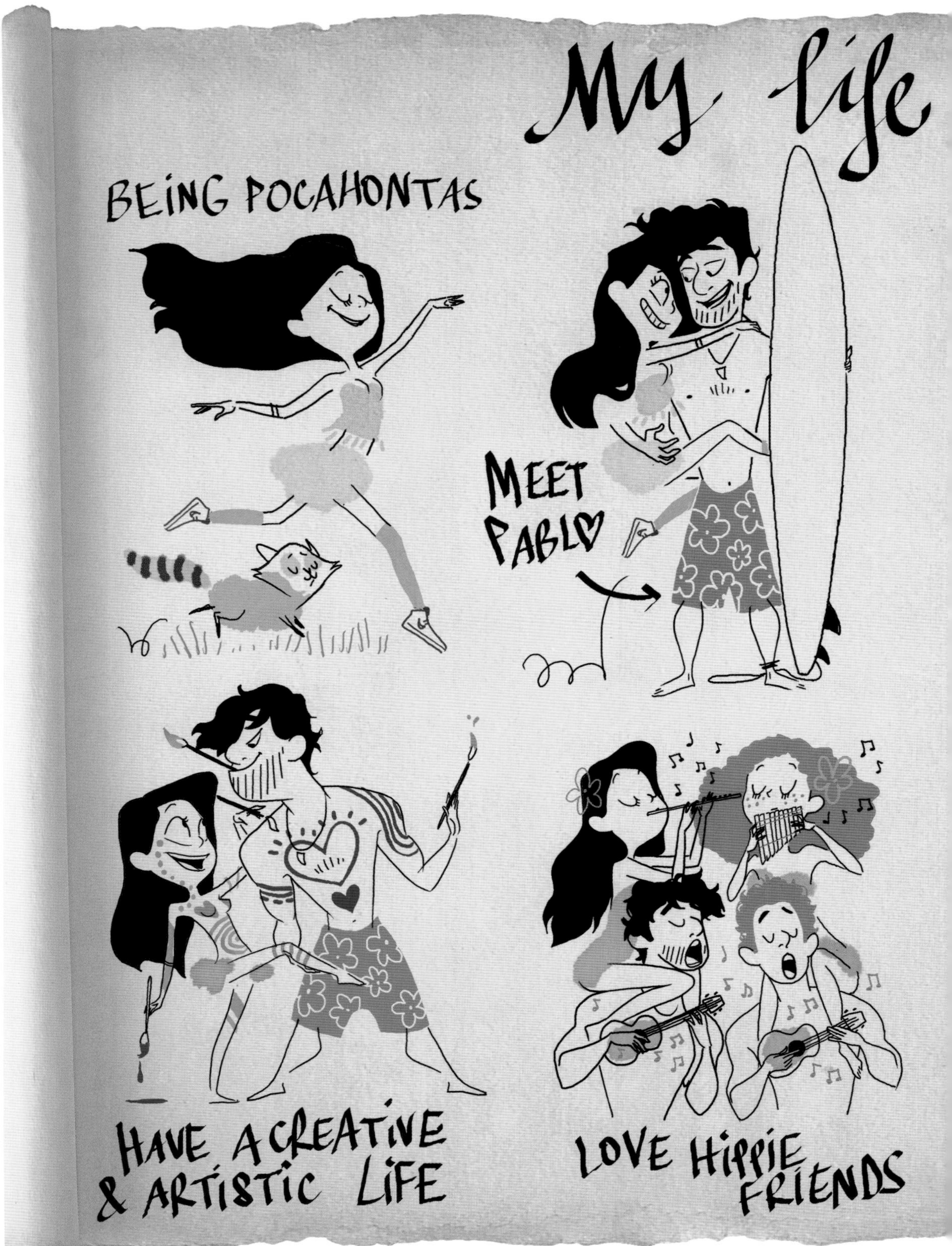

My life
BEING POCAHONTAS
MEET PABLO
HAVE A CREATIVE & ARTISTIC LIFE
LOVE HIPPIE FRIENDS

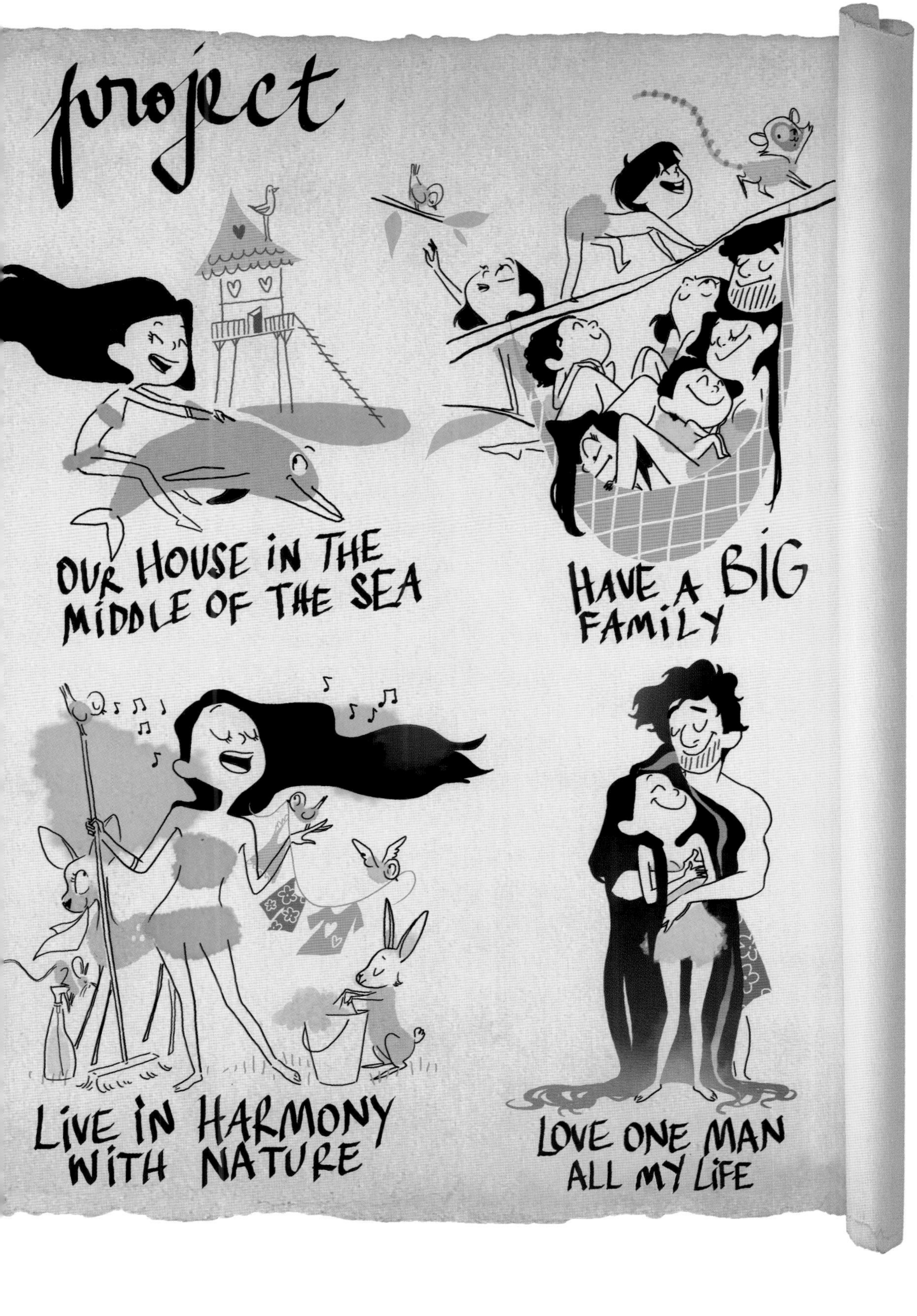
project
OUR HOUSE IN THE MIDDLE OF THE SEA
HAVE A BIG FAMILY
LIVE IN HARMONY WITH NATURE
LOVE ONE MAN ALL MY LIFE

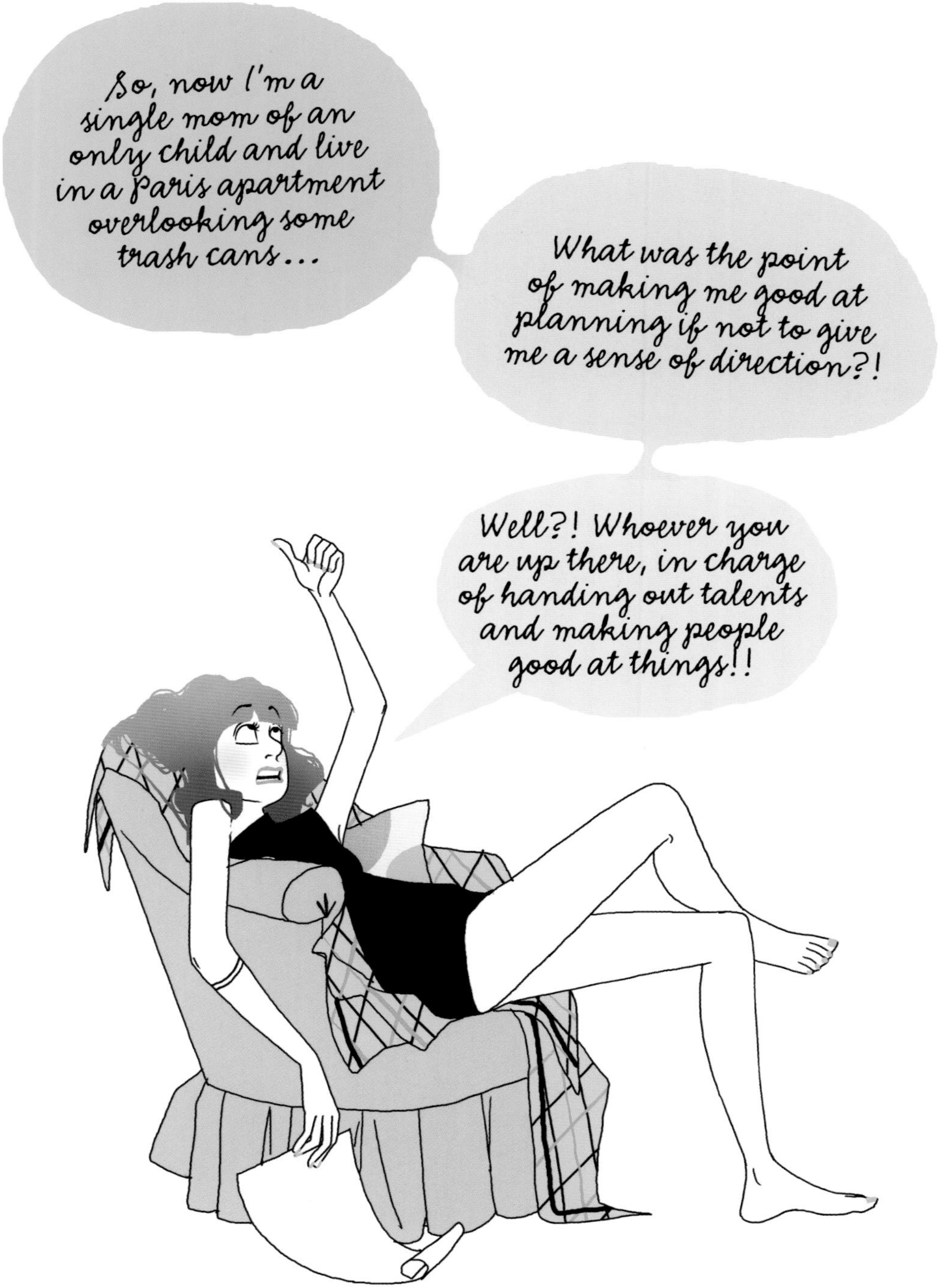
So, now I'm a single mom of an only child and live in a Paris apartment overlooking some trash cans...
What was the point of making me good at planning if not to give me a sense of direction?!
Well?! Whoever you are up there, in charge of handing out talents and making people good at things!!

Heroes Corp.

When girlfriends get together, their strength increases tenfold, suffusing them with powerful energy and giving them motivation beyond normal to face down trials and accomplish great things...

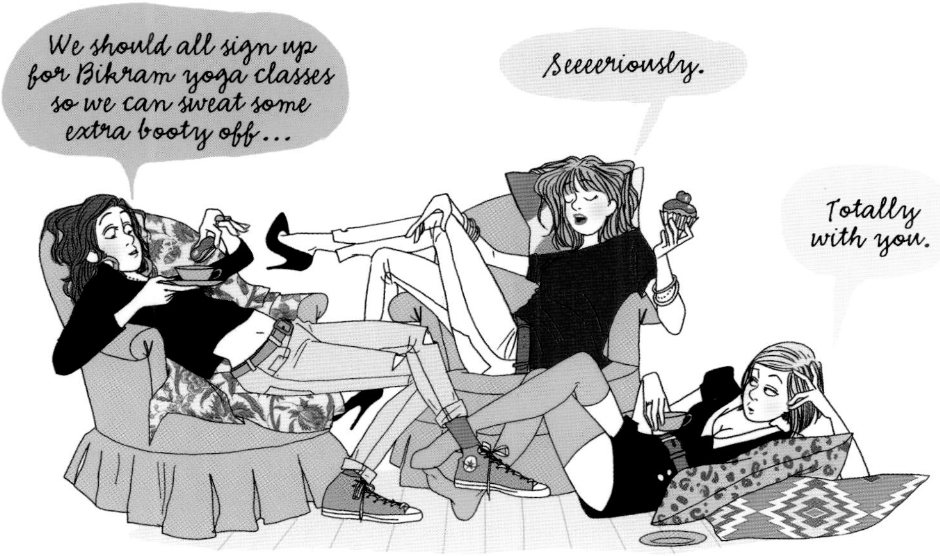
We should all sign up for Bikram yoga classes so we can sweat some extra booty off...
Seeeeriously.
Totally with you.

...or just goof off.

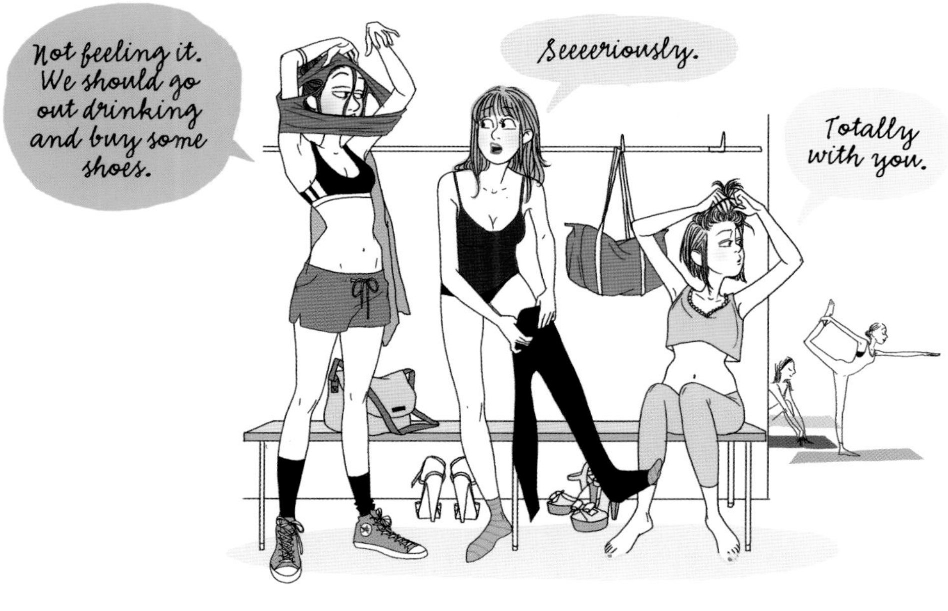
Not feeling it. We should go out drinking and buy some shoes.
Seeeeriously.
Totally with you.

So all that girly stuff totally made her a delicate flower

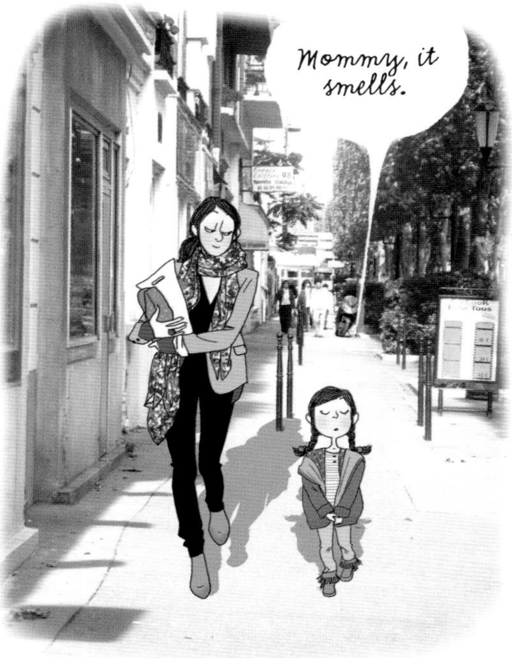
Mommy, it smells.

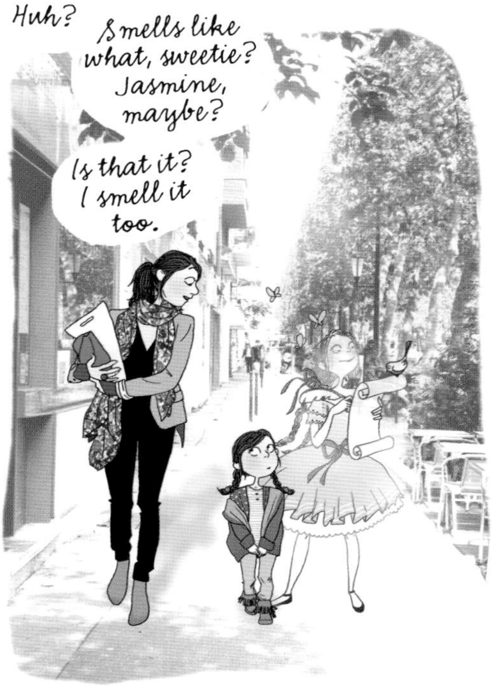
Huh?
Smells like what, sweetie? Jasmine, maybe?
Is that it? I smell it too.

Smells like sunshine after rain, right? Like the end of summer, and shared happiness, and warmth…

The aroma of loooove?

NOPE.

It smells like a dead bird.

Blue Skies

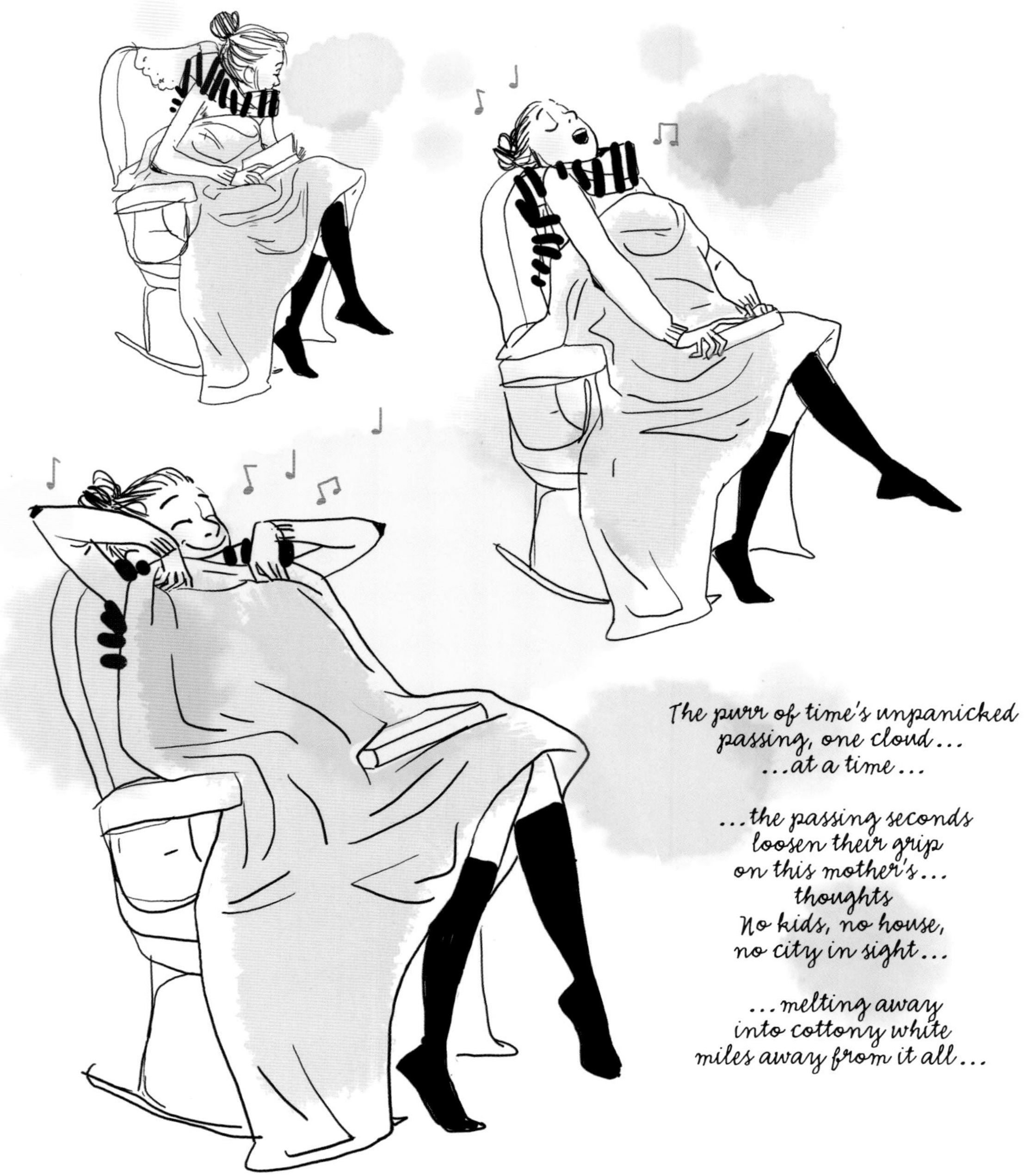
The purr of time's unpanicked passing, one cloud... ...at a time...
...the passing seconds loosen their grip on this mother's... thoughts
No kids, no house, no city in sight...
...melting away into cottony white miles away from it all...

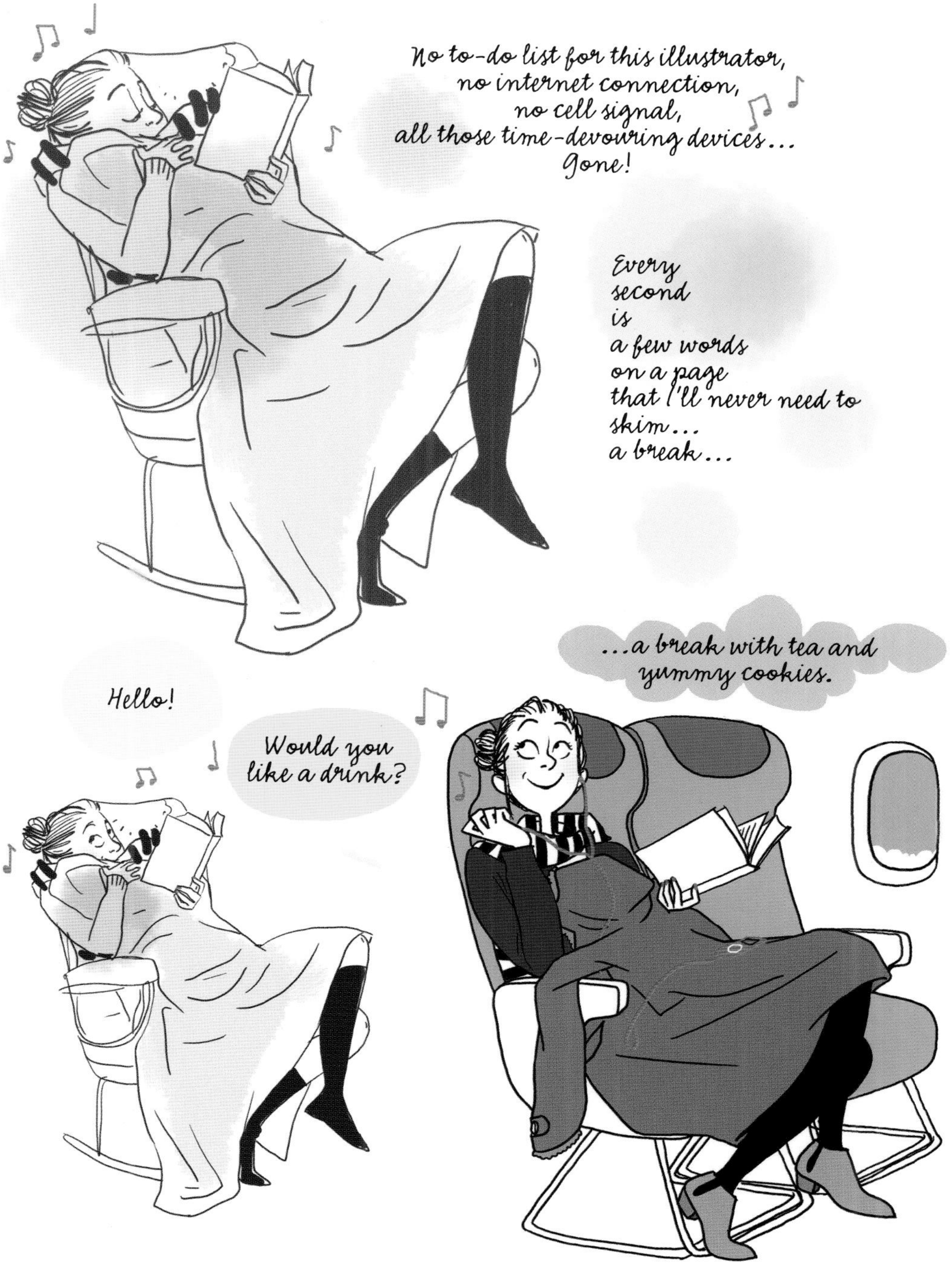
No to-do list for this illustrator,
no internet connection,
no cell signal,
all those time-devouring devices...
Gone!
Every
second
is
a few words
on a page
that I'll never need to
skim...
a break...
...a break with tea and
yummy cookies.
Hello!
Would you
like a drink?

Girls Just Wanna Have Fun

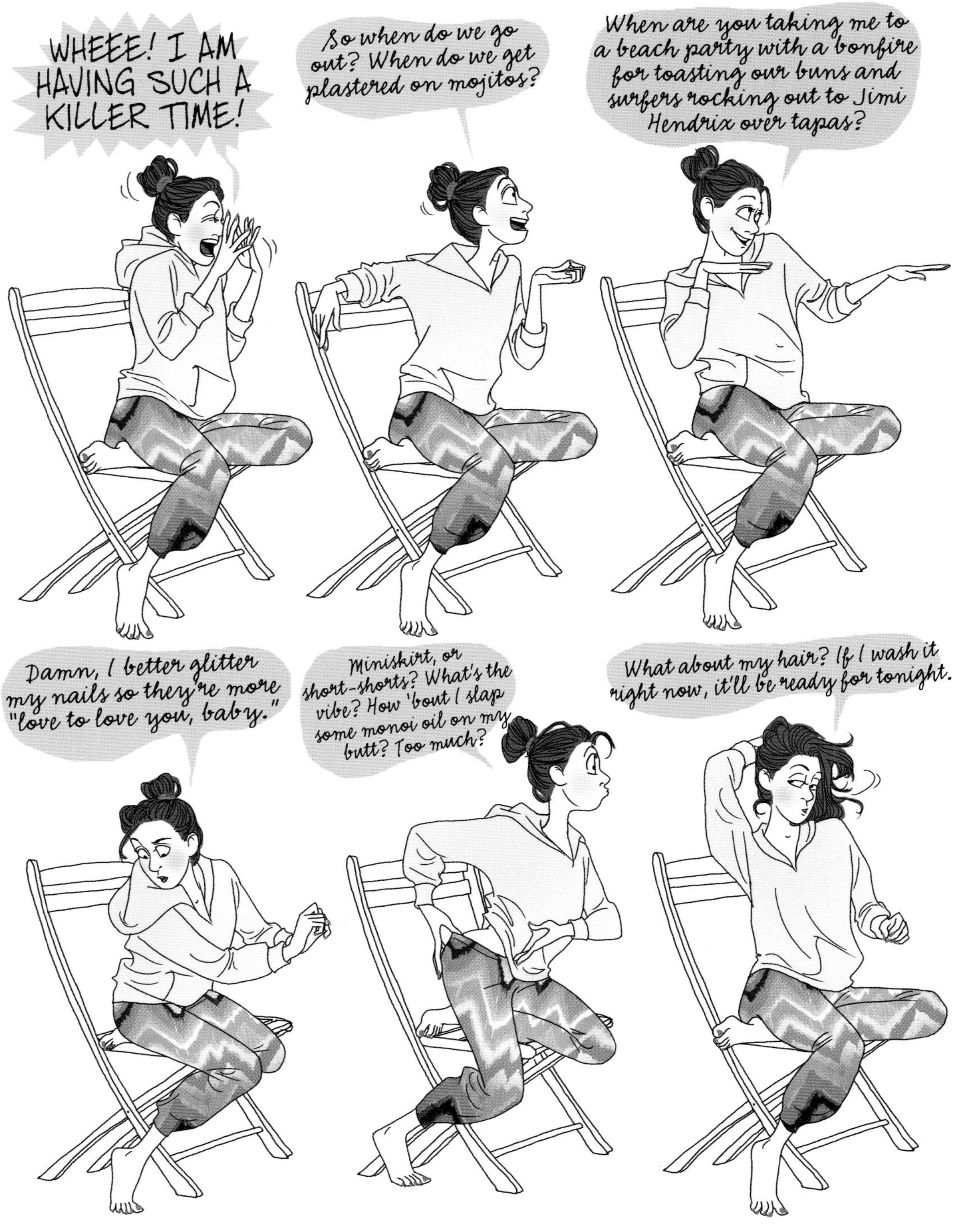
WHEEE! I AM HAVING SUCH A KILLER TIME!
So when do we go out? When do we get plastered on mojitos?
When are you taking me to a beach party with a bonfire for toasting our buns and surfers rocking out to Jimi Hendrix over tapas?
Damn, I better glitter my nails so they're more "love to love you, baby."
Miniskirt, or short-shorts? What's the vibe? How 'bout I slap some monoi oil on my butt? Too much?
What about my hair? If I wash it right now, it'll be ready for tonight.

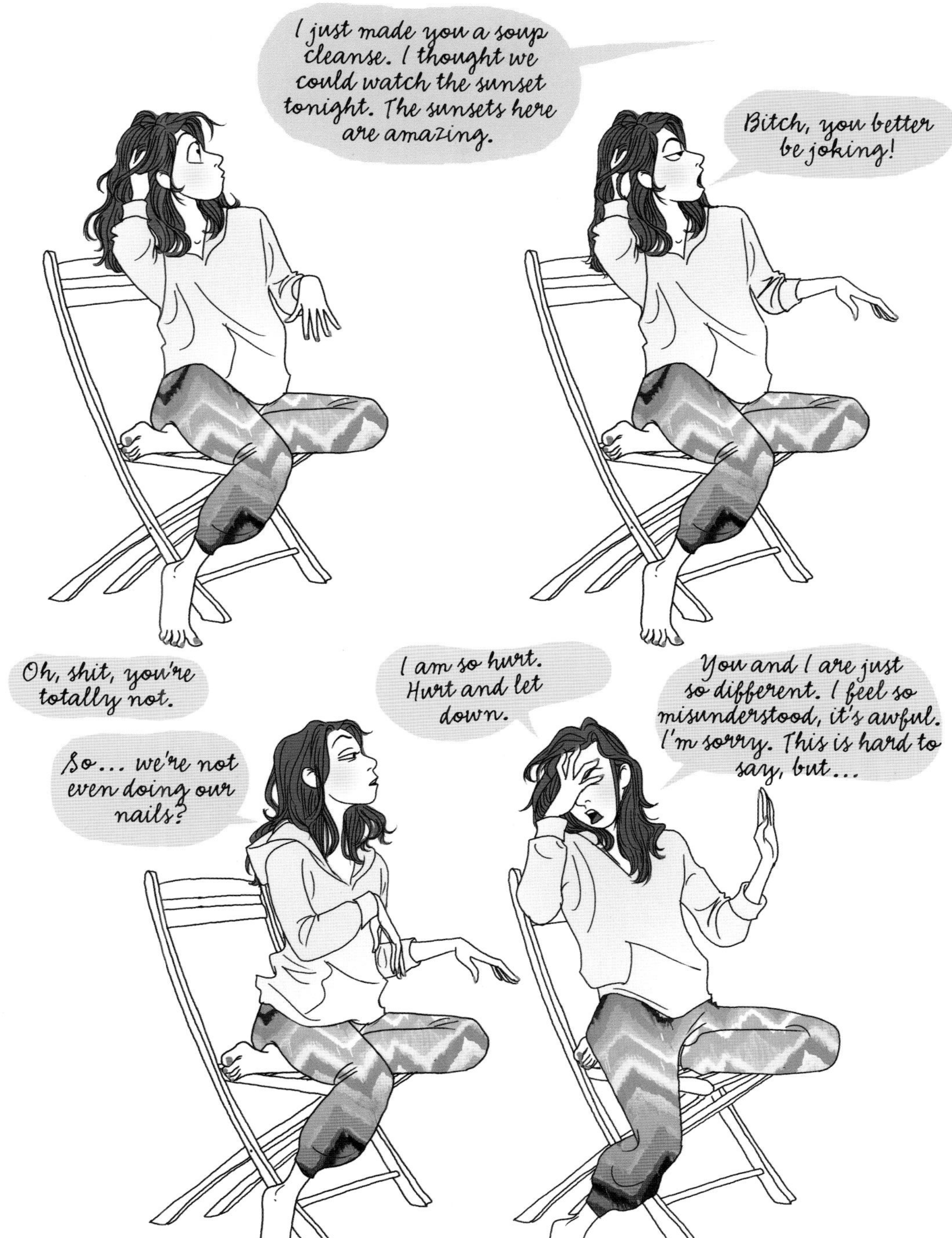
I just made you a soup cleanse. I thought we could watch the sunset tonight. The sunsets here are amazing.
Bitch, you better be joking!
Oh, shit, you're totally not.
So... we're not even doing our nails?
I am so hurt. Hurt and let down.
You and I are just so different. I feel so misunderstood, it's awful. I'm sorry. This is hard to say, but...

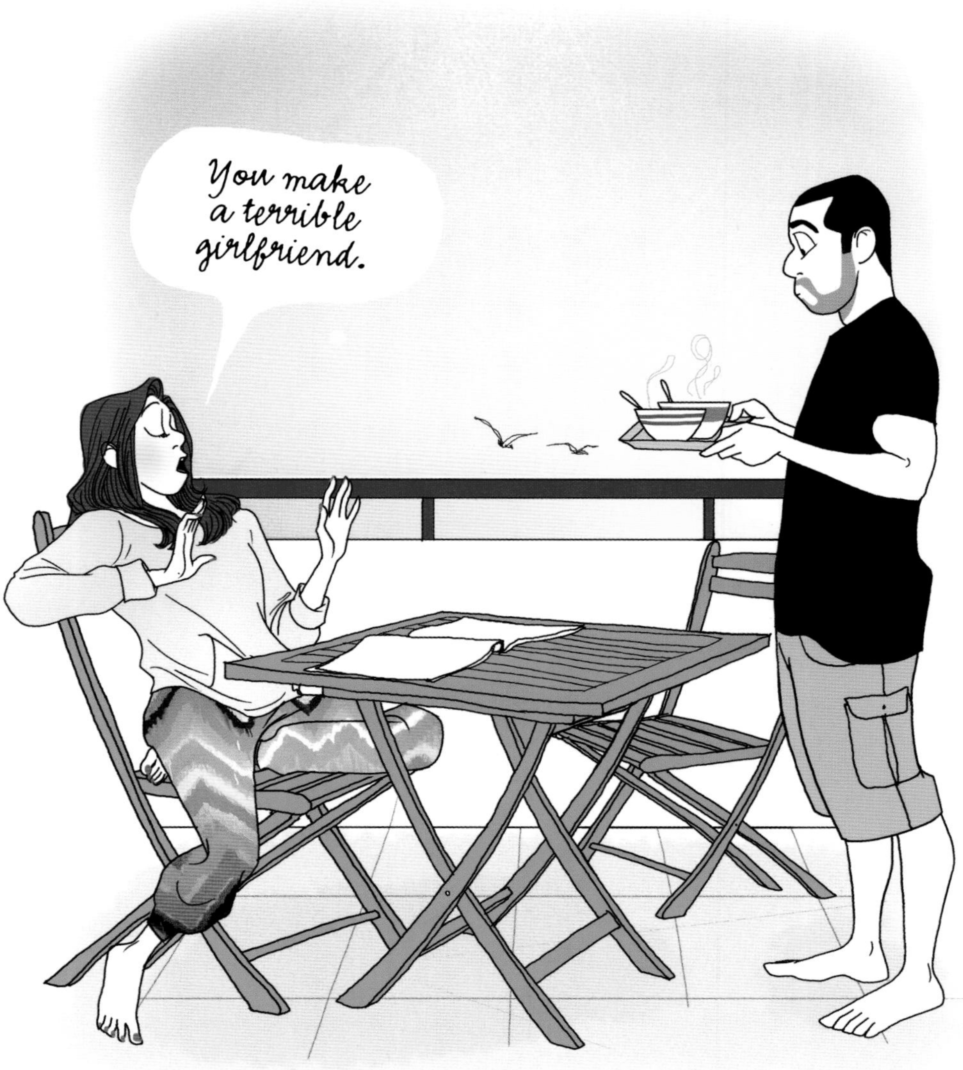
You make a terrible girlfriend.

Why The Man Friend Is Not Your Best Friend

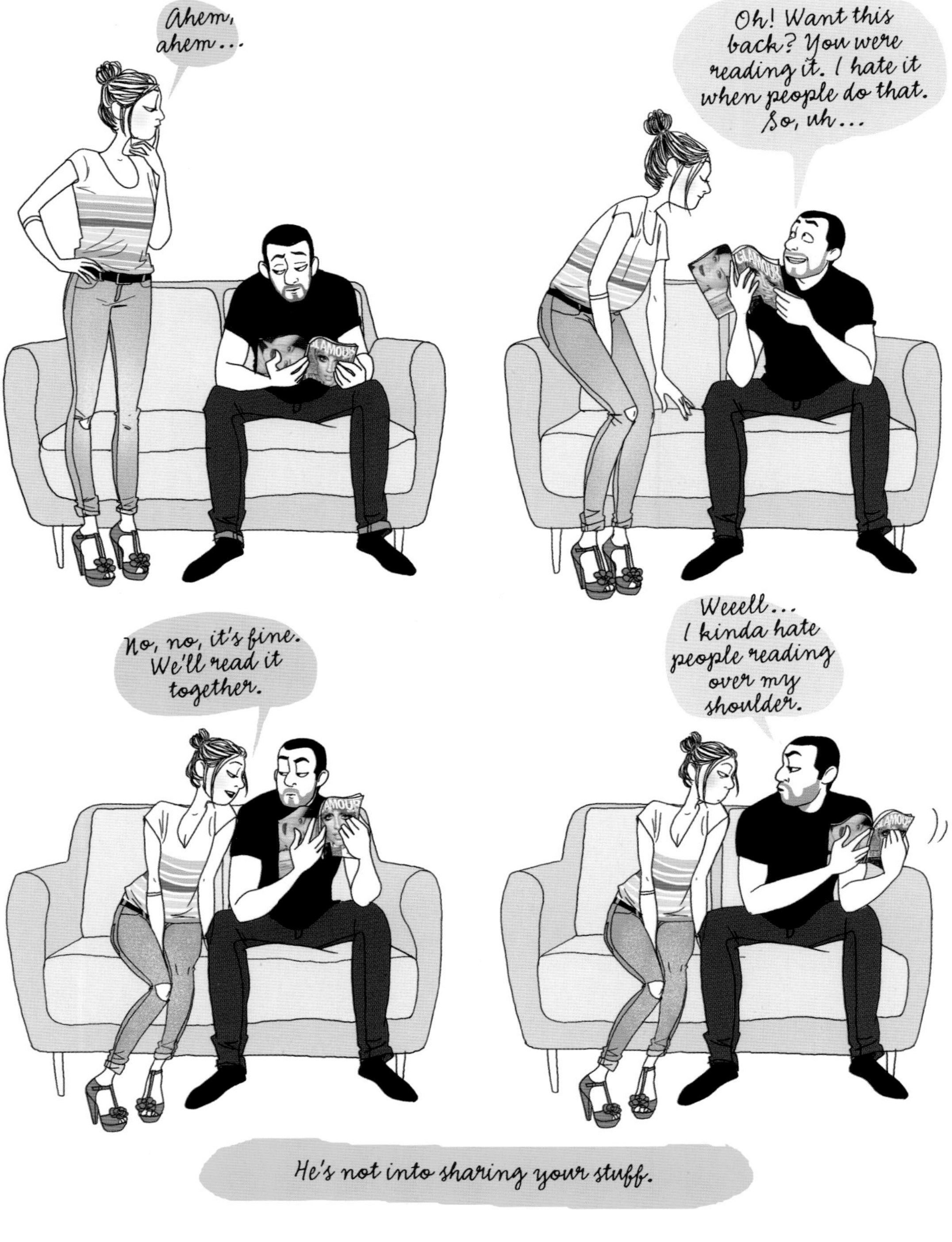
Ahem, ahem...
Oh! Want this back? You were reading it. I hate it when people do that. So, uh...
No, no, it's fine. We'll read it together.
Weeell... I kinda hate people reading over my shoulder.
He's not into sharing your stuff.

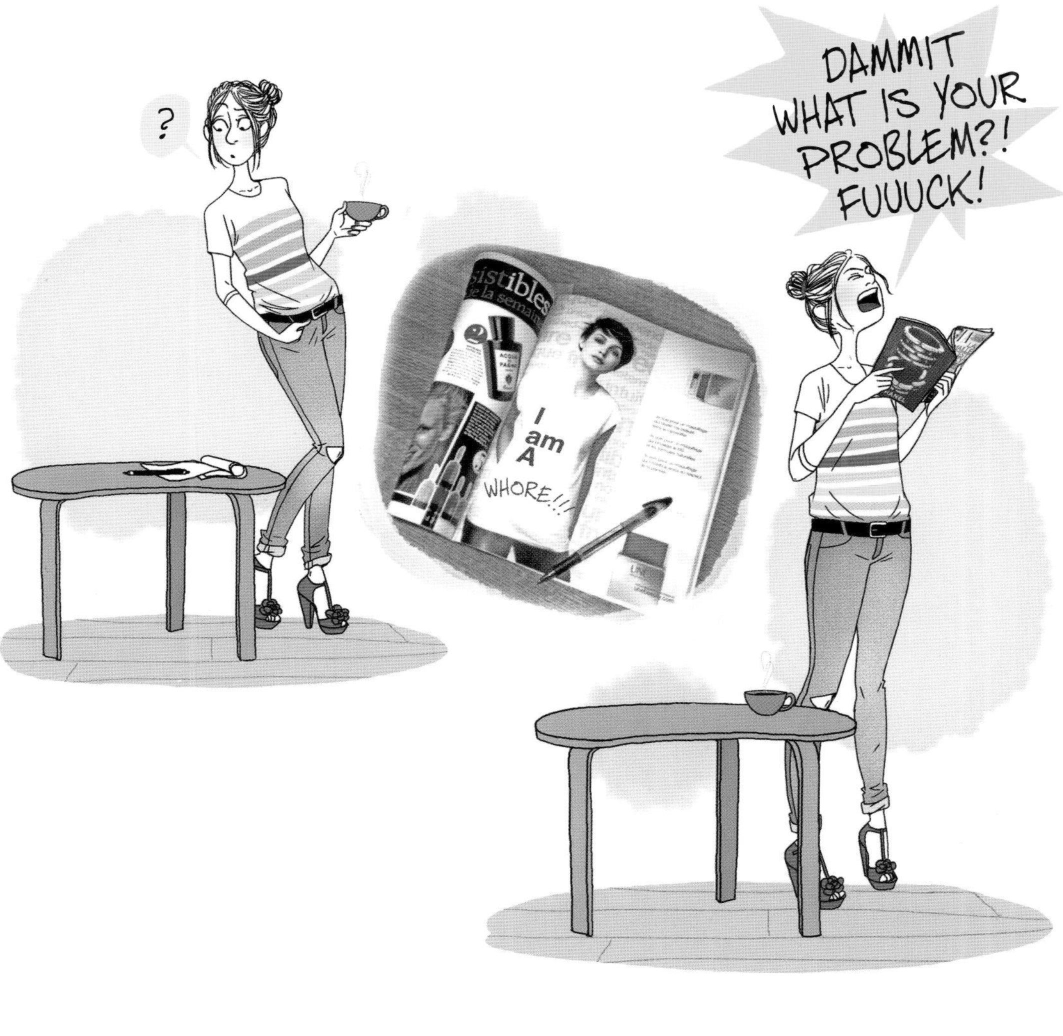
?
I am A
WHORE!!!
DAMMIT WHAT IS YOUR PROBLEM?! FUUUCK!

He doesn't respect your stuff.

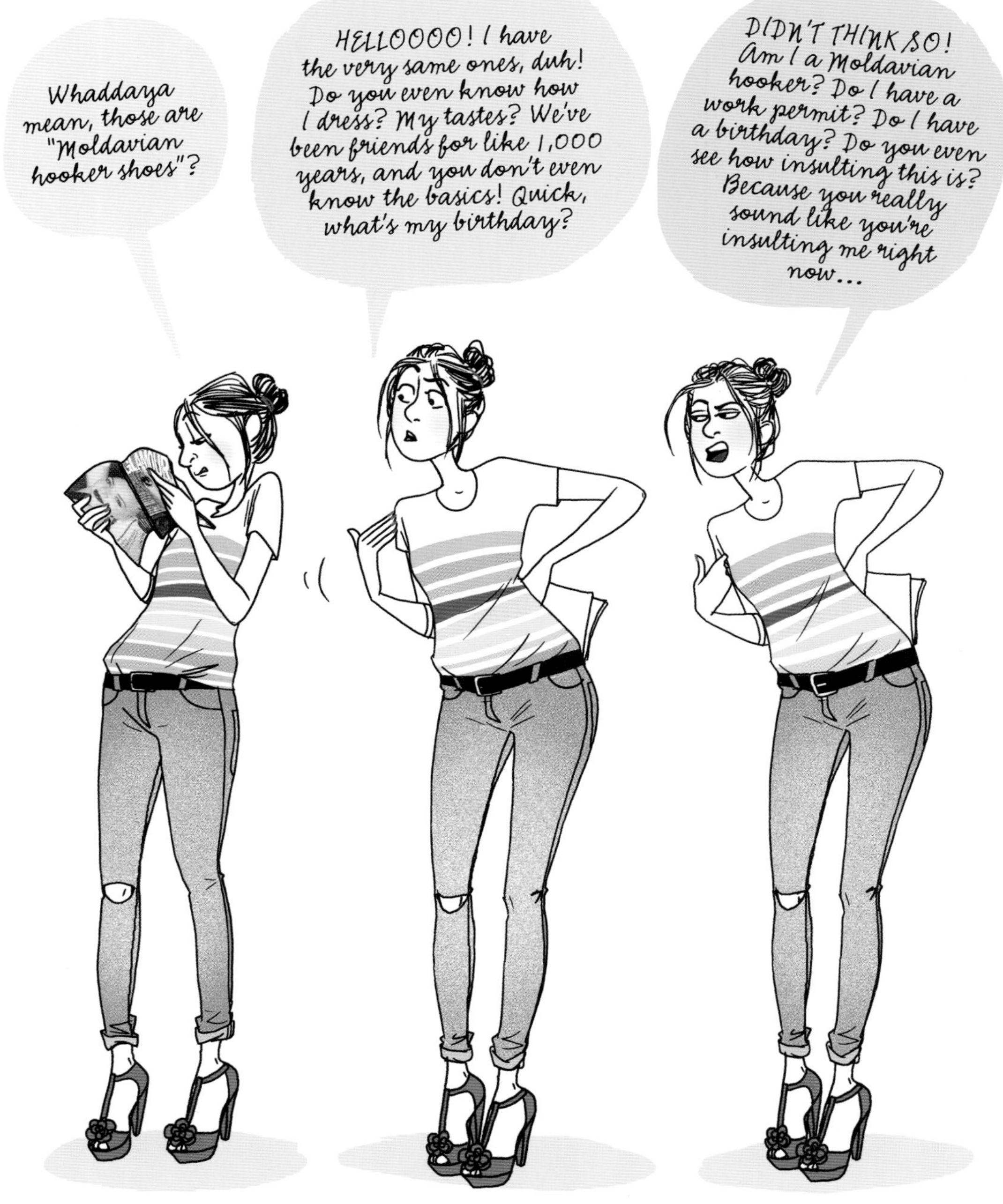
Whaddaya mean, those are "Moldavian hooker shoes"?
HELLOOOO! I have the very same ones, duh! Do you even know how I dress? My tastes? We've been friends for like 1,000 years, and you don't even know the basics! Quick, what's my birthday?
DIDN'T THINK SO! Am I a Moldavian hooker? Do I have a work permit? Do I have a birthday? Do you even see how insulting this is? Because you really sound like you're insulting me right now...

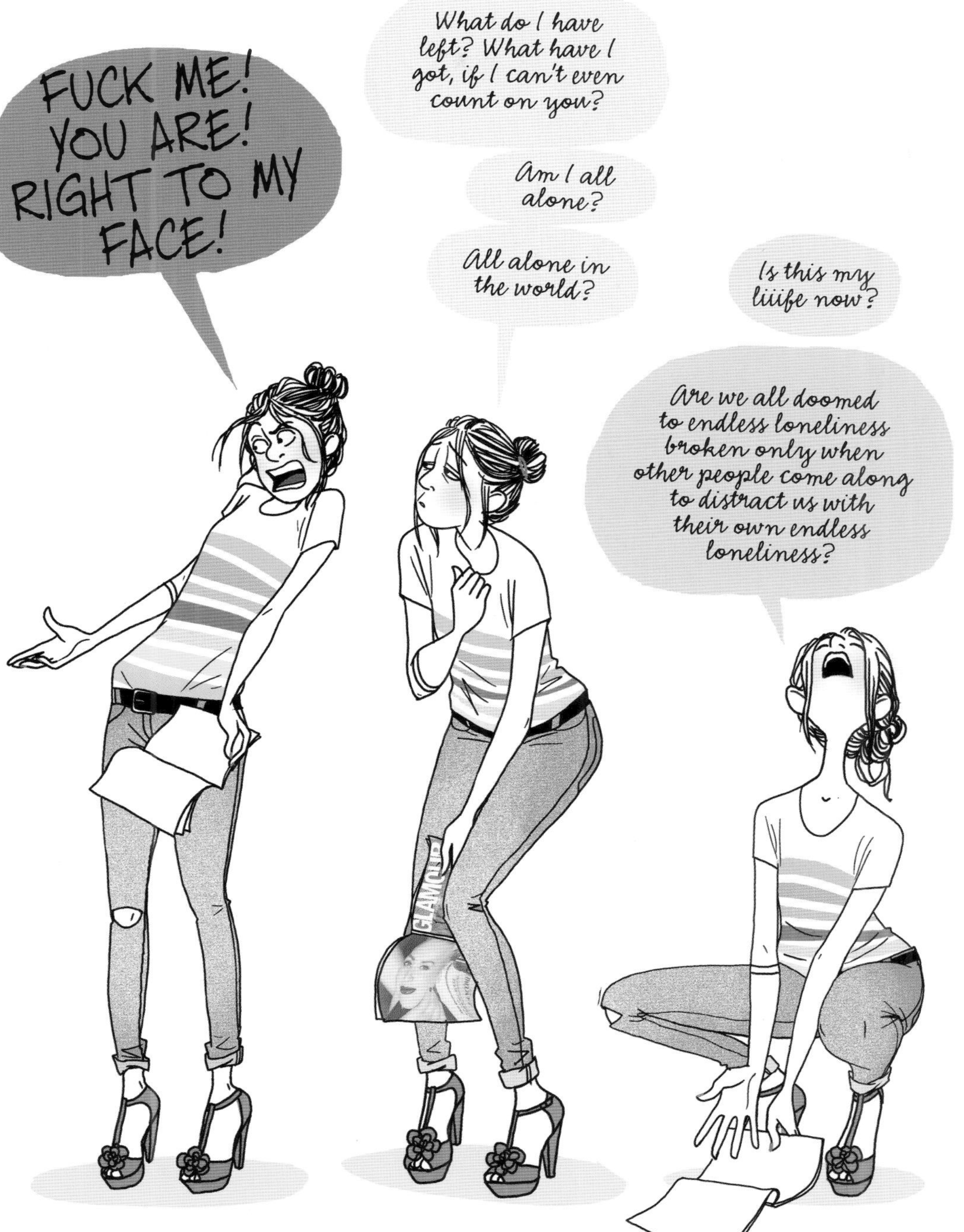
FUCK ME! YOU ARE! RIGHT TO MY FACE!
What do I have left? What have I got, if I can't even count on you?
Am I all alone?
All alone in the world?
Is this my liiife now?
Are we all doomed to endless loneliness broken only when other people come along to distract us with their own endless loneliness?
GLAMOUR

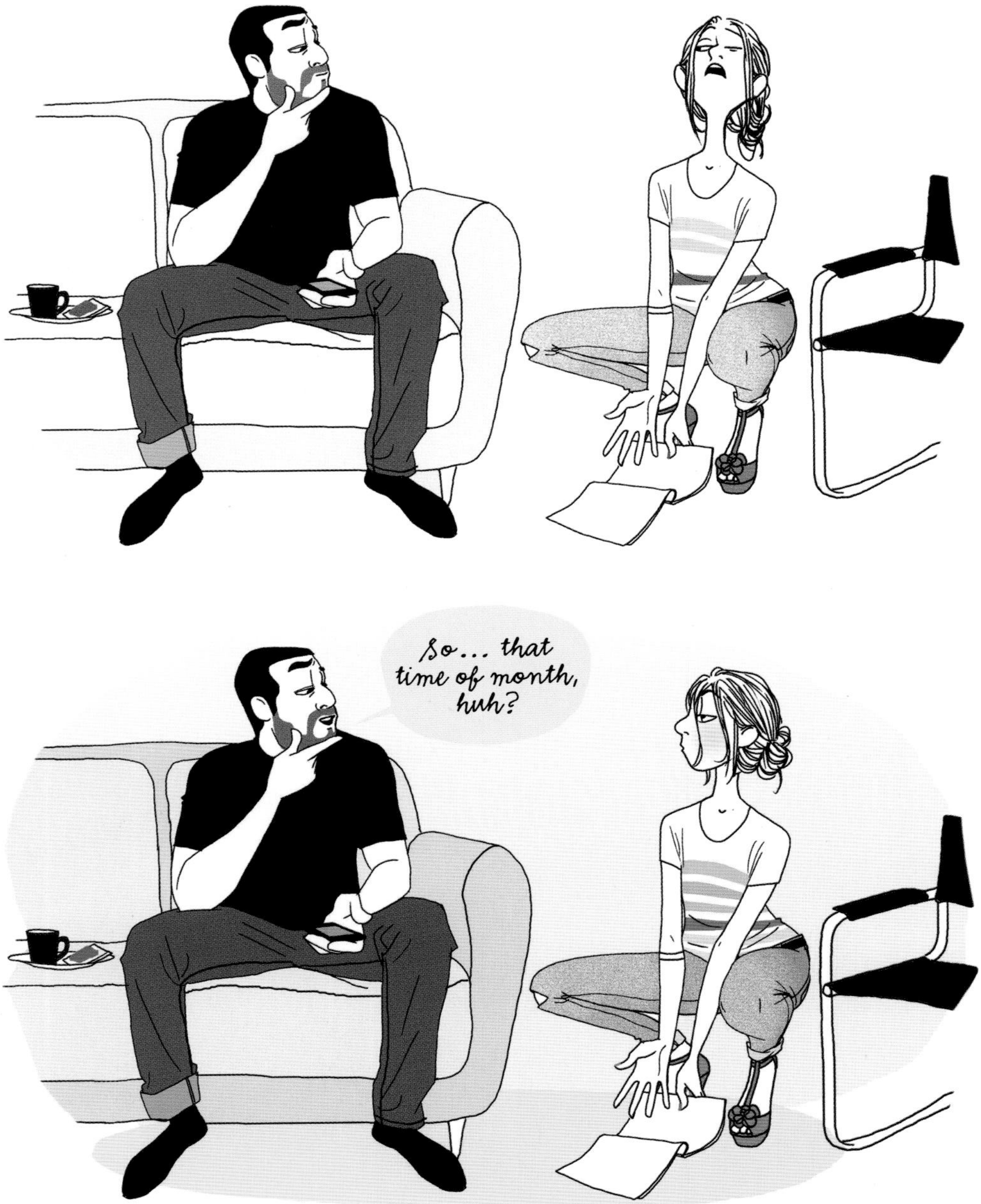
So... that time of month, huh?

You can't sync up your periods.

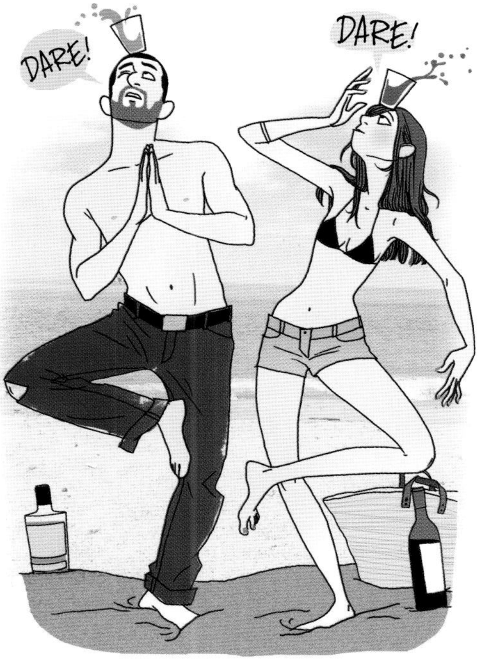
DARE!
DARE!

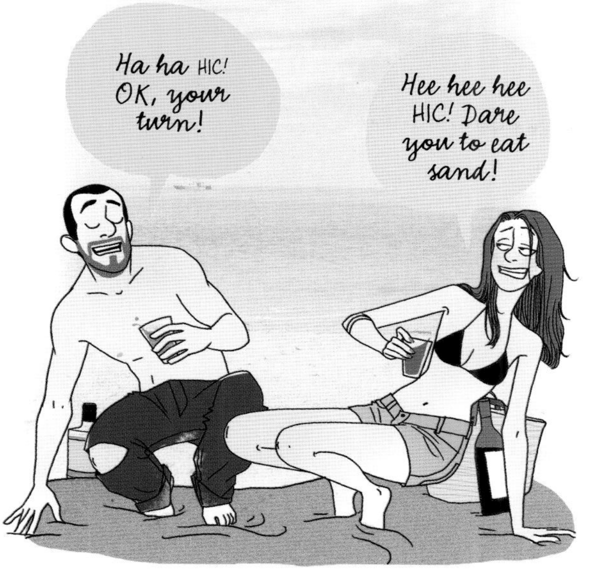
Ha ha HIC! OK, your turn!
Hee hee hee HIC! Dare you to eat sand!

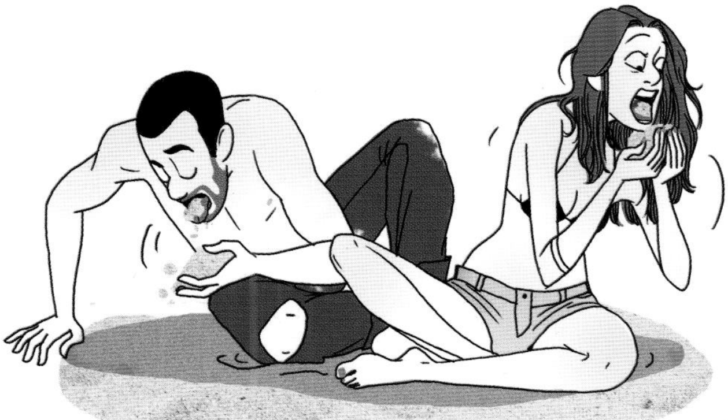

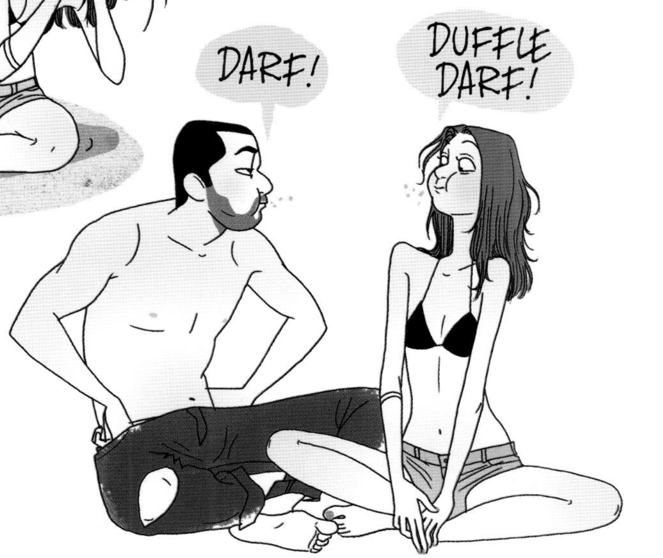
DARF!
DUFFLE DARF!

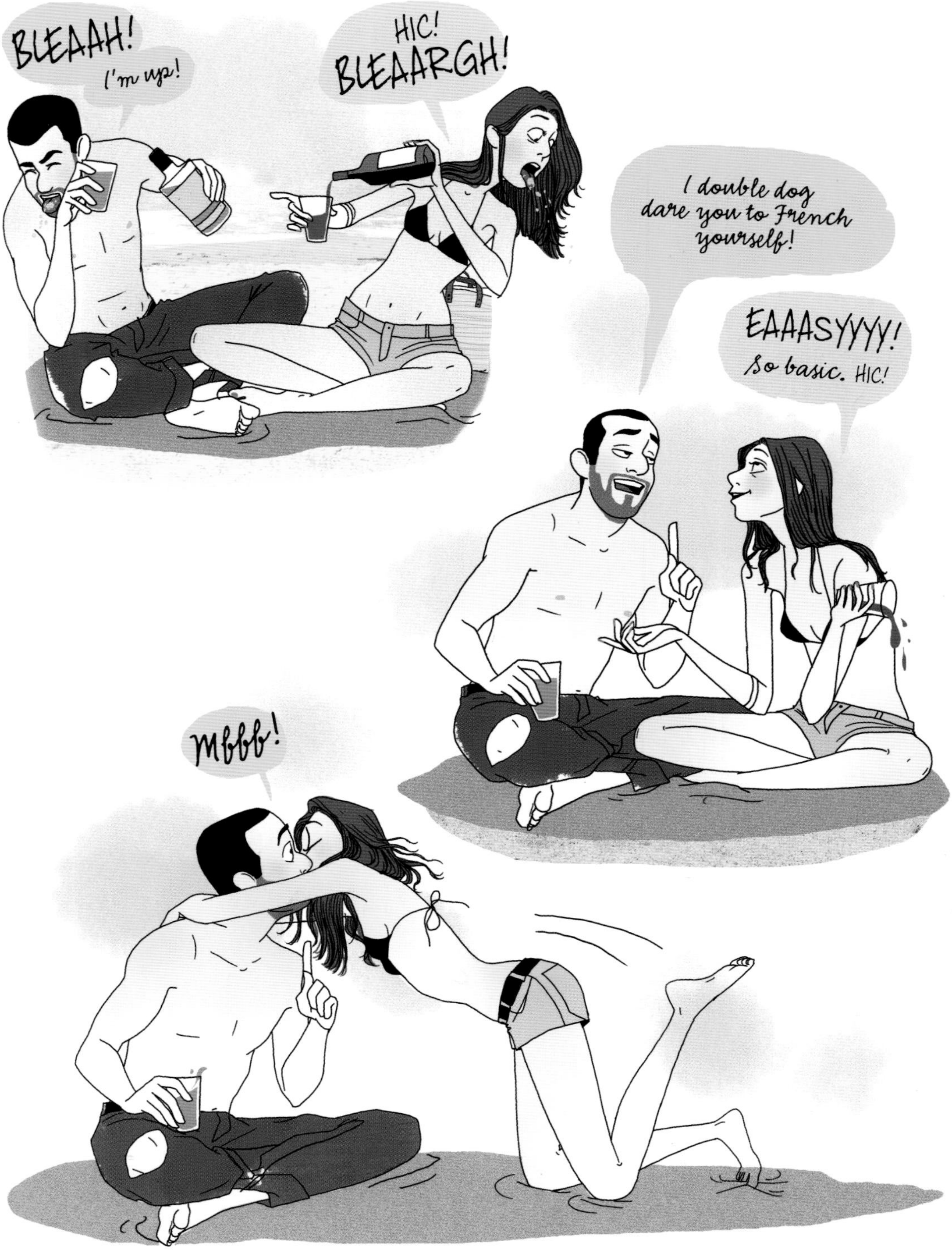
BLEAAH!
I'm up!
HIC!
BLEAARGH!
I double dog dare you to French yourself!
EAAASYYYY!
So basic. HIC!
Mbbb!

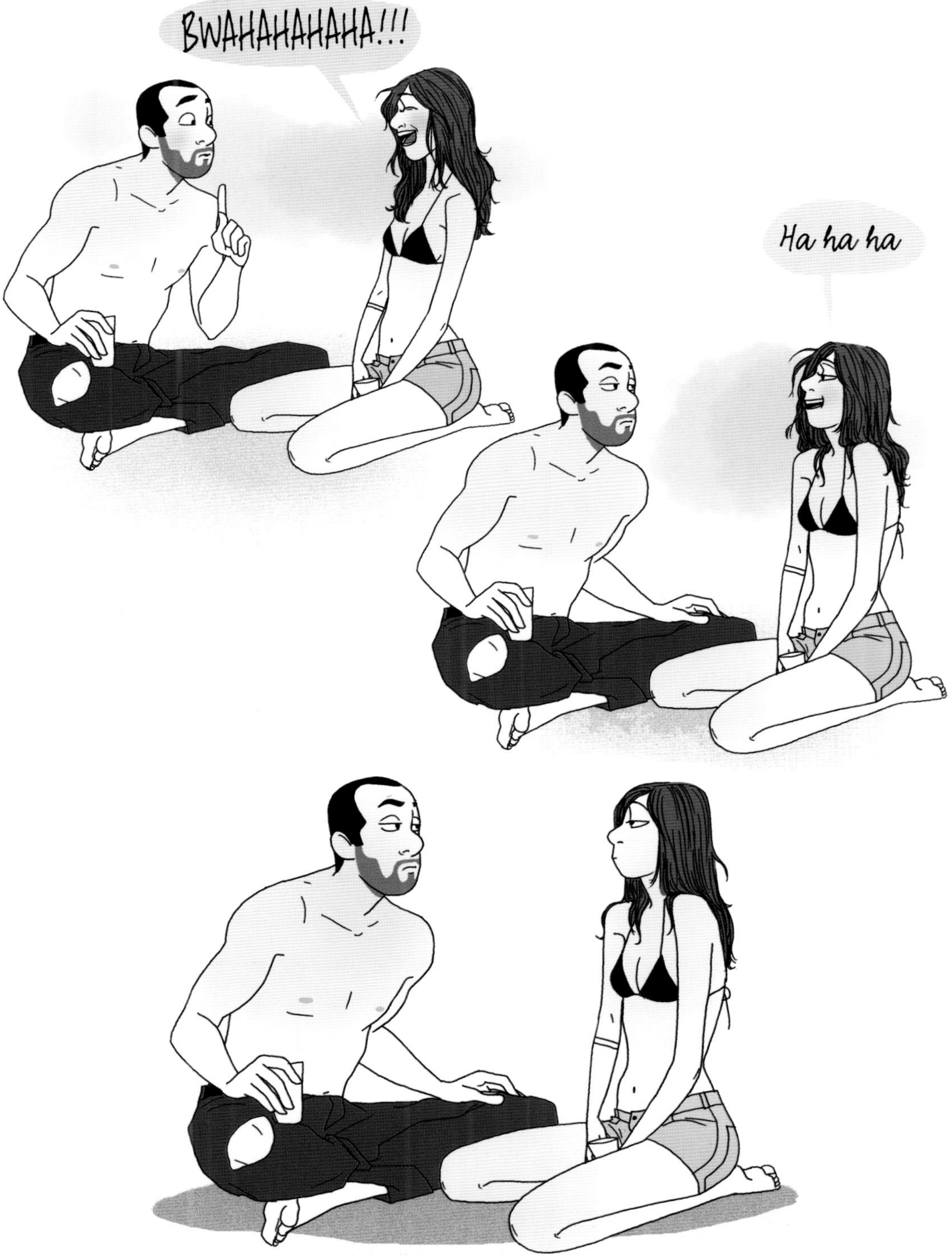
BWAHAHAHAHA!!!
Ha ha ha

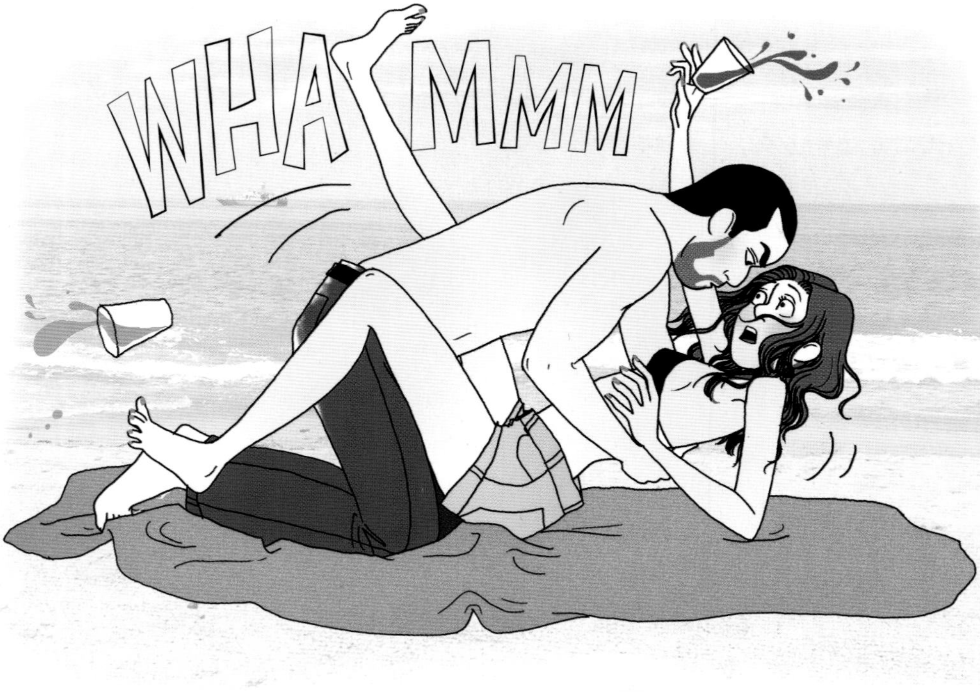
WHAMMM

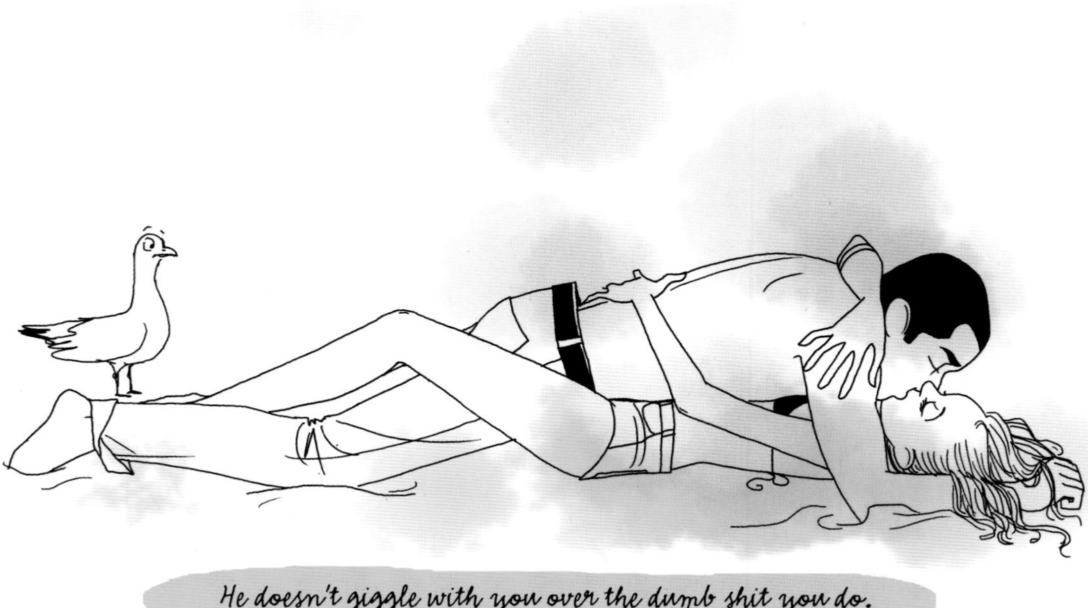

He doesn't giggle with you over the dumb shit you do.

Birds of a Feather

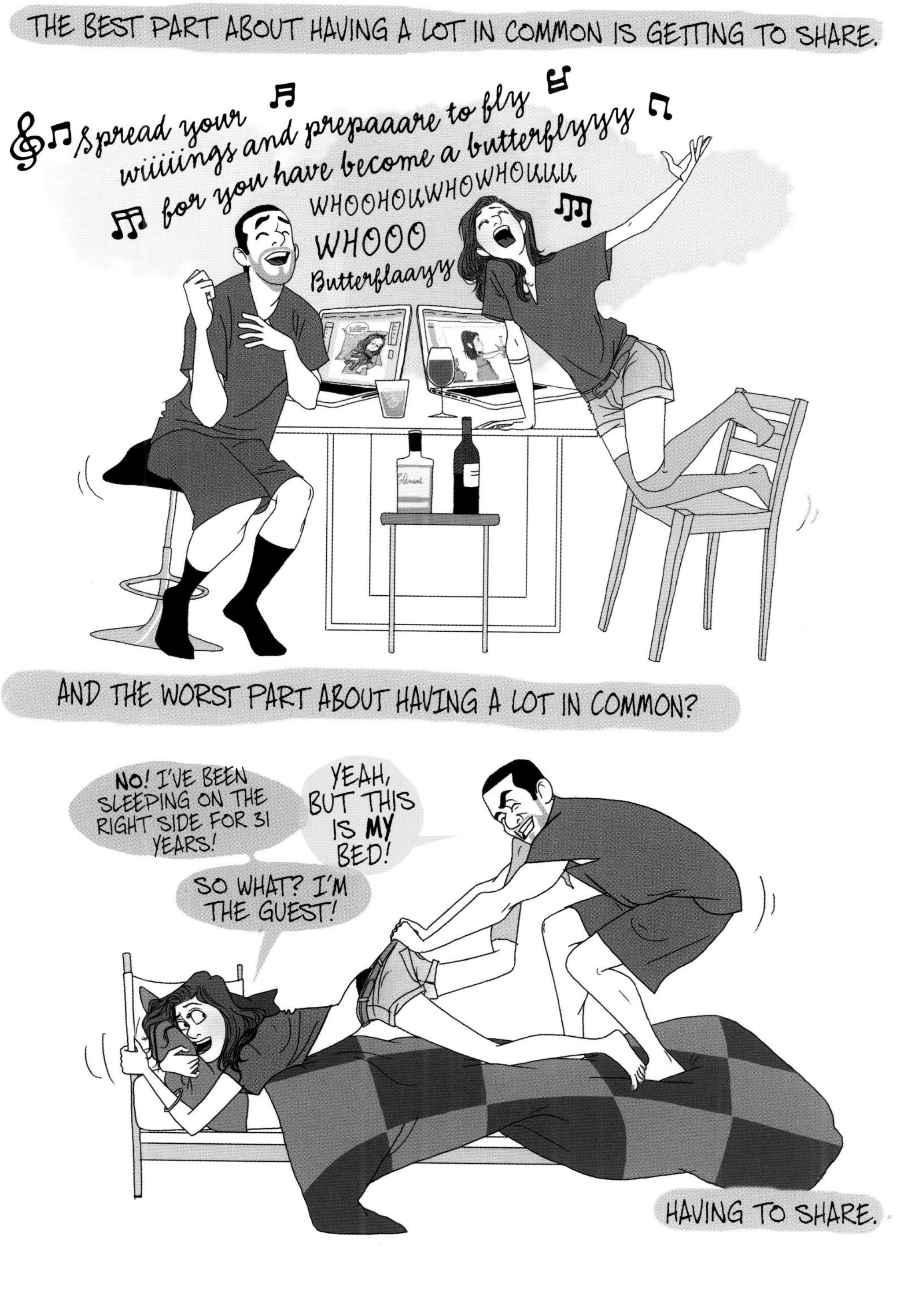
THE BEST PART ABOUT HAVING A LOT IN COMMON IS GETTING TO SHARE.
Spread your wiiiiings and prepaaare to fly for you have become a butterflyyy
WHOOHOUWHOWHOUUU
WHOOO
Butterflaayy
AND THE WORST PART ABOUT HAVING A LOT IN COMMON?
NO! I'VE BEEN SLEEPING ON THE RIGHT SIDE FOR 31 YEARS!
YEAH, BUT THIS IS MY BED!
SO WHAT? I'M THE GUEST!
HAVING TO SHARE.

*Mariah Carey "Butterfly"

The Dark Side of the Bed

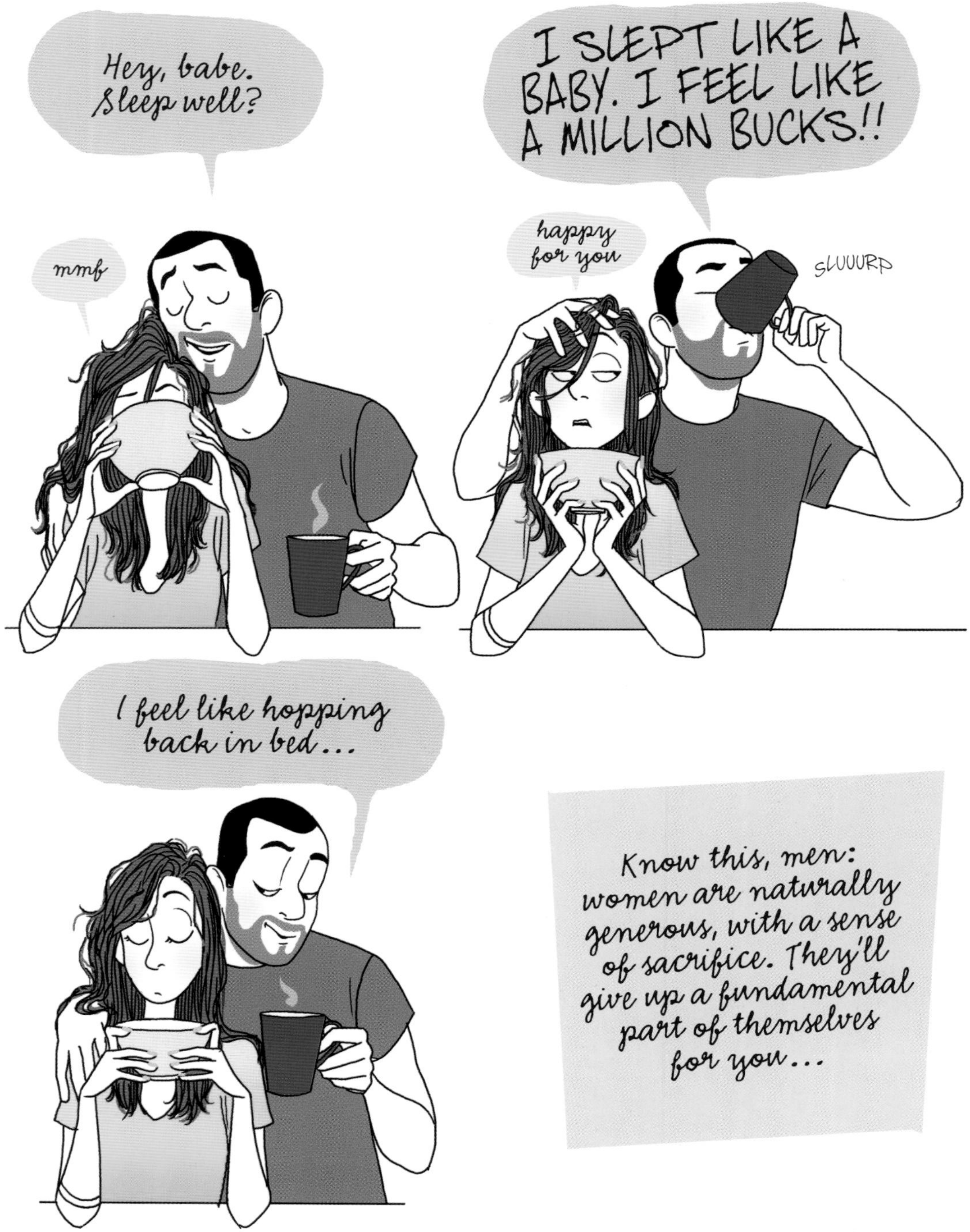

Hey, babe. Sleep well?
mmf
I SLEPT LIKE A BABY. I FEEL LIKE A MILLION BUCKS!!
happy for you
SLUUURP
I feel like hopping back in bed...
Know this, men: women are naturally generous, with a sense of sacrifice. They'll give up a fundamental part of themselves for you...

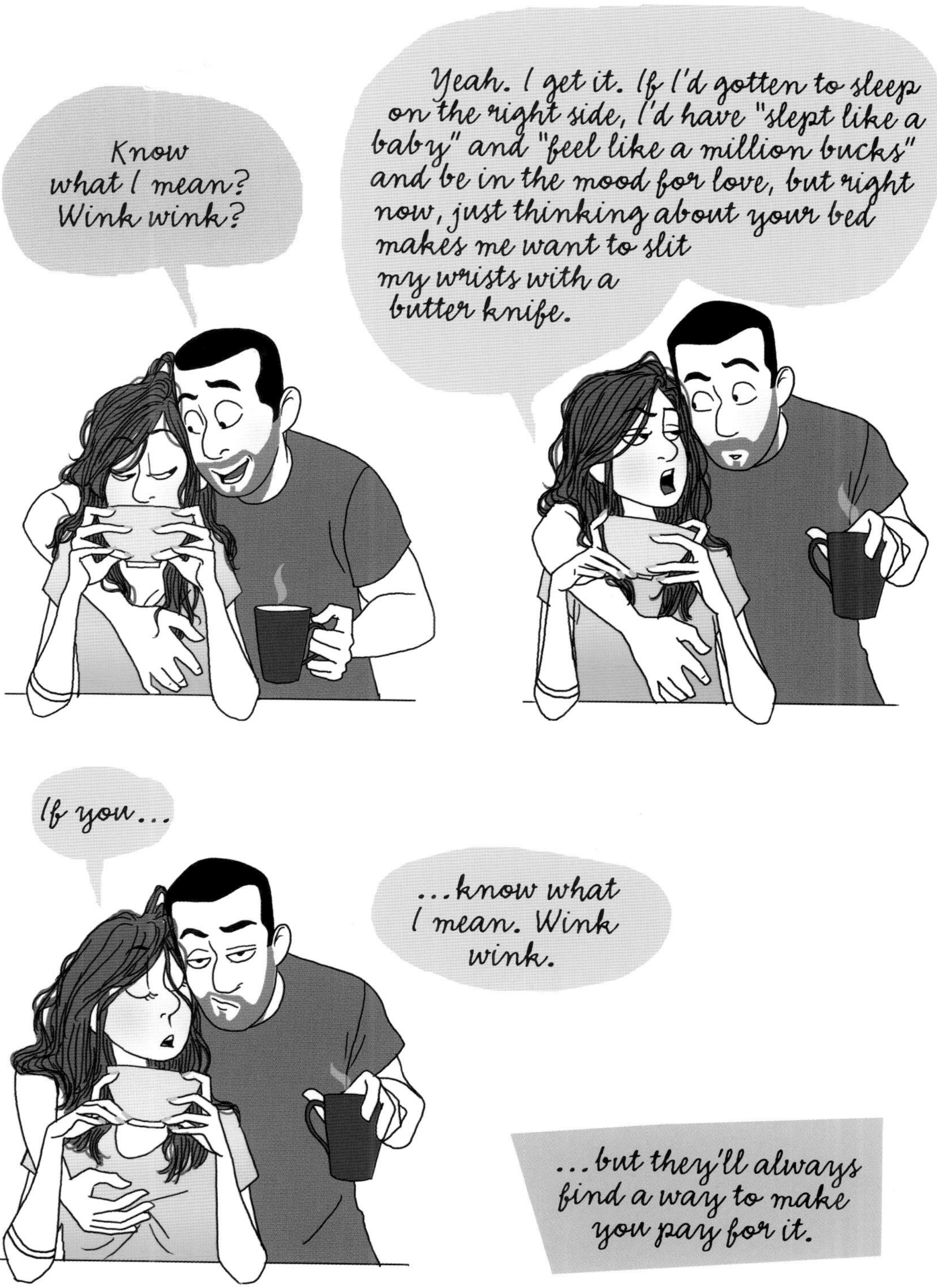
Know what I mean? Wink wink?
Yeah. I get it. If I'd gotten to sleep on the right side, I'd have "slept like a baby" and "feel like a million bucks" and be in the mood for love, but right now, just thinking about your bed makes me want to slit my wrists with a butter knife.
If you...
...know what I mean. Wink wink.
...but they'll always find a way to make you pay for it.

Your first time in bed with a new guy, you don't sleep a wink

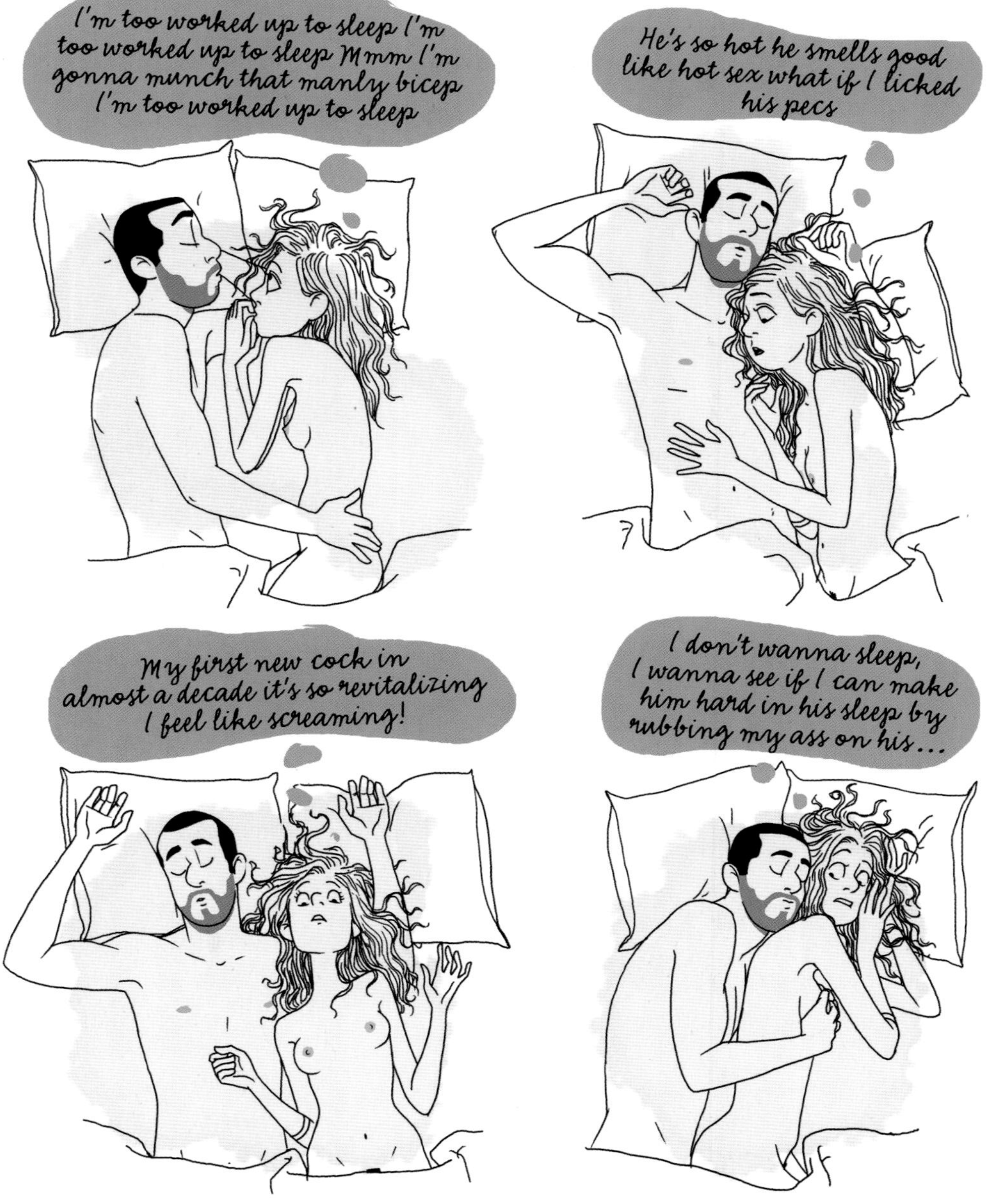

I'm too worked up to sleep I'm too worked up to sleep Mmm I'm gonna munch that manly bicep I'm too worked up to sleep
He's so hot he smells good like hot sex what if I licked his pecs
My first new cock in almost a decade it's so revitalizing I feel like screaming!
I don't wanna sleep, I wanna see if I can make him hard in his sleep by rubbing my ass on his...

They say it's 'cause of all the excitement burning inside us, like a raging volcano ready to erupt all over, passionate princesses of glamorous sexuality...

But we'd rather die than let all this come spurting out, this one truth NO ONE IN THE WORLD seems ready to admit:

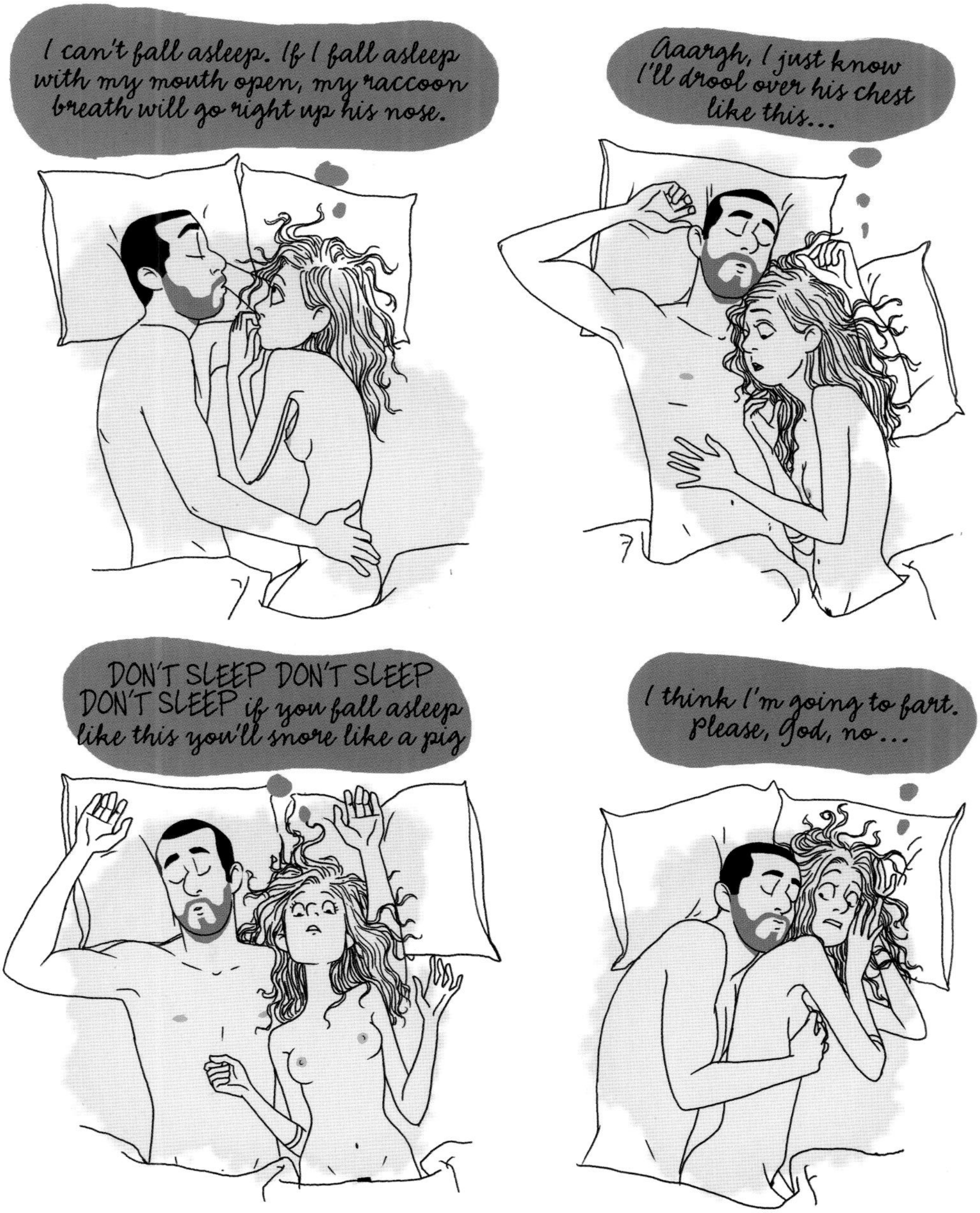
I can't fall asleep. If I fall asleep with my mouth open, my raccoon breath will go right up his nose.
Aaargh, I just know I'll drool over his chest like this...
DON'T SLEEP DON'T SLEEP DON'T SLEEP if you fall asleep like this you'll snore like a pig
I think I'm going to fart. Please, God, no...

DEEP DOWN, WOMEN ARE JUST LIKE MEN.

Fantasies

I've been making movies all my life. It's a gift. In my head, I know exactly what the first phases of a new romance should look like.

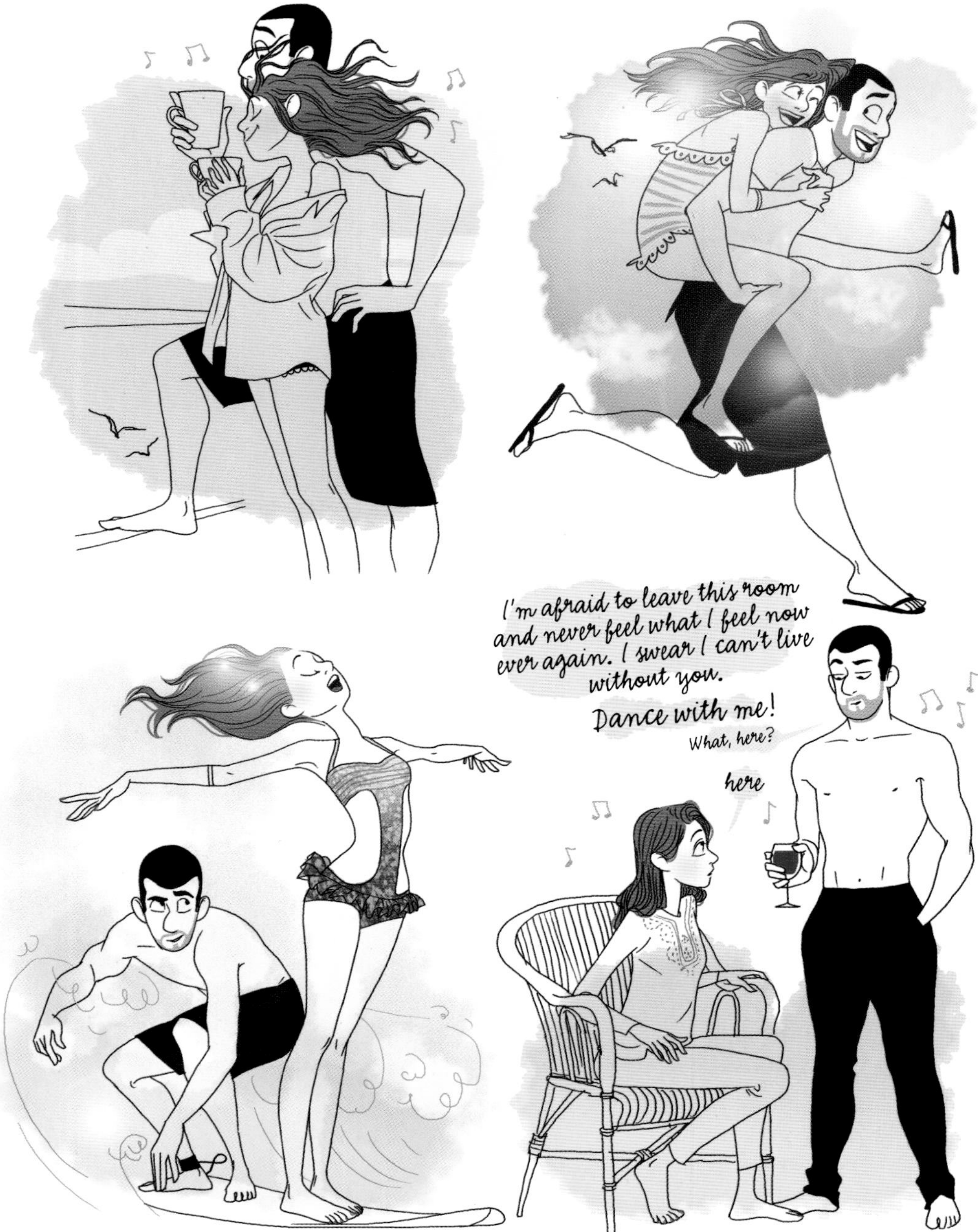
I'm afraid to leave this room and never feel what I feel now ever again. I swear I can't live without you.
Dance with me!
What, here?
here

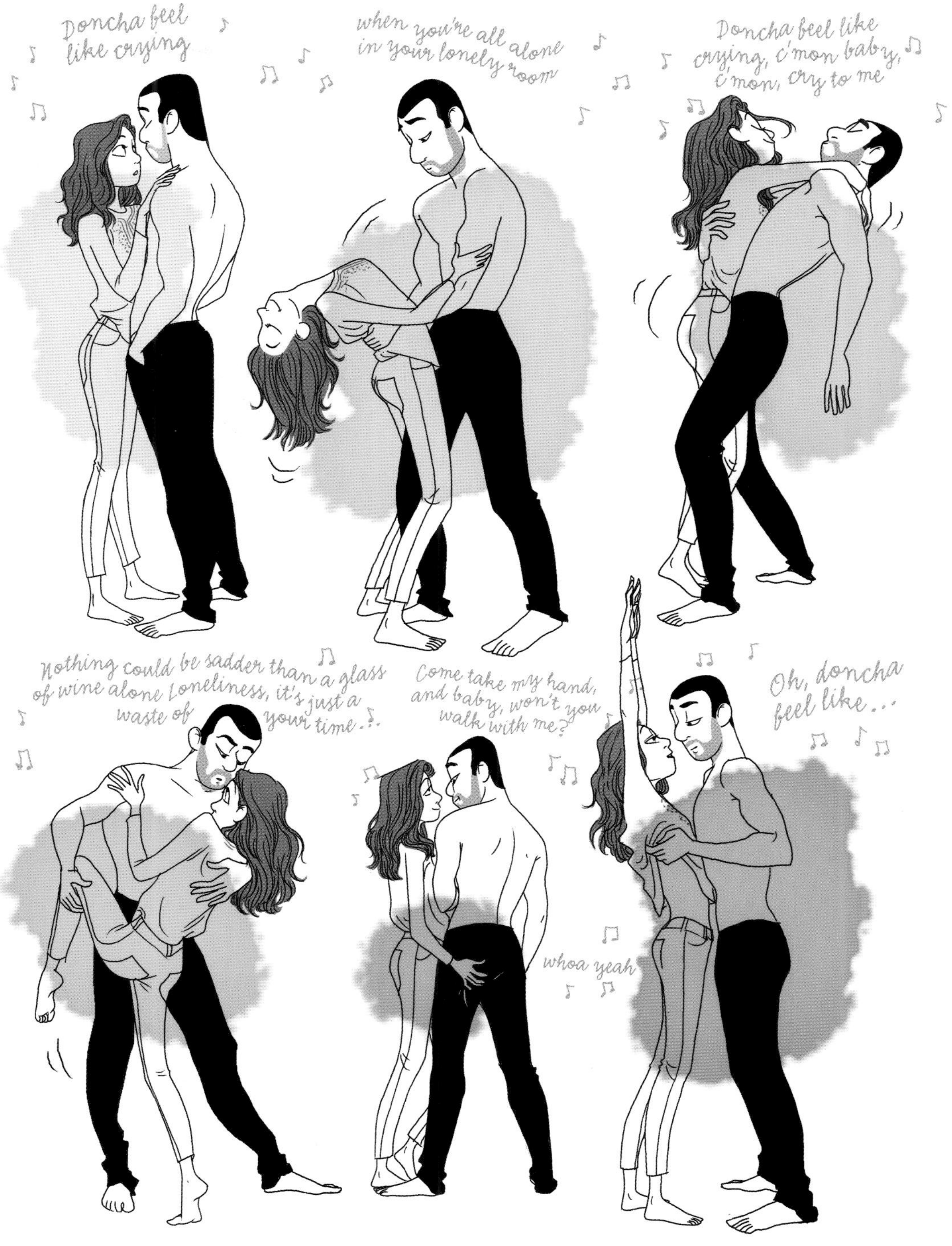
Doncha feel like crying
when you're all alone in your lonely room
Doncha feel like crying, c'mon baby, c'mon, cry to me
Nothing could be sadder than a glass of wine alone Loneliness, it's just a waste of your time.
Come take my hand, and baby, won't you walk with me?
whoa yeah
Oh, doncha feel like...

In my head, it's so magical...

...that I'm often a wee bit disappointed in how things really pan out.

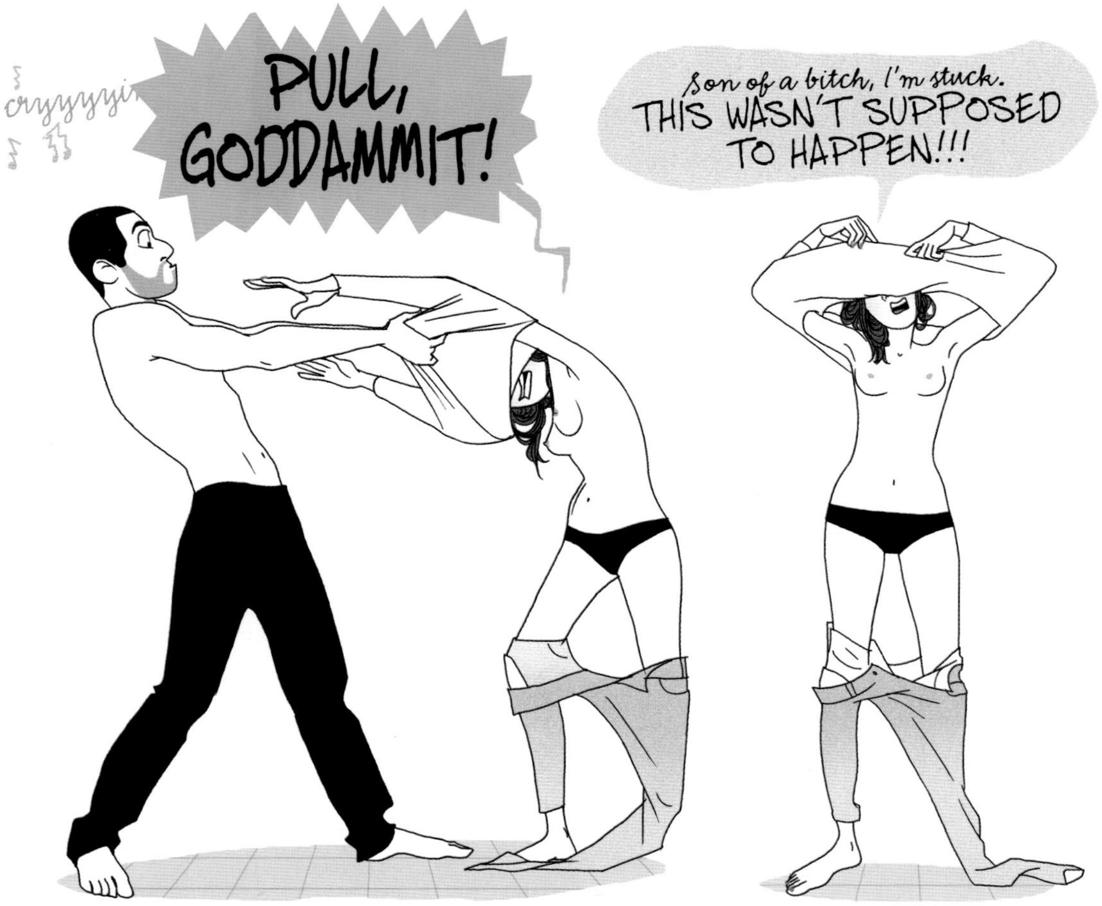
cryyyyi
PULL, GODDAMMIT!
Son of a bitch, I'm stuck.
THIS WASN'T SUPPOSED TO HAPPEN!!!

Uh...
coming?

NEVER!!!

*Solomon Burke "Cry to Me"

St. Jean de Luz

Paris

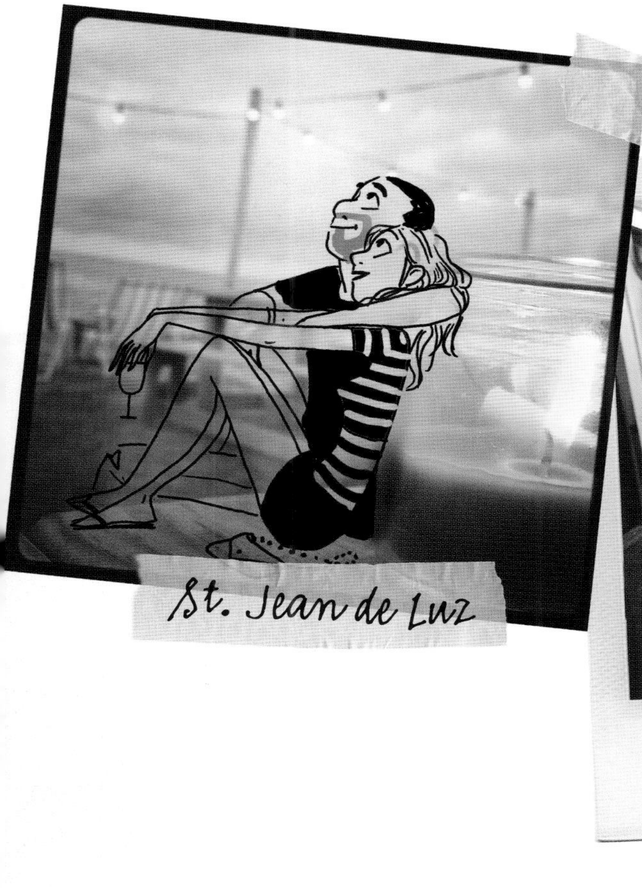
St. Jean de Luz

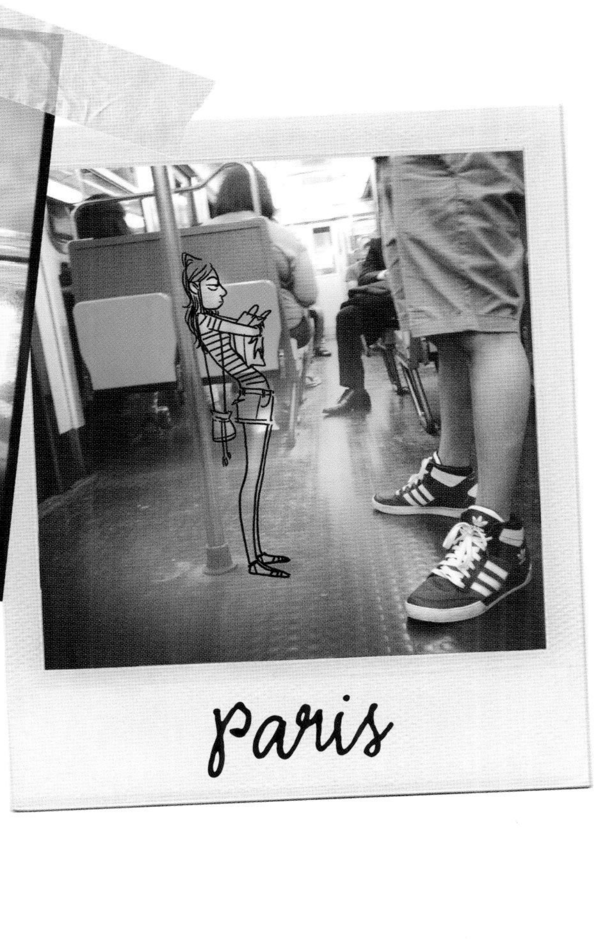
paris

The Art of Anticipation

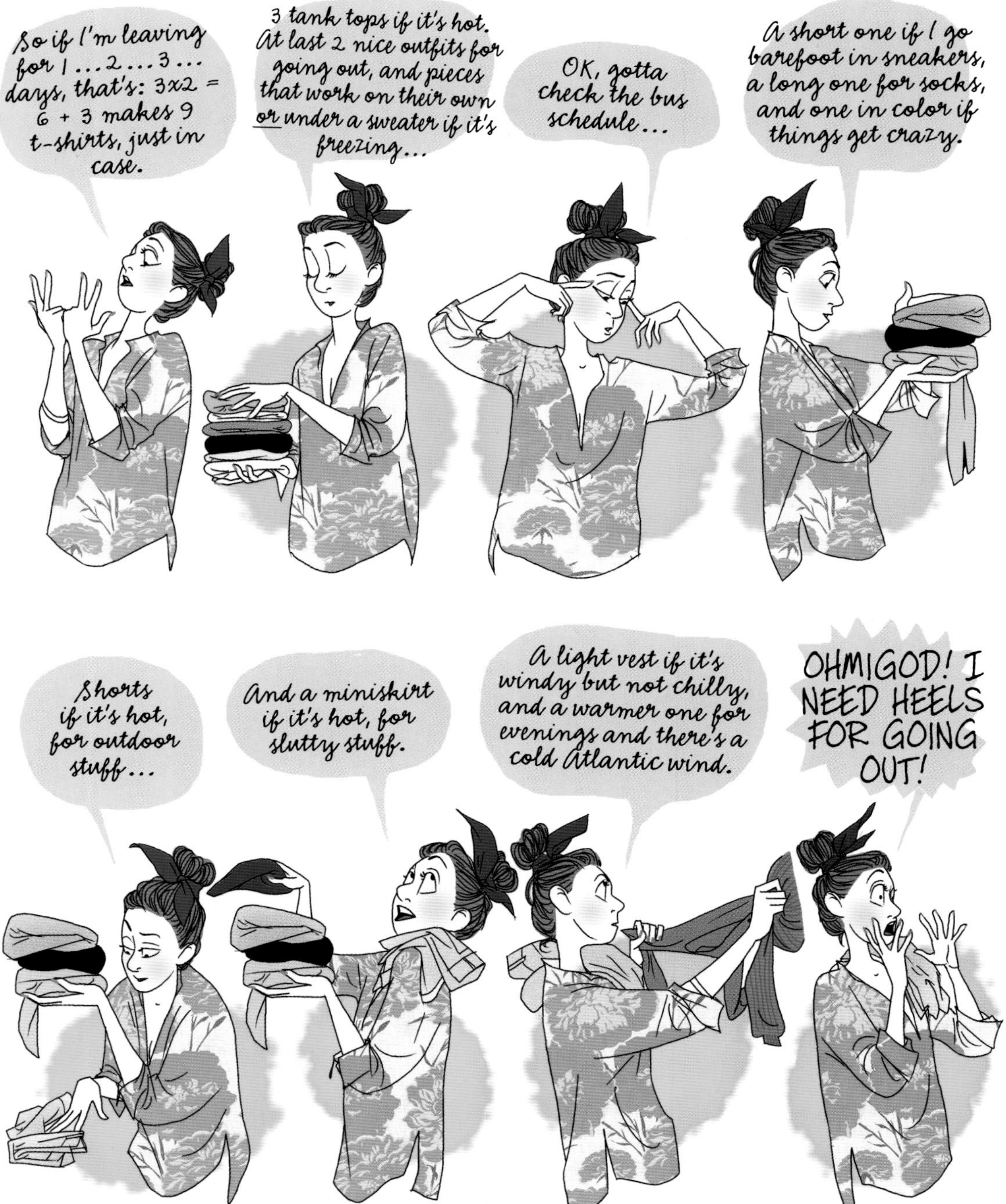

So if I'm leaving for 1... 2... 3... days, that's: 3x2 = 6 + 3 makes 9 t-shirts, just in case.
3 tank tops if it's hot. At last 2 nice outfits for going out, and pieces that work on their own or under a sweater if it's freezing...
OK, gotta check the bus schedule...
A short one if I go barefoot in sneakers, a long one for socks, and one in color if things get crazy.
Shorts if it's hot, for outdoor stuff...
And a miniskirt if it's hot, for slutty stuff.
A light vest if it's windy but not chilly, and a warmer one for evenings and there's a cold Atlantic wind.
OHMIGOD! I NEED HEELS FOR GOING OUT!

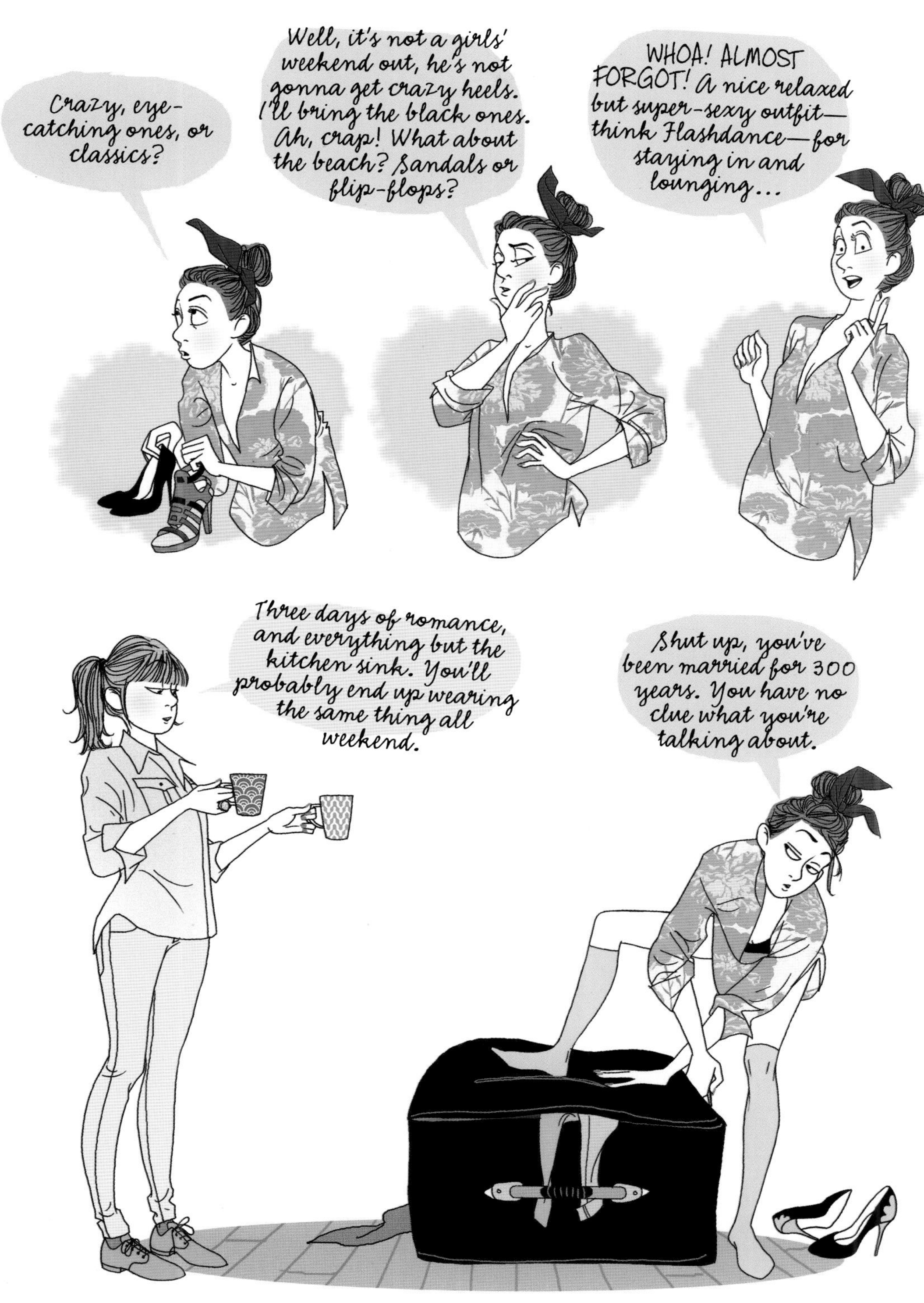
Crazy, eye-catching ones, or classics?
Well, it's not a girls' weekend out, he's not gonna get crazy heels. I'll bring the black ones. Ah, crap! What about the beach? Sandals or flip-flops?
WHOA! ALMOST FORGOT! A nice relaxed but super-sexy outfit—think Flashdance—for staying in and lounging...
Three days of romance, and everything but the kitchen sink. You'll probably end up wearing the same thing all weekend.
Shut up, you've been married for 300 years. You have no clue what you're talking about.

Friday

Saturday

Saturday night

Sunday

There you have it.

In All Honesty

Sometimes, I wonder what the "director's commentary" option the DVD of my life would look like...

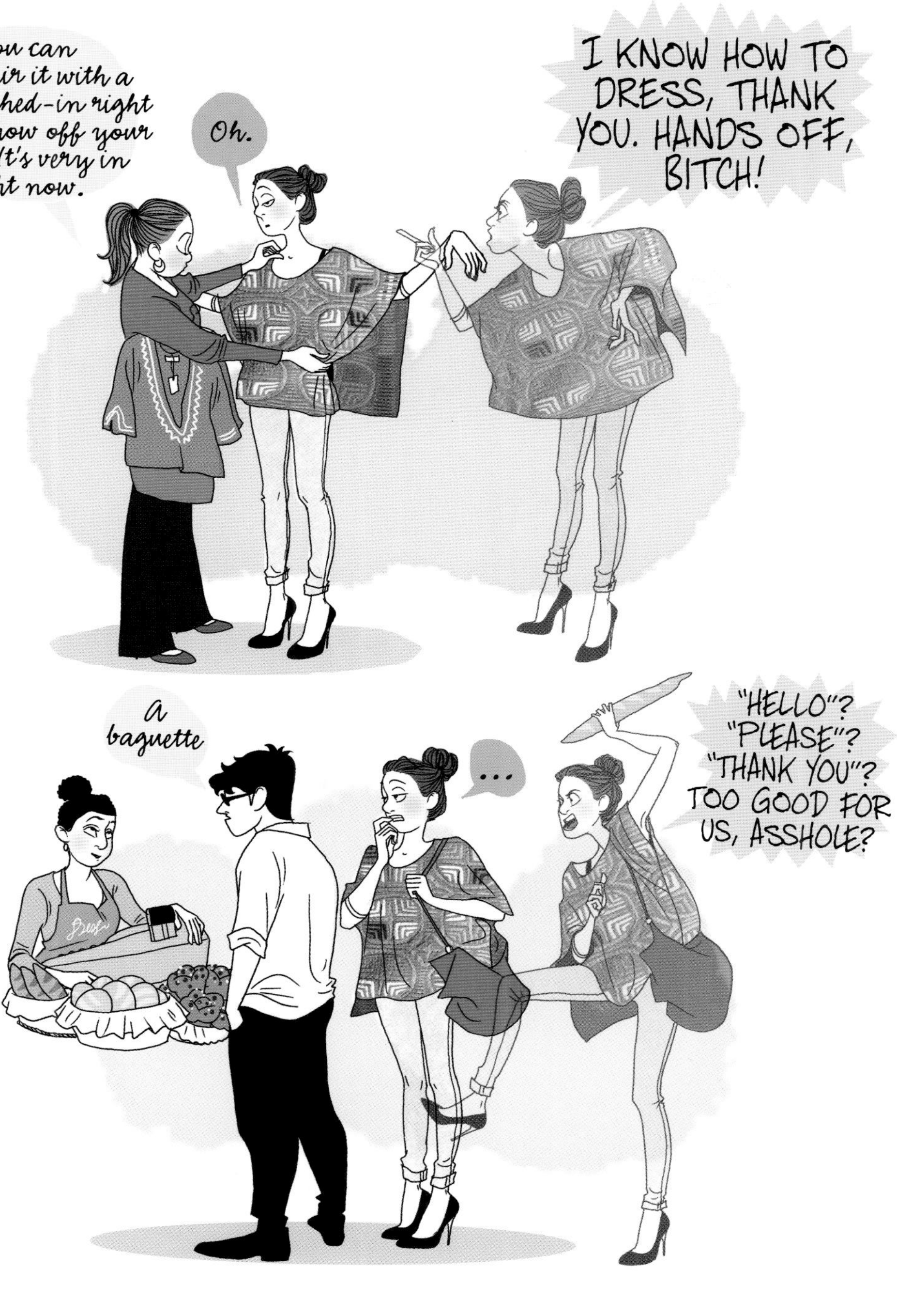
You can also pair it with a belt cinched-in right here to show off your waist. It's very in right now.
Oh.
I KNOW HOW TO DRESS, THANK YOU. HANDS OFF, BITCH!
a baguette
...
"HELLO"? "PLEASE"? "THANK YOU"? TOO GOOD FOR US, ASSHOLE?

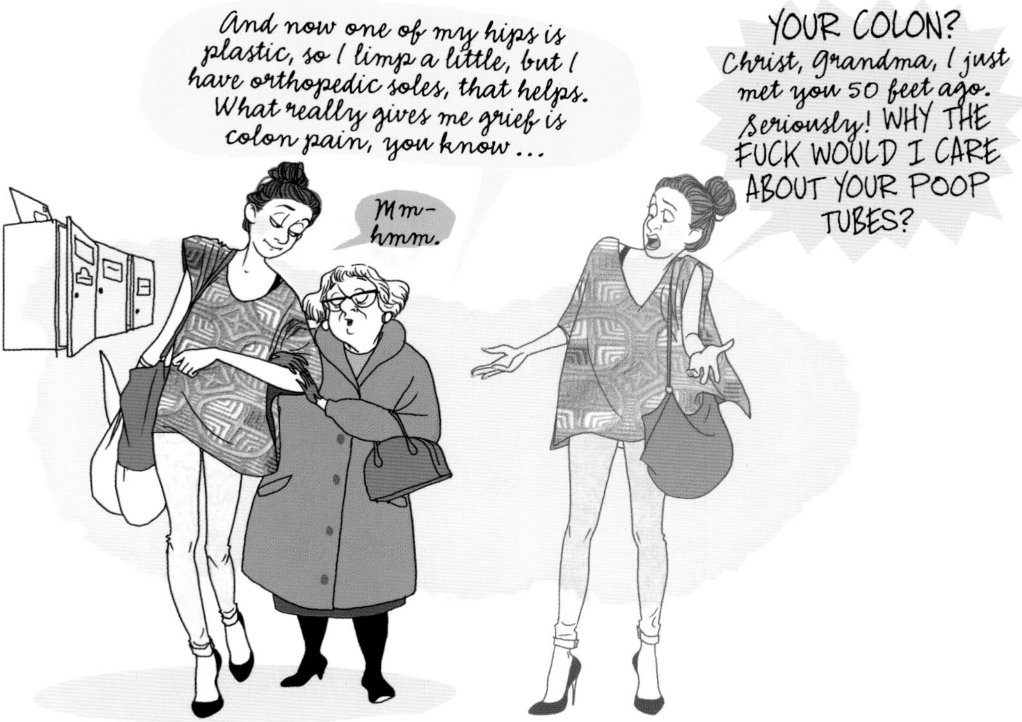
And now one of my hips is plastic, so I limp a little, but I have orthopedic soles, that helps. What really gives me grief is colon pain, you know...
Mm-hmm.
YOUR COLON? Christ, Grandma, I just met you 50 feet ago. Seriously! WHY THE FUCK WOULD I CARE ABOUT YOUR POOP TUBES?

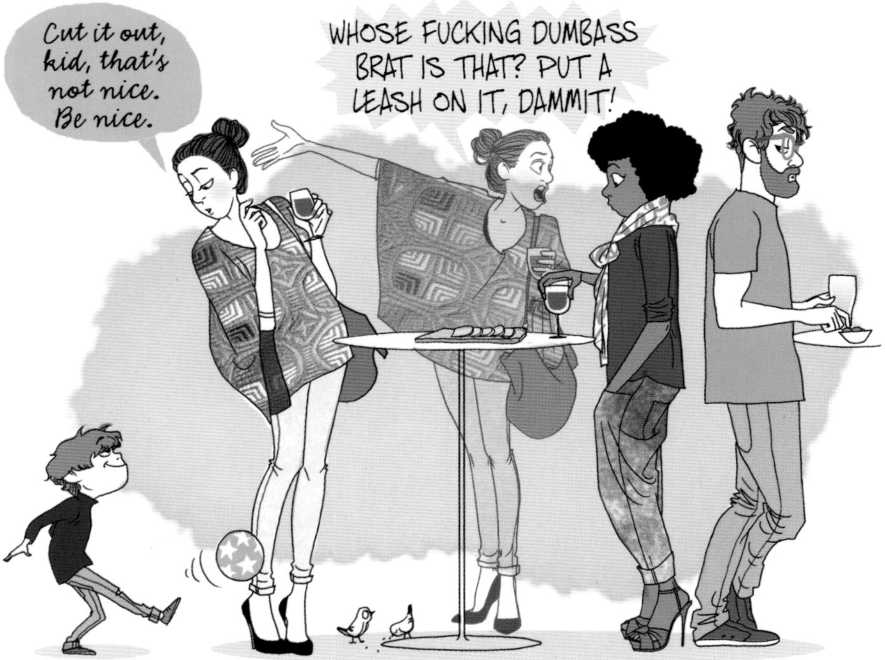
Cut it out, kid, that's not nice. Be nice.
WHOSE FUCKING DUMBASS BRAT IS THAT? PUT A LEASH ON IT, DAMMIT!

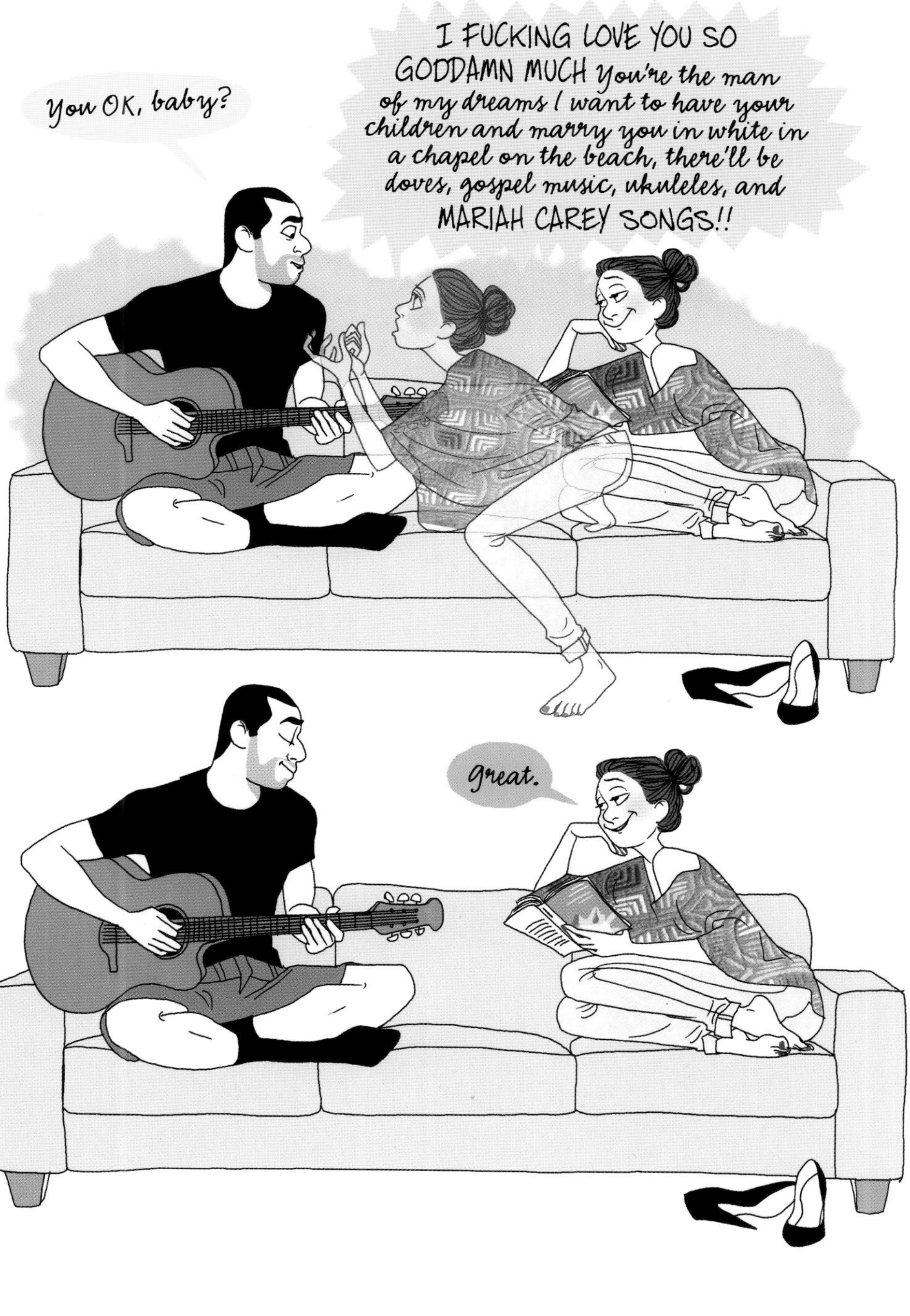
You OK, baby?
I FUCKING LOVE YOU SO GODDAMN MUCH You're the man of my dreams I want to have your children and marry you in white in a chapel on the beach, there'll be doves, gospel music, ukuleles, and MARIAH CAREY SONGS!!
Great.

Thank God there's a button on the remote control of my life that says: "Keep your mouth shut, you jackass."

Don't Say I Didn't Warn You

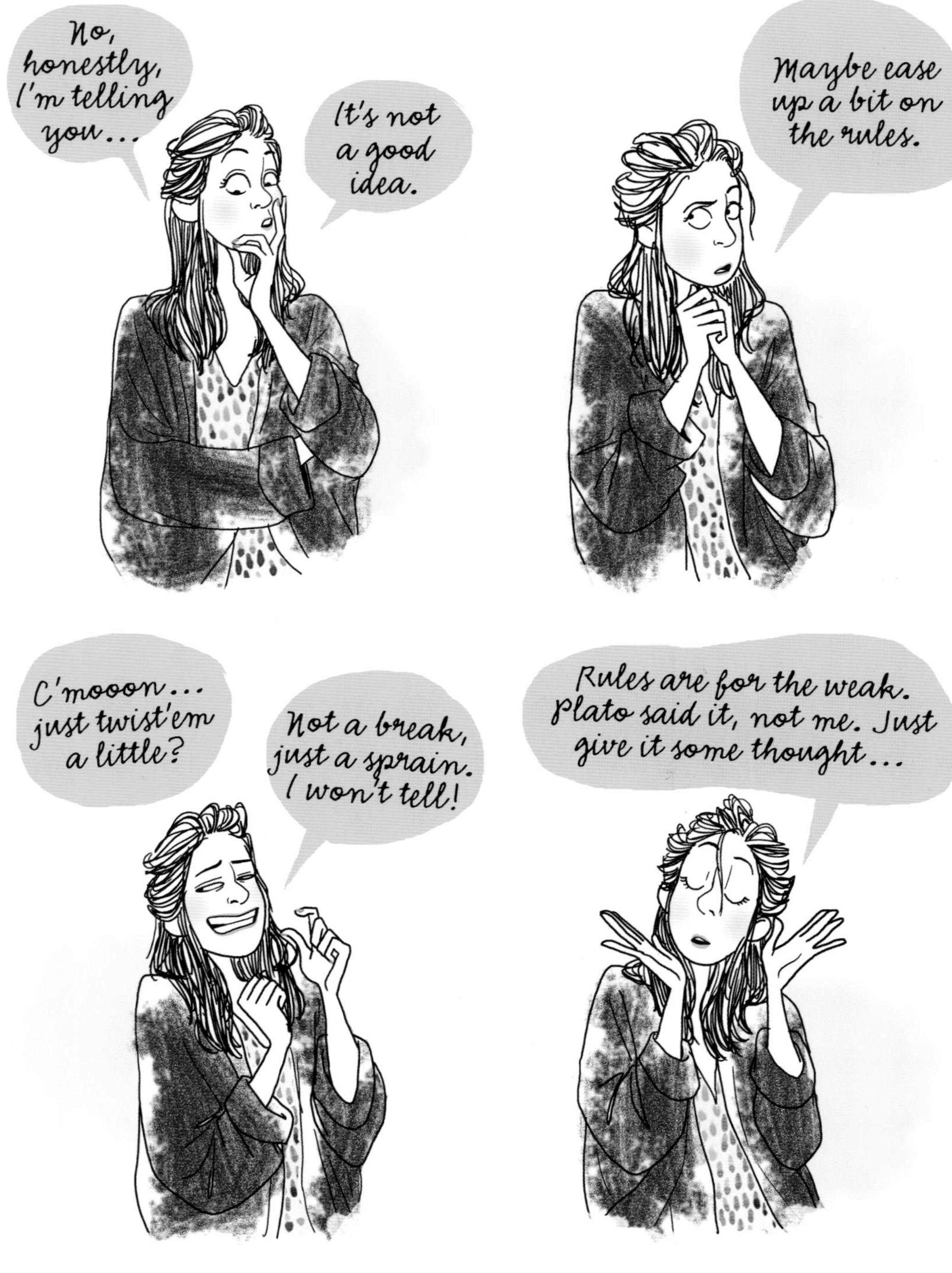
No, honestly, I'm telling you...
It's not a good idea.
Maybe ease up a bit on the rules.
C'mooon... just twist'em a little?
Not a break, just a sprain. I won't tell!
Rules are for the weak. Plato said it, not me. Just give it some thought...

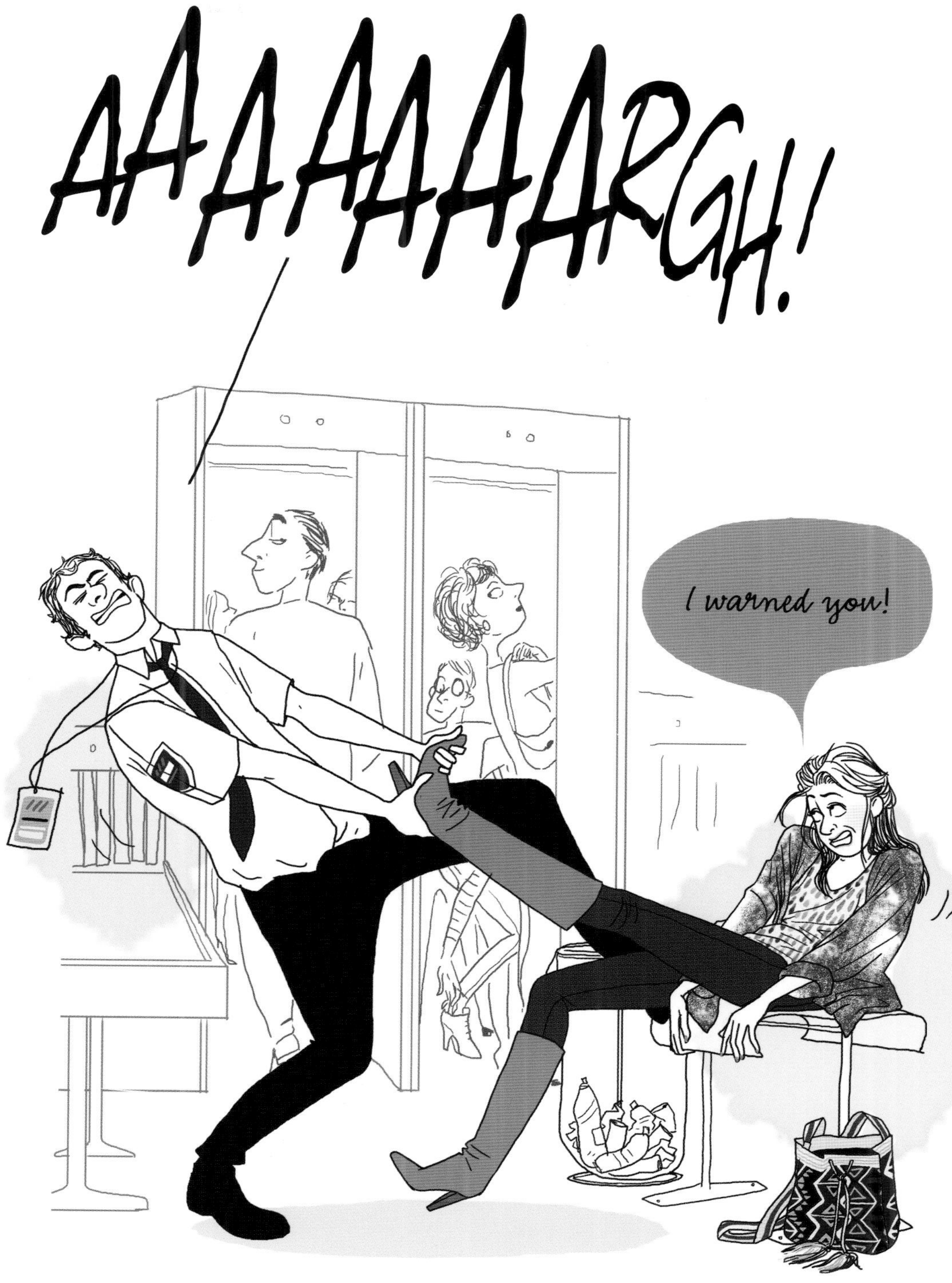
AAAAAAARGH!
I warned you!

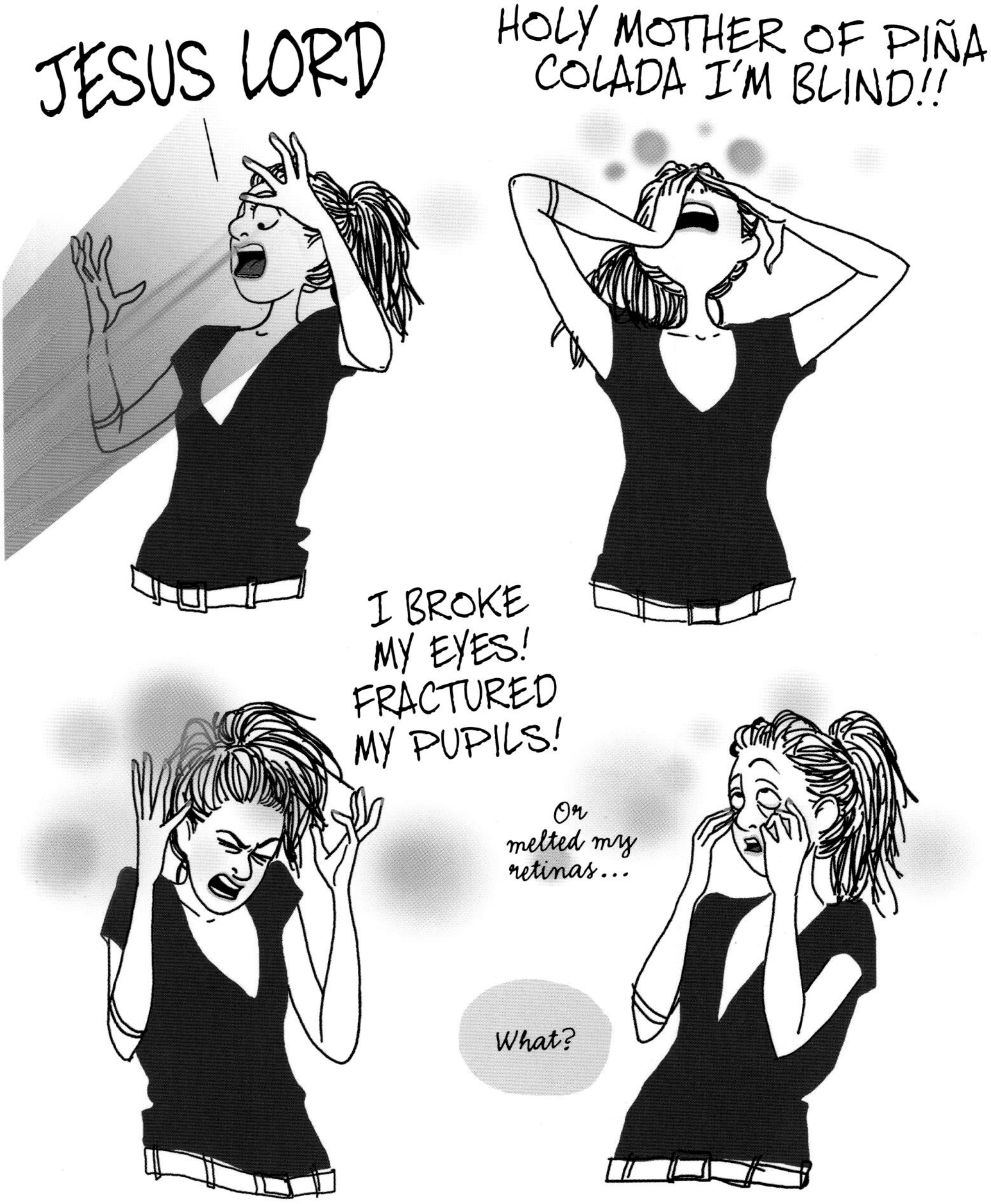
JESUS LORD
HOLY MOTHER OF PIÑA COLADA I'M BLIND!!
I BROKE MY EYES! FRACTURED MY PUPILS!
Or melted my retinas...
What?

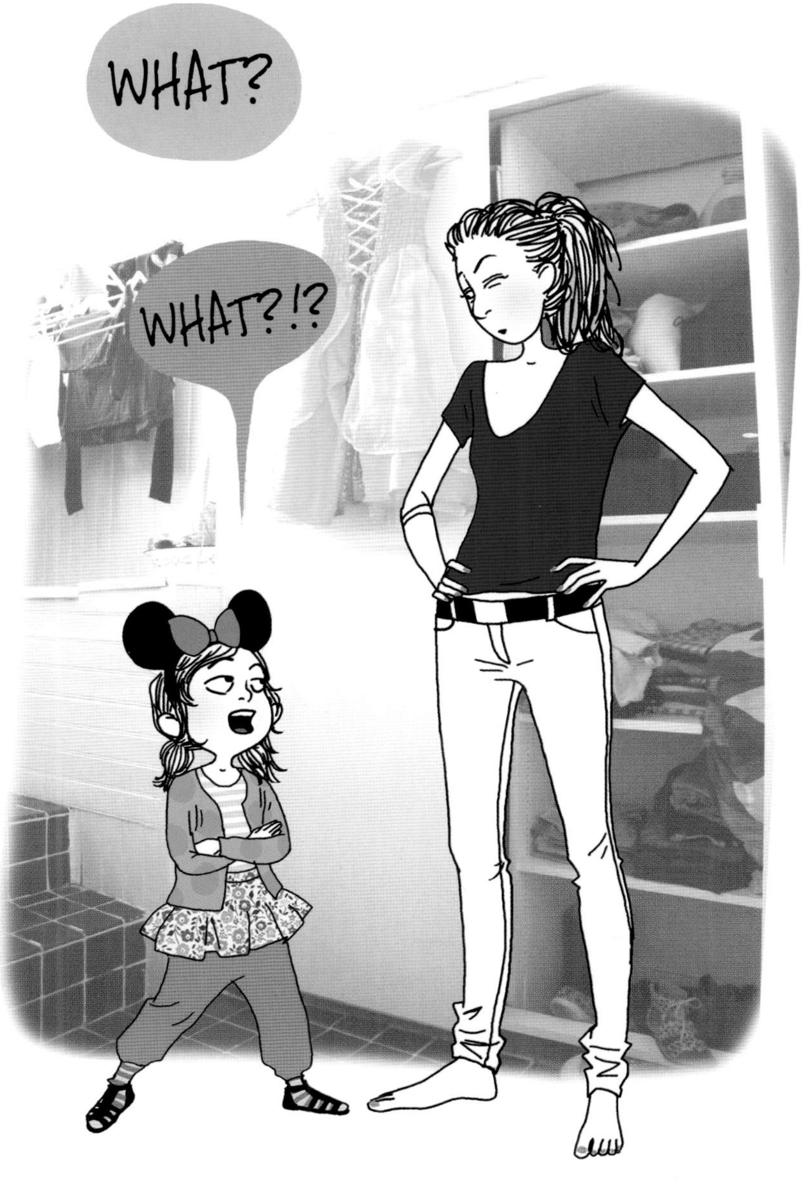
WHAT?
WHAT?!?

I've lost half my vision in both eyes since Pumpkin started dressing herself in the morning.

ALL MOTHERS HAVE SUPERPOWERS #2

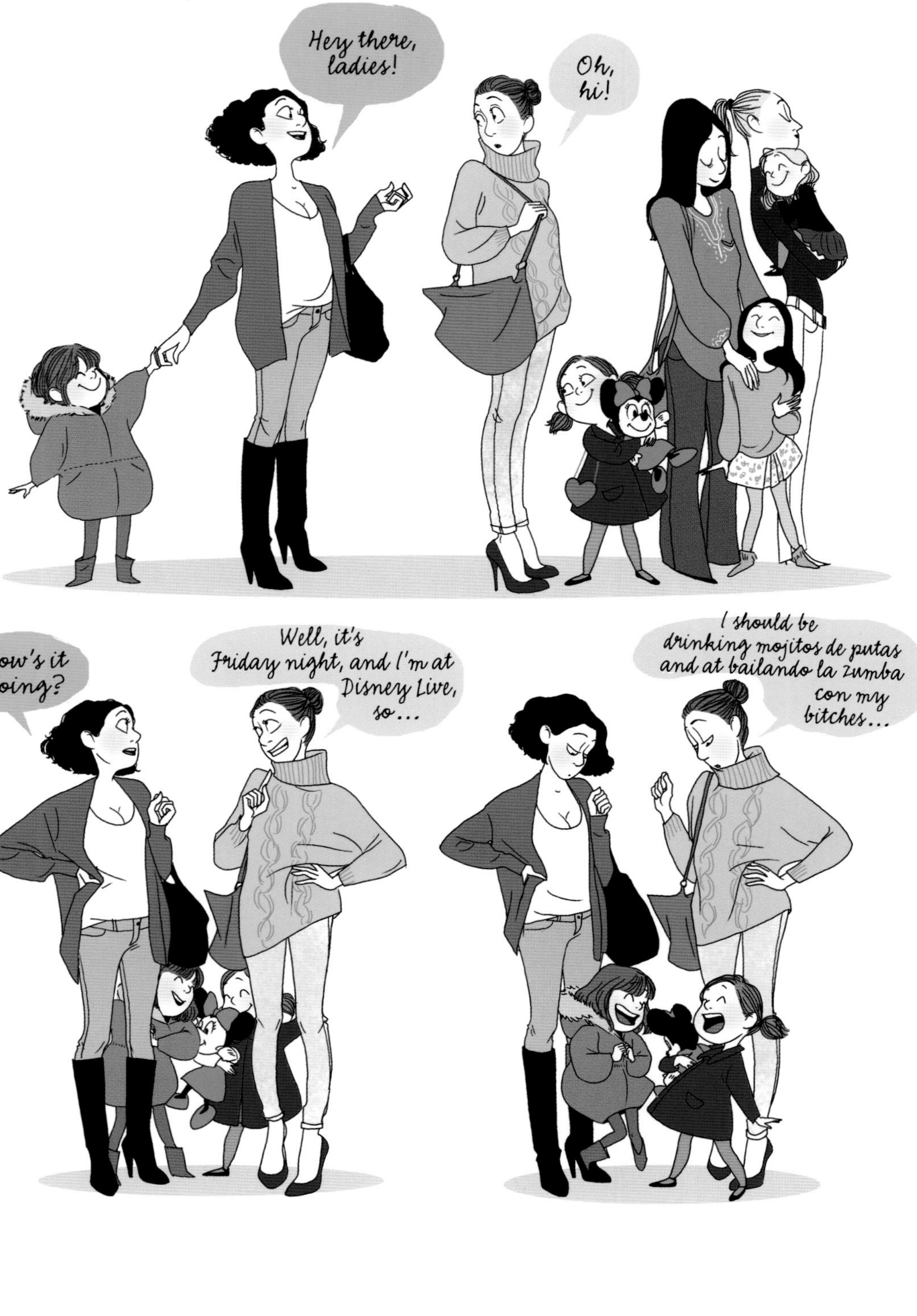
Hey there, ladies!
Oh, hi!
How's it going?
Well, it's Friday night, and I'm at Disney Live, so...
I should be drinking mojitos de putas and at bailando la zumba con my bitches...

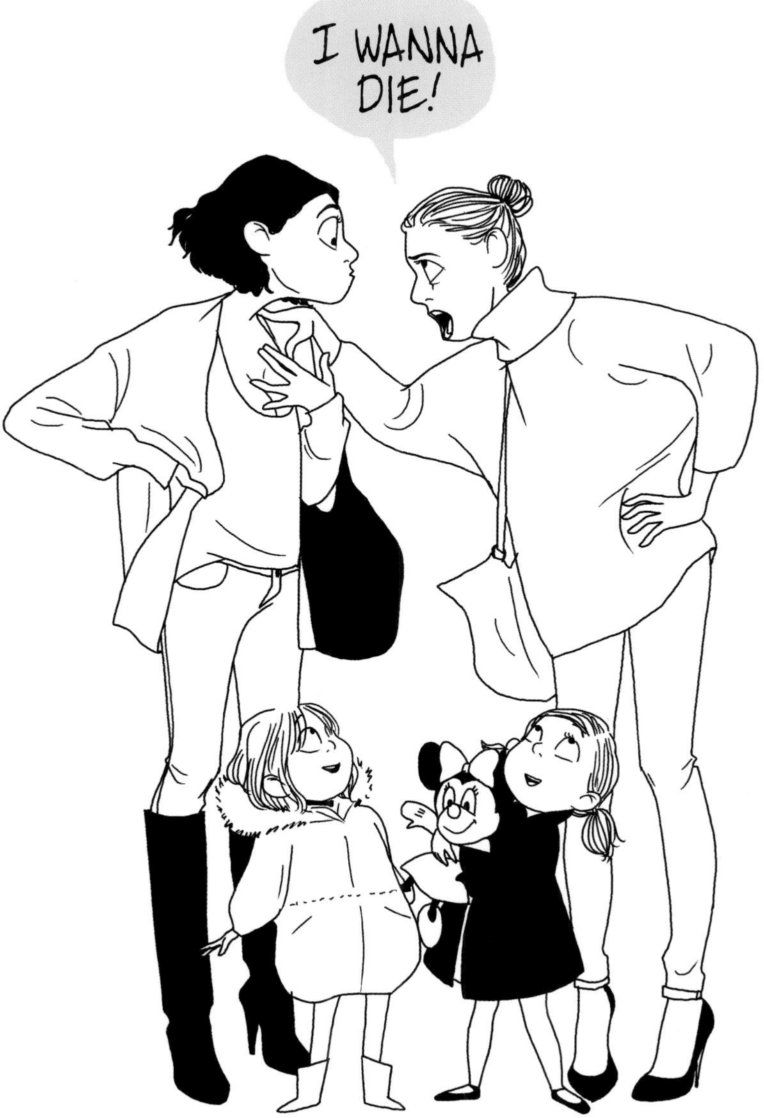
I WANNA DIE!

SUPERPOWER #2: **MULTILINGUALISM.**

What? He's 500 miles away, it's
not like he's gonna check

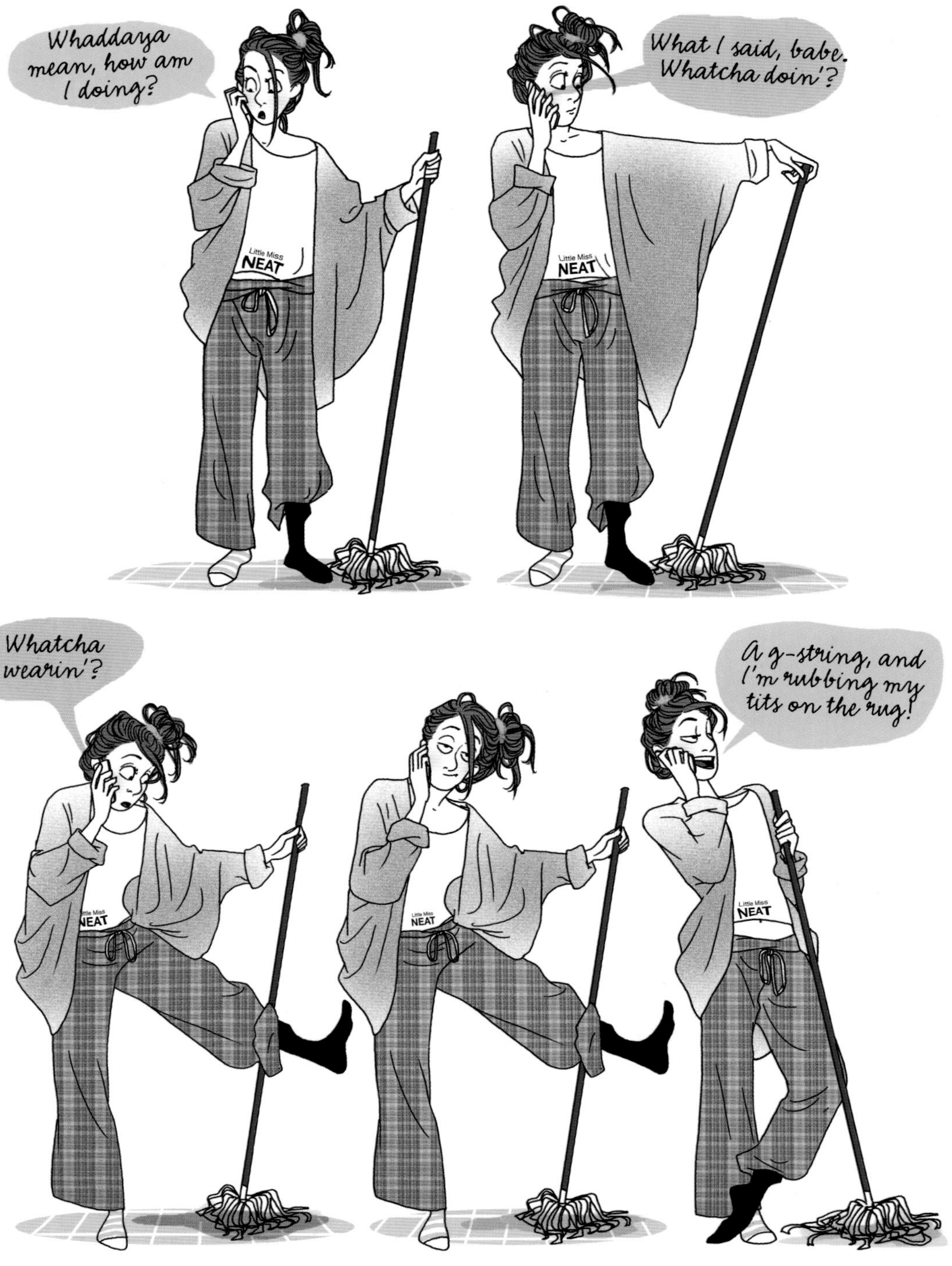
Whaddaya mean, how am I doing?
What I said, babe. Whatcha doin'?
Whatcha wearin'?
A g-string, and I'm rubbing my tits on the rug!

It's all relative

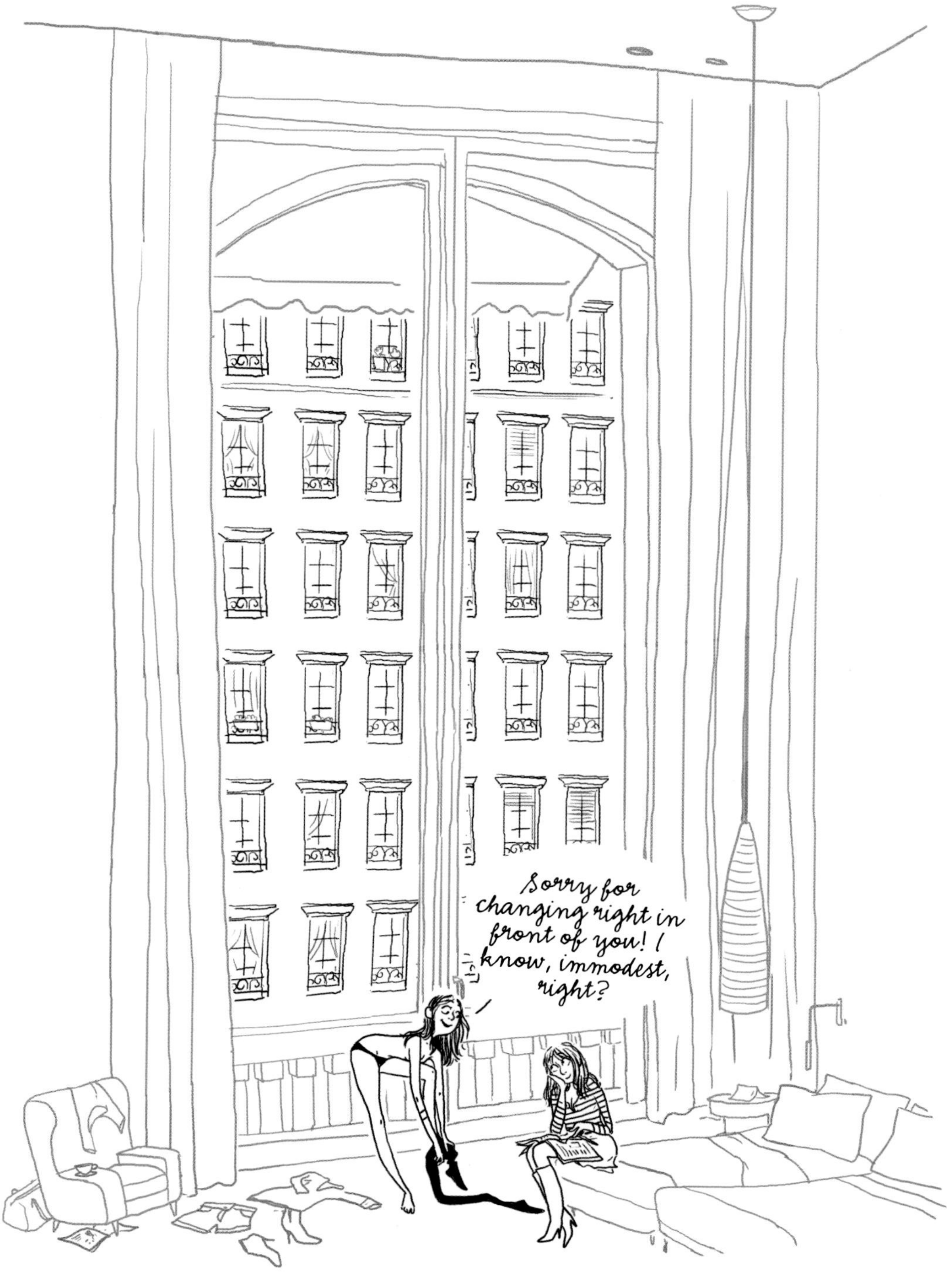
Sorry for changing right in front of you! I know, immodest, right?

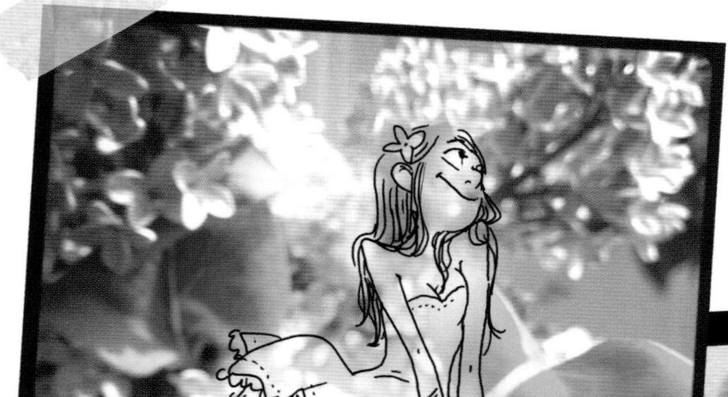

St. Jean

Paris

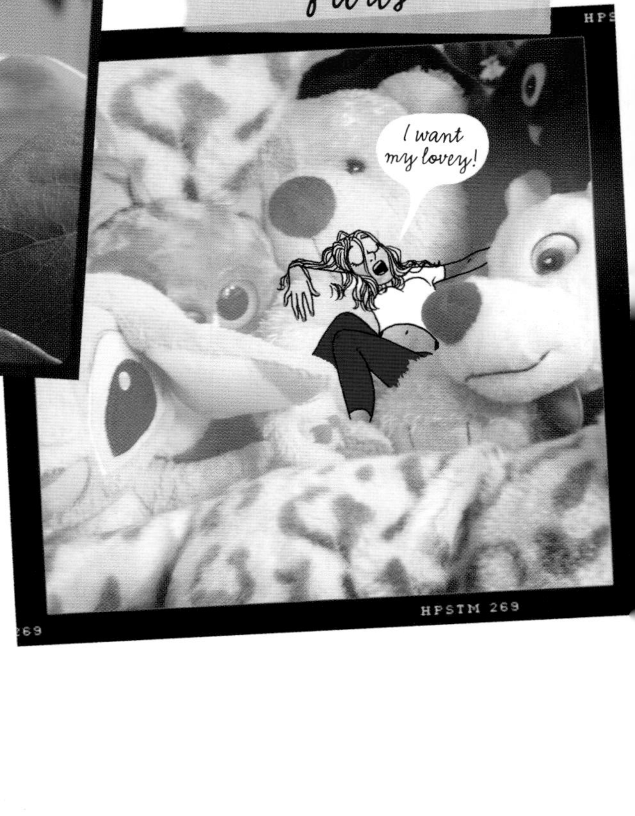
I want my lovey!
HPSTM 269

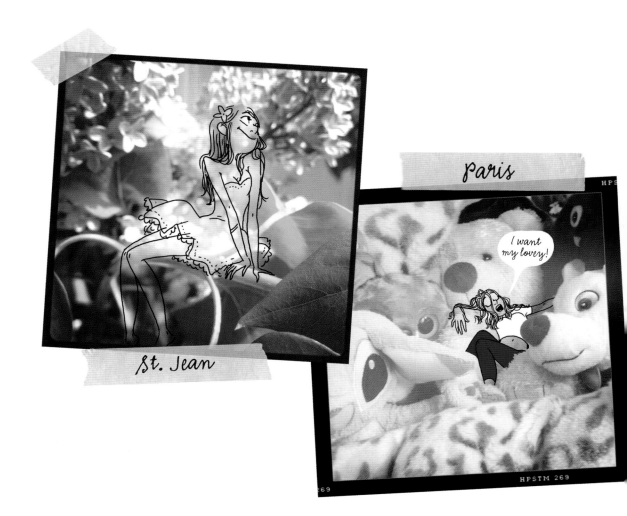

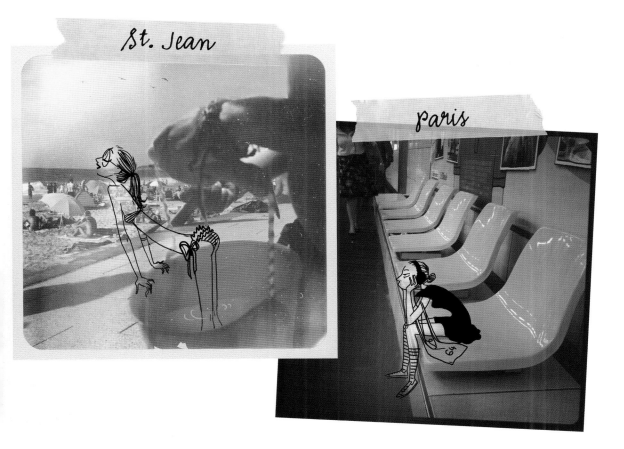

St. Jean

Paris

Sleeping Beauty

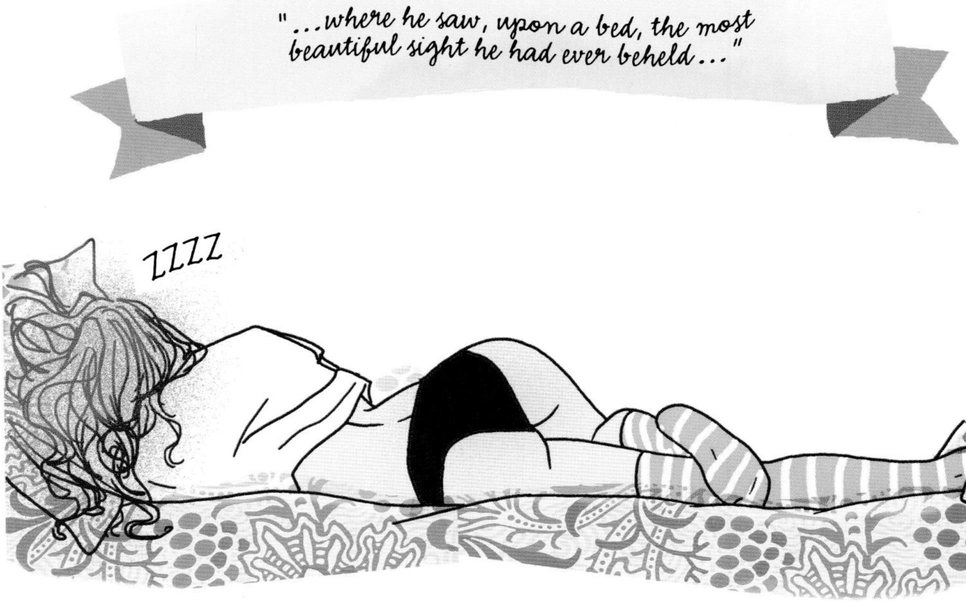
"...where he saw, upon a bed, the most beautiful sight he had ever beheld..."
ZZZZ

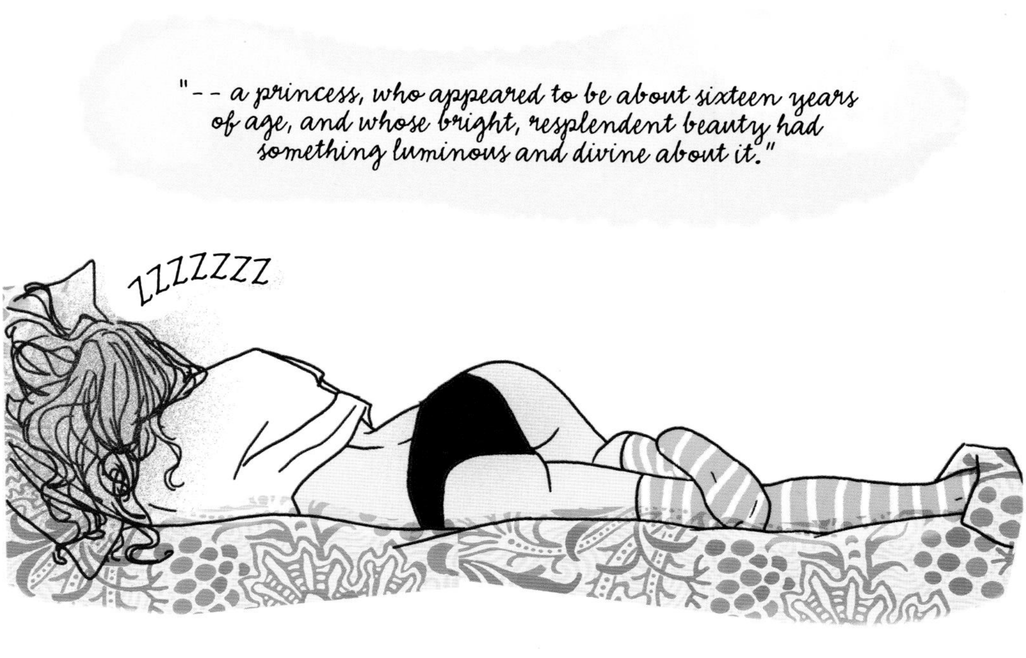
"-- a princess, who appeared to be about sixteen years of age, and whose bright, resplendent beauty had something luminous and divine about it."
ZZZZZZZ

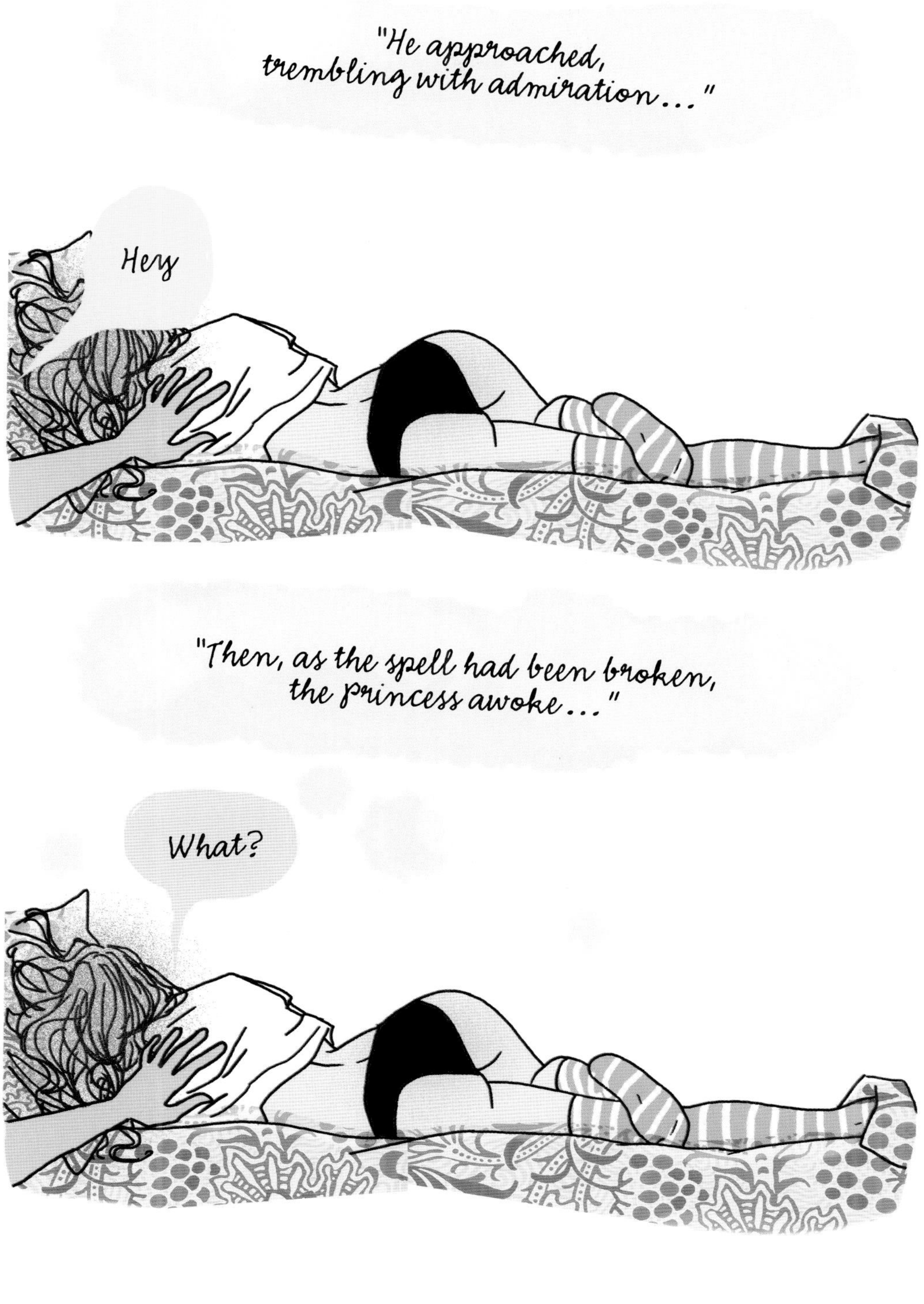
"He approached, trembling with admiration..."
Hey
"Then, as the spell had been broken, the princess awoke..."
What?

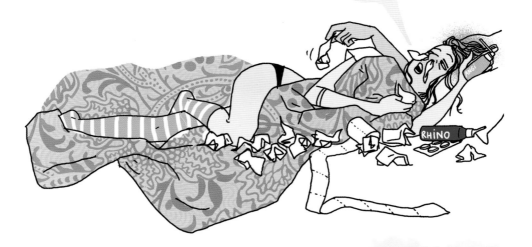

You're snoring.

"And looking upon him with a gaze more tender than could have been expected at first sight, said: 'Is it you, my Prince? You have waited a long while.'"

NO WAY! AS IF!

"The Prince, charmed by these words, and much more by the manner in which they were spoken, knew not how to show his joy and gratitude; he assured her that he loved her better than he did himself."

No, I swear. You snore like a pig.

Hurts So Good

Demons and wonders
Winds and waves
The tide has receded toward the horizon
But in your half-open eyes
Two tiny waves still remain
Demons and wonders
Winds and waves
Two tiny eddies to drown in.

"Quicksand" by Jacques Prévert

The Mentalist

A power I have as a chick is reading my boo's thoughts.

CHRIST, JUST SAY IT. Why won't you say it? I can smell it on you. I'm not stupid!
OUT WITH IT. No point hiding. I KNOW EVERYTHING. 'FESS UP!
OOOOH your pupils are dilated and you won't look me in the eye. That's a tell.
C'mon, SAY IT! Even your cock wants to say it. C'MOOON!

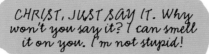

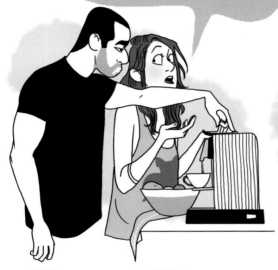

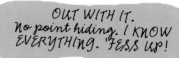

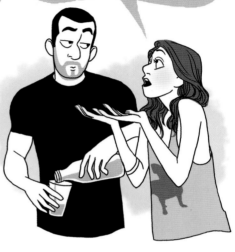

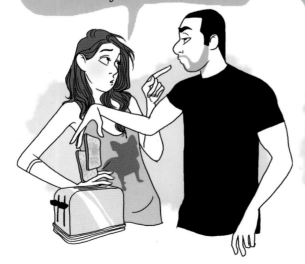

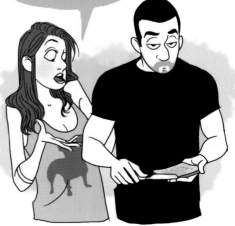

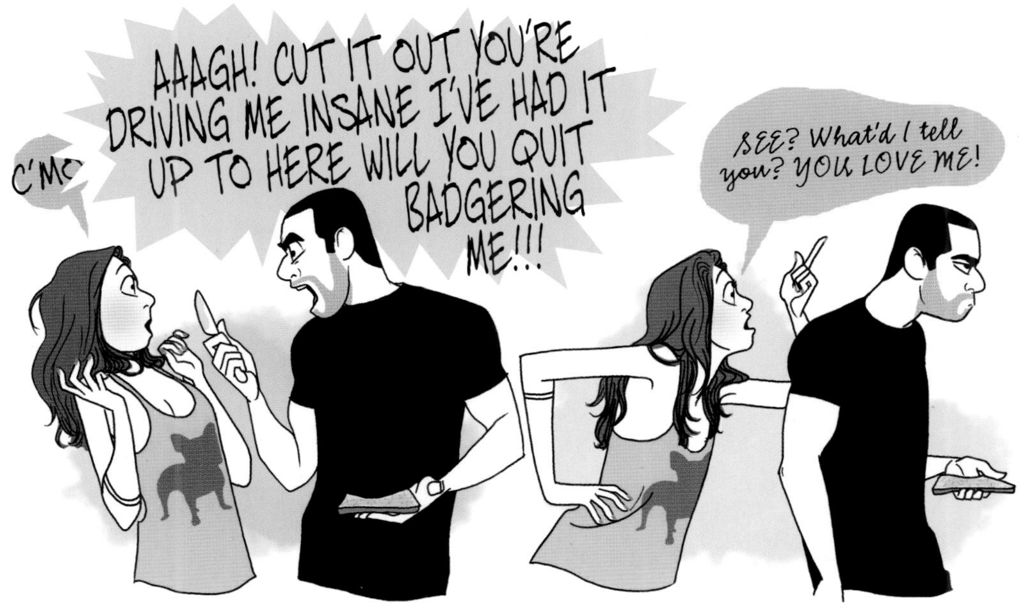
C'MO
AAAGH! CUT IT OUT YOU'RE DRIVING ME INSANE I'VE HAD IT UP TO HERE WILL YOU QUIT BADGERING ME!!!
SEE? What'd I tell you? YOU LOVE ME!

He was obviously refusing to believe in my power. I know things about him he doesn't know about himself, and it scares him. THANK GOD I'm not alone. There are others endowed with the same vast telepathic powers. Together, I think we're strong enough to expose the truth...

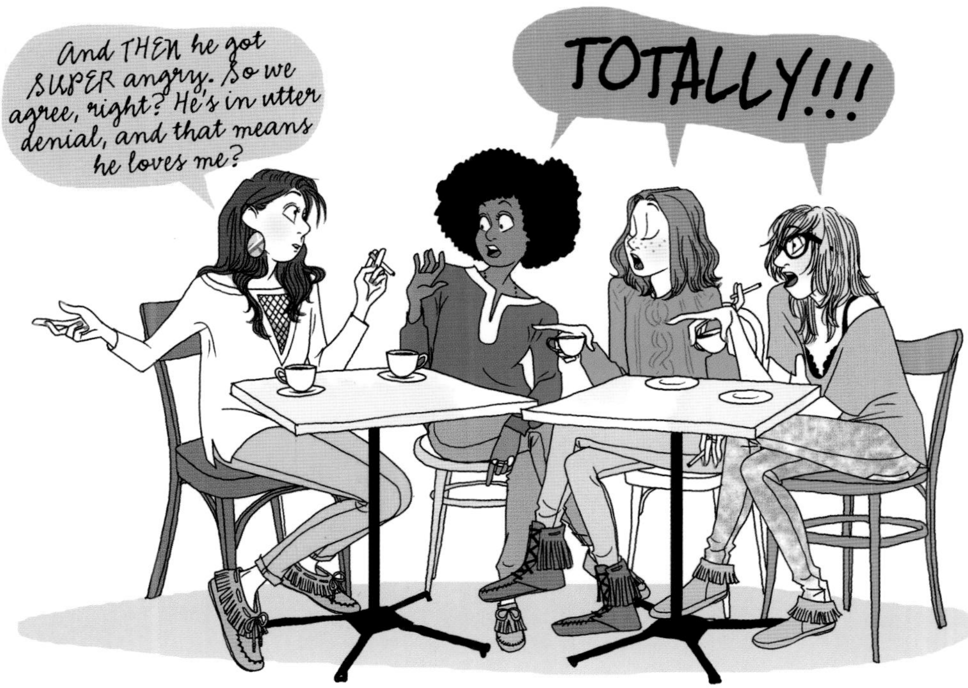
And THEN he got SUPER angry. So we agree, right? He's in utter denial, and that means he loves me?
TOTALLY!!!

Never Happy

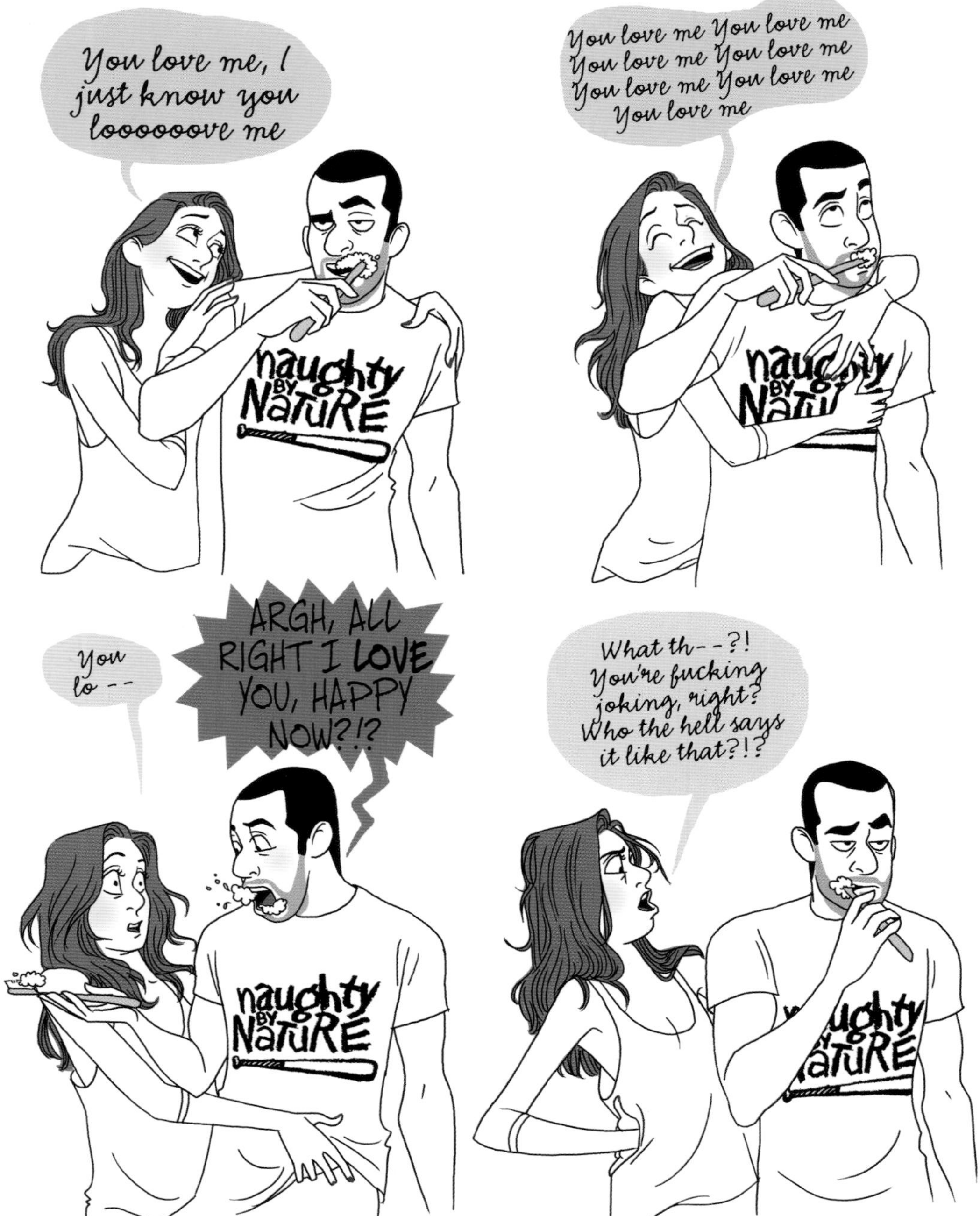
You love me, I just know you loooooove me
naughty BY NATURE
You love me You love me You love me You love me You love me You love me You love me
You lo --
ARGH, ALL RIGHT I LOVE YOU, HAPPY NOW?!?
What th--?! You're fucking joking, right? Who the hell says it like that?!?

Ain't No Sunshine

I put your photos in my songs
And sailboats in my house
I wanted to get away, but I can't anymore
I'm all upside down, I can't stand where I live now
I used to be 100, don't recognize myself anymore
Don't like people now that I've seen you
Don't want to dream anymore, just want you to come
and fly me away…

United States of Margaux

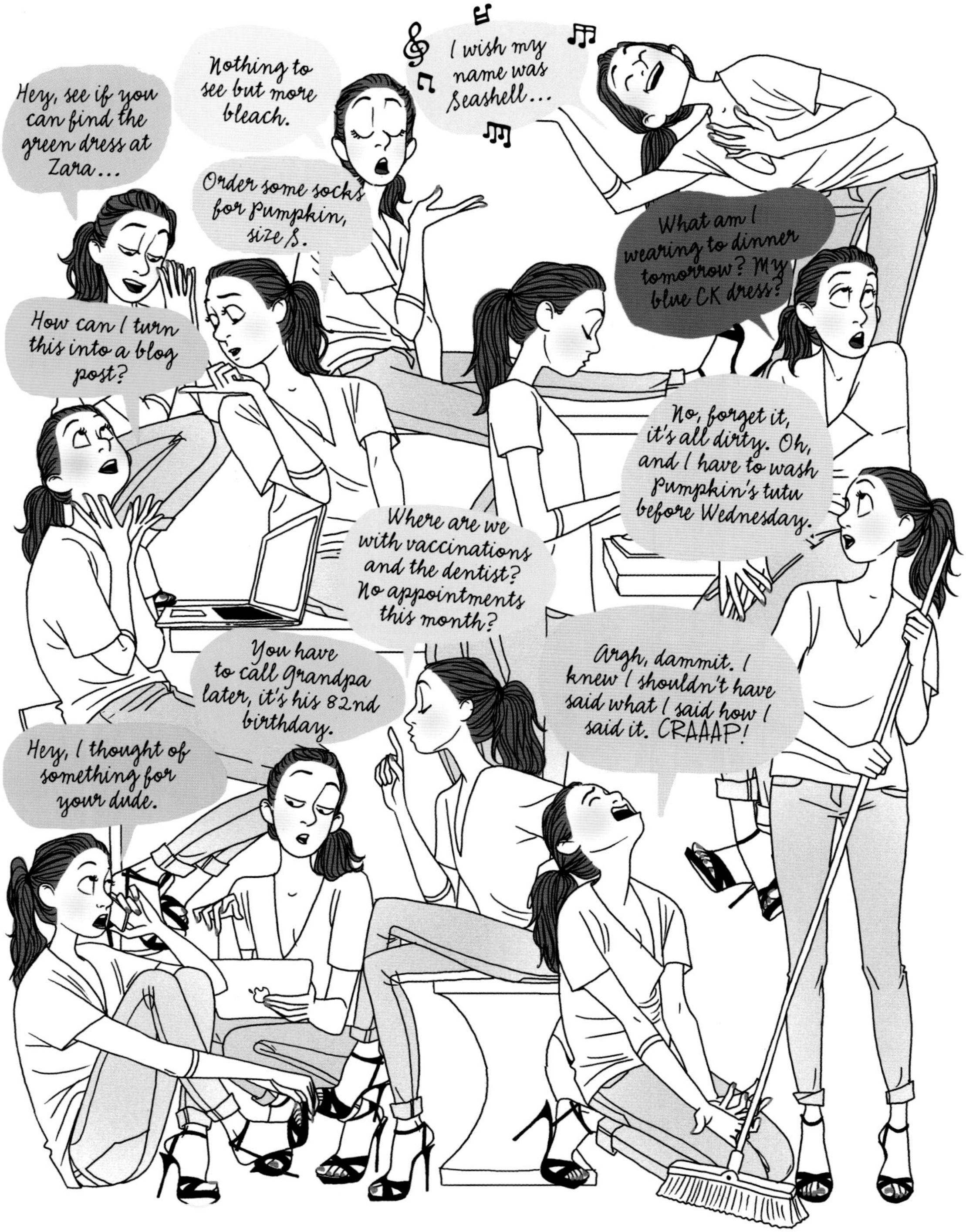

Hey, see if you can find the green dress at Zara...
Nothing to see but more bleach.
I wish my name was Seashell...
Order some socks for Pumpkin, size S.
What am I wearing to dinner tomorrow? My blue CK dress?
How can I turn this into a blog post?
No, forget it, it's all dirty. Oh, and I have to wash Pumpkin's tutu before Wednesday.
Where are we with vaccinations and the dentist? No appointments this month?
You have to call Grandpa later, it's his 82nd birthday.
Argh, dammit. I knew I shouldn't have said what I said how I said it. CRAAAP!
Hey, I thought of something for your dude.

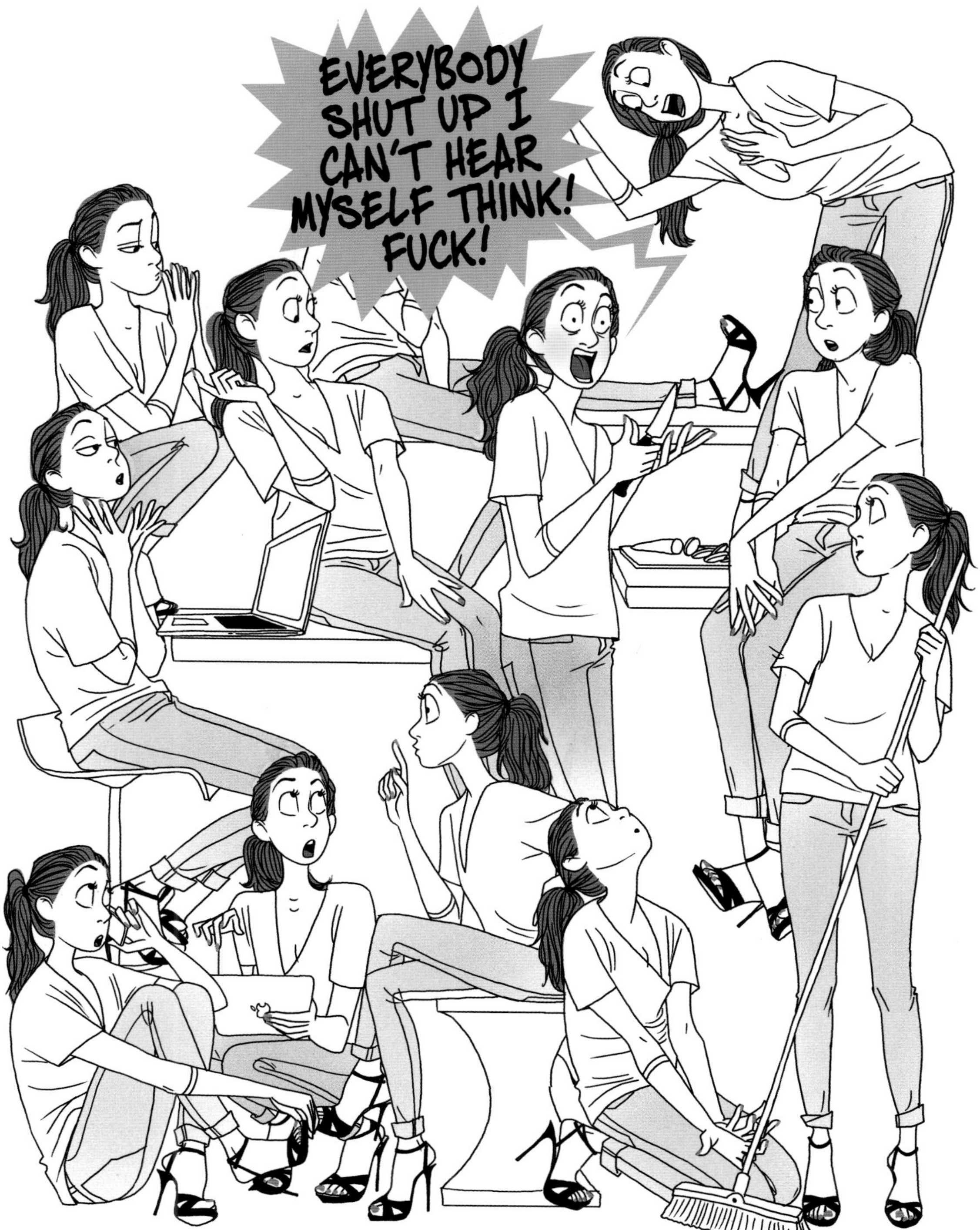
EVERYBODY SHUT UP I CAN'T HEAR MYSELF THINK! FUCK!

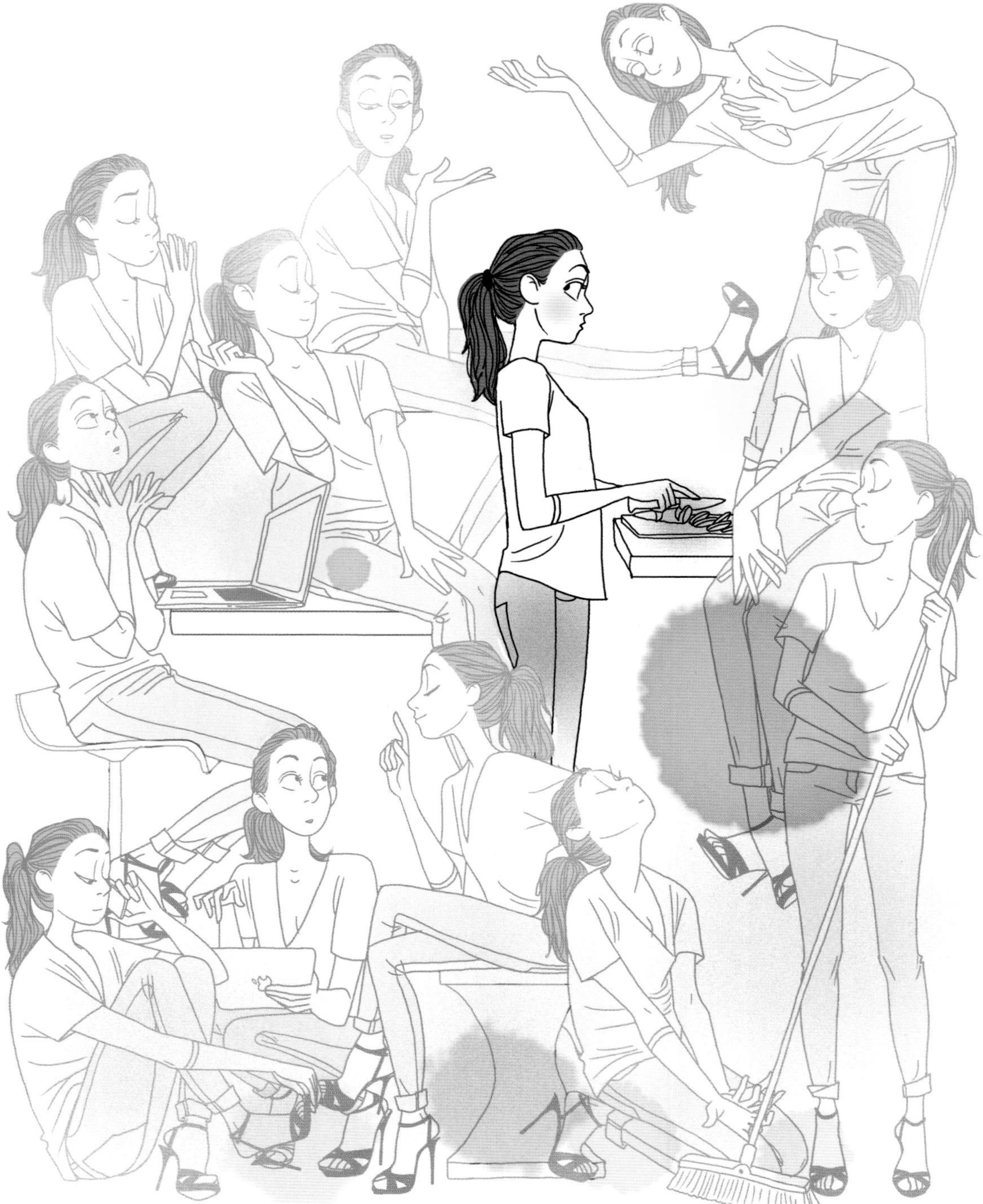

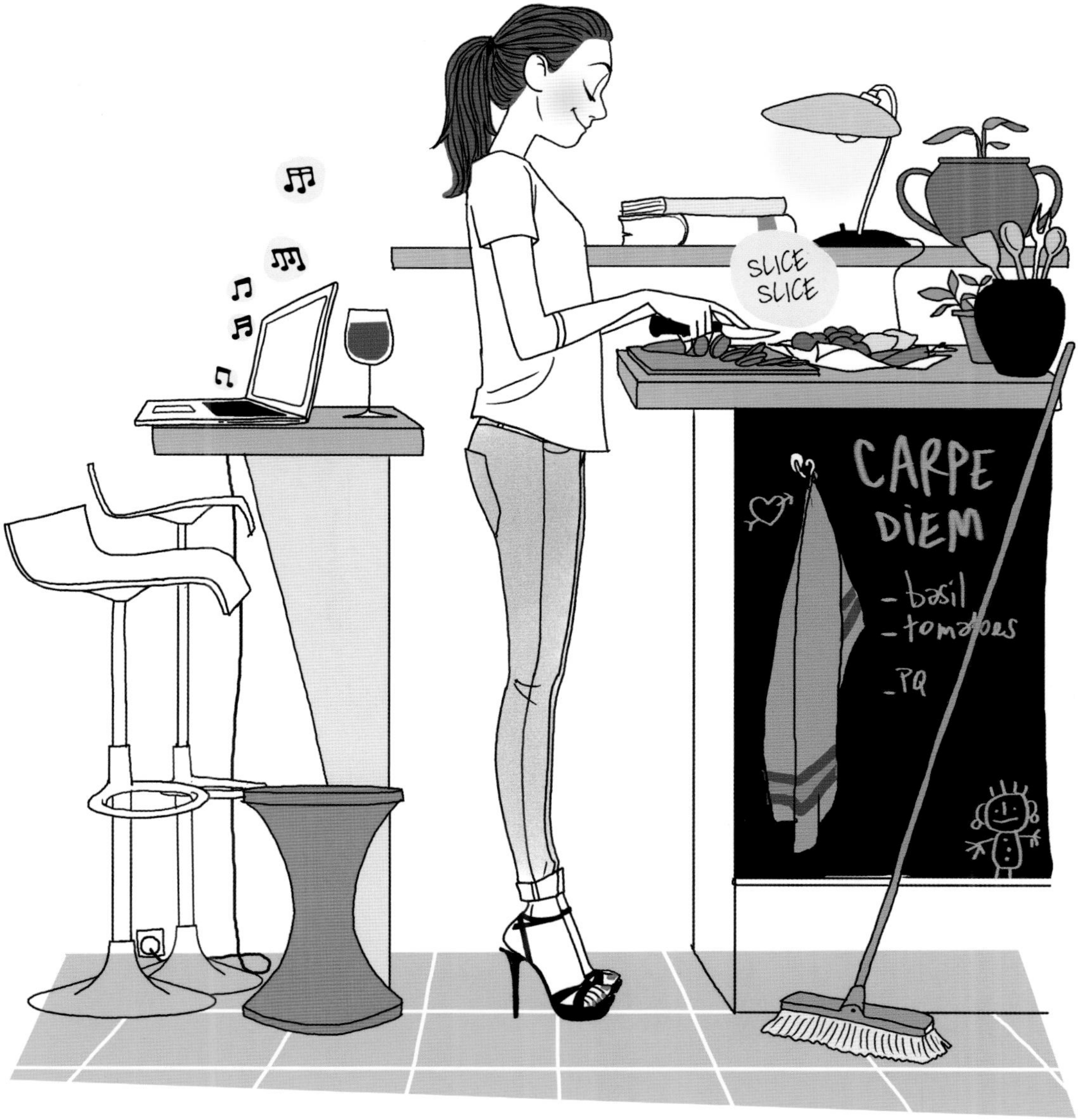
SLICE
SLICE
CARPE
DIEM
_basil
_tomatoes
_PQ

"C'mon, I'll take you to fairyland, at the back of the wind..."

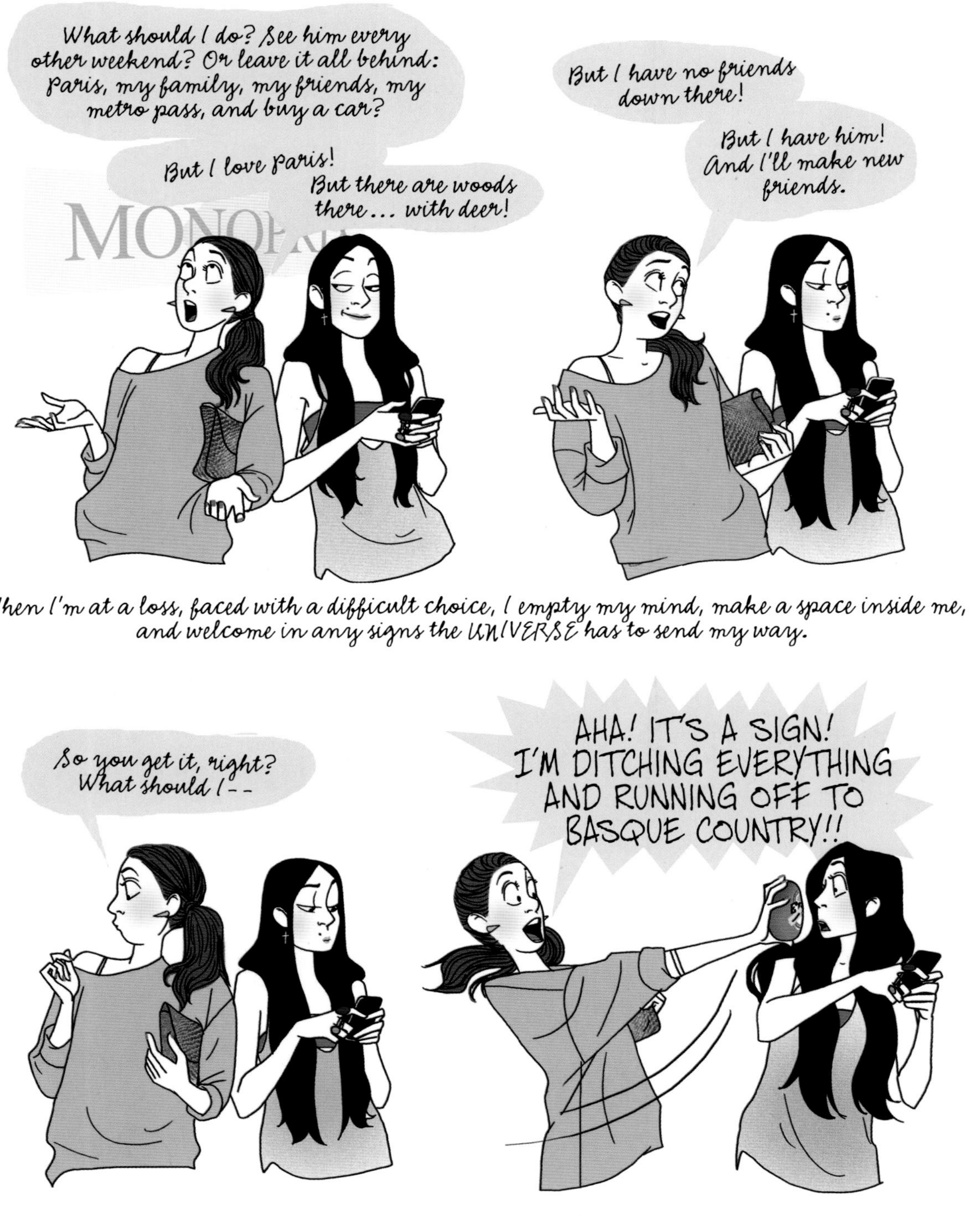
What should I do? See him every other weekend? Or leave it all behind: Paris, my family, my friends, my metro pass, and buy a car?
But I love Paris!
But there are woods there... with deer!
But I have no friends down there!
But I have him! And I'll make new friends.
When I'm at a loss, faced with a difficult choice, I empty my mind, make a space inside me, and welcome in any signs the UNIVERSE has to send my way.
So you get it, right? What should I--
AHA! IT'S A SIGN! I'M DITCHING EVERYTHING AND RUNNING OFF TO BASQUE COUNTRY!!

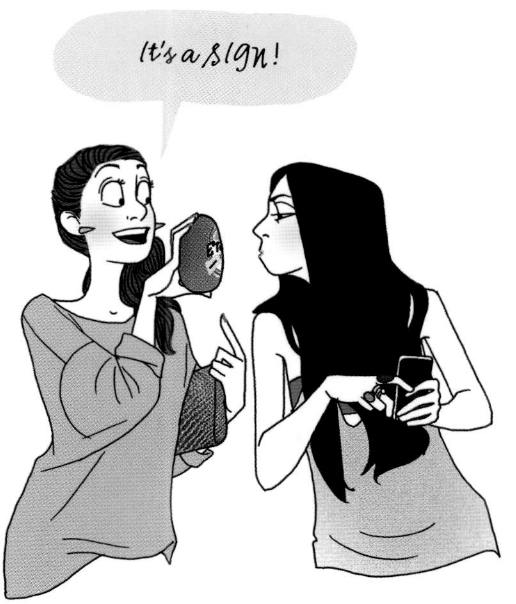
It's a SIGN!

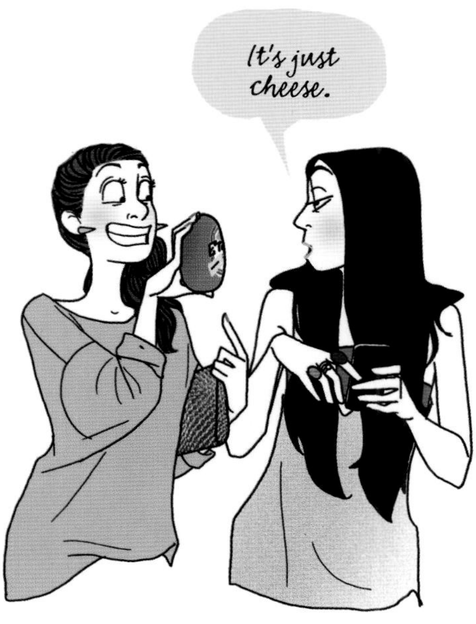
It's just cheese.

Look, my guy can be subtle, but my artistic sensibilities are attuned to sussing out the messages he sends.

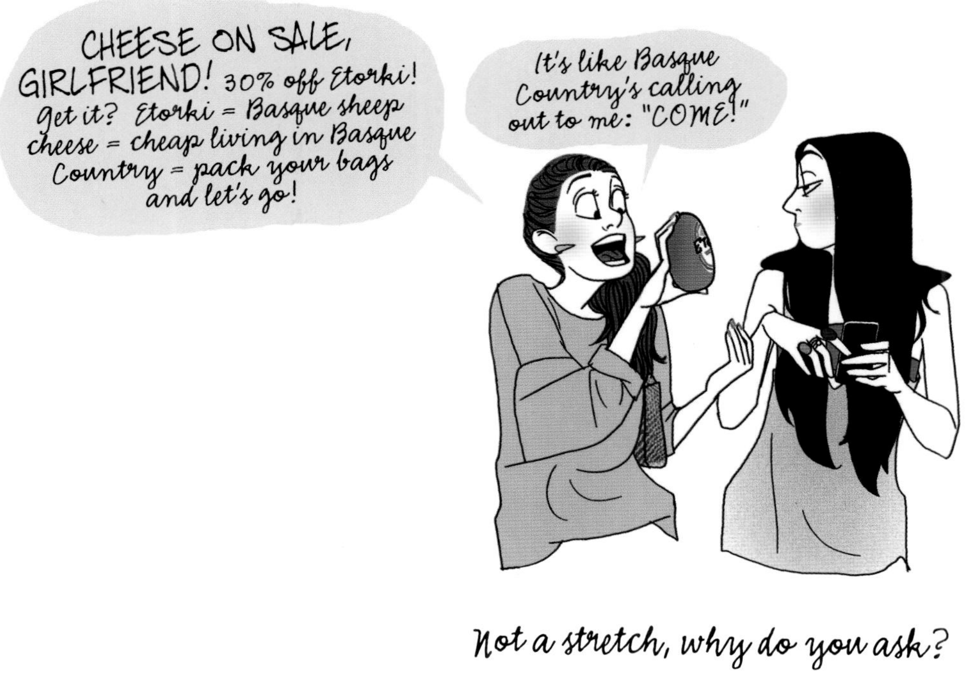
CHEESE ON SALE, GIRLFRIEND! 30% off Etorki! Get it? Etorki = Basque sheep cheese = cheap living in Basque Country = pack your bags and let's go!
It's like Basque Country's calling out to me: "COME!"

Not a stretch, why do you ask?

Moving, or successfully introducing a species to a new habitat

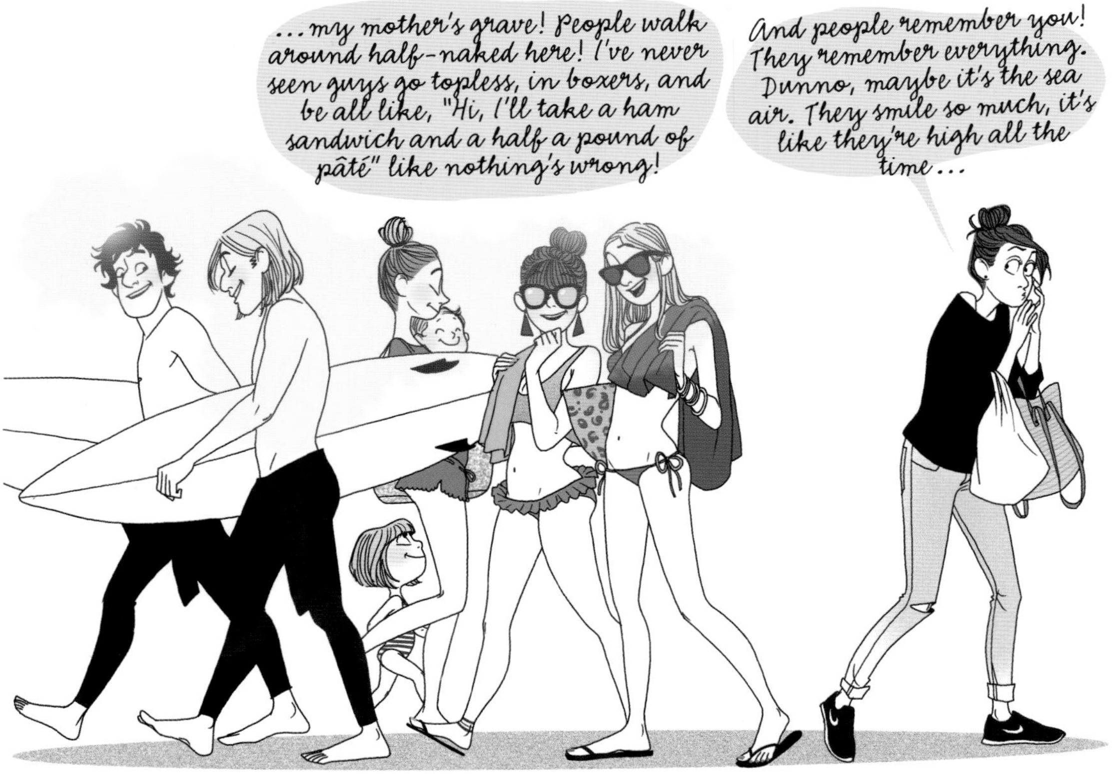
...my mother's grave! People walk around half-naked here! I've never seen guys go topless, in boxers, and be all like, "Hi, I'll take a ham sandwich and a half a pound of pâté" like nothing's wrong!
And people remember you! They remember everything. Dunno, maybe it's the sea air. They smile so much, it's like they're high all the time...

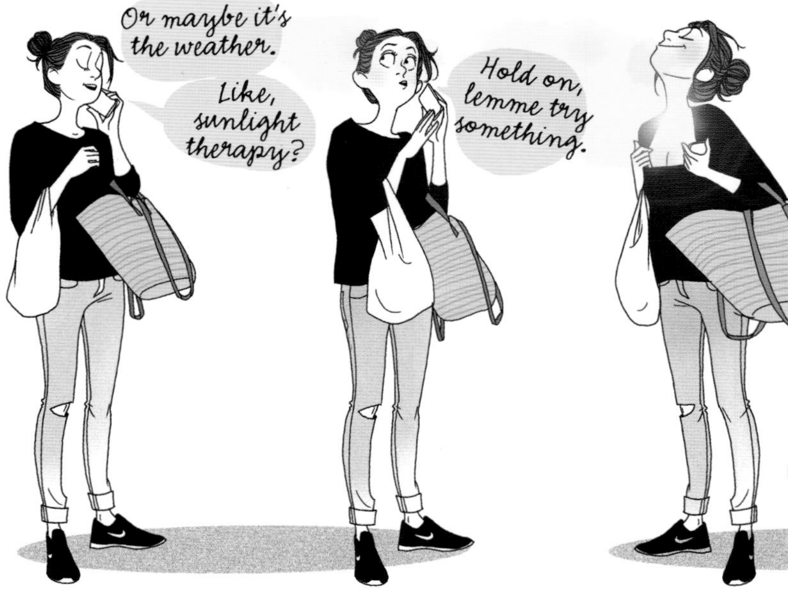
Or maybe it's the weather.
Like, sunlight therapy?
Hold on, lemme try something.

PHASE NO. 1:
Recreate suitable living conditions and an environment suited to the species in question.

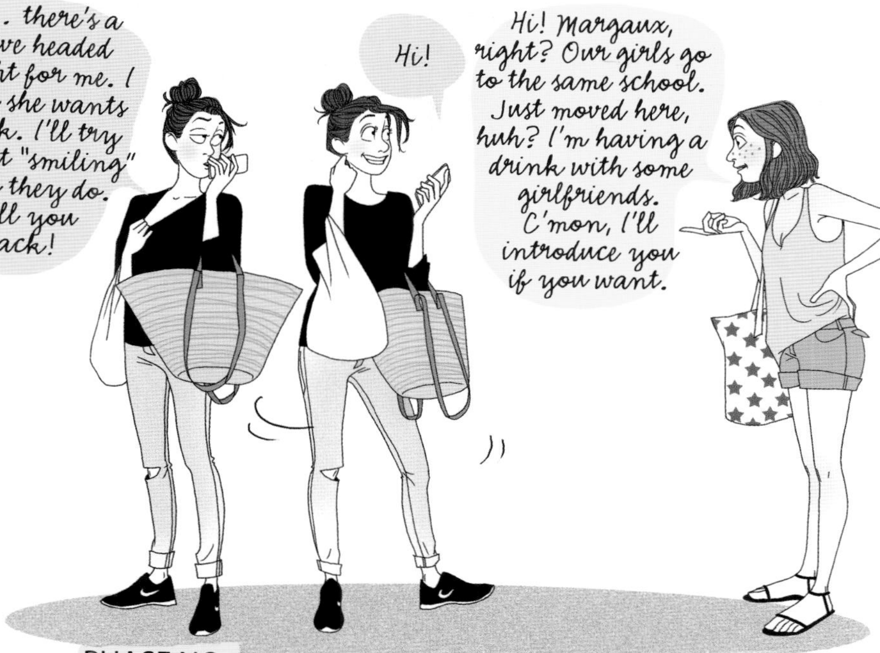
Uh... there's a native headed straight for me. I think she wants to talk. I'll try out that "smiling" thing they do. Call you back!
Hi!
Hi! Margaux, right? Our girls go to the same school. Just moved here, huh? I'm having a drink with some girlfriends. C'mon, I'll introduce you if you want.

PHASE NO. 2: Social acceptance from the local population.

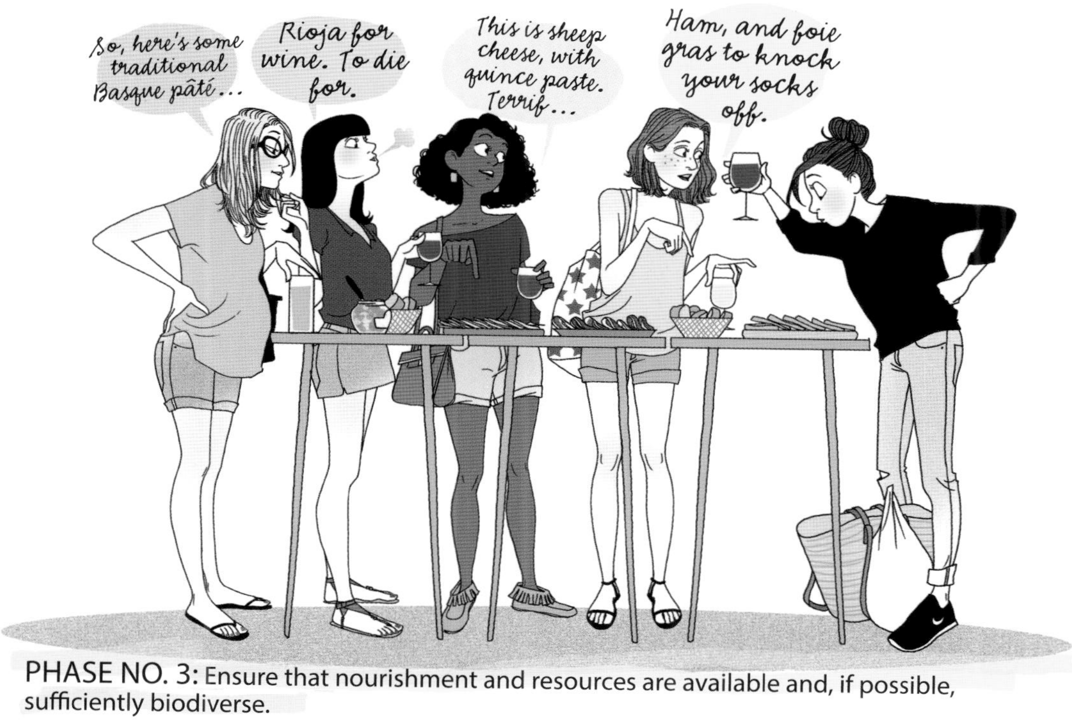
So, here's some traditional Basque pâté...
Rioja for wine. To die for.
This is sheep cheese, with quince paste. Terrif...
Ham, and foie gras to knock your socks off.

PHASE NO. 3: Ensure that nourishment and resources are available and, if possible, sufficiently biodiverse.

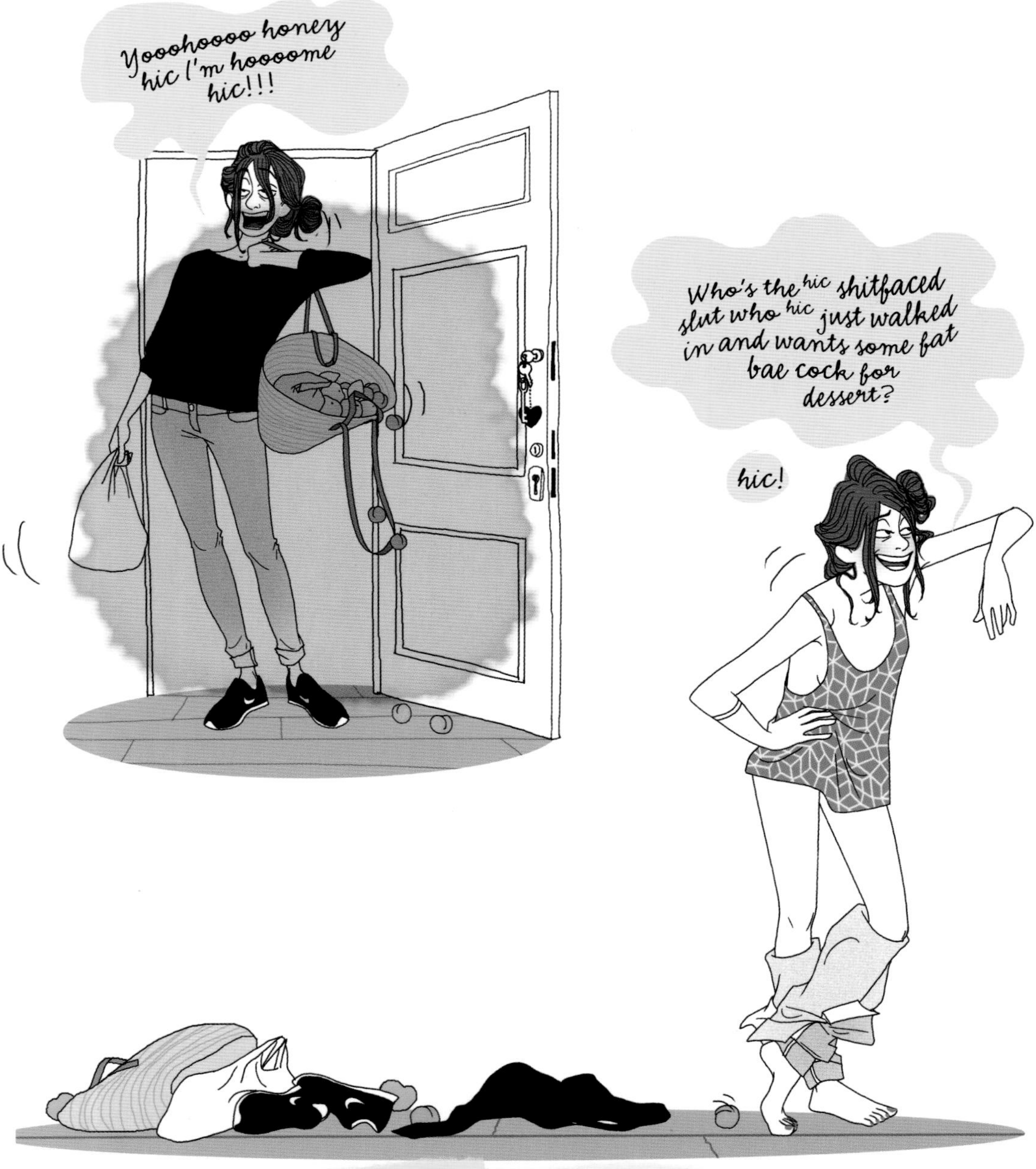
Yooohoooo honey hic I'm hoooome hic!!!
Who's the hic shitfaced slut who hic just walked in and wants some fat bae cock for dessert?
hic!

FINAL PHASE: Conditions conducive to reproduction.

Let me tell you, I think moving down here was a great idea.

Glitching

When I'm tired and overwhelmed, there's something mechanical about how I run through my daily tasks: wake up, turn off the gas, lock the front door...

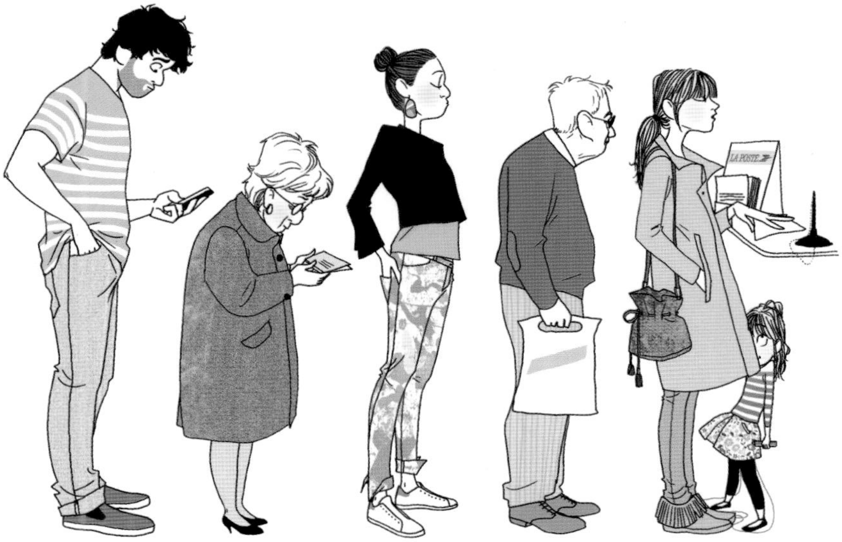
LA POSTE

Only much later do I get a creeping sensation of spine-tingling terror: "Did mechanical me perform that daily task correctly?"

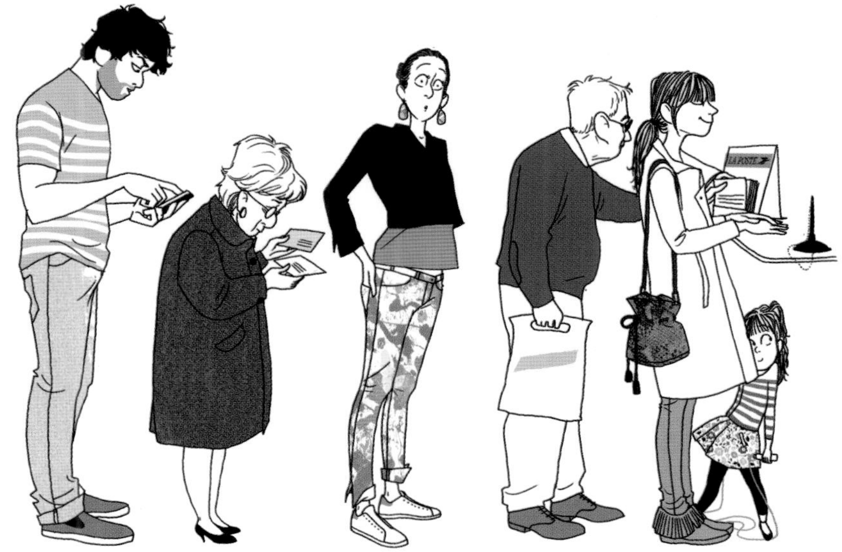
LA POSTE

No matter how I rack my brain, I can't remember.

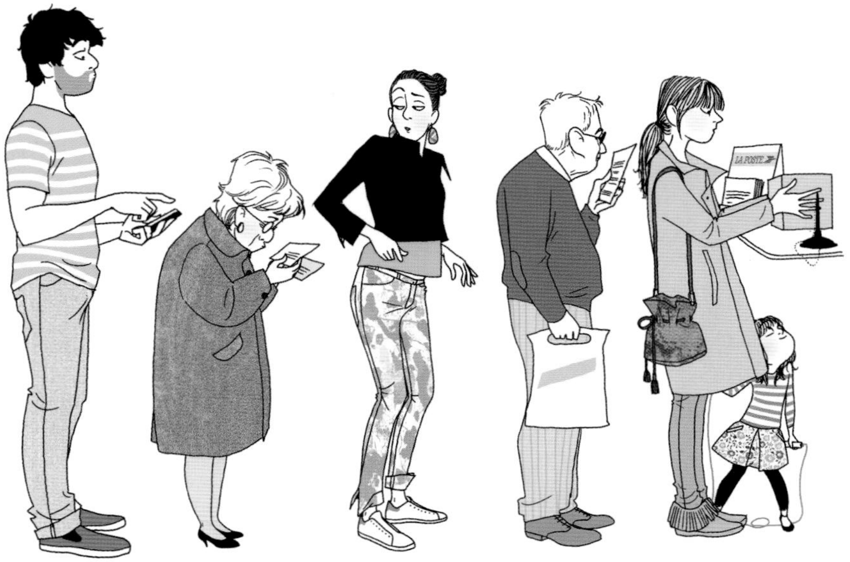
LA POSTE

I have to return to the scene of the crime to check with my own eyes...

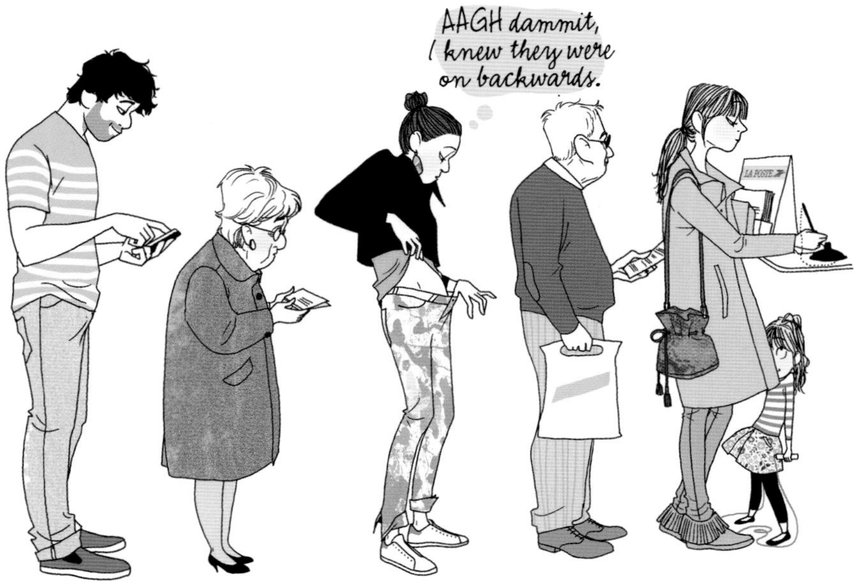
AAGH dammit, I knew they were on backwards.
LA POSTE

I'm getting better. Last time, I forgot to put shoes on.

Out of the Mouths of Babes

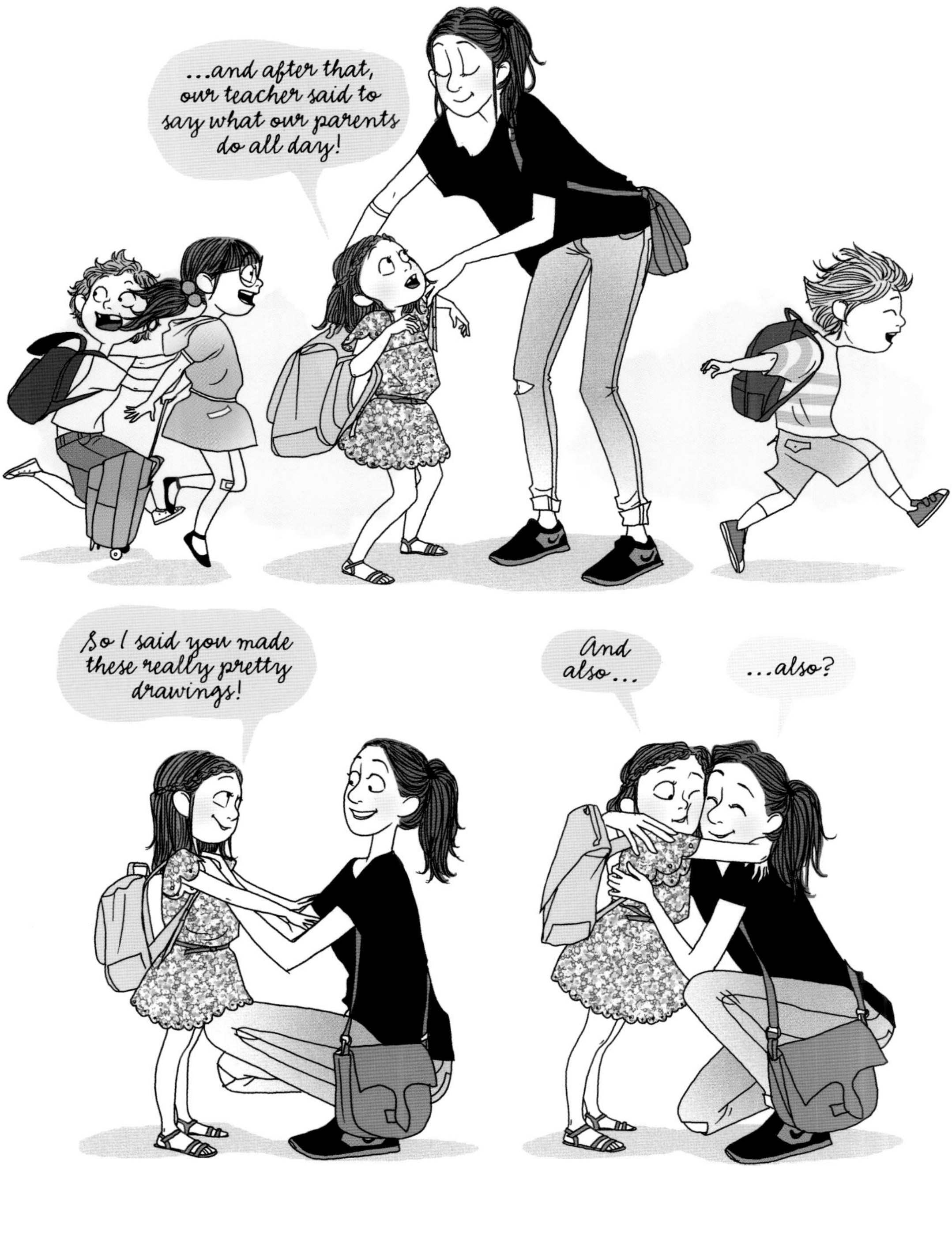
...and after that, our teacher said to say what our parents do all day!
So I said you made these really pretty drawings!
And also...
...also?

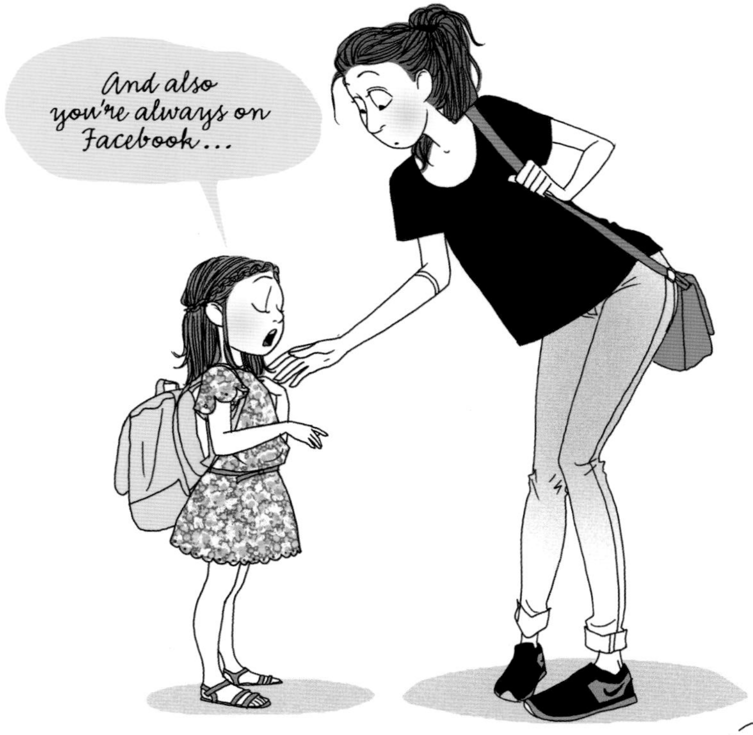
And also you're always on Facebook...

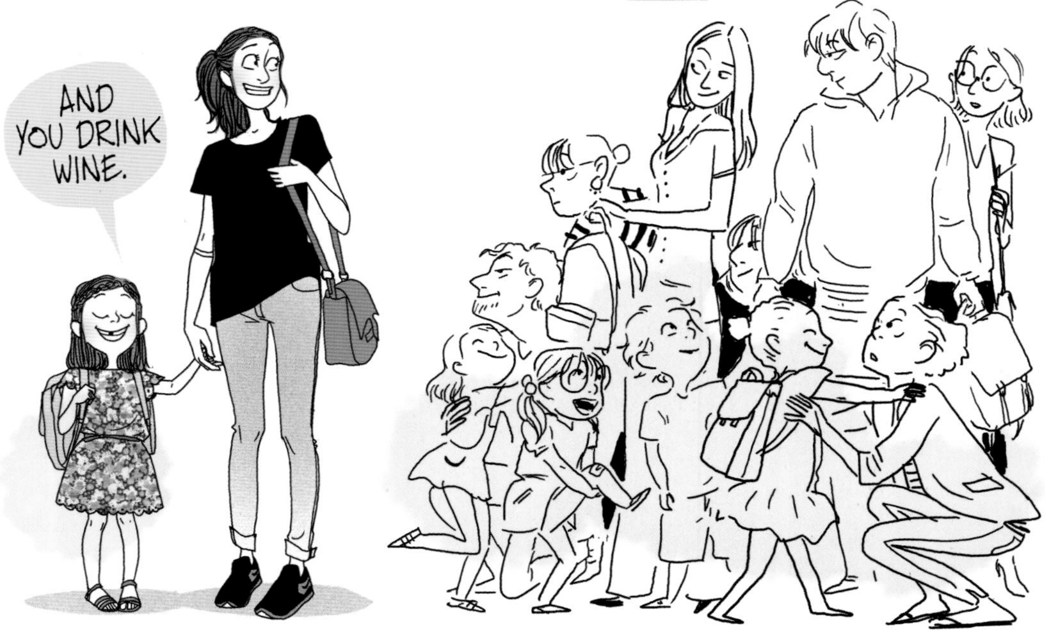
AND YOU DRINK WINE.

Still, it'd be nice if they shut their tiny traps sometimes.

I Have a Serious Mental Condition

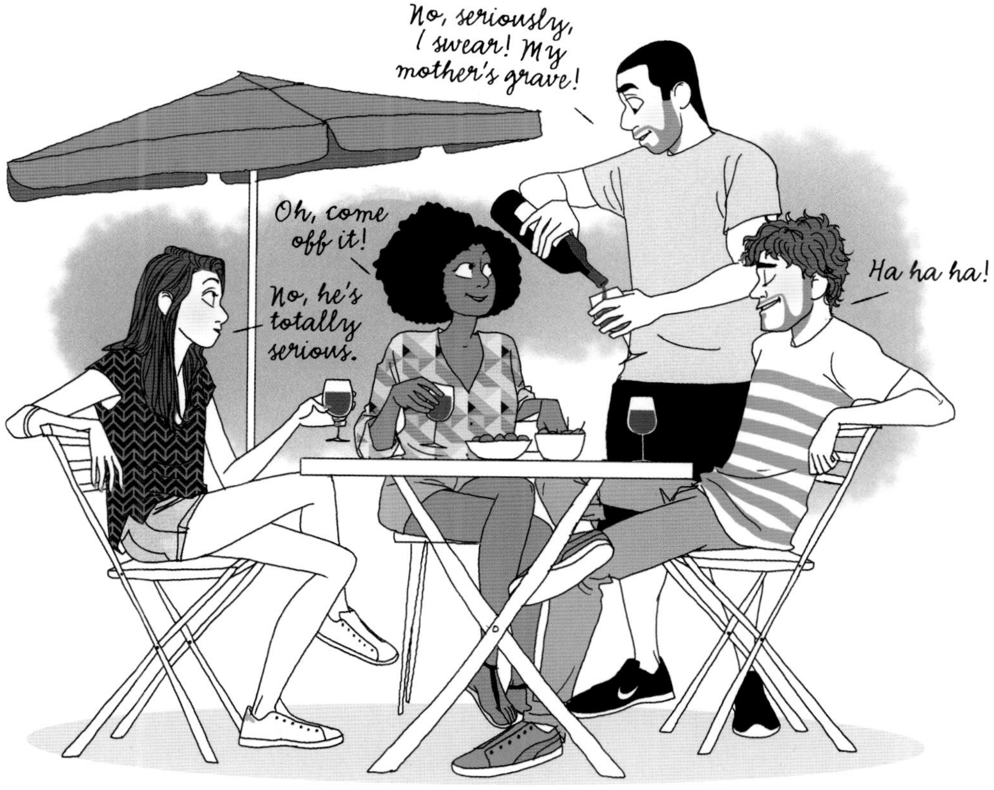
No, seriously, I swear! My mother's grave!
Oh, come off it!
No, he's totally serious.
Ha ha ha!

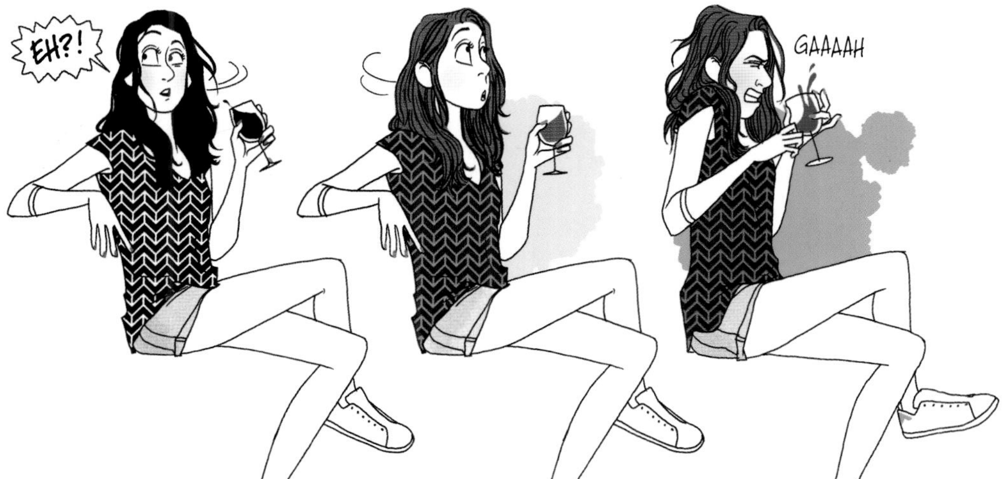
EH?!
GAAAAH

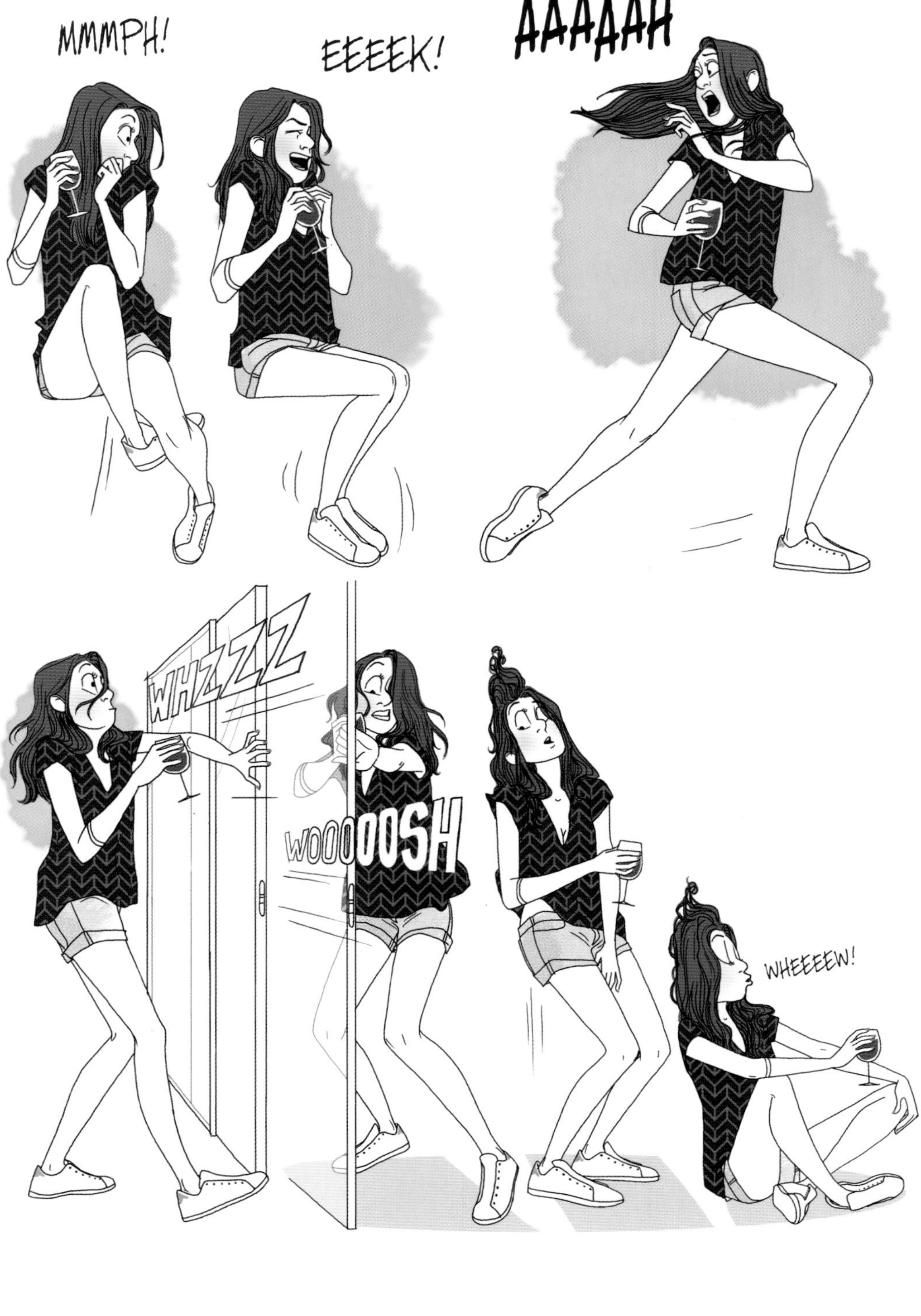
MMMPH!
EEEEK!
AAAAAH
WHZZZ
WOOOOOSH
WHEEEEW!

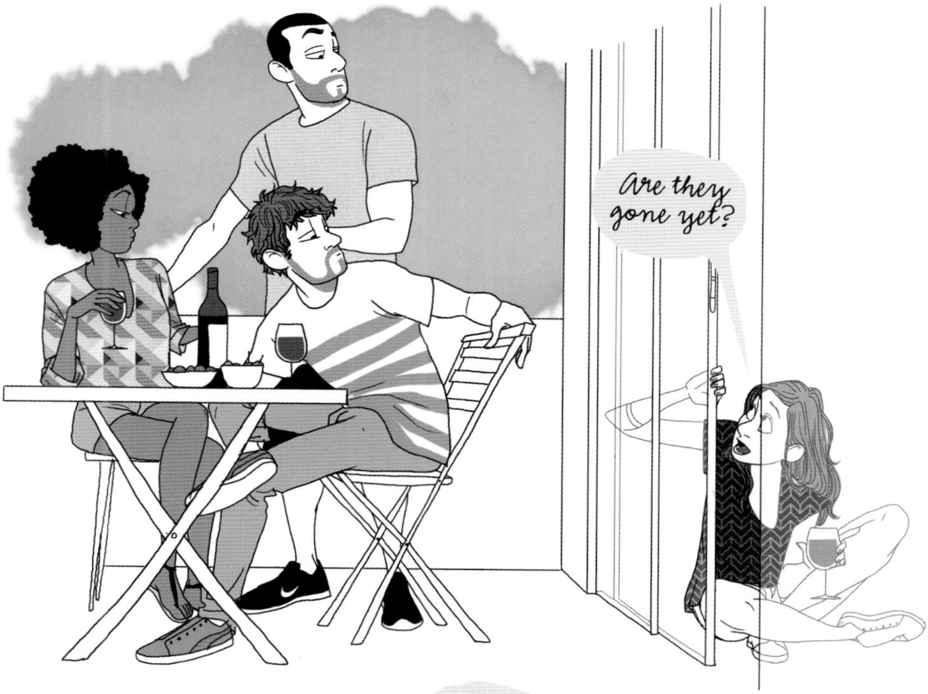
Are they gone yet?

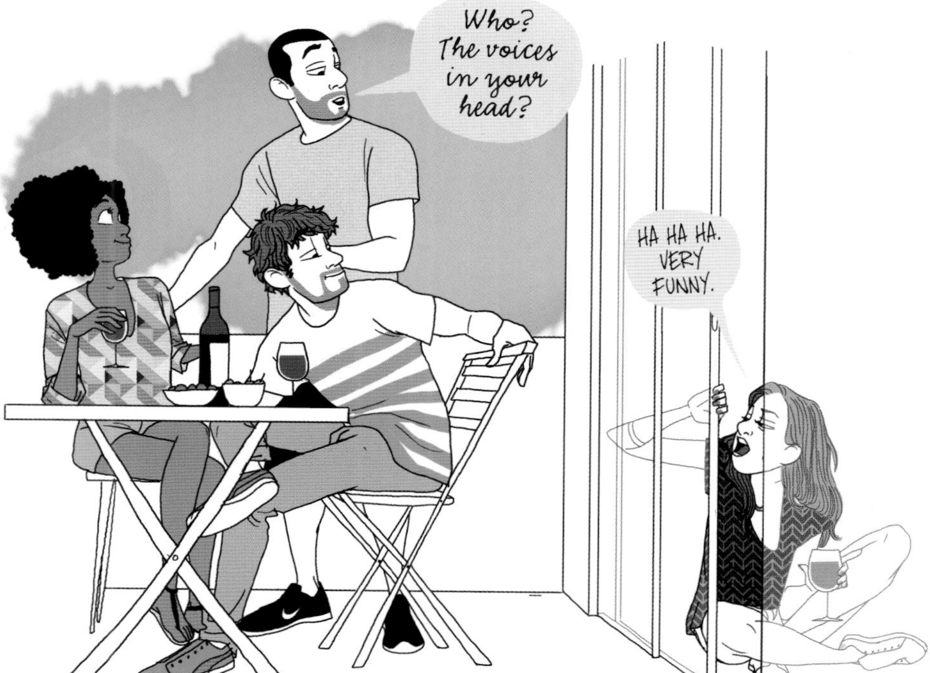
Who? The voices in your head?
HA HA HA. VERY FUNNY.

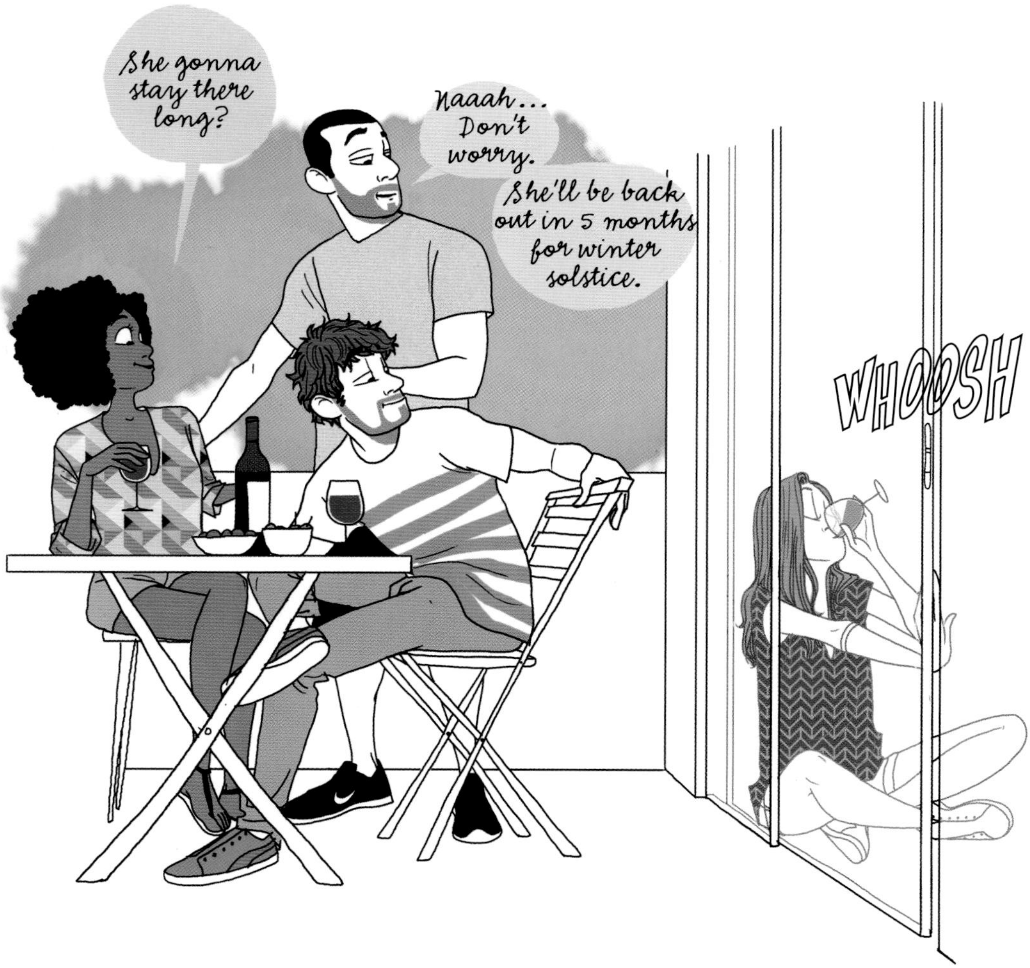
She gonna stay there long?
Naaah... Don't worry.
She'll be back out in 5 months for winter solstice.
WHOOSH

I AM AFRAID OF WASPS.

"Insane in the Brain"

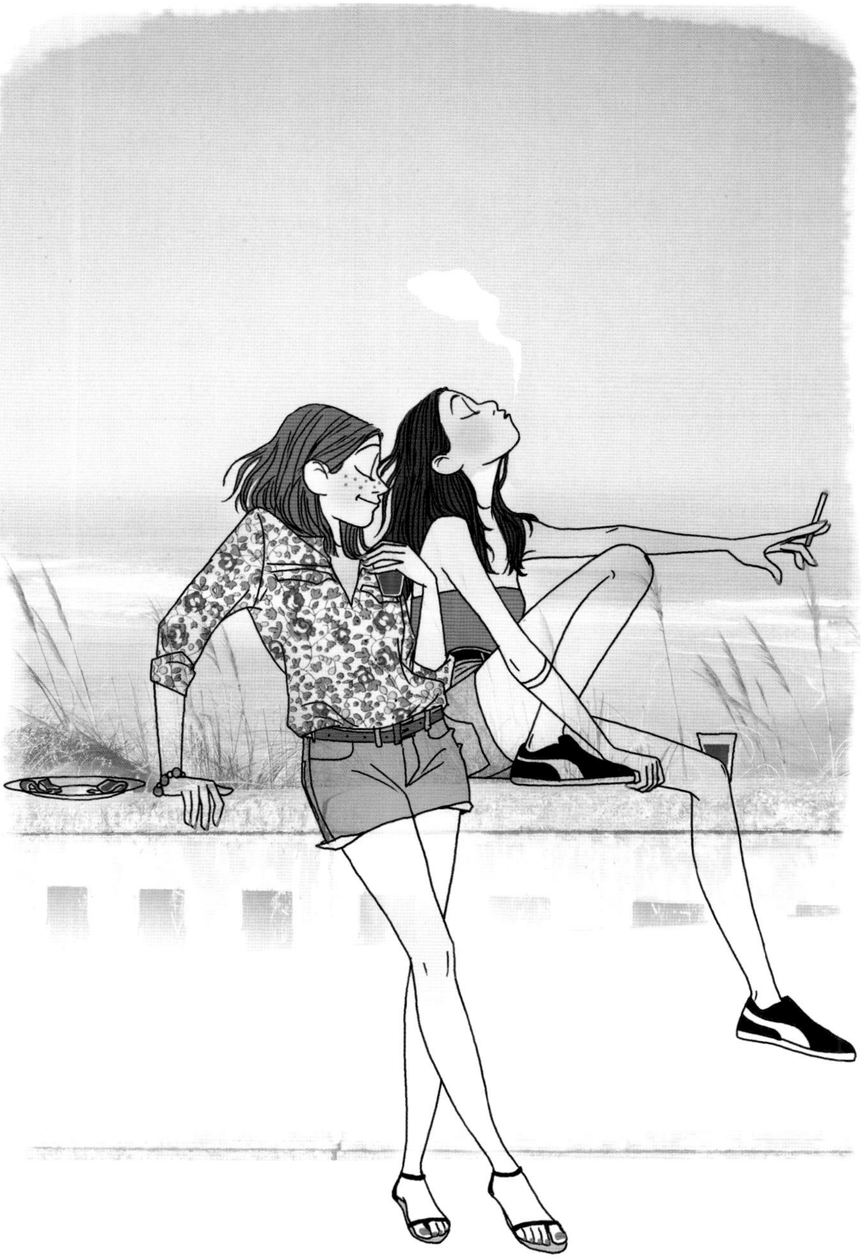

*Cypress Hill "Insane In The Brain"

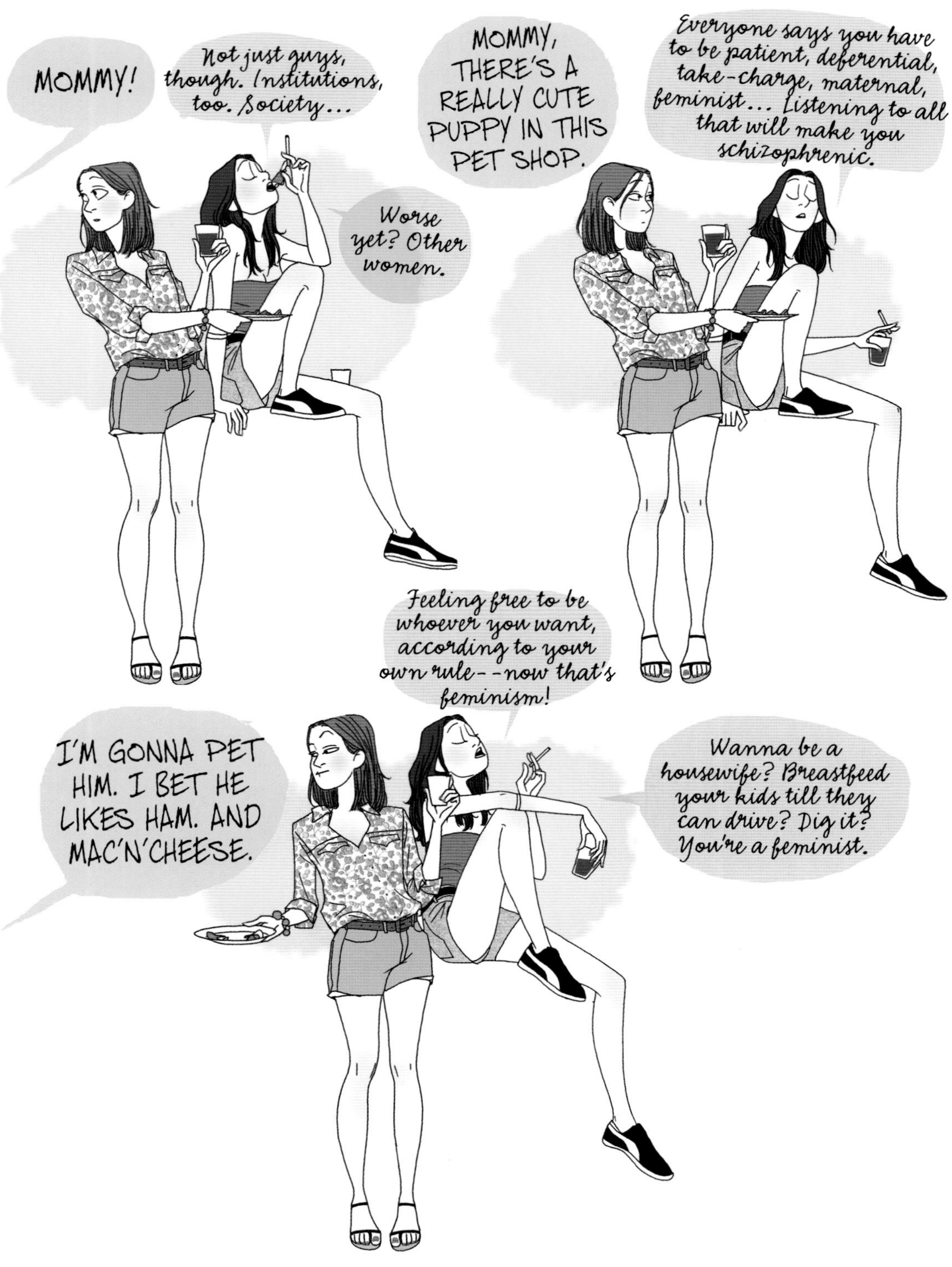
MOMMY!
Not just guys, though. Institutions, too. Society...
Worse yet? Other women.
MOMMY, THERE'S A REALLY CUTE PUPPY IN THIS PET SHOP.
Everyone says you have to be patient, deferential, take-charge, maternal, feminist... Listening to all that will make you schizophrenic.
Feeling free to be whoever you want, according to your own rule--now that's feminism!
I'M GONNA PET HIM. I BET HE LIKES HAM. AND MAC'N'CHEESE.
Wanna be a housewife? Breastfeed your kids till they can drive? Dig it? You're a feminist.

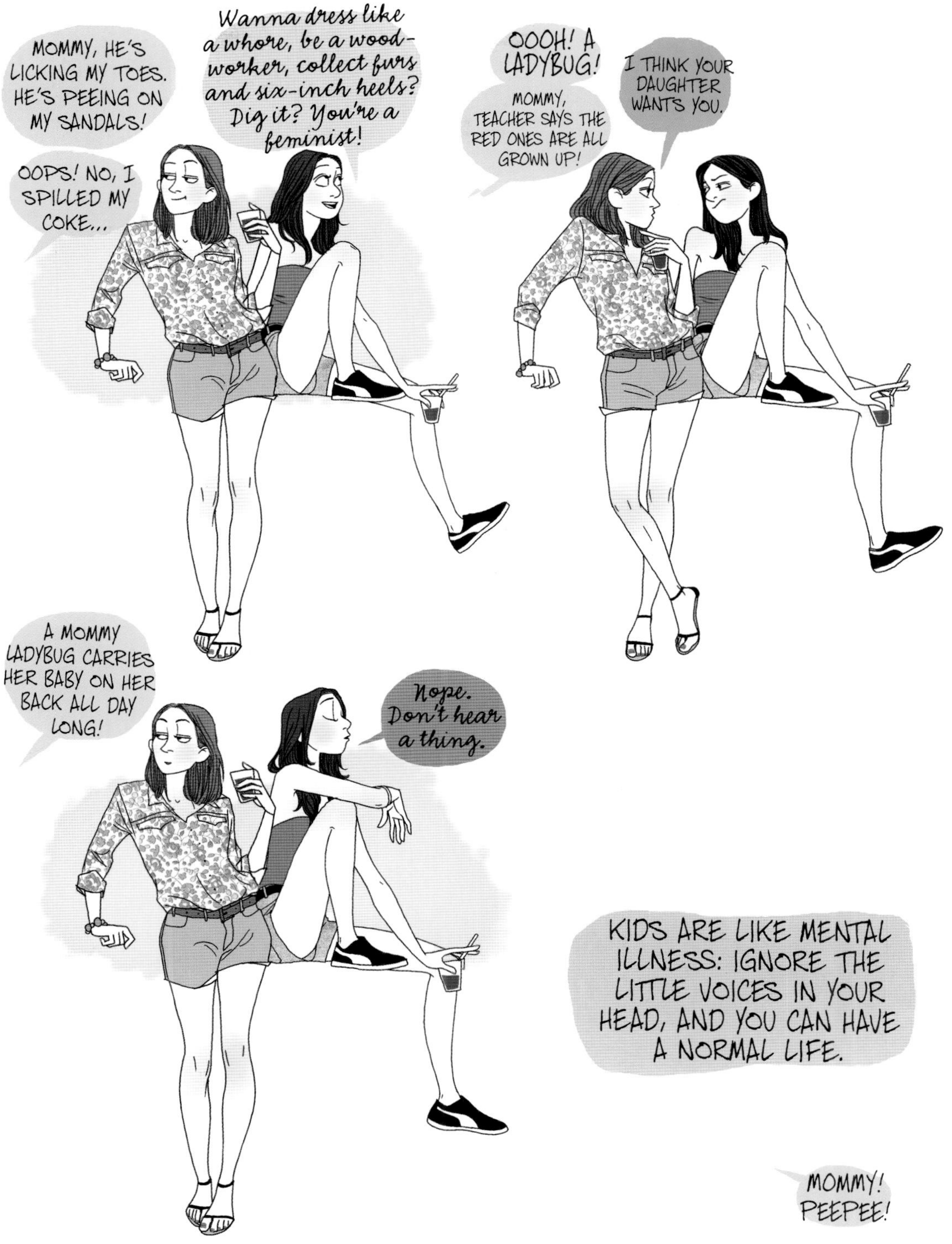
MOMMY, HE'S LICKING MY TOES. HE'S PEEING ON MY SANDALS!
OOPS! NO, I SPILLED MY COKE...
Wanna dress like a whore, be a wood-worker, collect furs and six-inch heels? Dig it? You're a feminist!
OOOH! A LADYBUG!
MOMMY, TEACHER SAYS THE RED ONES ARE ALL GROWN UP!
I THINK YOUR DAUGHTER WANTS YOU.
A MOMMY LADYBUG CARRIES HER BABY ON HER BACK ALL DAY LONG!
Nope. Don't hear a thing.
KIDS ARE LIKE MENTAL ILLNESS: IGNORE THE LITTLE VOICES IN YOUR HEAD, AND YOU CAN HAVE A NORMAL LIFE.
MOMMY! PEEPEE!

Home

There rise the thousand walls
Of our houses, aging well,
And mothers from a thousand houses
There, waves of tiles slumber
Renewed by the sun
Buoying bird shadows
As the waters buoy the fish…
There I soar off into space
There I return to the entire world
I speak of a time freed
From reason's gravediggers
I speak of freedom

Paul Éluard, *"Elsewhere Here Everywhere"*
from *Uninterrupted Poetry*

What the—?! Was that some kind of regional dialect?

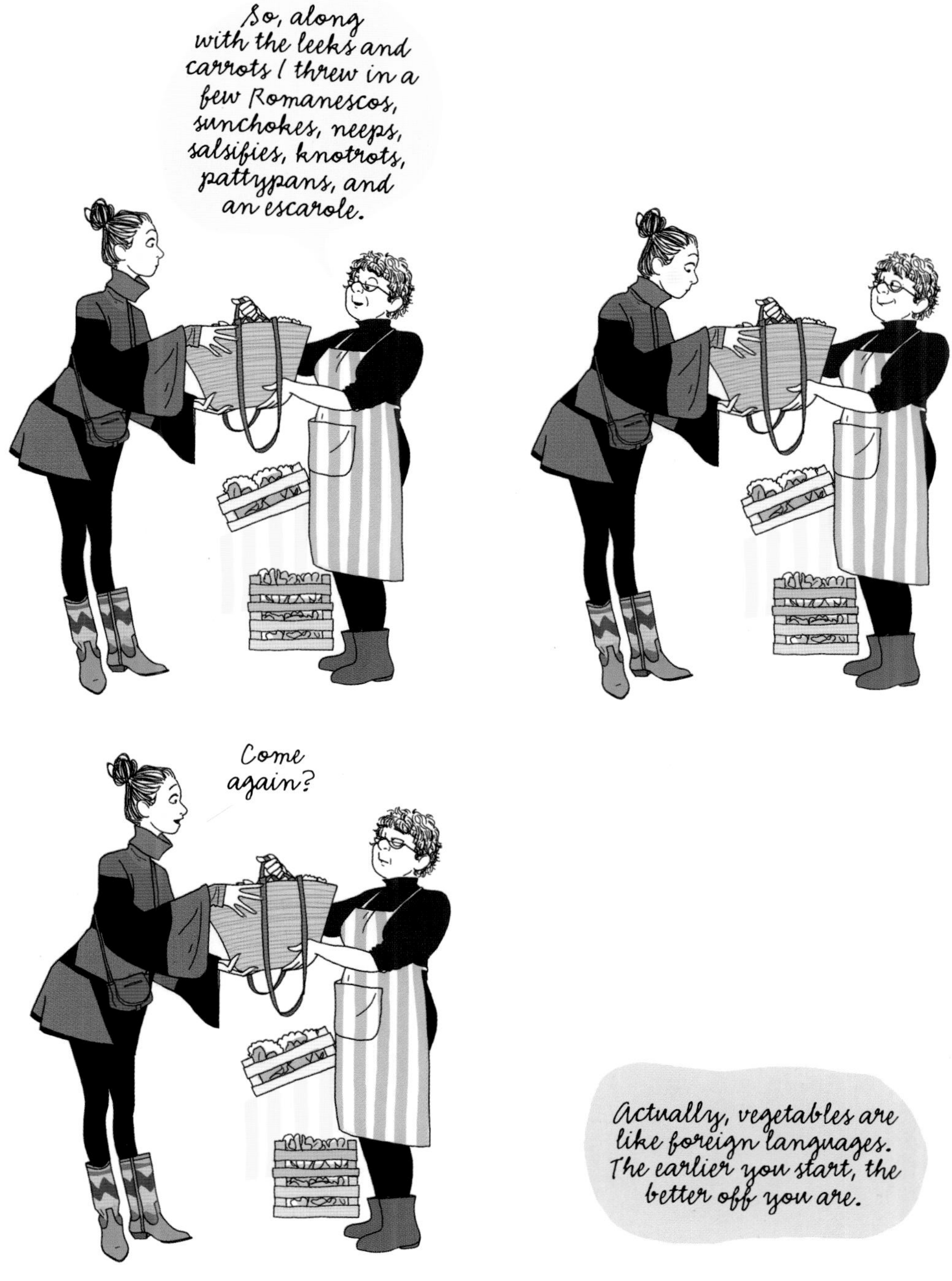
So, along with the leeks and carrots I threw in a few Romanescos, sunchokes, neeps, salsifies, knotrots, pattypans, and an escarole.
Come again?
Actually, vegetables are like foreign languages. The earlier you start, the better off you are.

Desperate Housewife

I LIKE TO THINK OF MYSELF AS DESPERATE HOUSEWIVES' GABRIELLE SOLIS.

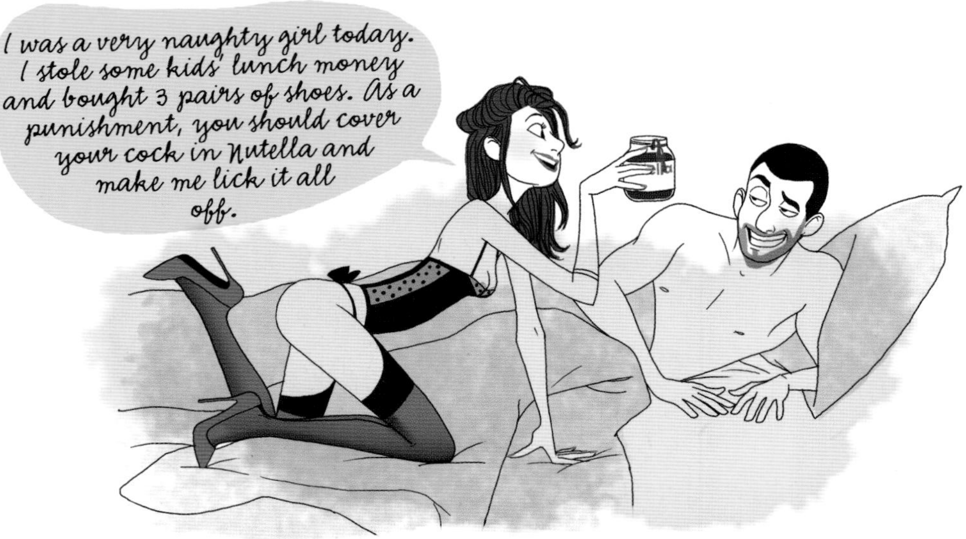
I was a very naughty girl today. I stole some kids' lunch money and bought 3 pairs of shoes. As a punishment, you should cover your cock in Nutella and make me lick it all off.

BUT LET'S FACE FACTS:

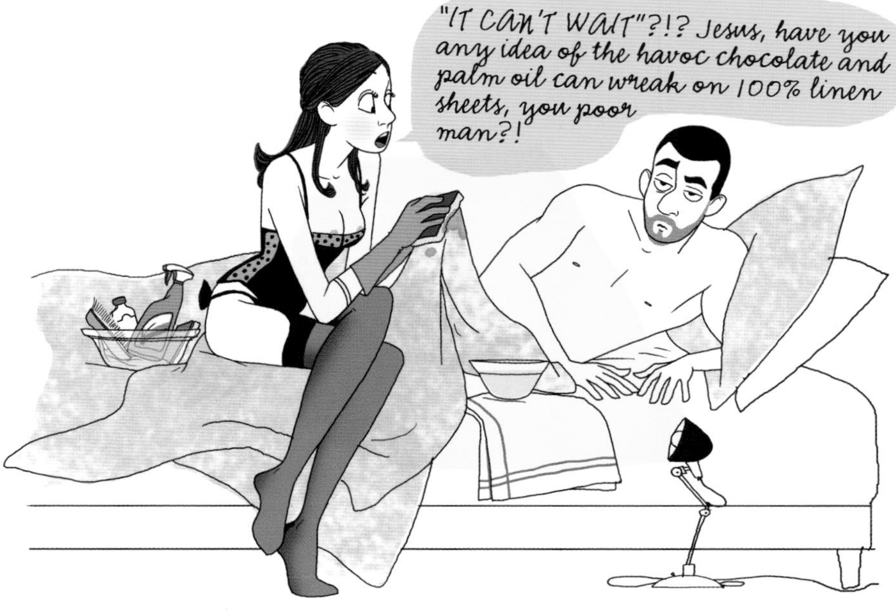
"IT CAN'T WAIT"?!? Jesus, have you any idea of the havoc chocolate and palm oil can wreak on 100% linen sheets, you poor man?!

I'M BREE VAN DE KAMP.

Guilty Pleasures

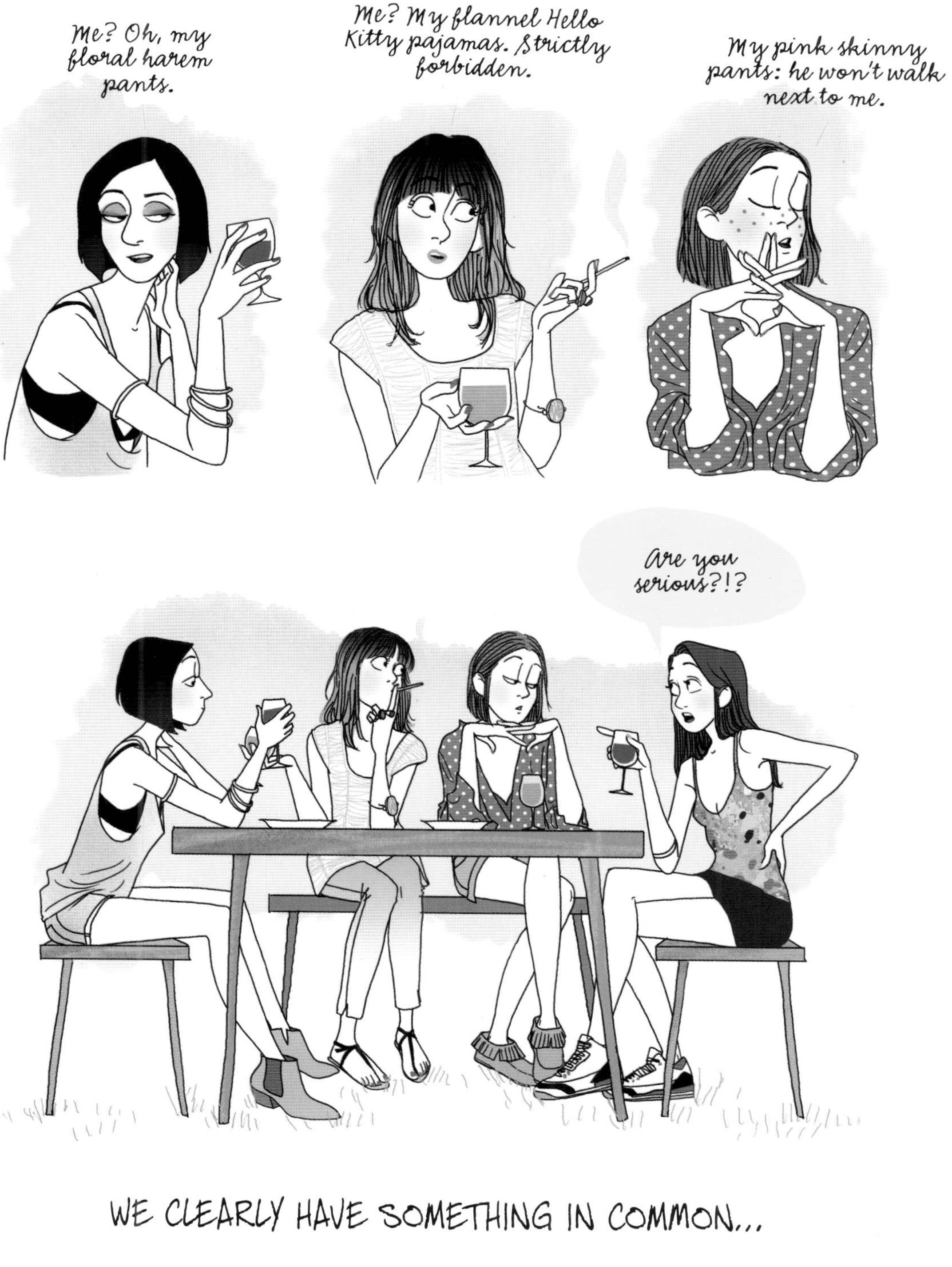
Me? Oh, my floral harem pants.
Me? My flannel Hello Kitty pajamas. Strictly forbidden.
My pink skinny pants: he won't walk next to me.
Are you serious?!?
WE CLEARLY HAVE SOMETHING IN COMMON...

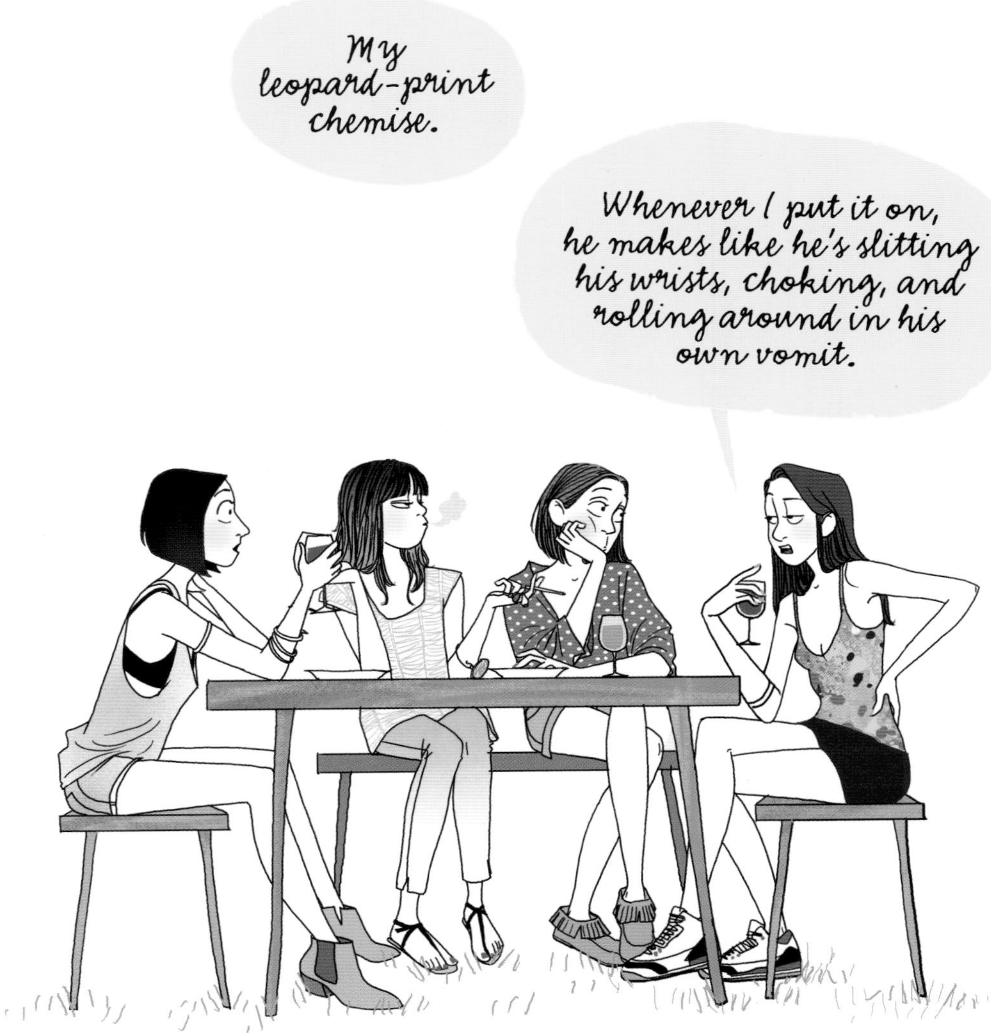
My leopard-print chemise.
Whenever I put it on, he makes like he's slitting his wrists, choking, and rolling around in his own vomit.

...WE ALL HAVE BOYFRIENDS.

The Secret

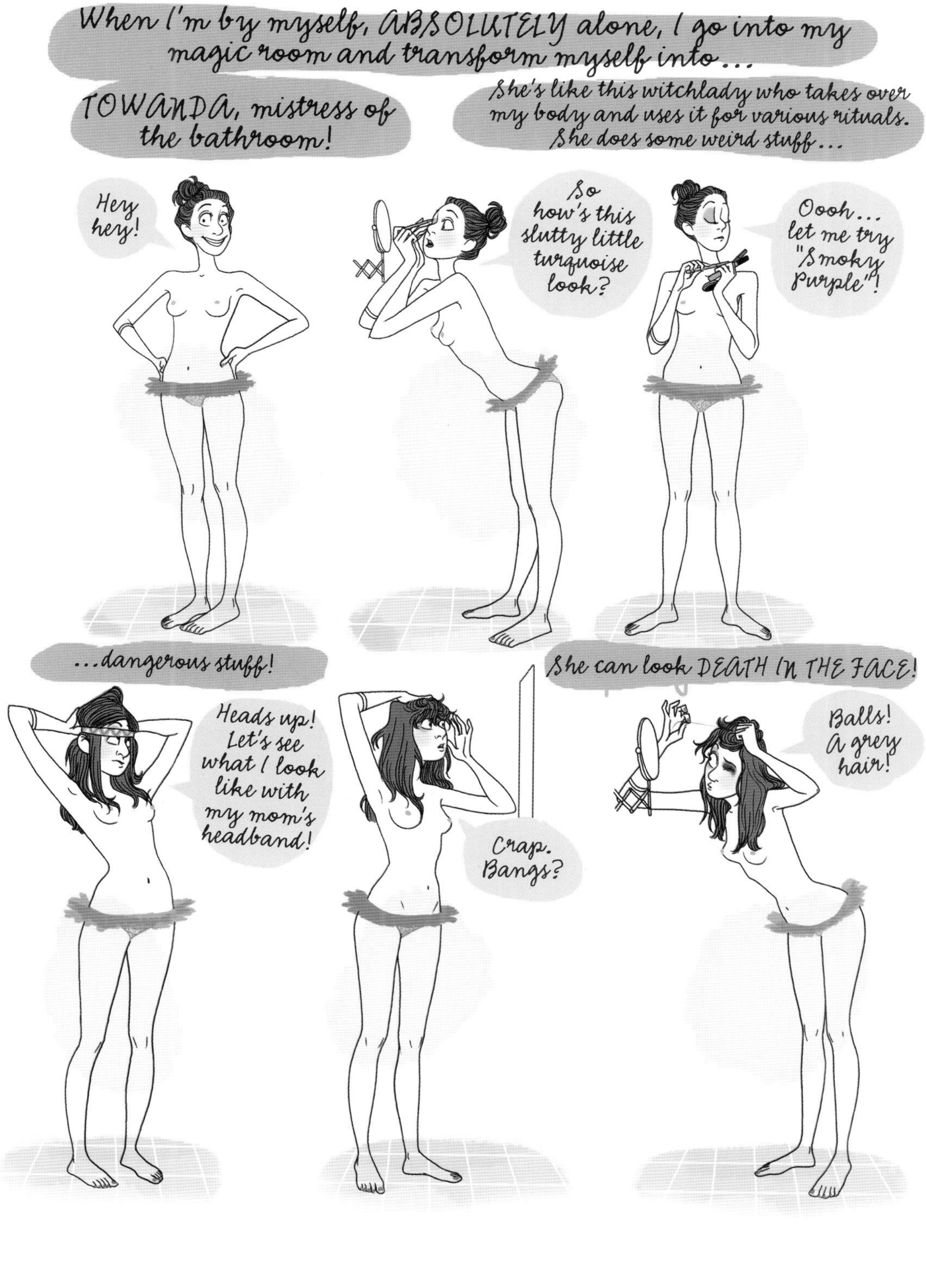
When I'm by myself, ABSOLUTELY alone, I go into my magic room and transform myself into...
TOWANDA, mistress of the bathroom!
She's like this witchlady who takes over my body and uses it for various rituals. She does some weird stuff...
Hey hey!
So how's this slutty little turquoise look?
Oooh... let me try "Smoky Purple"!
...dangerous stuff!
Heads up! Let's see what I look like with my mom's headband!
Crap. Bangs?
She can look DEATH IN THE FACE!
Balls! A grey hair!

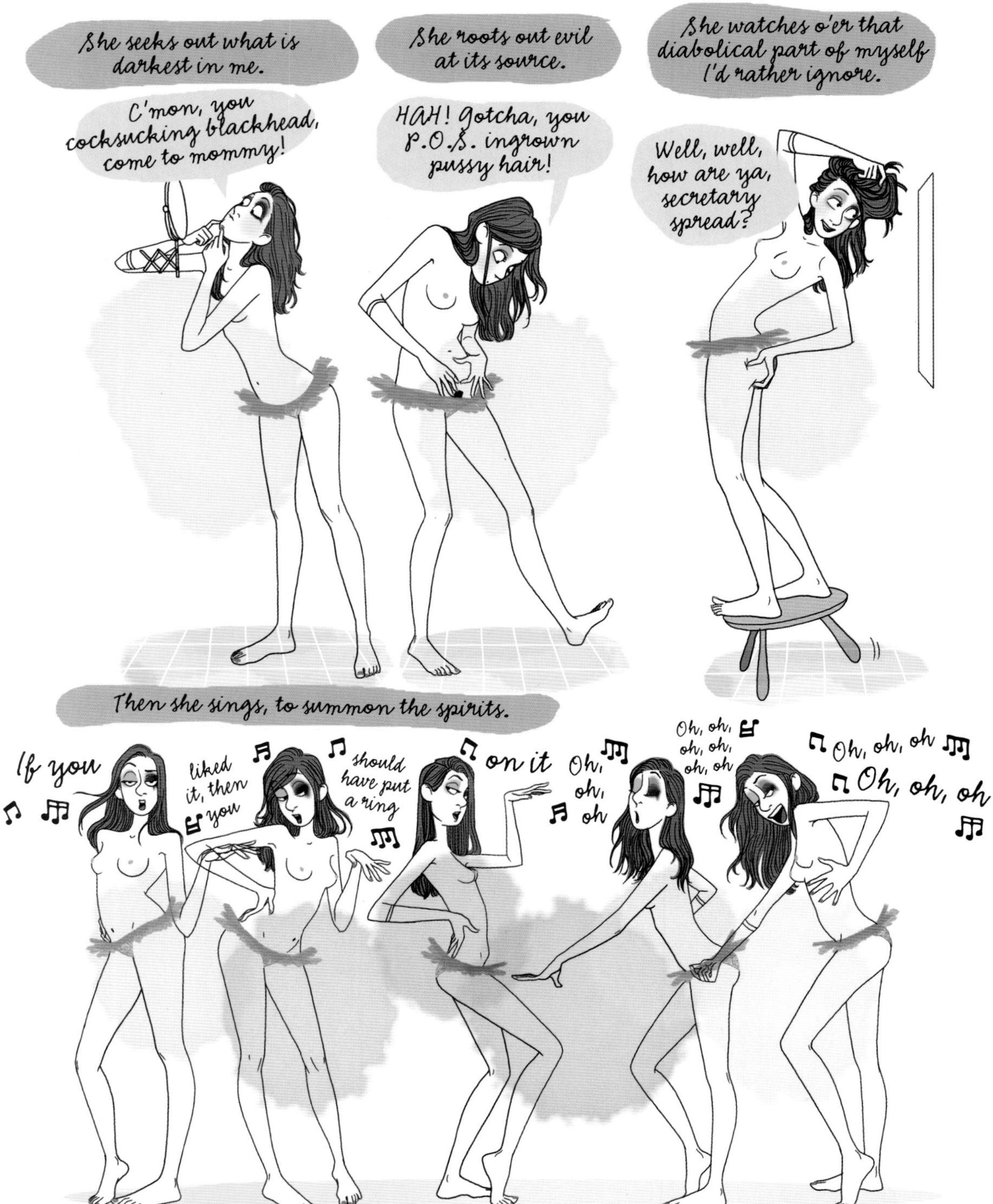

She seeks out what is darkest in me.
C'mon, you cocksucking blackhead, come to mommy!
She roots out evil at its source.
HAH! Gotcha, you P.O.S. ingrown pussy hair!
She watches o'er that diabolical part of myself I'd rather ignore.
Well, well, how are ya, secretary spread?
Then she sings, to summon the spirits.
If you
liked it, then you
should have put a ring
on it
Oh, oh, oh
Oh, oh, oh, oh, oh, oh
Oh, oh, oh
Oh, oh, oh

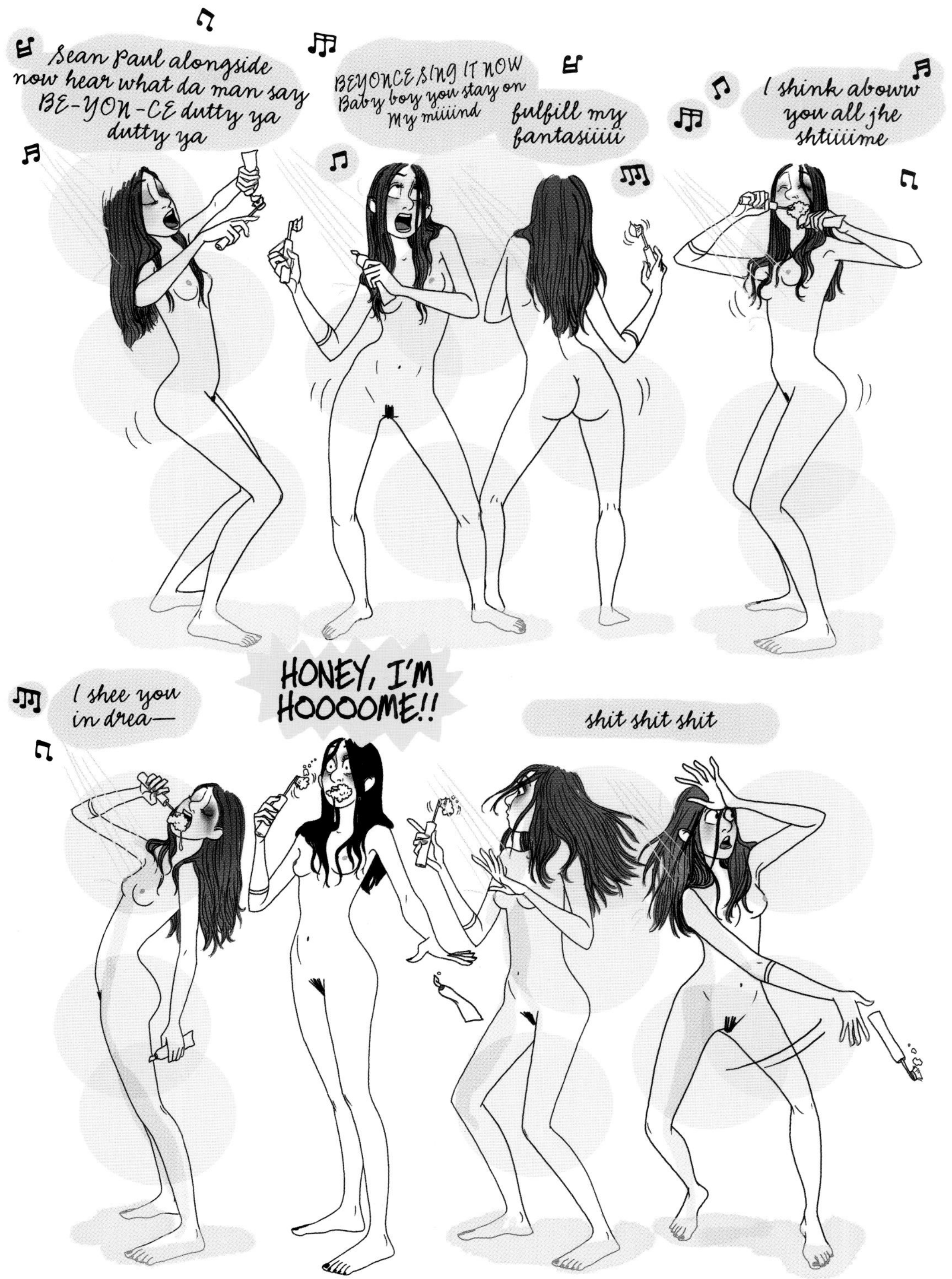

Sean Paul alongside now hear what da man say BE-YON-CE dutty ya dutty ya
BEYONCE SING IT NOW Baby boy you stay on My miiiind
fulfill my fantasiiiii
I shink aboww you all jhe shtiiiime
I shee you in drea—
HONEY, I'M HOOOOME!!
shit shit shit

*Beyonce "Baby Boy (Junior's World Mixshow)

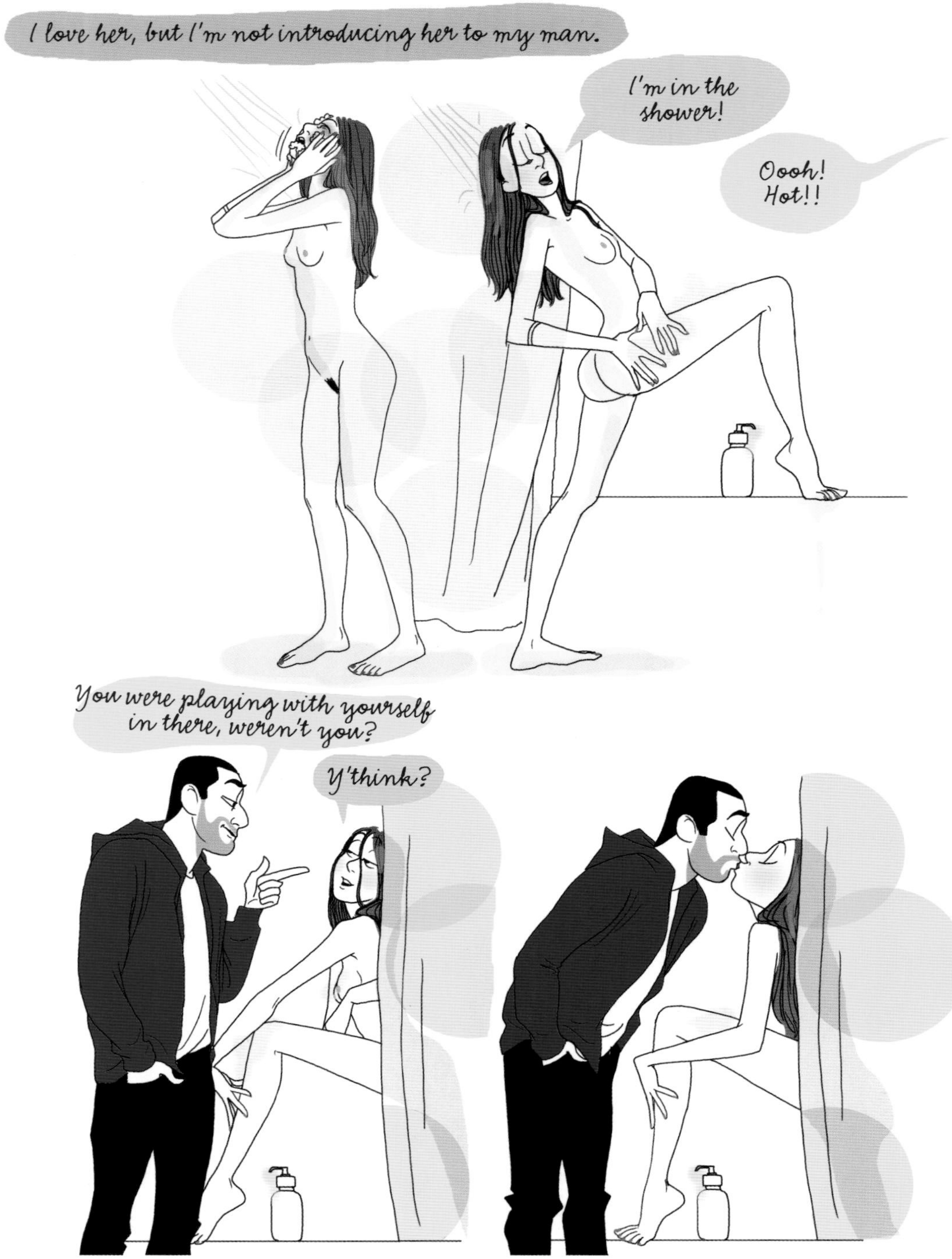
I love her, but I'm not introducing her to my man.
I'm in the shower!
Oooh! Hot!!
You were playing with yourself in there, weren't you?
Y'think?

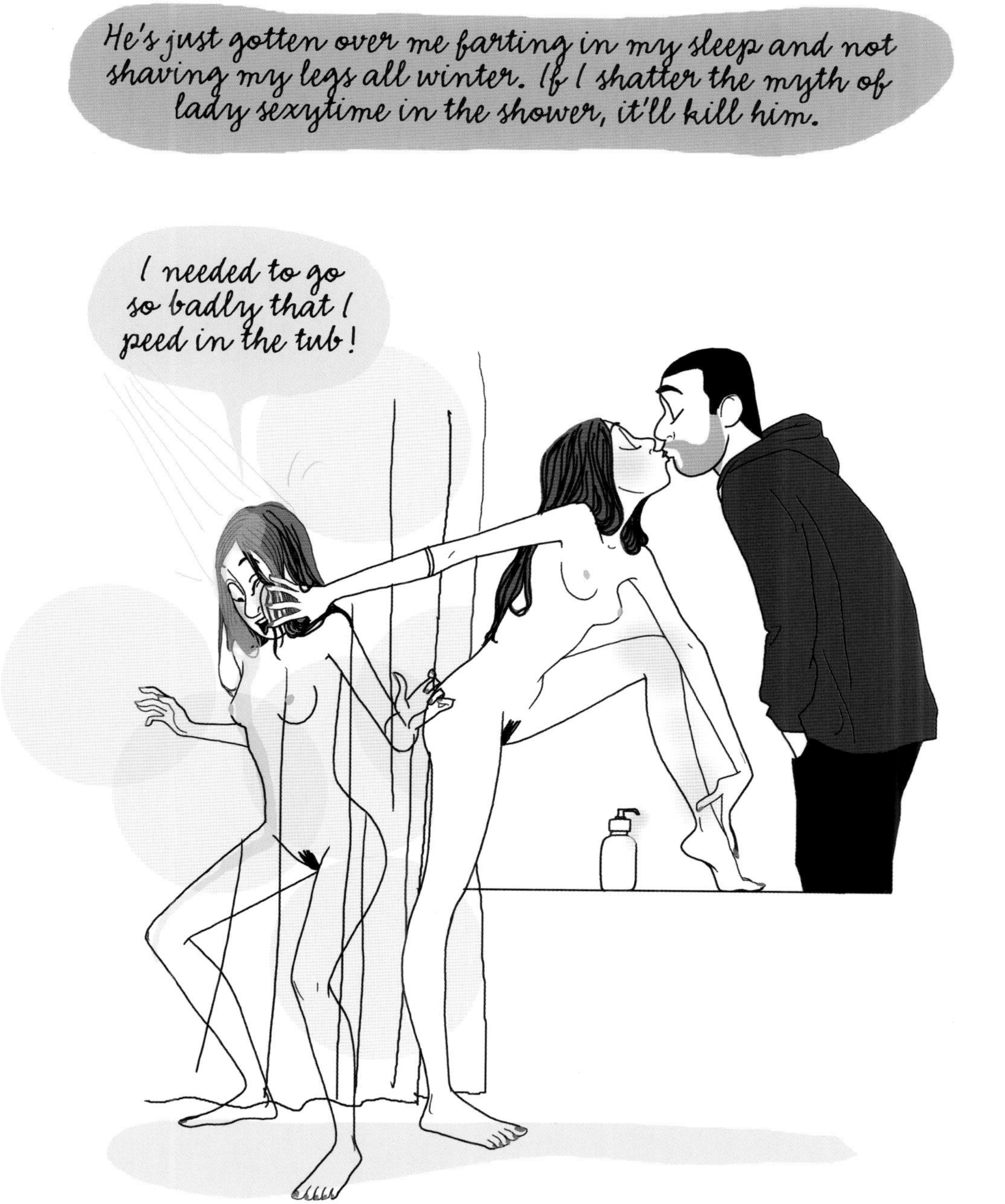
He's just gotten over me farting in my sleep and not shaving my legs all winter. If I shatter the myth of lady sexytime in the shower, it'll kill him.
I needed to go so badly that I peed in the tub!

Holy shit this language barrier business is for realz

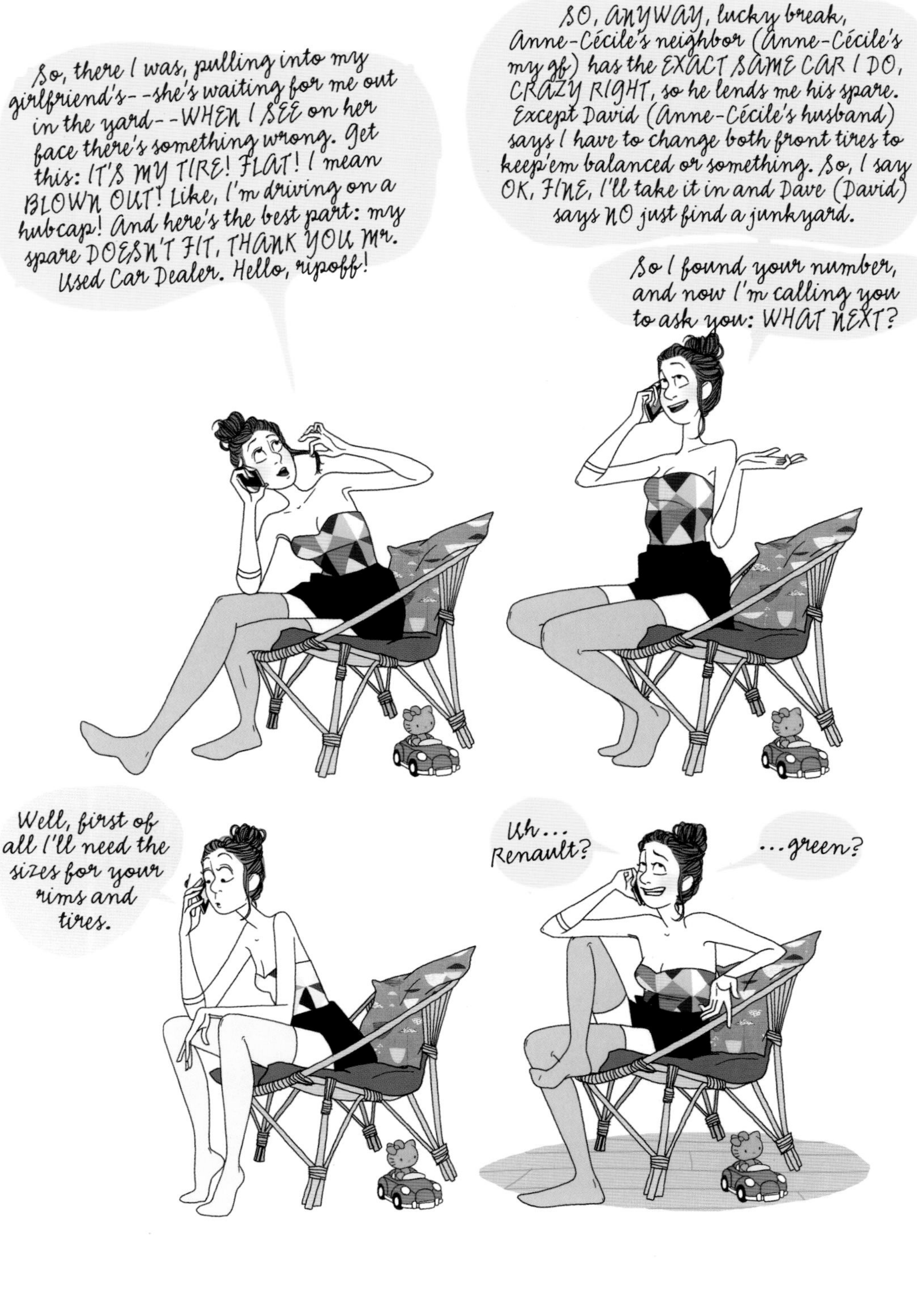
So, there I was, pulling into my girlfriend's--she's waiting for me out in the yard--WHEN I SEE on her face there's something wrong. Get this: IT'S MY TIRE! FLAT! I mean BLOWN OUT! Like, I'm driving on a hubcap! And here's the best part: my spare DOESN'T FIT, THANK YOU Mr. Used Car Dealer. Hello, ripoff!
SO, ANYWAY, lucky break, Anne-Cécile's neighbor (Anne-Cécile's my gf) has the EXACT SAME CAR I DO, CRAZY RIGHT, so he lends me his spare. Except David (Anne-Cécile's husband) says I have to change both front tires to keep'em balanced or something. So, I say OK, FINE, I'll take it in and Dave (David) says NO just find a junkyard.
So I found your number, and now I'm calling you to ask you: WHAT NEXT?
Well, first of all I'll need the sizes for your rims and tires.
Uh... Renault?
...green?

Fear first graders… for they can math.

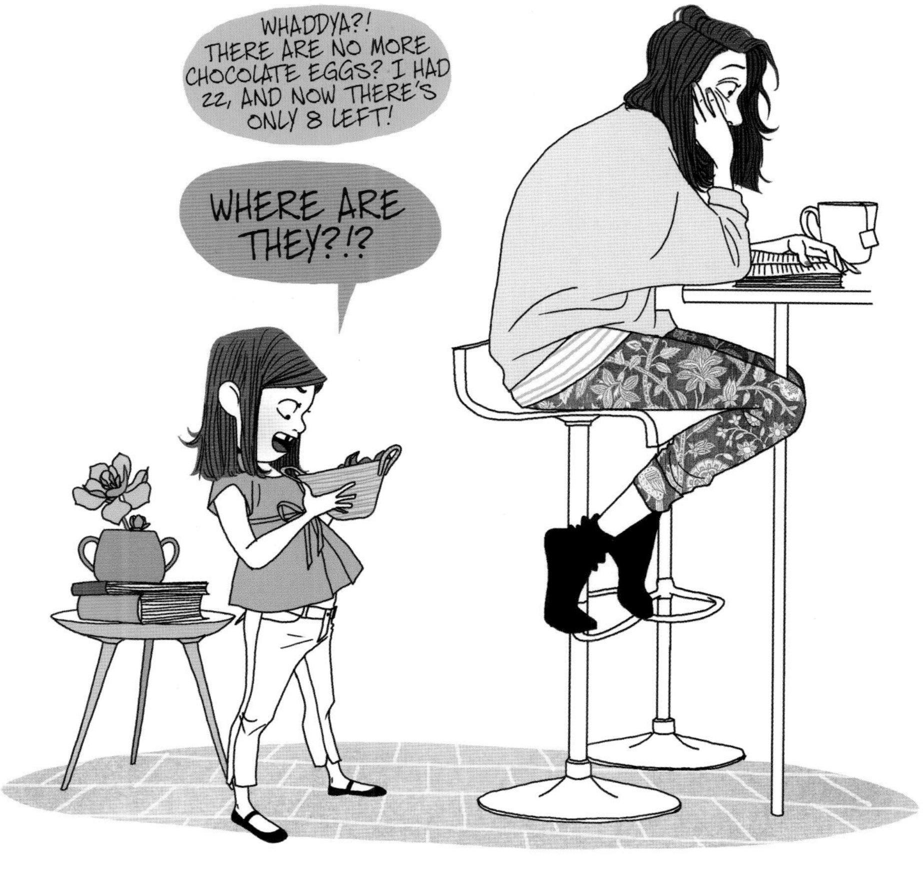
WHADDYA?! THERE ARE NO MORE CHOCOLATE EGGS? I HAD 22, AND NOW THERE'S ONLY 8 LEFT!
WHERE ARE THEY?!?

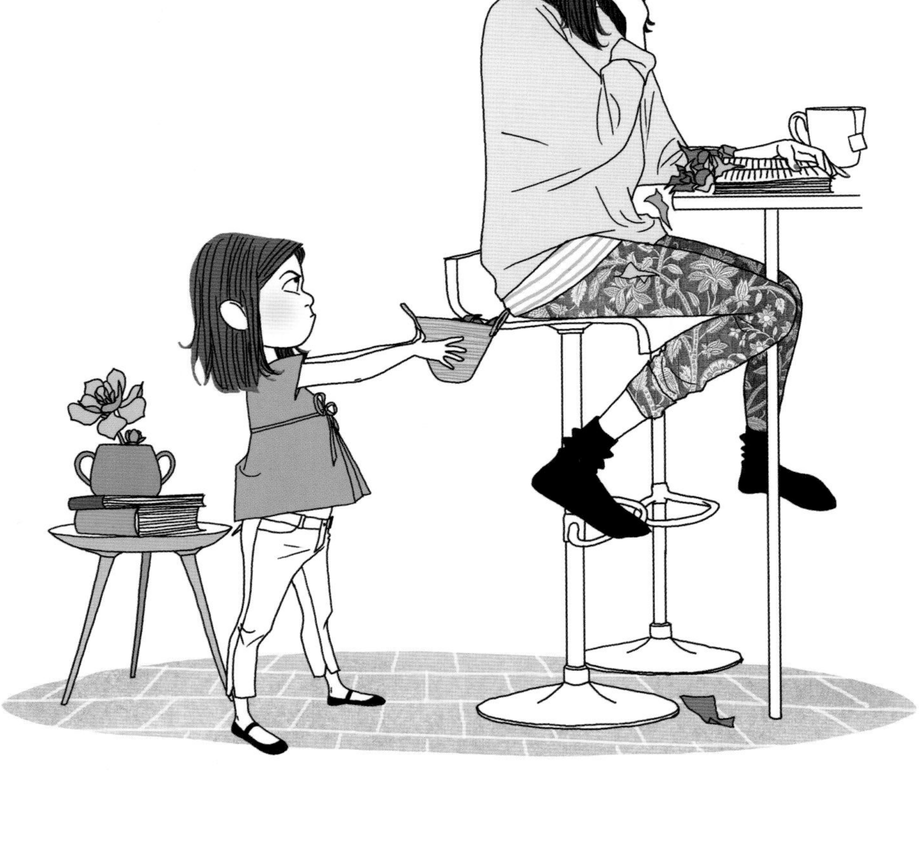
How mythteriouth...

Freedom

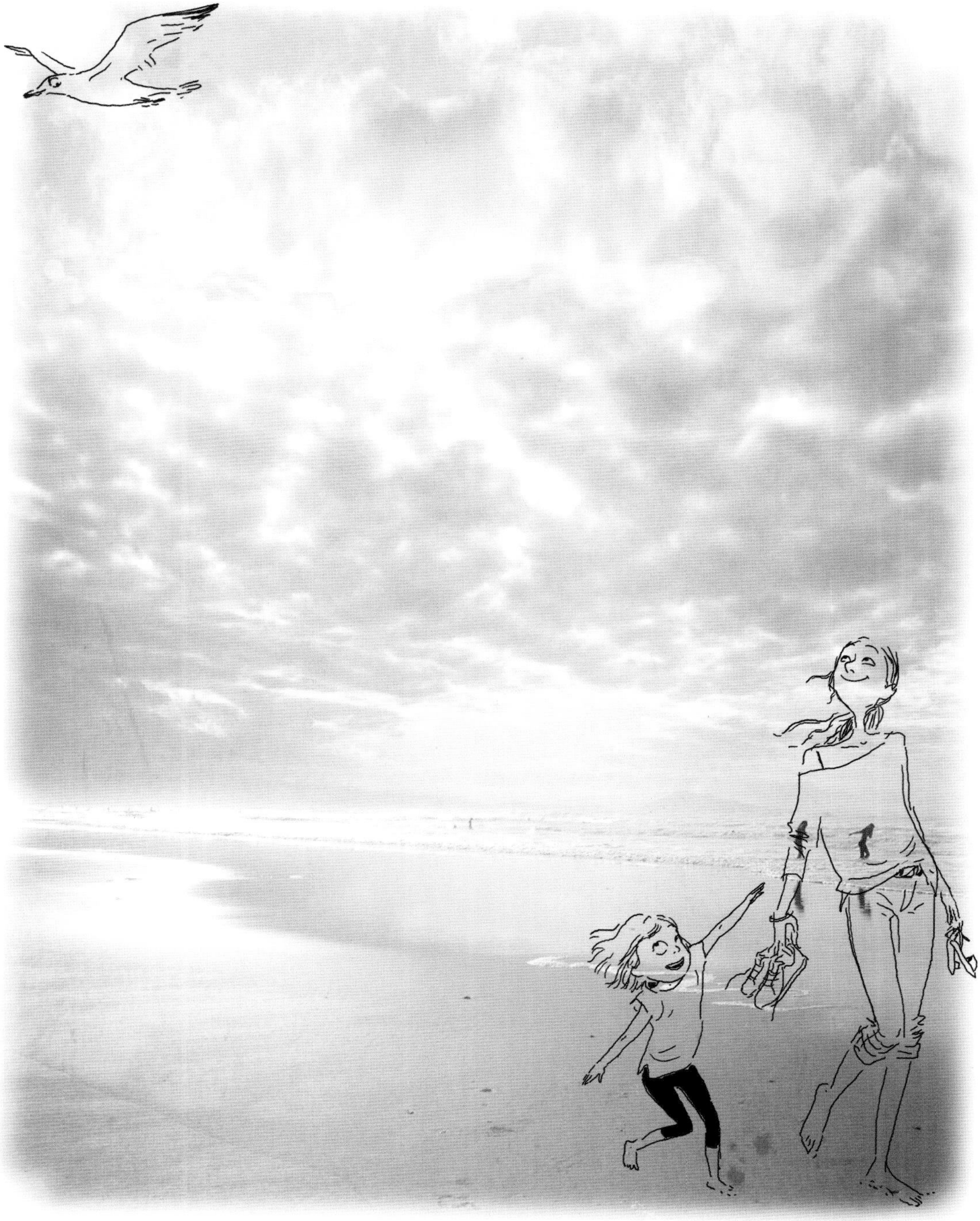

LOL

This is the story of a chick who had to go on maternity leave because she couldn't find childcare for her son, who wasn't high up on the childcare waiting list because she had no job and was on maternity leave because she couldn't find childcare for her son... LOL

Here, listen to this:

"Women's jobs support rising birth rates."

blabla blab la oh here

"Economists today attribute this increase in birth rates to women in the workforce and the quality services that allow them to maintain professional lives while having children."

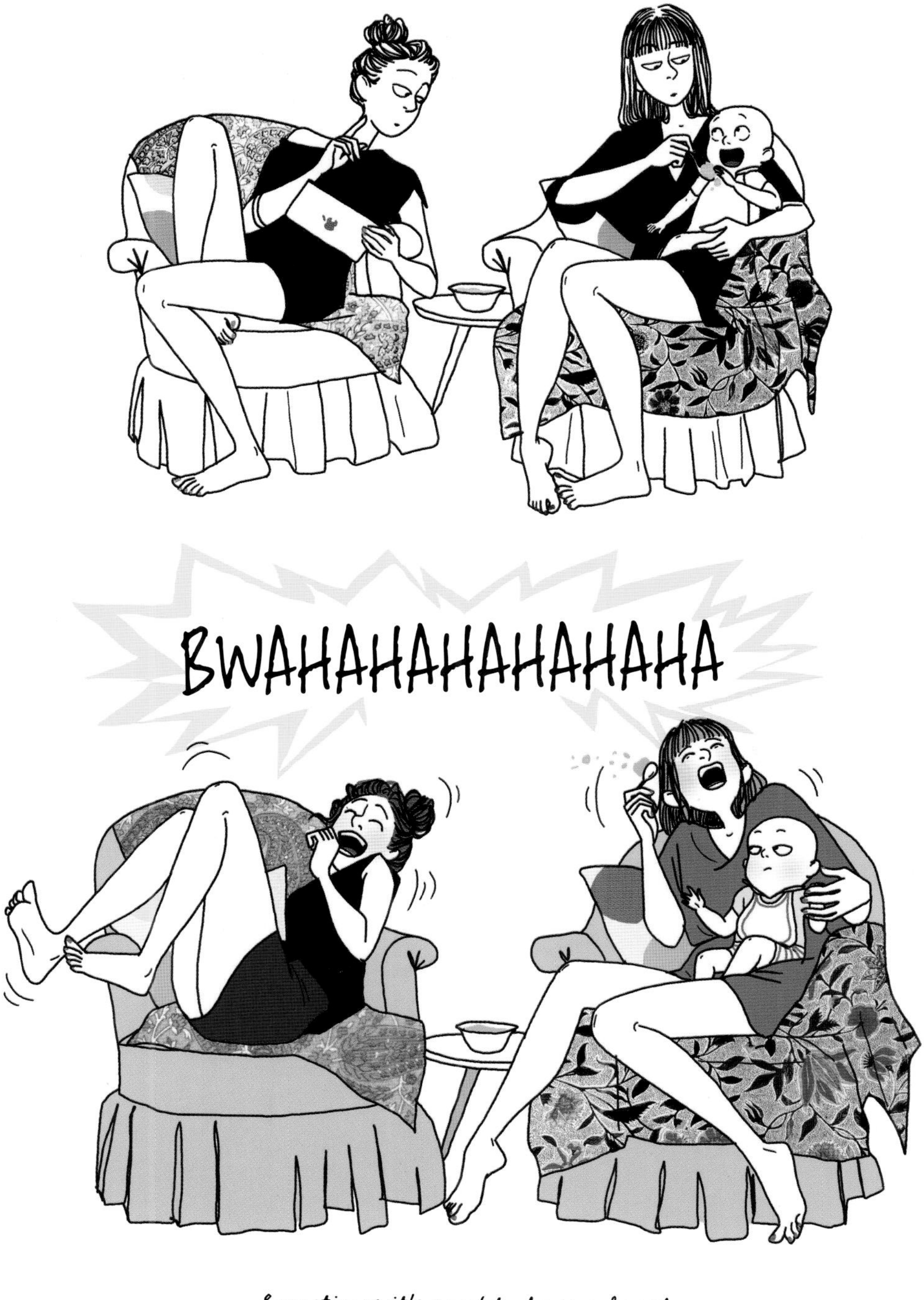
BWAHAHAHAHAHAHA

Sometimes it's good to have a laugh.

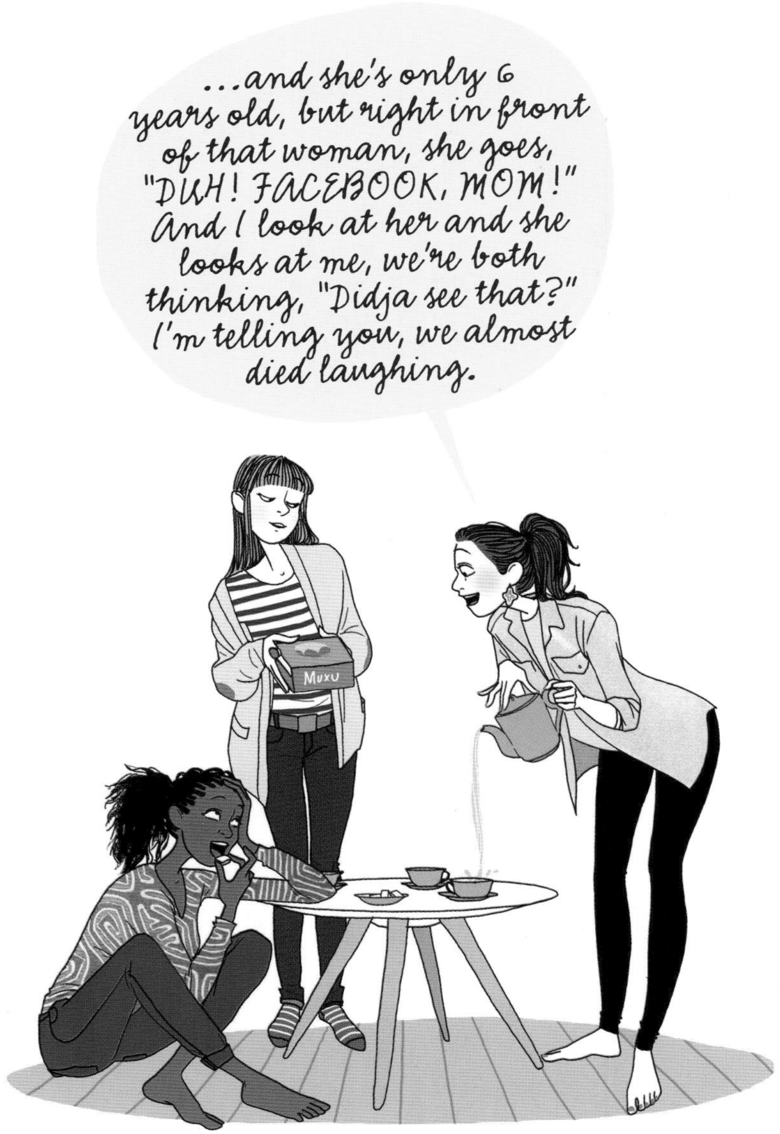
...and she's only 6 years old, but right in front of that woman, she goes, "DUH! FACEBOOK, MOM!" And I look at her and she looks at me, we're both thinking, "Didja see that?" I'm telling you, we almost died laughing.
MUXU

KIDS...

...WHEN THEY'RE NOT YOURS...

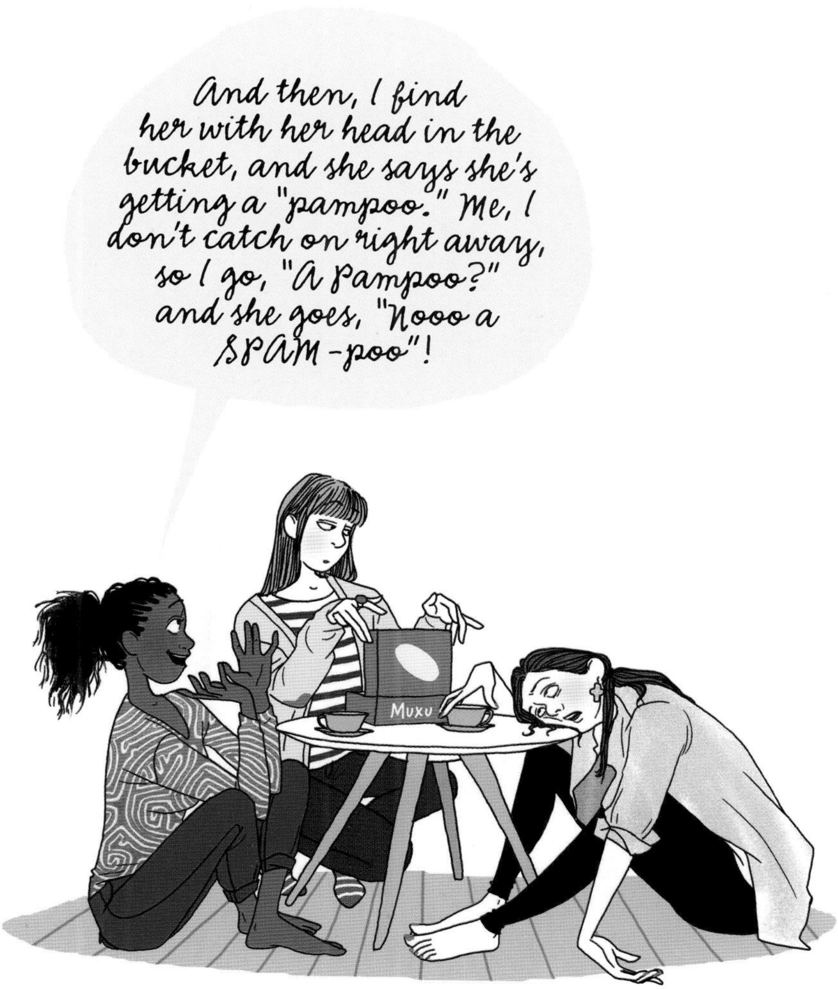
And then, I find her with her head in the bucket, and she says she's getting a "pampoo." Me, I don't catch on right away, so I go, "A pampoo?" and she goes, "Nooo a SPAM-poo"!
MUXU

...YOU DON'T EVEN HAVE A FUCK TO GIVE.

The Waiting Room

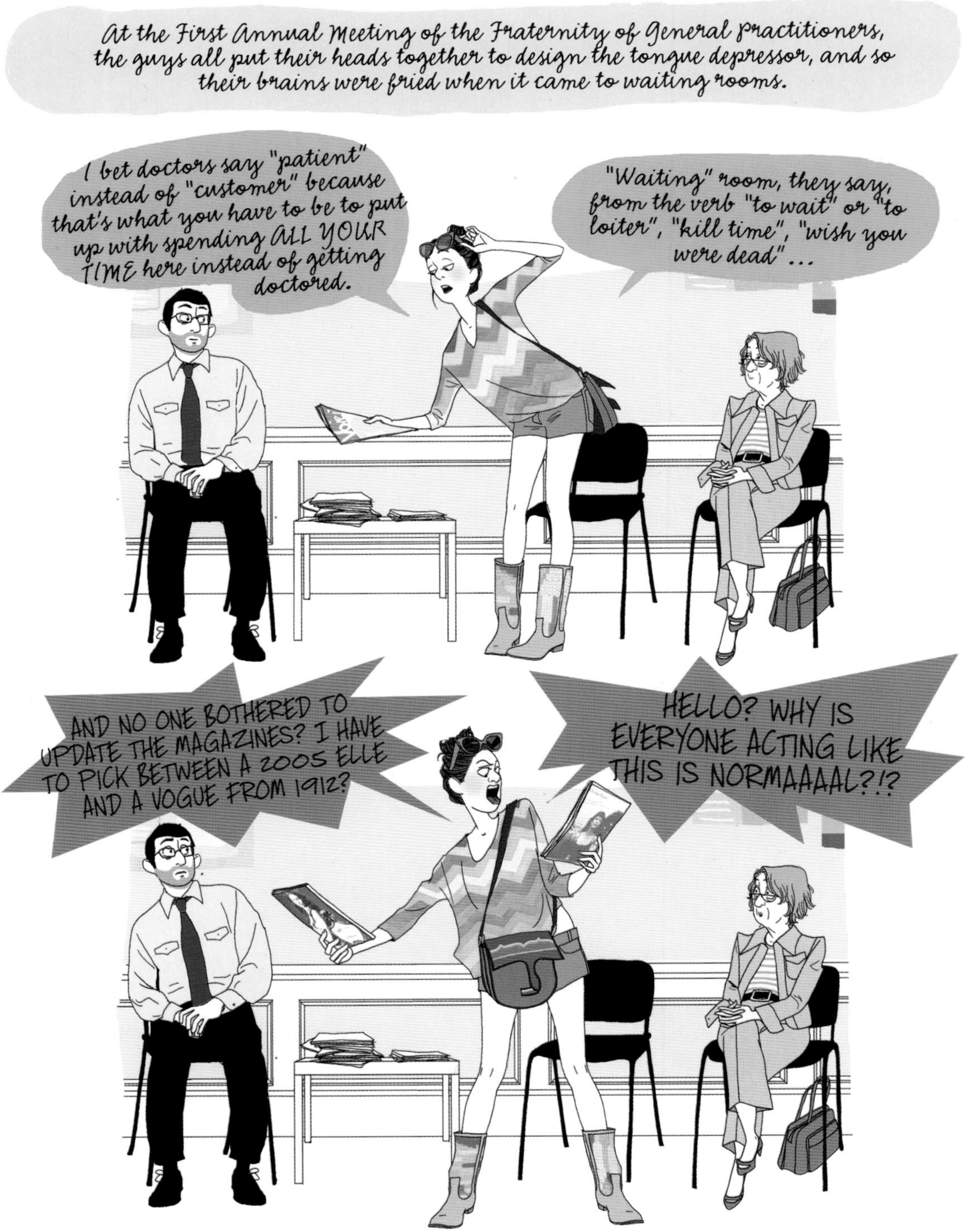
At the First Annual Meeting of the Fraternity of General practitioners, the guys all put their heads together to design the tongue depressor, and so their brains were fried when it came to waiting rooms.
I bet doctors say "patient" instead of "customer" because that's what you have to be to put up with spending ALL YOUR TIME here instead of getting doctored.
"Waiting" room, they say, from the verb "to wait" or "to loiter", "kill time", "wish you were dead"...
AND NO ONE BOTHERED TO UPDATE THE MAGAZINES? I HAVE TO PICK BETWEEN A 2005 ELLE AND A VOGUE FROM 1912?
HELLO? WHY IS EVERYONE ACTING LIKE THIS IS NORMAAAAL?!?

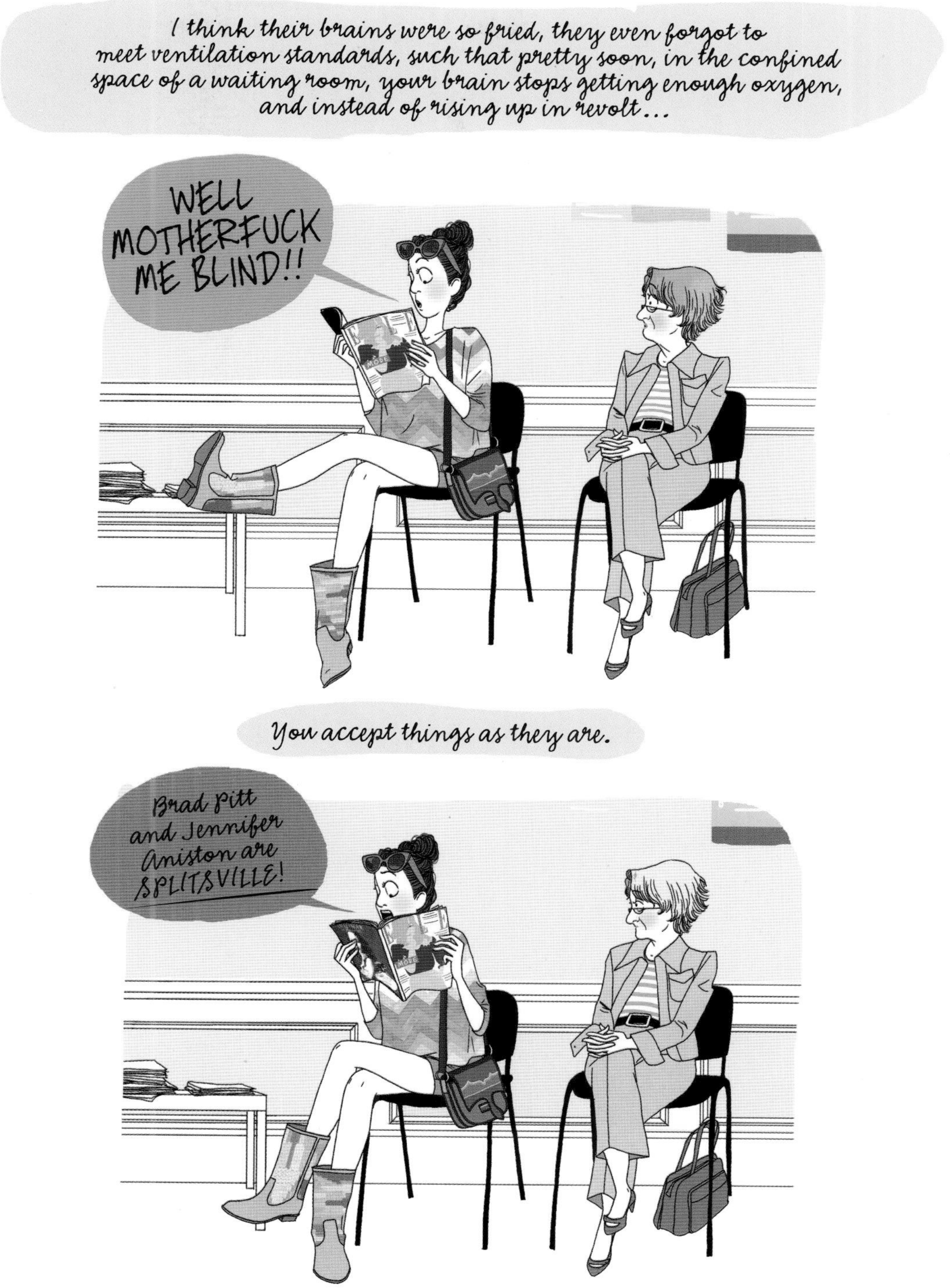
I think their brains were so fried, they even forgot to meet ventilation standards, such that pretty soon, in the confined space of a waiting room, your brain stops getting enough oxygen, and instead of rising up in revolt...
WELL MOTHERFUCK ME BLIND!!
You accept things as they are.
Brad Pitt and Jennifer Aniston are SPLITSVILLE!

Crying Freeman

As a little girl, I devised an unbeatable defense system against pain. A sort of ninja technique, fearsomely effective at anticipating attacks and paralyzing the enemy...

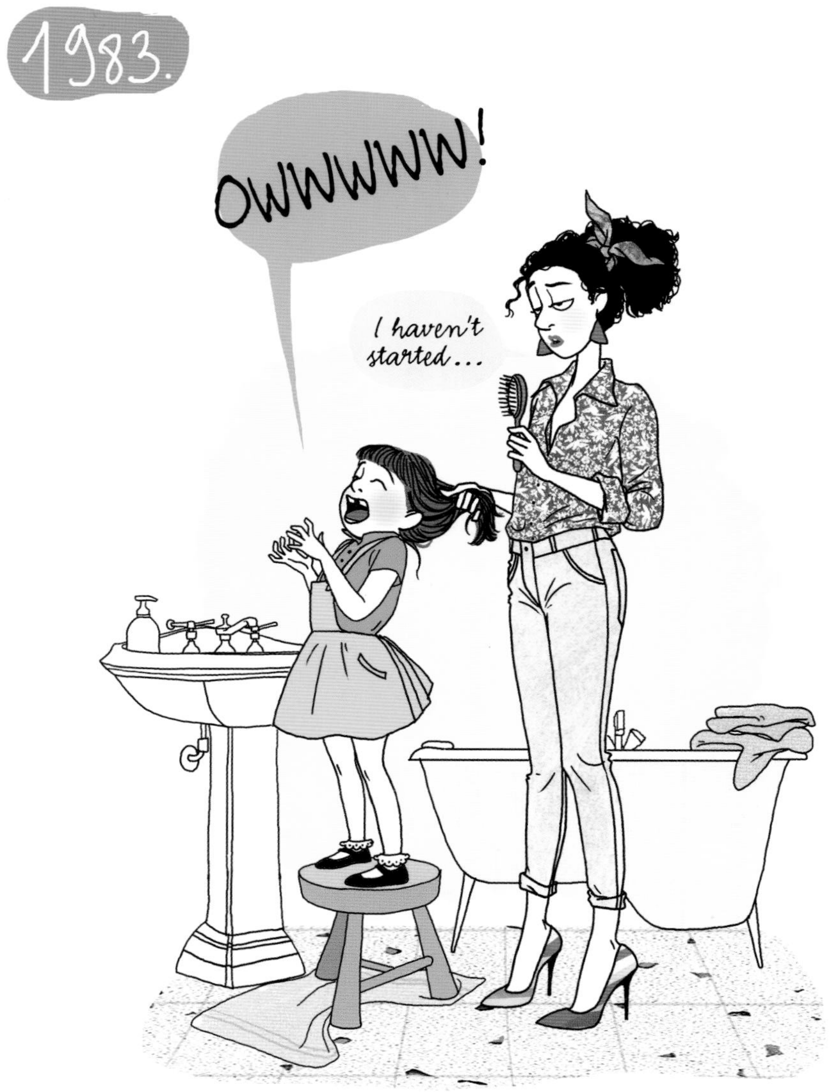
1983.
OWWWWW!
I haven't started...

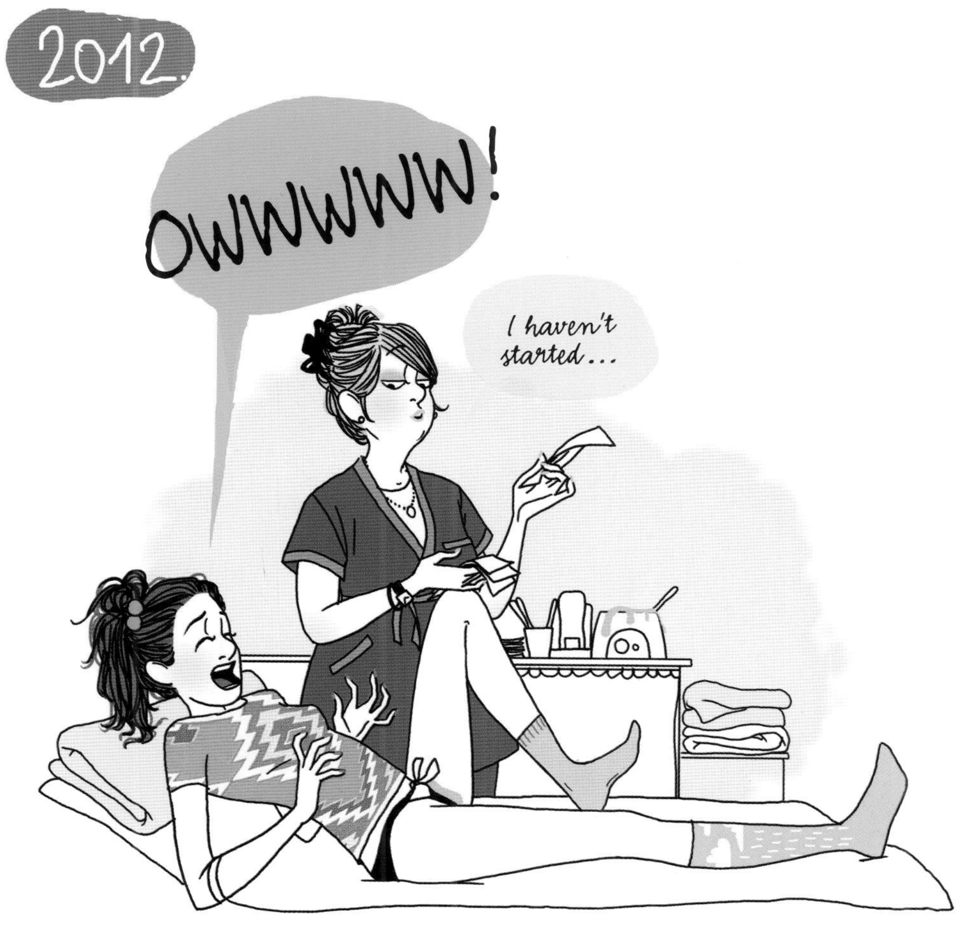
2012.
OWWWWW!
I haven't started...

...thus sparing me torture and suffering.

A Bad Rap

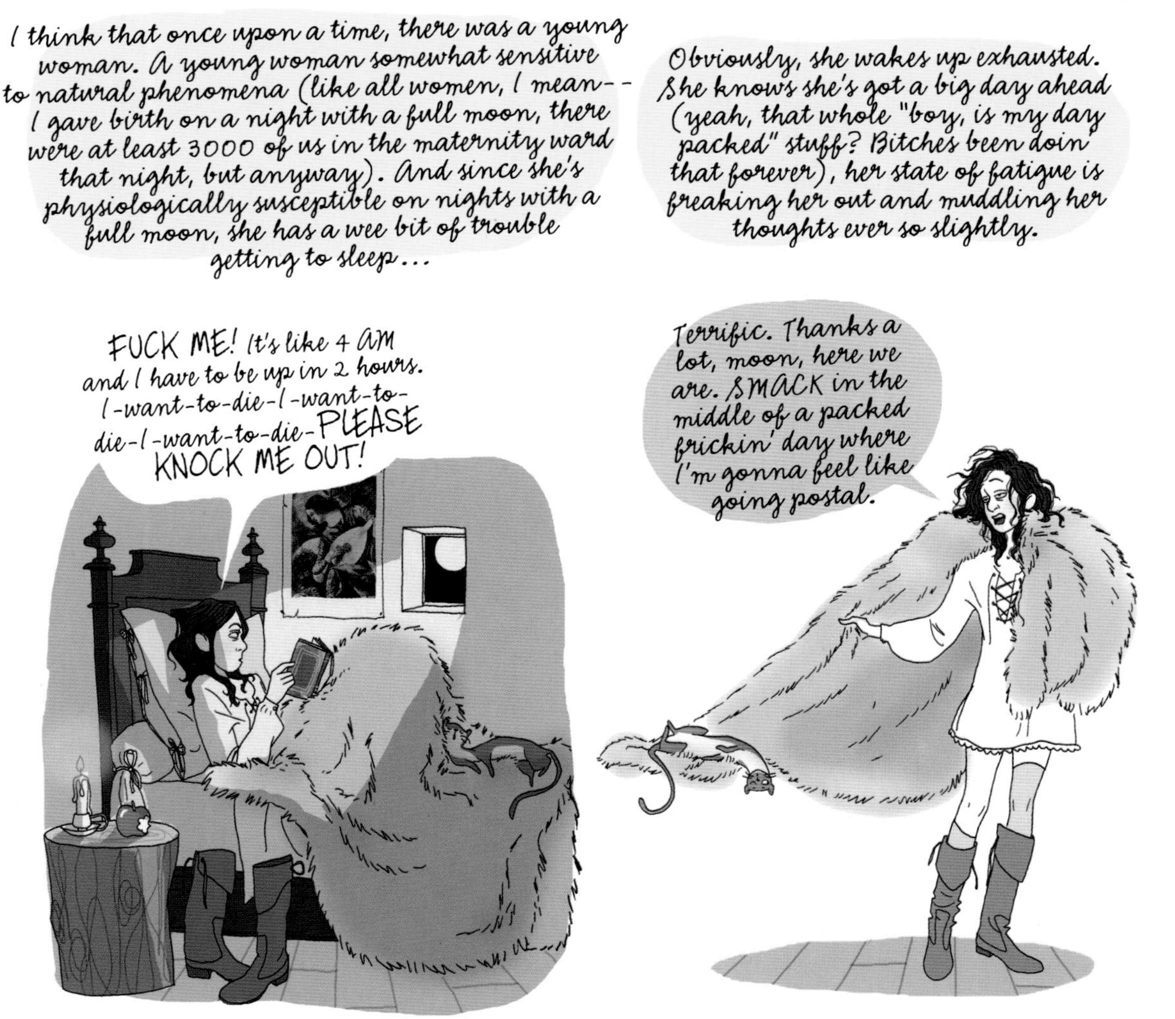
I think that once upon a time, there was a young woman. A young woman somewhat sensitive to natural phenomena (like all women, I mean-- I gave birth on a night with a full moon, there were at least 3000 of us in the maternity ward that night, but anyway). And since she's physiologically susceptible on nights with a full moon, she has a wee bit of trouble getting to sleep...
FUCK ME! It's like 4 AM and I have to be up in 2 hours. I-want-to-die-I-want-to-die-I-want-to-die-PLEASE KNOCK ME OUT!
Obviously, she wakes up exhausted. She knows she's got a big day ahead (yeah, that whole "boy, is my day packed" stuff? Bitches been doin' that forever), her state of fatigue is freaking her out and muddling her thoughts ever so slightly.
Terrific. Thanks a lot, moon, here we are. SMACK in the middle of a packed frickin' day where I'm gonna feel like going postal.

Somewhere out there, a worn-out young woman in need of some solace and tenderness...
A normal young woman jonesing for sleep who needs a protein-rich breakfast to bring up her magnesium levels.
FUCK the corset and the scratchy lace skirt, today I'm going schlubby.
I'm jittery. I could eat a horse!

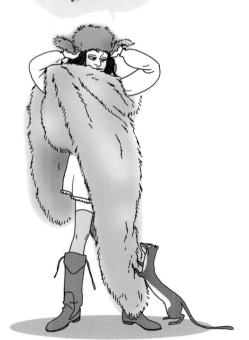

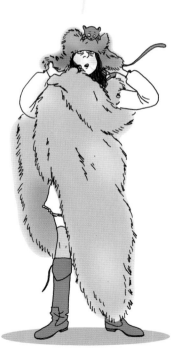

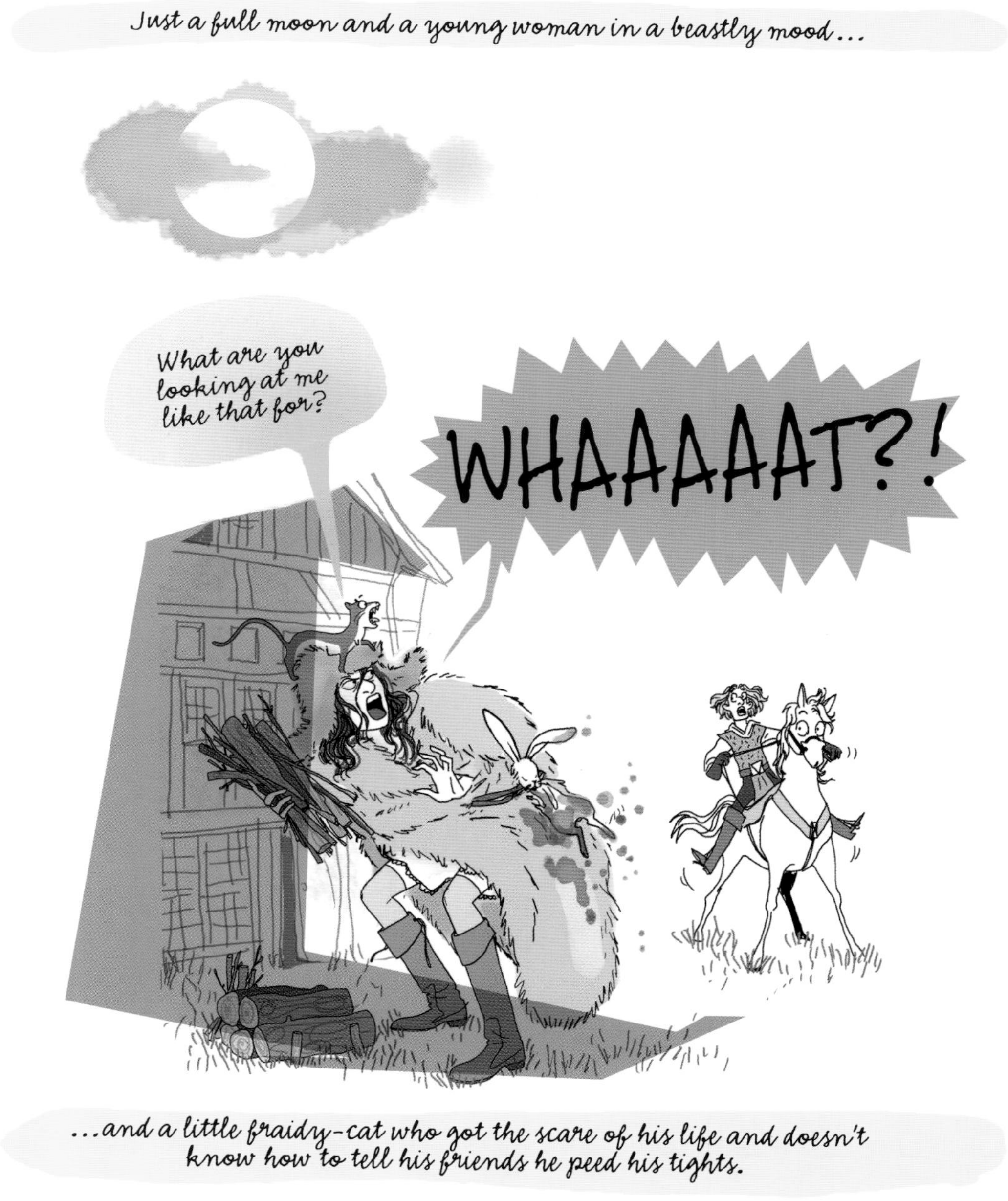
Just a full moon and a young woman in a beastly mood...
What are you looking at me like that for?
WHAAAAAT?!
...and a little fraidy-cat who got the scare of his life and doesn't know how to tell his friends he peed his tights.

I've thought it over lots, and I'm convinced that's how the werewolf myth got started. You're welcome.

Aaah, crap.

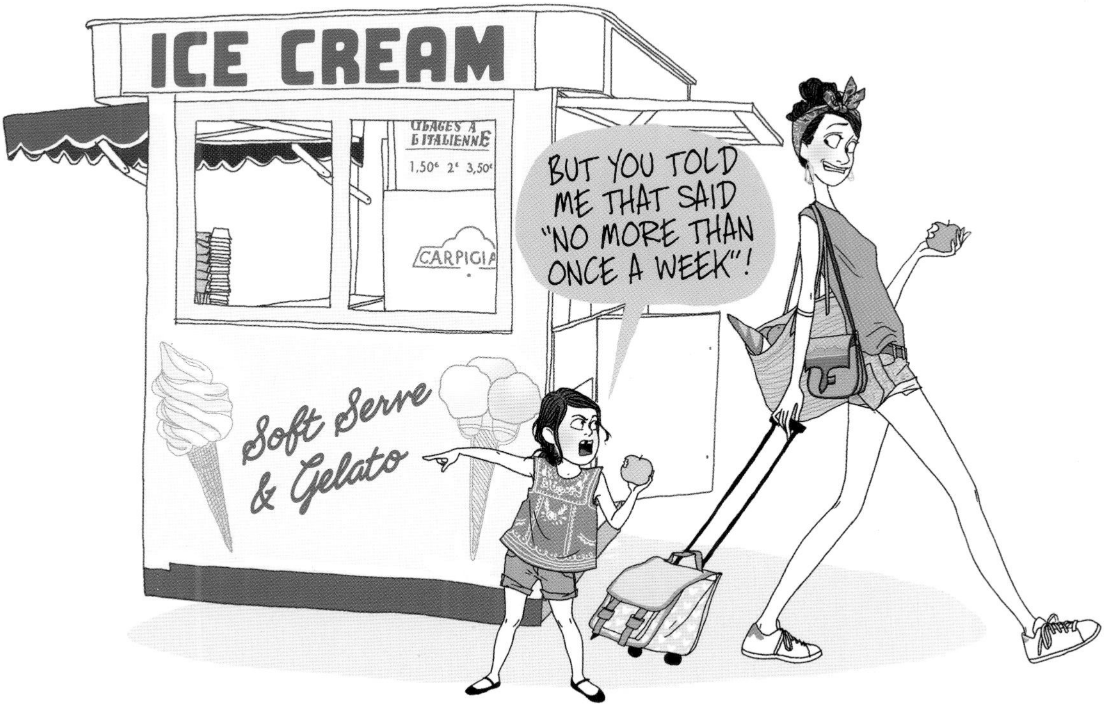
ICE CREAM
CARPIGIA
Soft Serve & Gelato
BUT YOU TOLD ME THAT SAID "NO MORE THAN ONCE A WEEK"!

...She can read now.

What are they teaching kids these days?

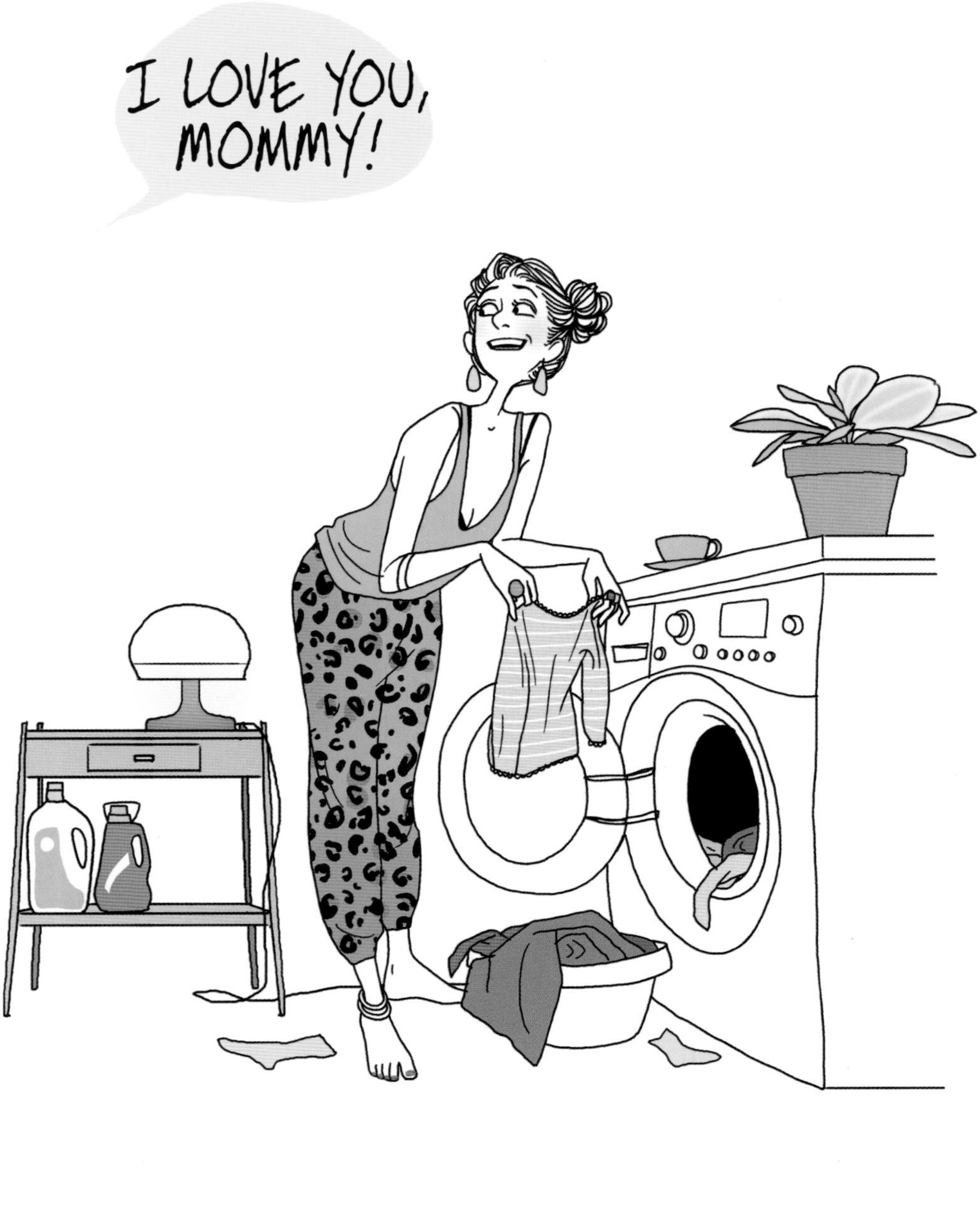
I LOVE YOU, MOMMY!

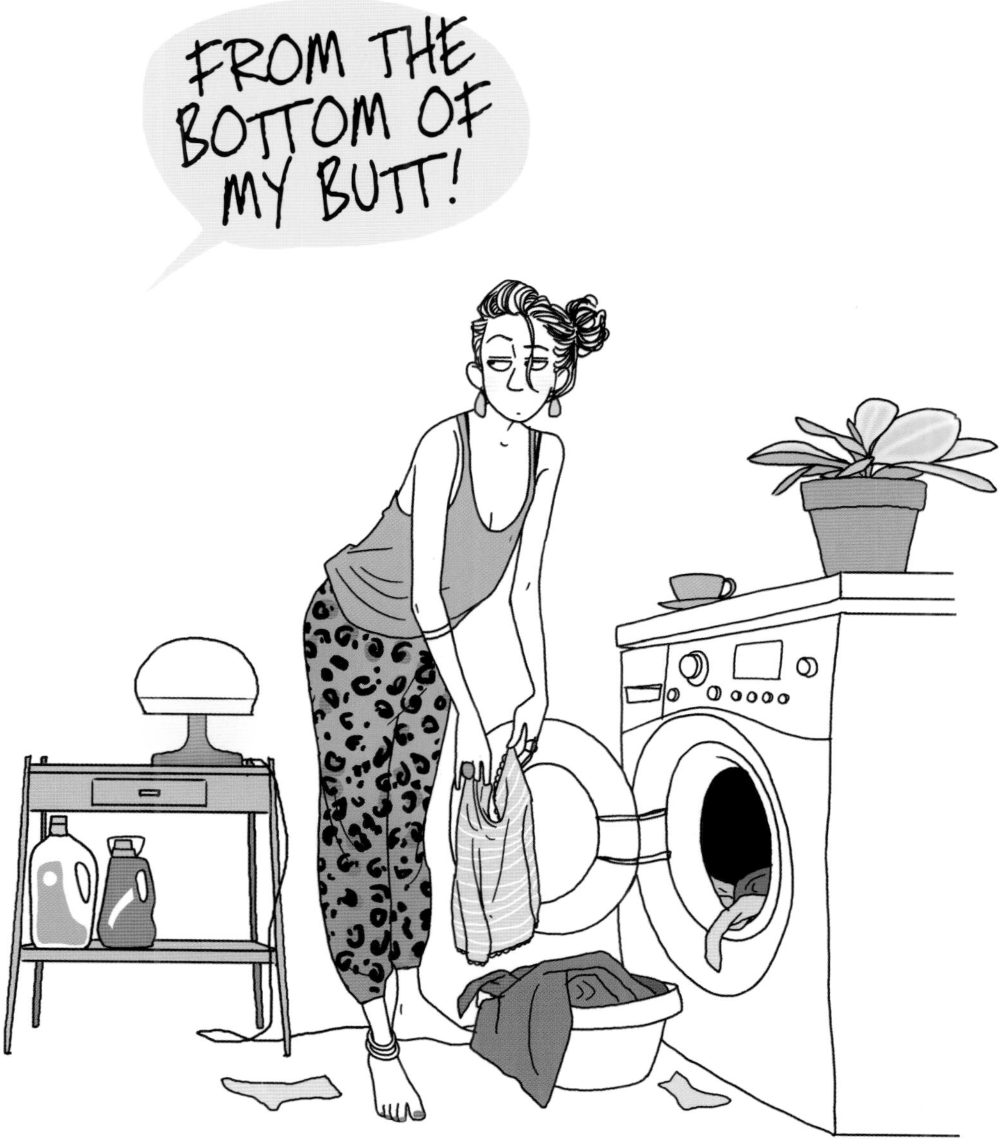
FROM THE BOTTOM OF MY BUTT!

"Running away from happiness before it runs away from me..." ~ Jane Birkin sang in 1982

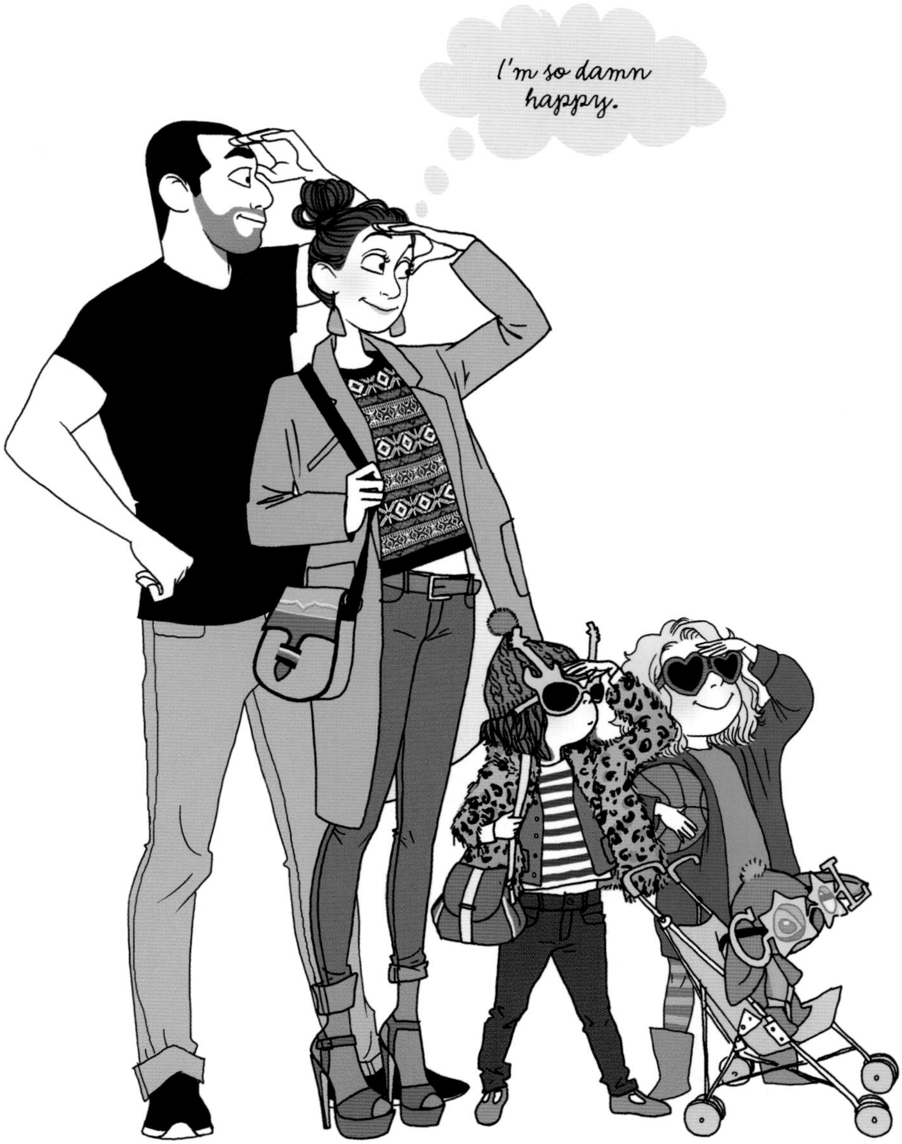
I'm so damn happy.

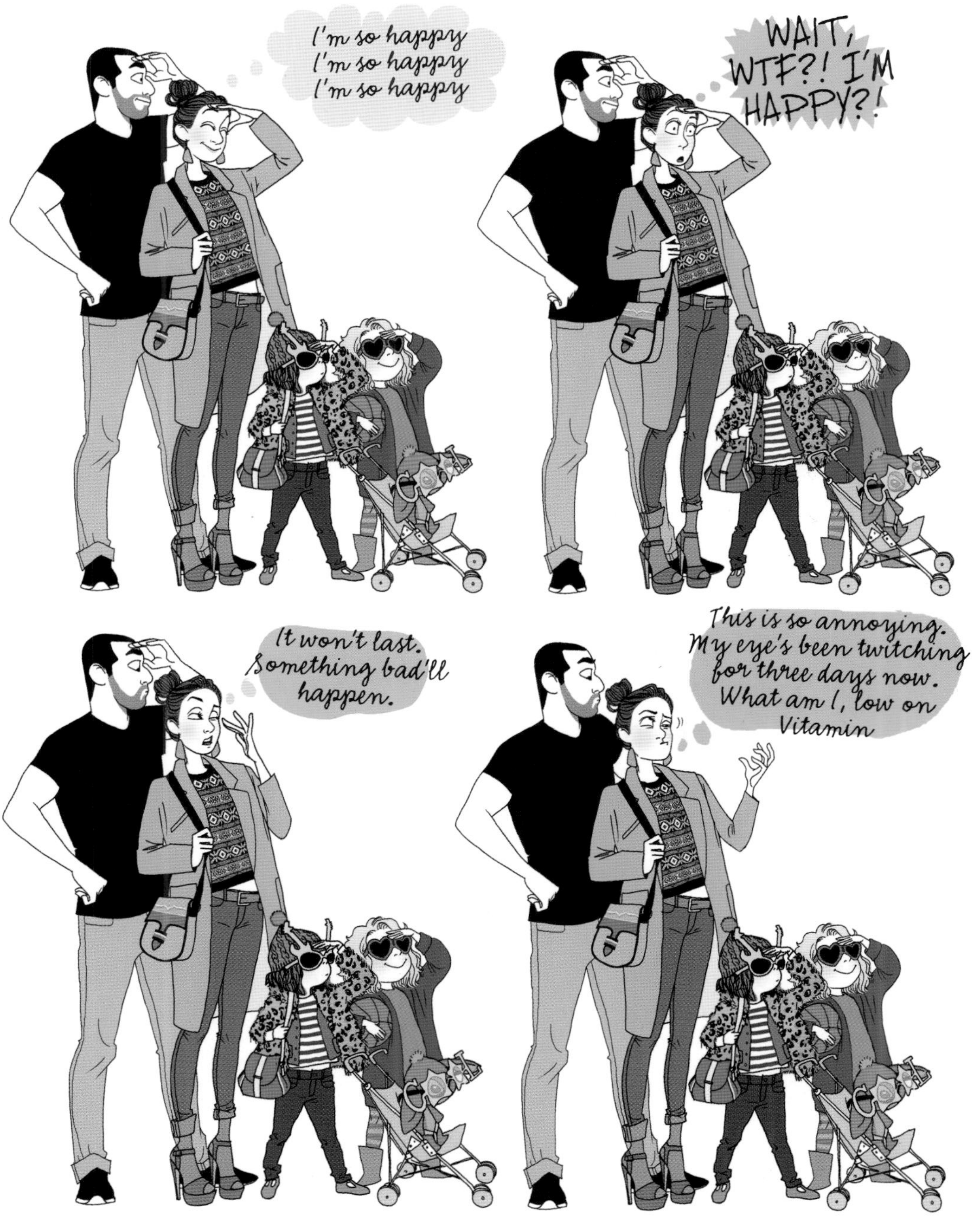
I'm so happy
I'm so happy
I'm so happy
WAIT, WTF?! I'M HAPPY?!
It won't last. Something bad'll happen.
This is so annoying. My eye's been twitching for three days now. What am I, low on Vitamin

Admit it: it's stupid to sweat the small stuff and let it ruin your life...

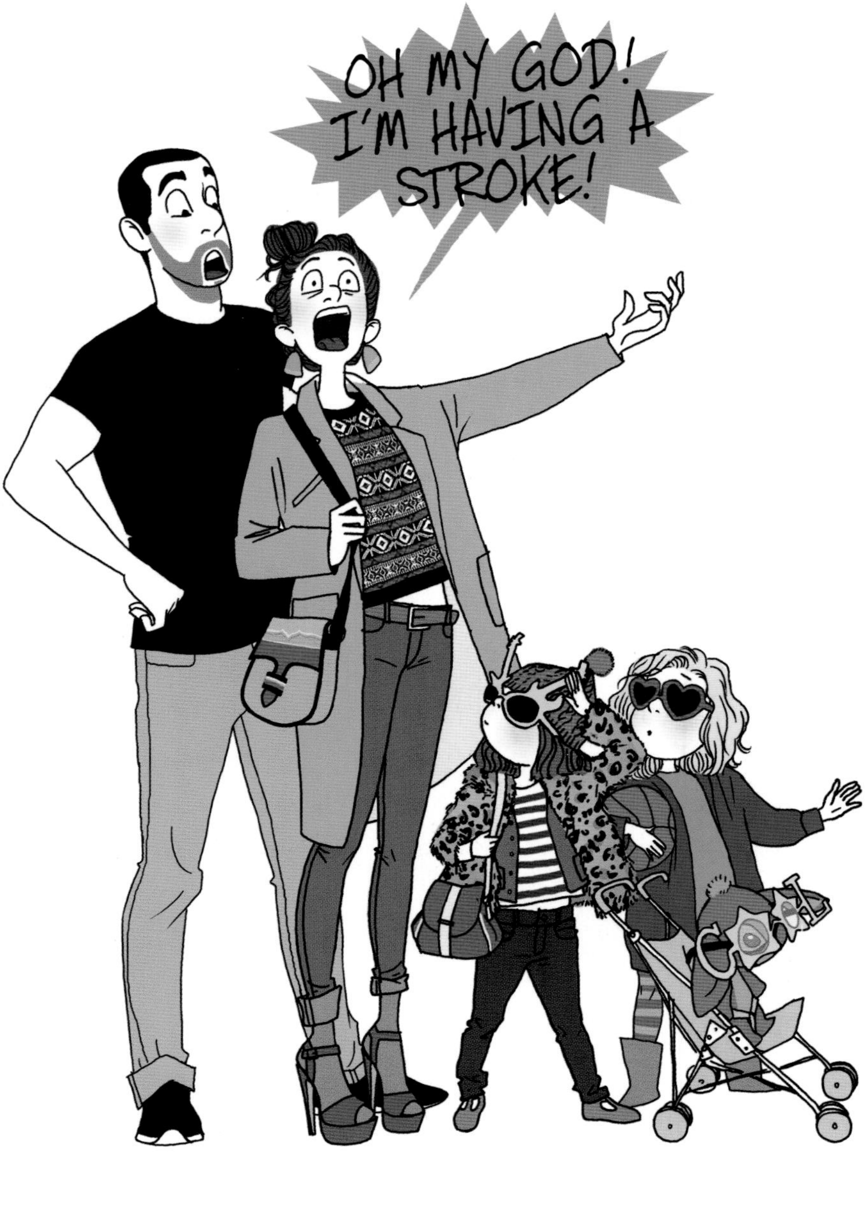
OH MY GOD! I'M HAVING A STROKE!

THERE! Not so small now, huh?

"A Dream of Blue"

It'll laaaaast for you and meee....

The rest of our lives

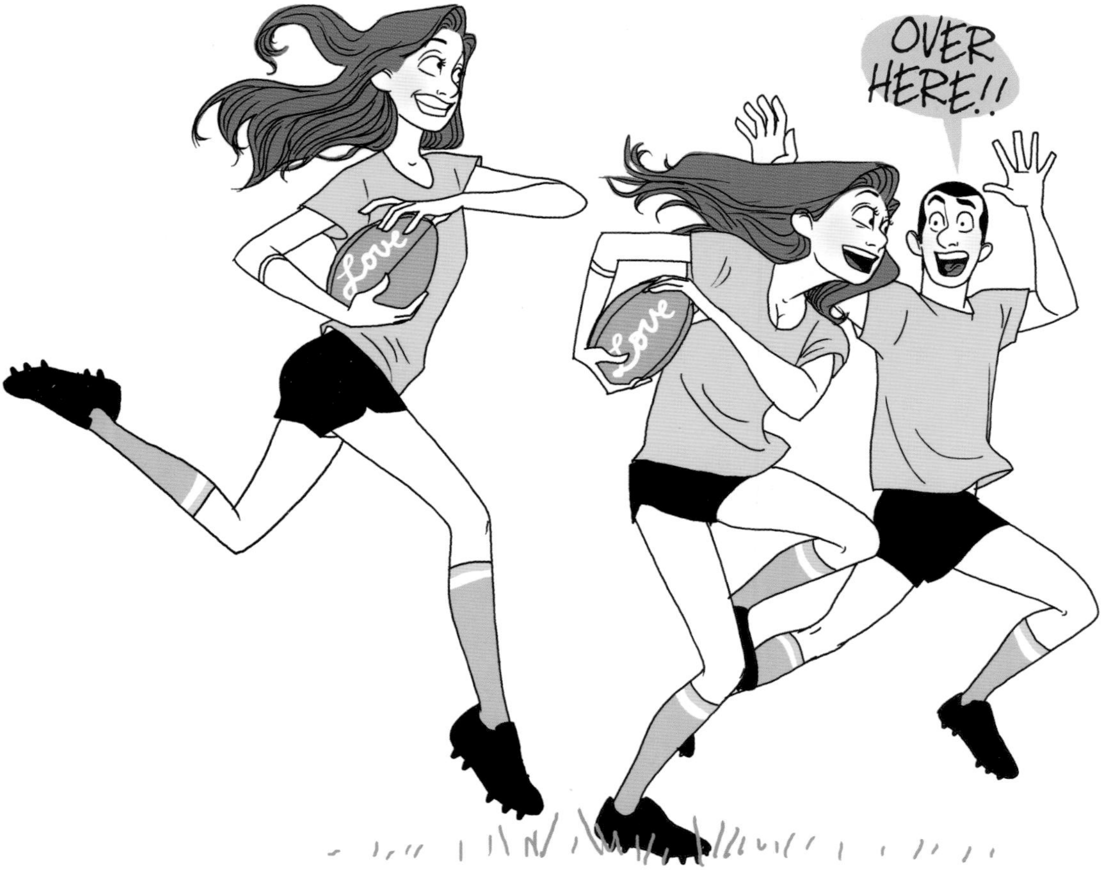

Love
Love
OVER HERE!!

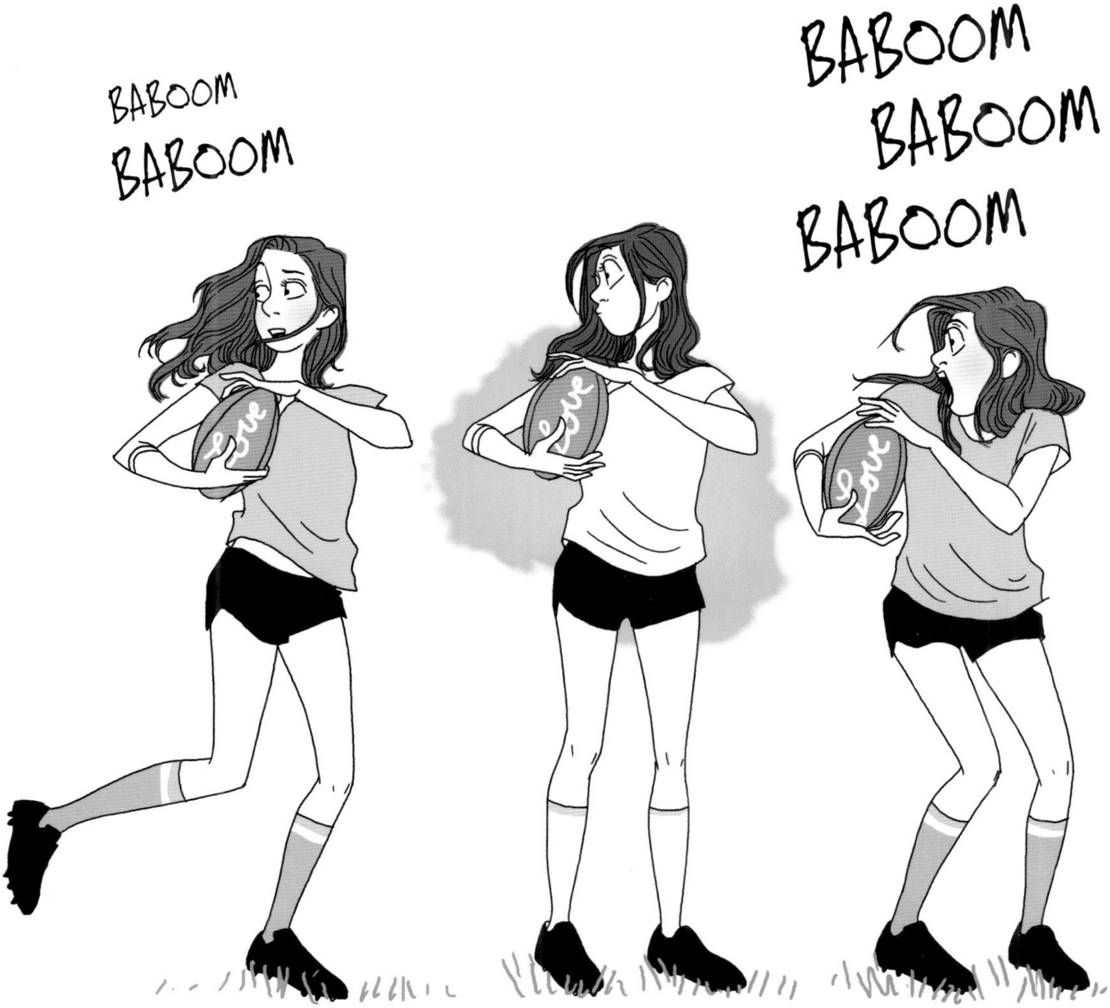
BABOOM
BABOOM
Love
Love
BABOOM
BABOOM
BABOOM
Love

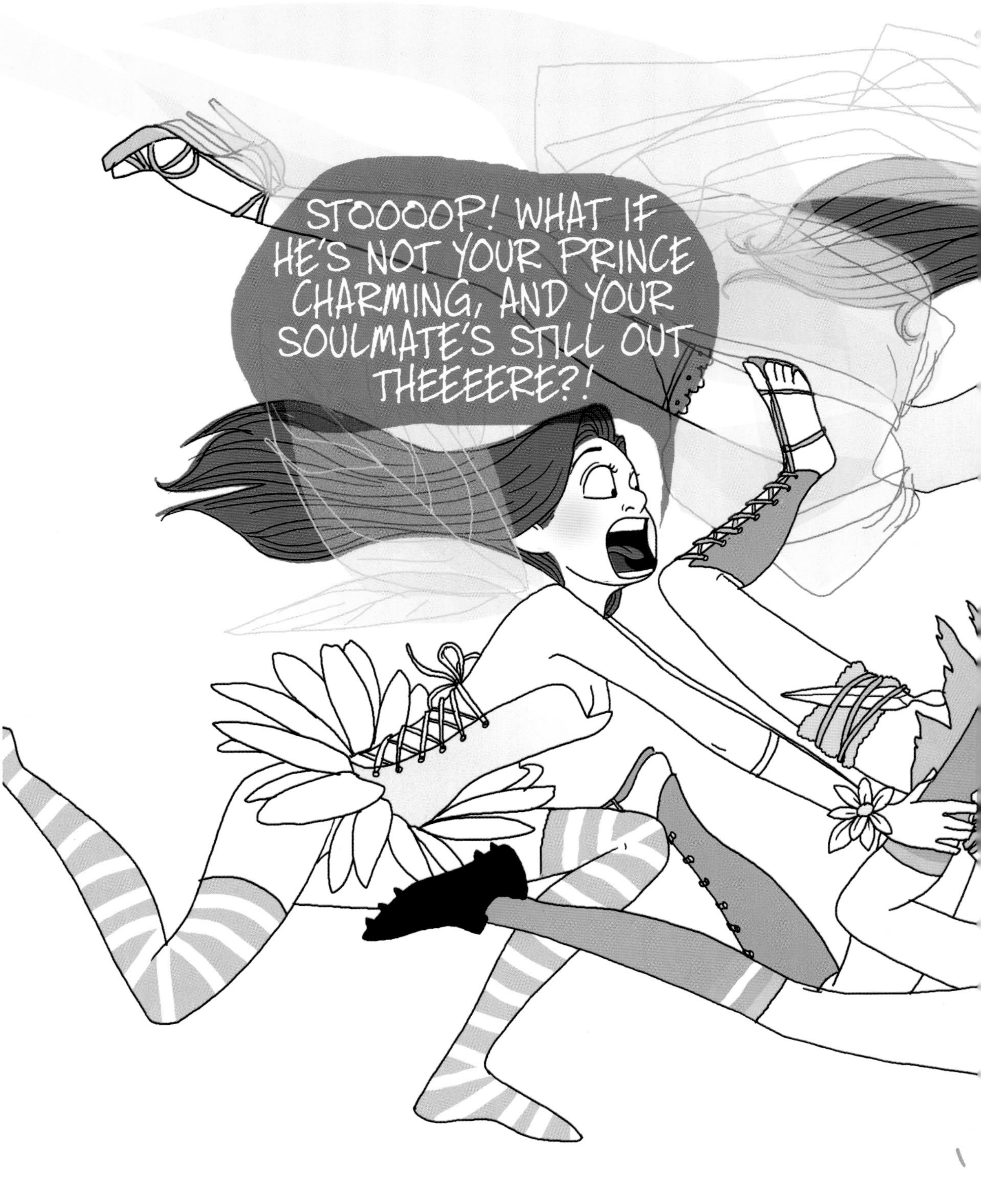
STOOOOP! WHAT IF HE'S NOT YOUR PRINCE CHARMING, AND YOUR SOULMATE'S STILL OUT THEEEERE?!

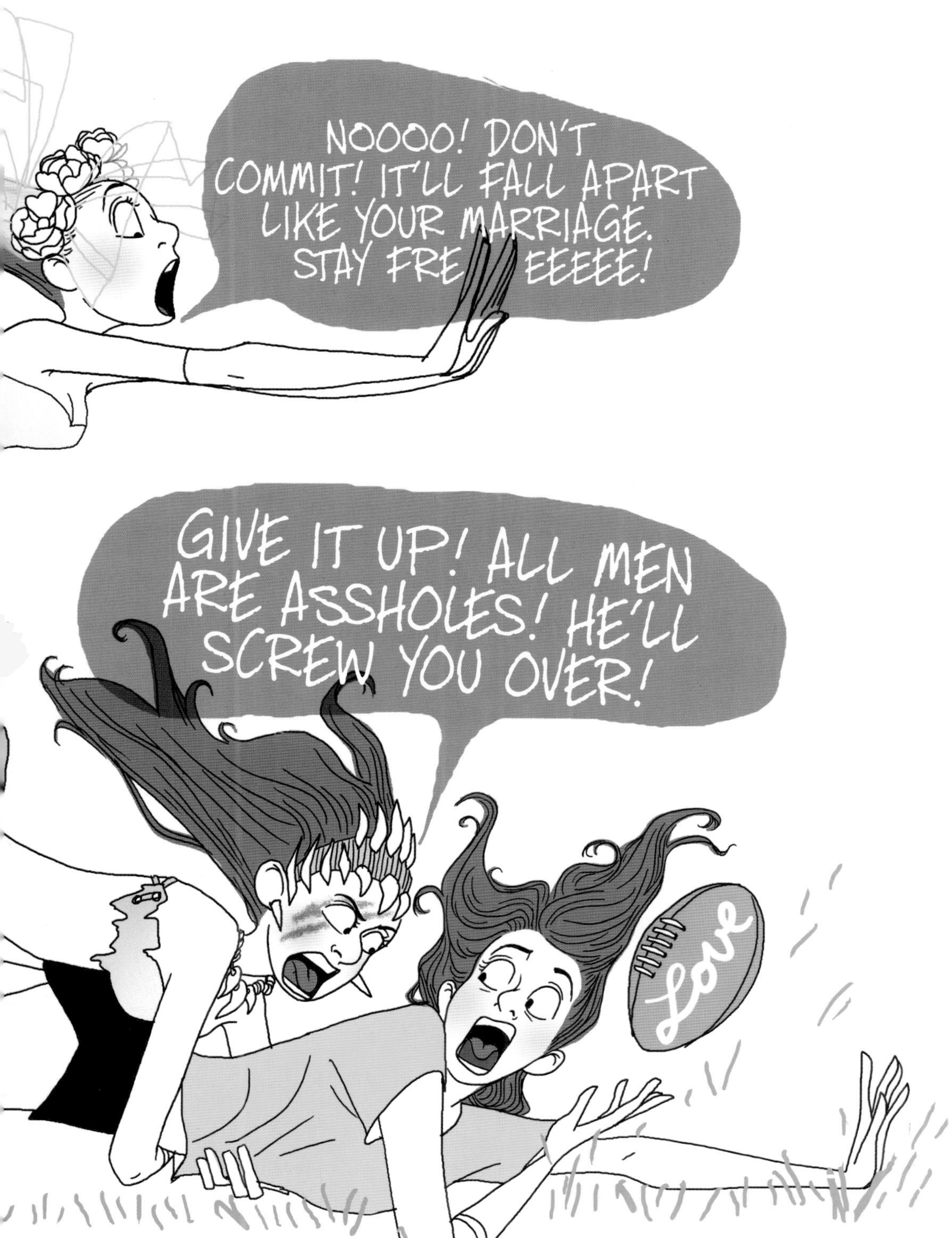
NOOOO! DON'T COMMIT! IT'LL FALL APART LIKE YOUR MARRIAGE. STAY FREEEEEE!
GIVE IT UP! ALL MEN ARE ASSHOLES! HE'LL SCREW YOU OVER!
Love

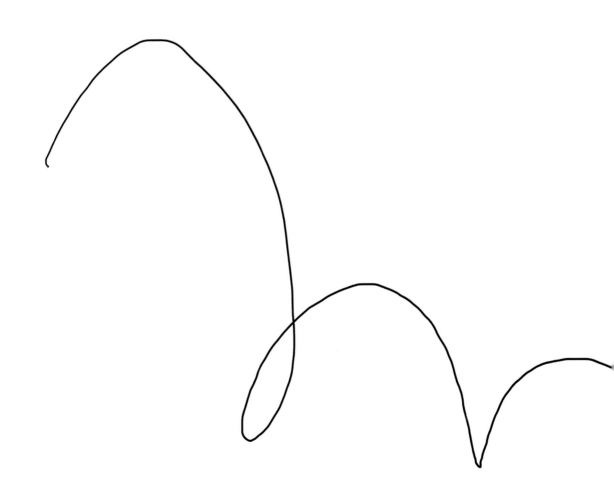

Love

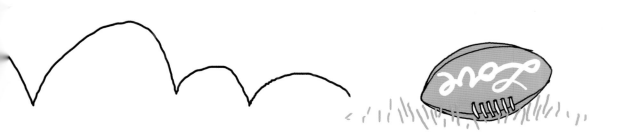

It was supposed to be the rest of our lives...

Thank You, Bitches

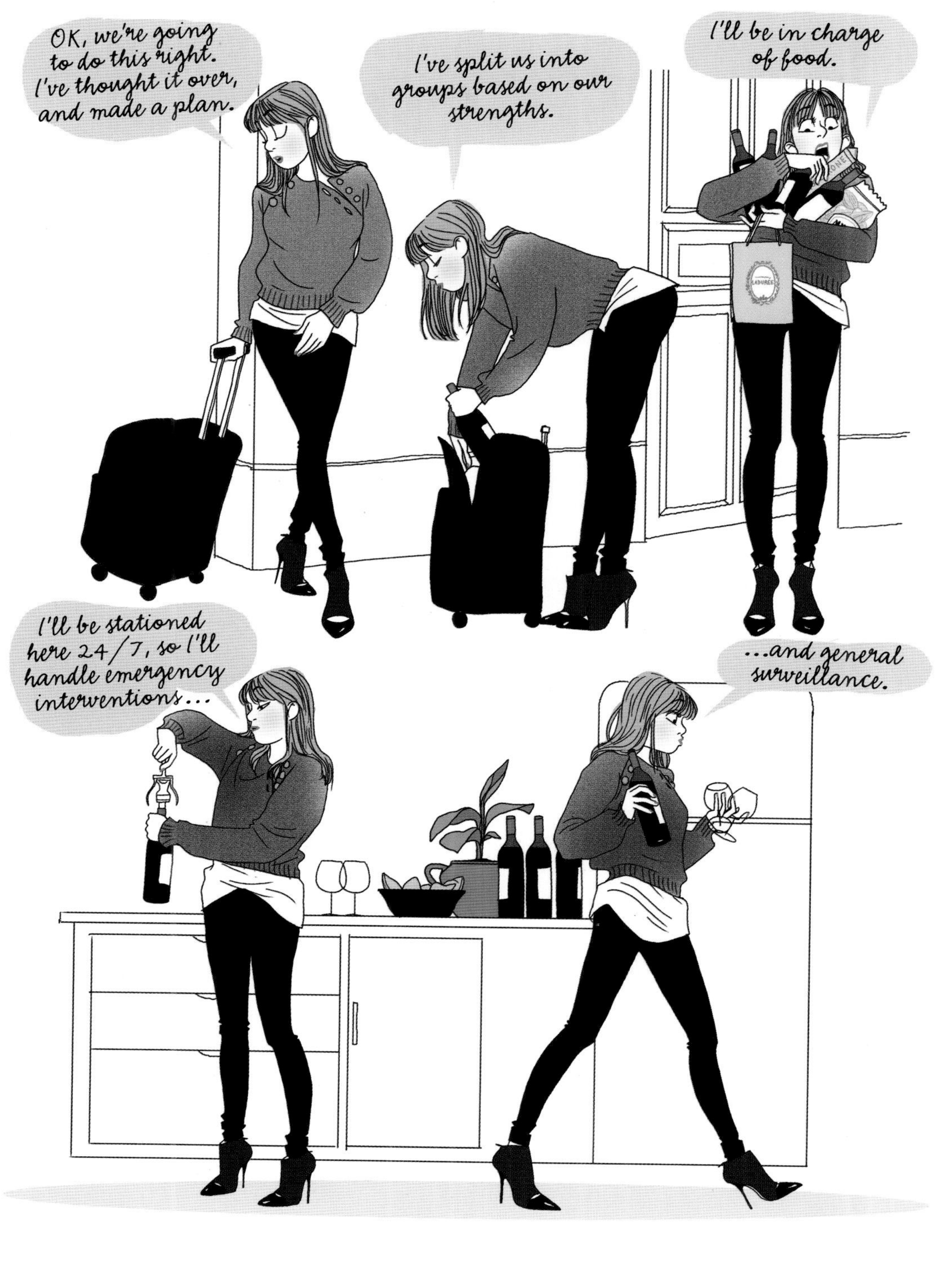

OK, we're going to do this right. I've thought it over, and made a plan.
I've split us into groups based on our strengths.
I'll be in charge of food.
I'll be stationed here 24/7, so I'll handle emergency interventions...
...and general surveillance.

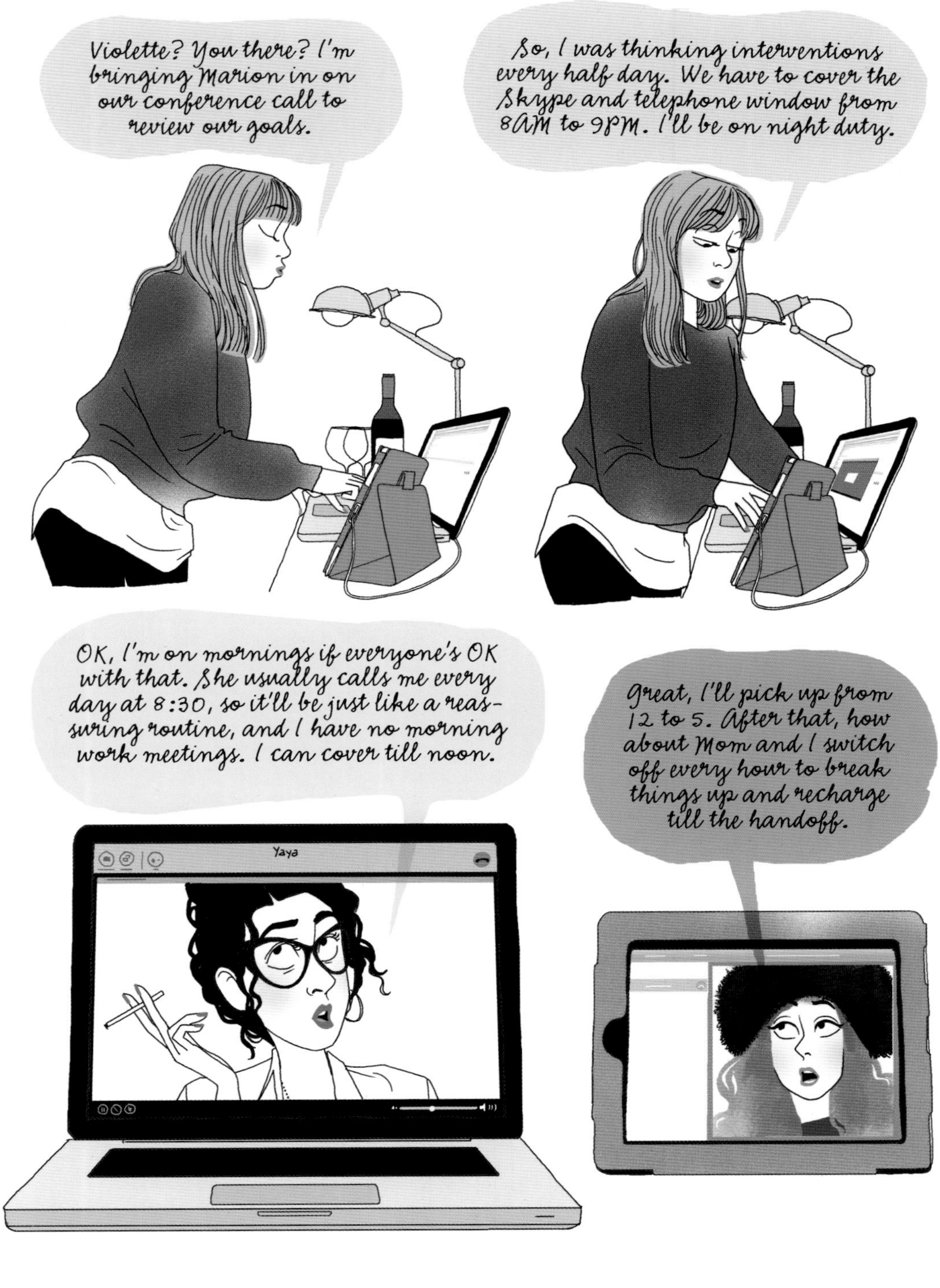
Violette? You there? I'm bringing Marion in on our conference call to review our goals.
So, I was thinking interventions every half day. We have to cover the Skype and telephone window from 8AM to 9PM. I'll be on night duty.
OK, I'm on mornings if everyone's OK with that. She usually calls me every day at 8:30, so it'll be just like a reassuring routine, and I have no morning work meetings. I can cover till noon.
Yaya
Great, I'll pick up from 12 to 5. After that, how about Mom and I switch off every hour to break things up and recharge till the handoff.

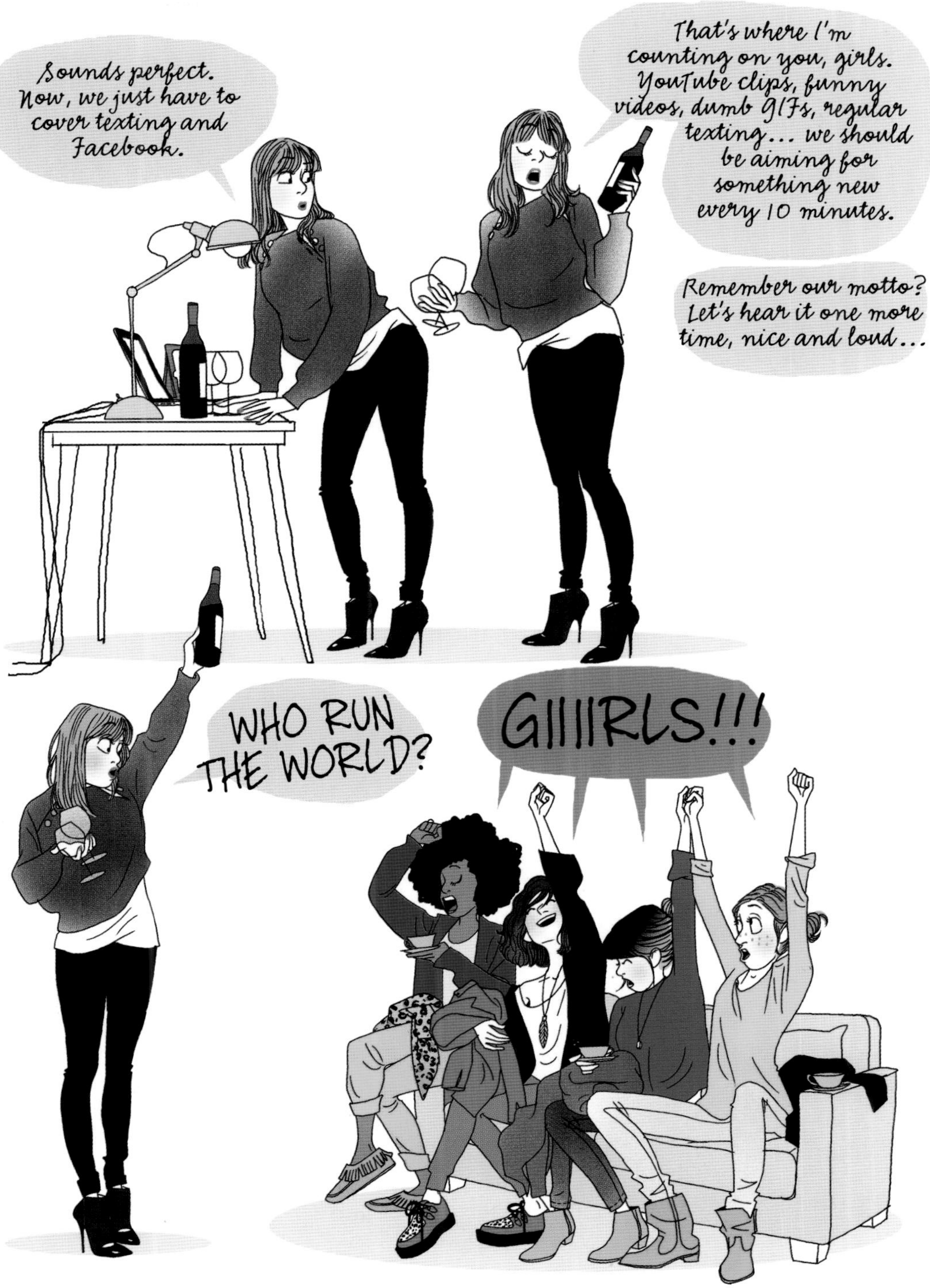
Sounds perfect. Now, we just have to cover texting and Facebook.
That's where I'm counting on you, girls. YouTube clips, funny videos, dumb GIFs, regular texting... we should be aiming for something new every 10 minutes.
Remember our motto? Let's hear it one more time, nice and loud...
WHO RUN THE WORLD?
GIIIIRLS!!!

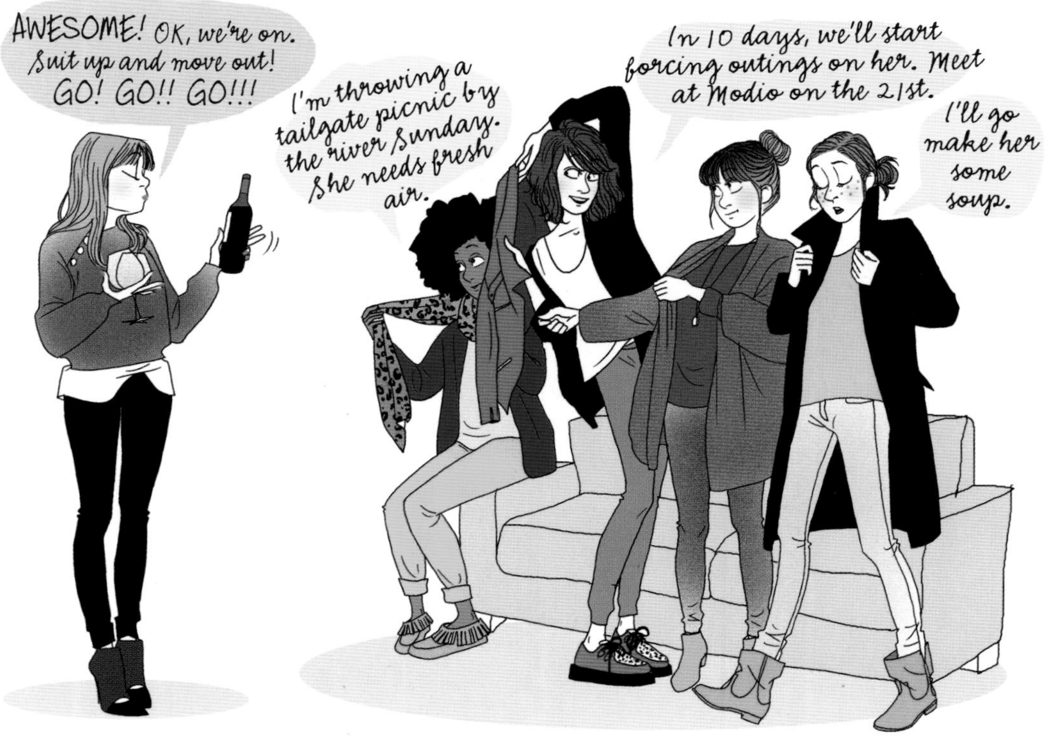
AWESOME! OK, we're on. Suit up and move out! GO! GO!! GO!!!
I'm throwing a tailgate picnic by the river Sunday. She needs fresh air.
In 10 days, we'll start forcing outings on her. Meet at Modio on the 21st.
I'll go make her some soup.

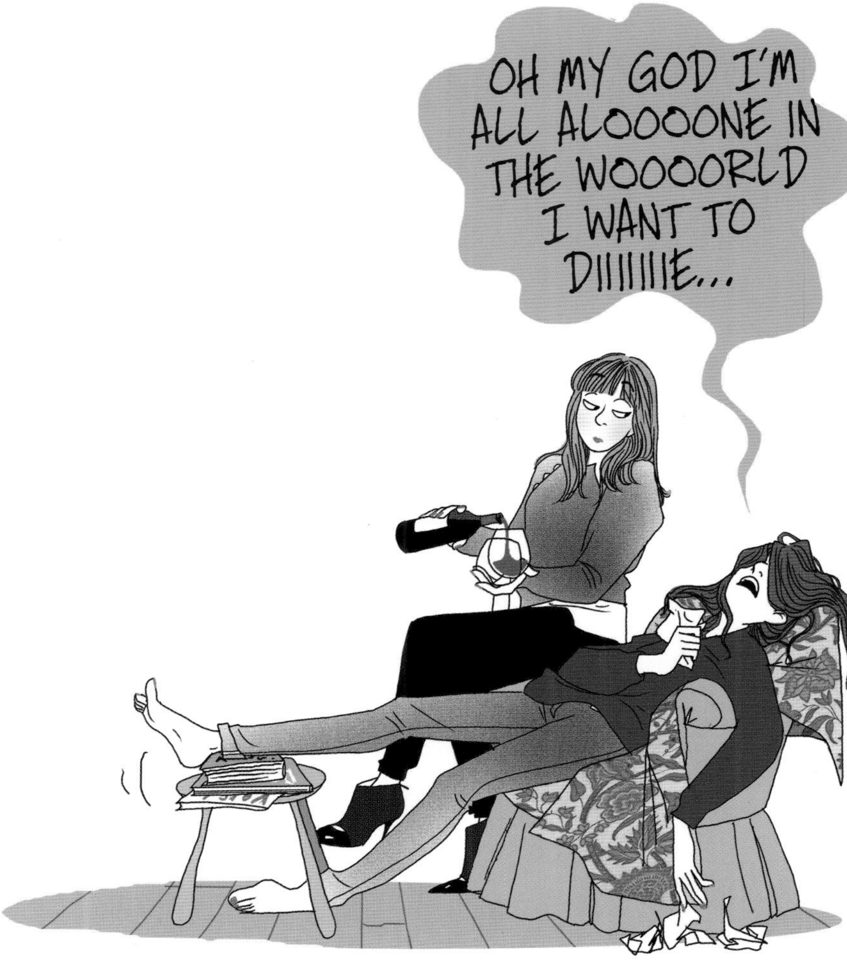
OH MY GOD I'M ALL ALOOOONE IN THE WOOOORLD I WANT TO DIIIIIIIE...

"Emotional Support Volunteer": a thankless and unsung calling.
I have a ton of respect for those people.

Surviving a Breakup, or The 7 Stages of Grief

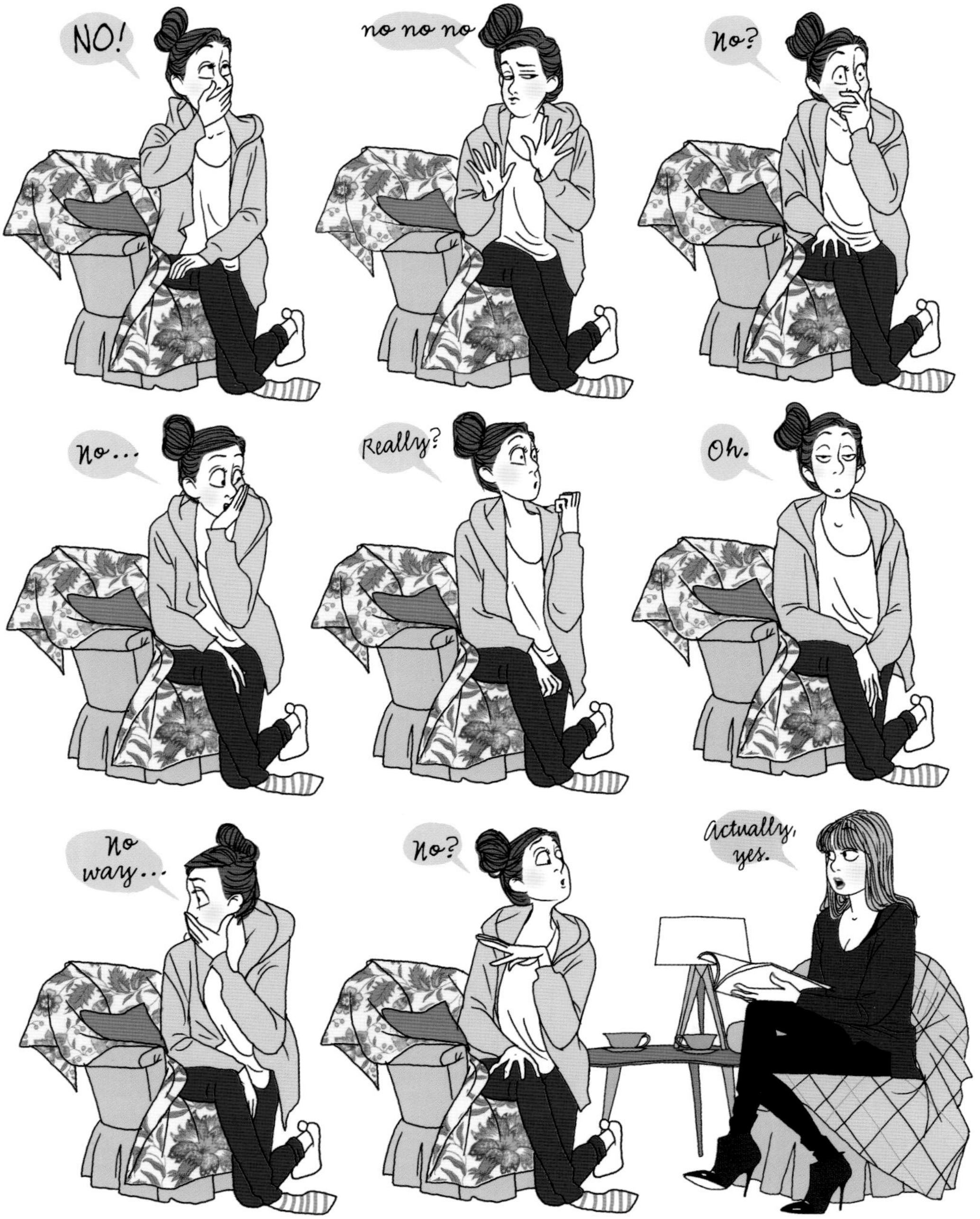
NO!
no no no
no?
no...
Really?
Oh.
no way...
no?
actually, yes.

I. SHOCK

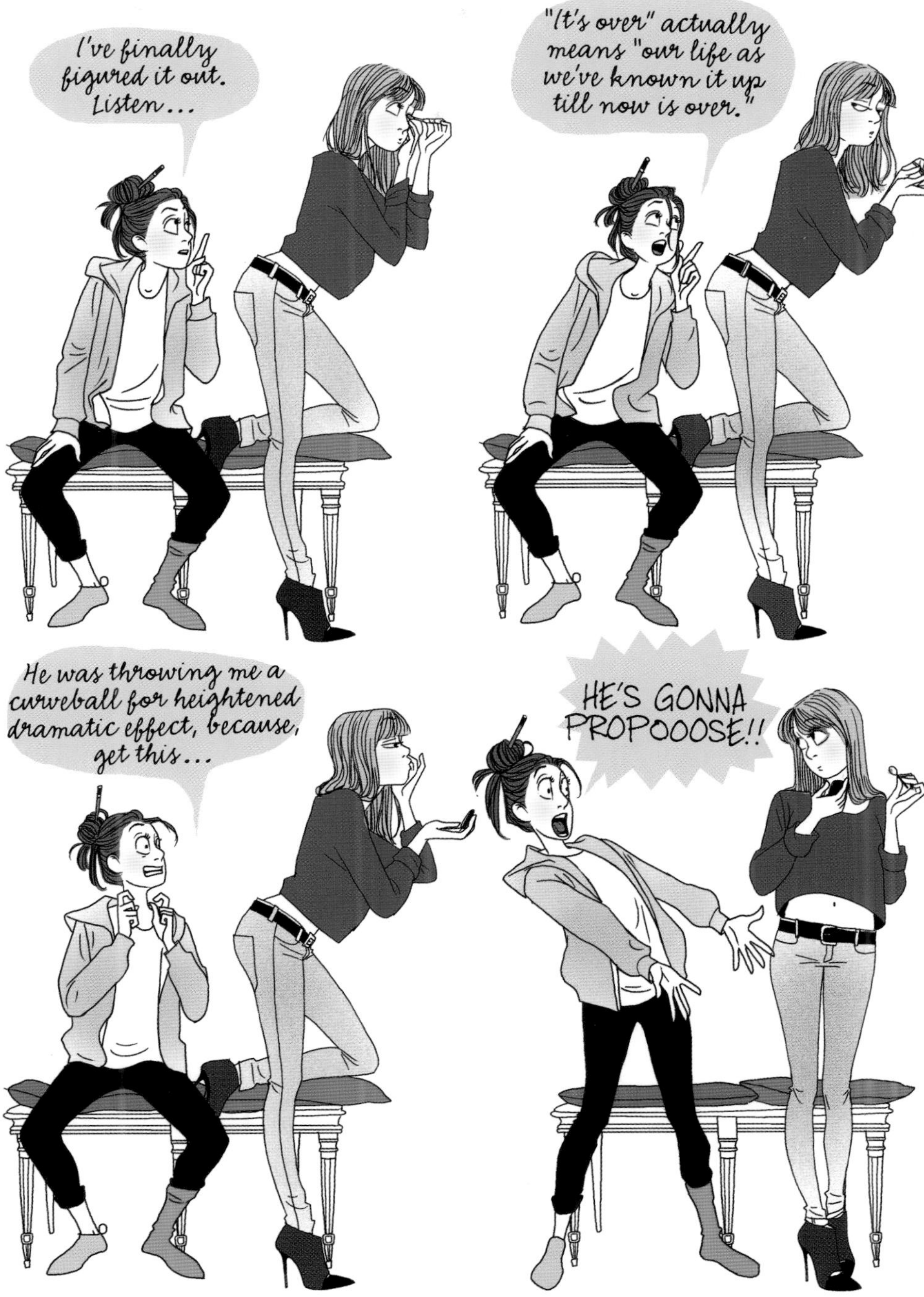
I've finally figured it out. Listen...
"It's over" actually means "our life as we've known it up till now is over."
He was throwing me a curveball for heightened dramatic effect, because, get this...
HE'S GONNA PROPOOOSE!!

2. DENIAL

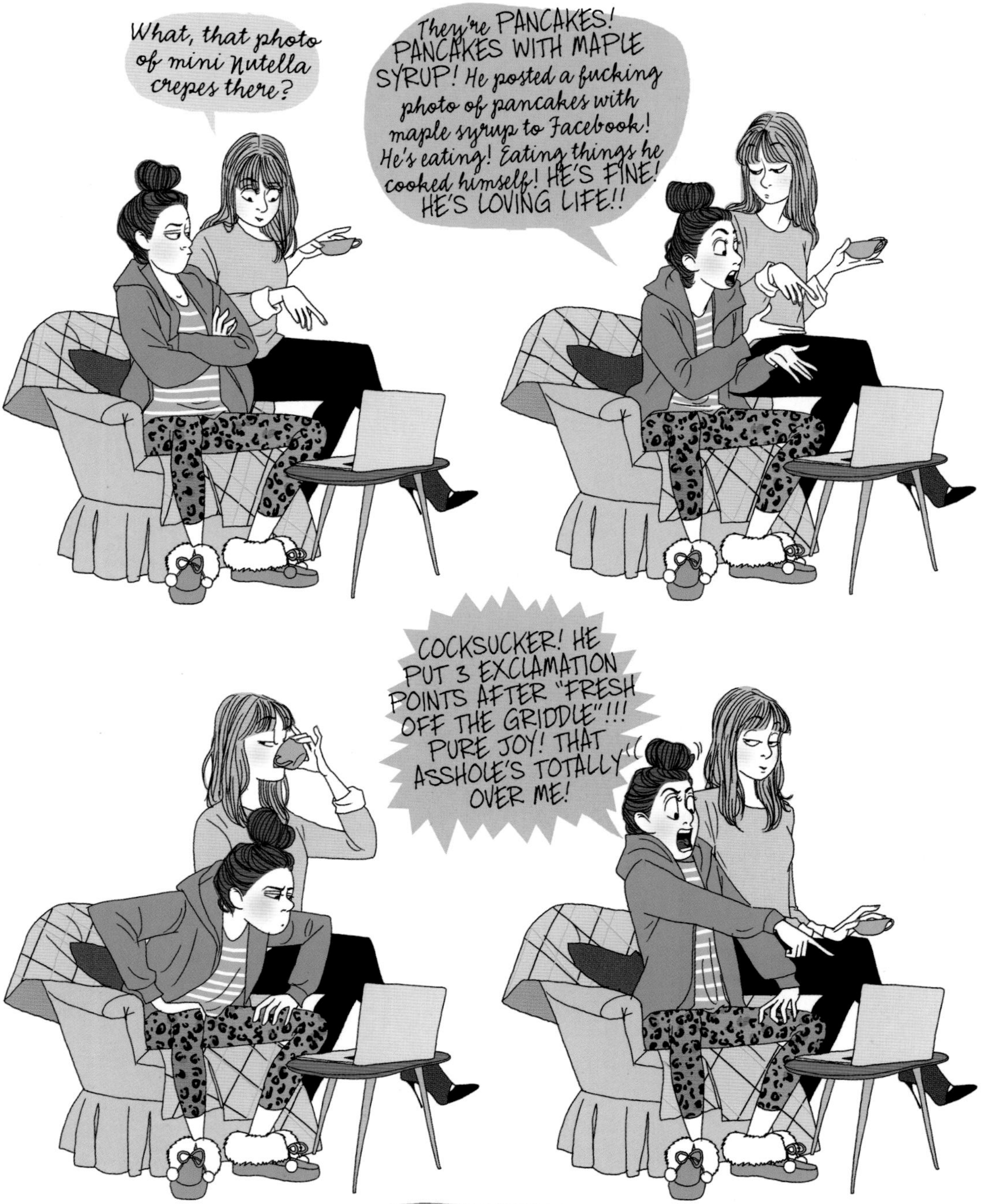
What, that photo of mini Nutella crepes there?
They're PANCAKES! PANCAKES WITH MAPLE SYRUP! He posted a fucking photo of pancakes with maple syrup to Facebook! He's eating! Eating things he cooked himself! HE'S FINE! HE'S LOVING LIFE!!
COCKSUCKER! HE PUT 3 EXCLAMATION POINTS AFTER "FRESH OFF THE GRIDDLE"!!! PURE JOY! THAT ASSHOLE'S TOTALLY OVER ME!

3. ANGER

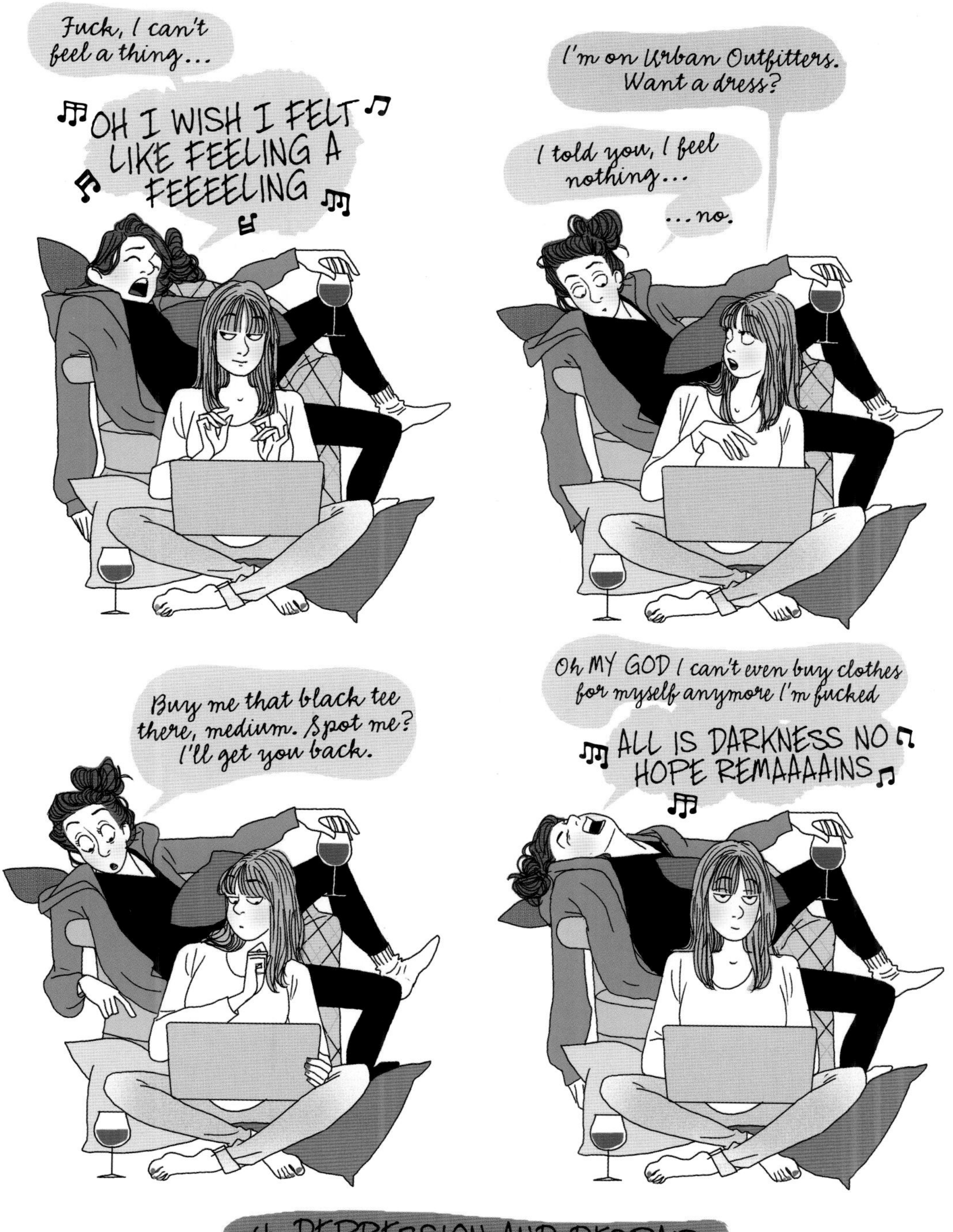
Fuck, I can't feel a thing...
OH I WISH I FELT LIKE FEELING A FEEEELING
I'm on Urban Outfitters. Want a dress?
I told you, I feel nothing...
...no.
Buy me that black tee there, medium. Spot me? I'll get you back.
Oh MY GOD I can't even buy clothes for myself anymore I'm fucked
ALL IS DARKNESS NO HOPE REMAAAAINS
4. DEPRESSION AND DESPAIR

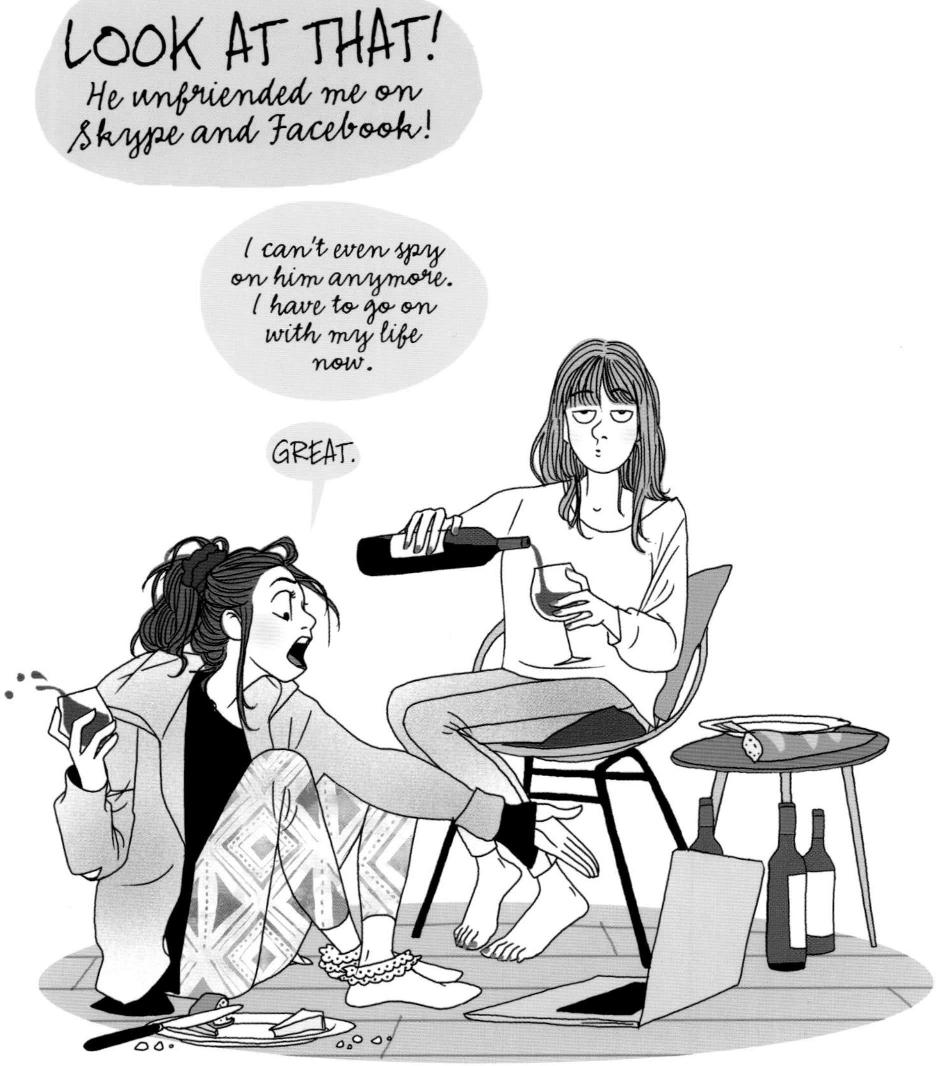
LOOK AT THAT!
He unfriended me on Skype and Facebook!
I can't even spy on him anymore. I have to go on with my life now.
GREAT.

5. RESIGNATION

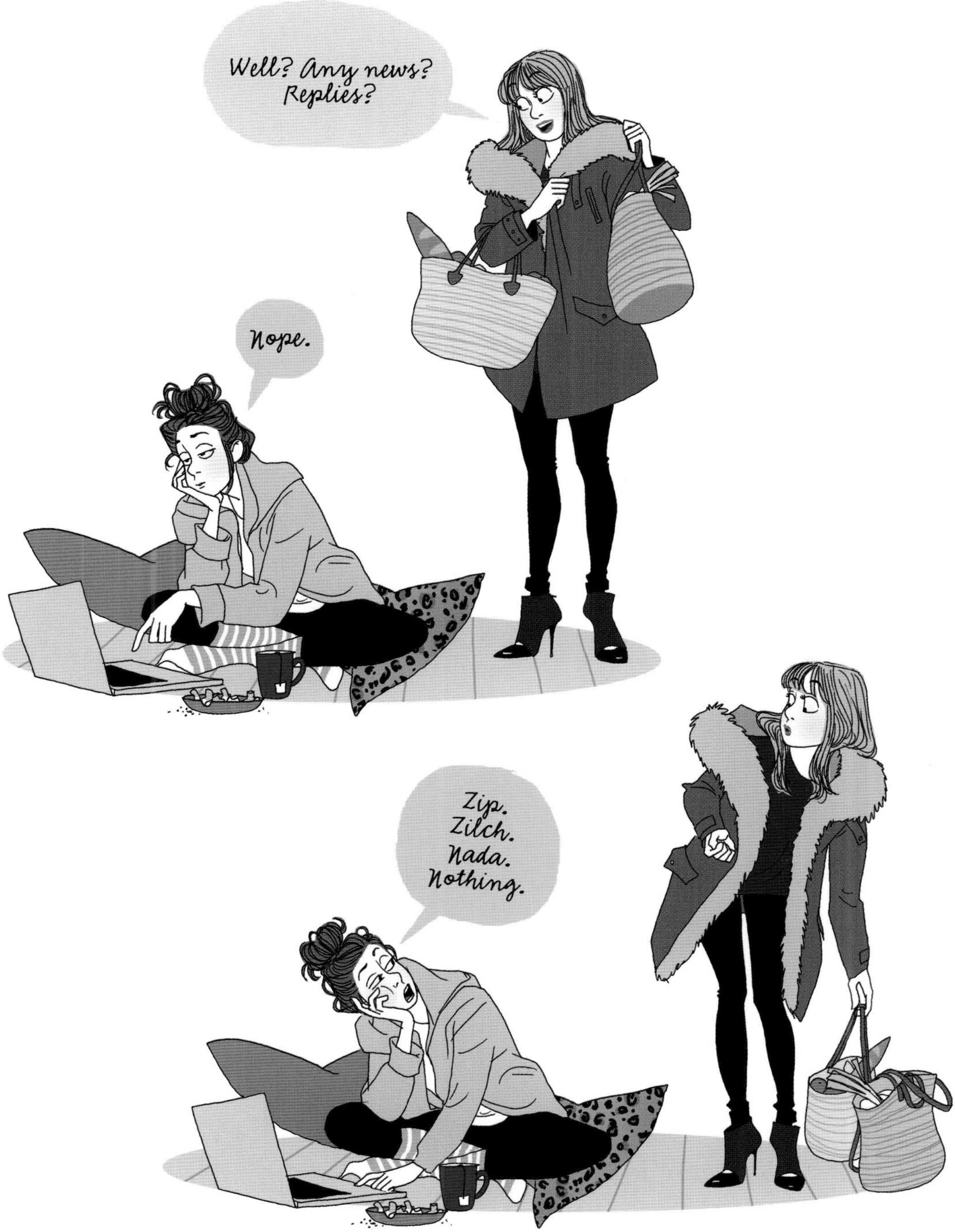
Well? Any news? Replies?
Nope.
Zip. Zilch. Nada. Nothing.

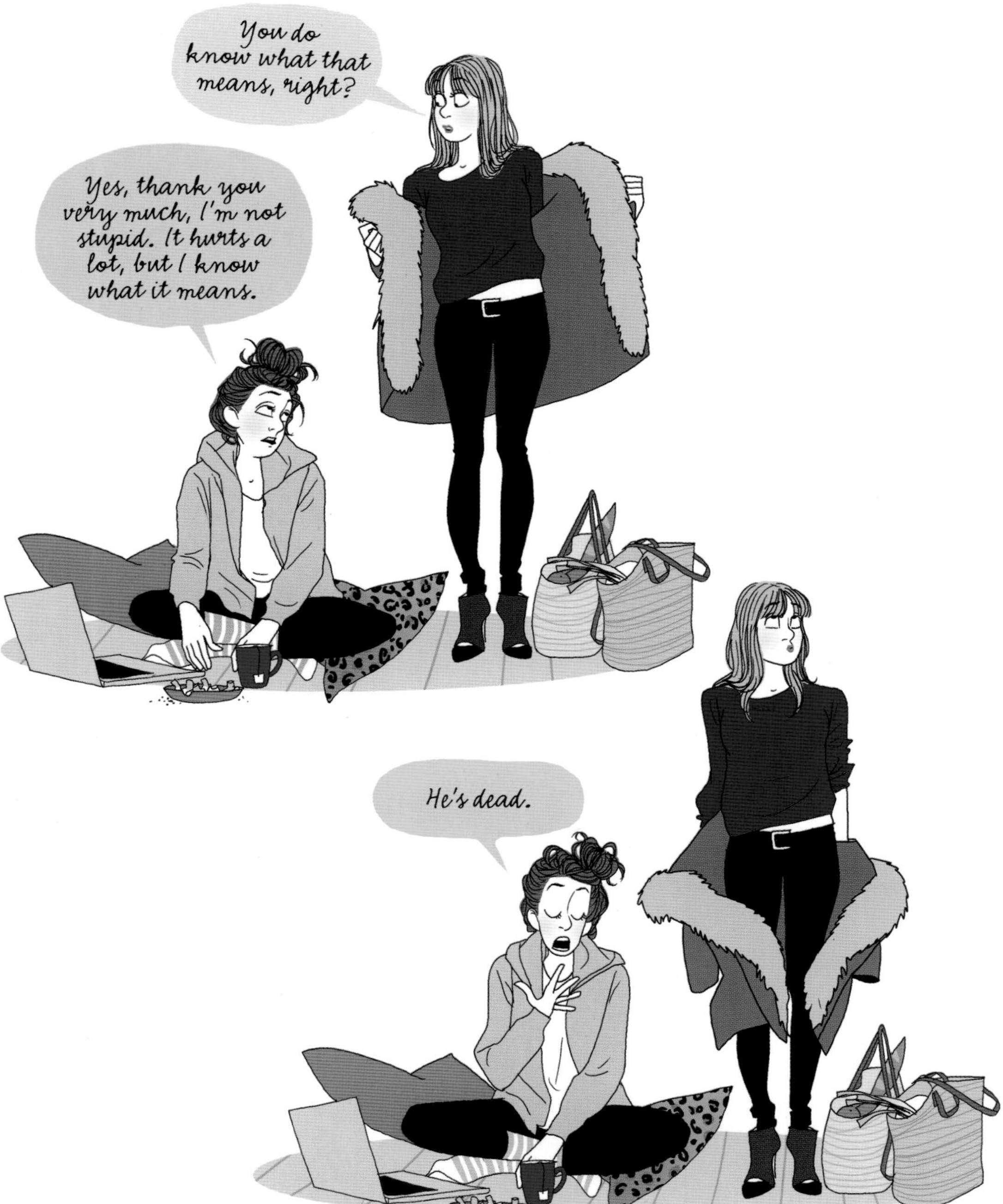
You do know what that means, right?
Yes, thank you very much, I'm not stupid. It hurts a lot, but I know what it means.
He's dead.

6. ACCEPTANCE

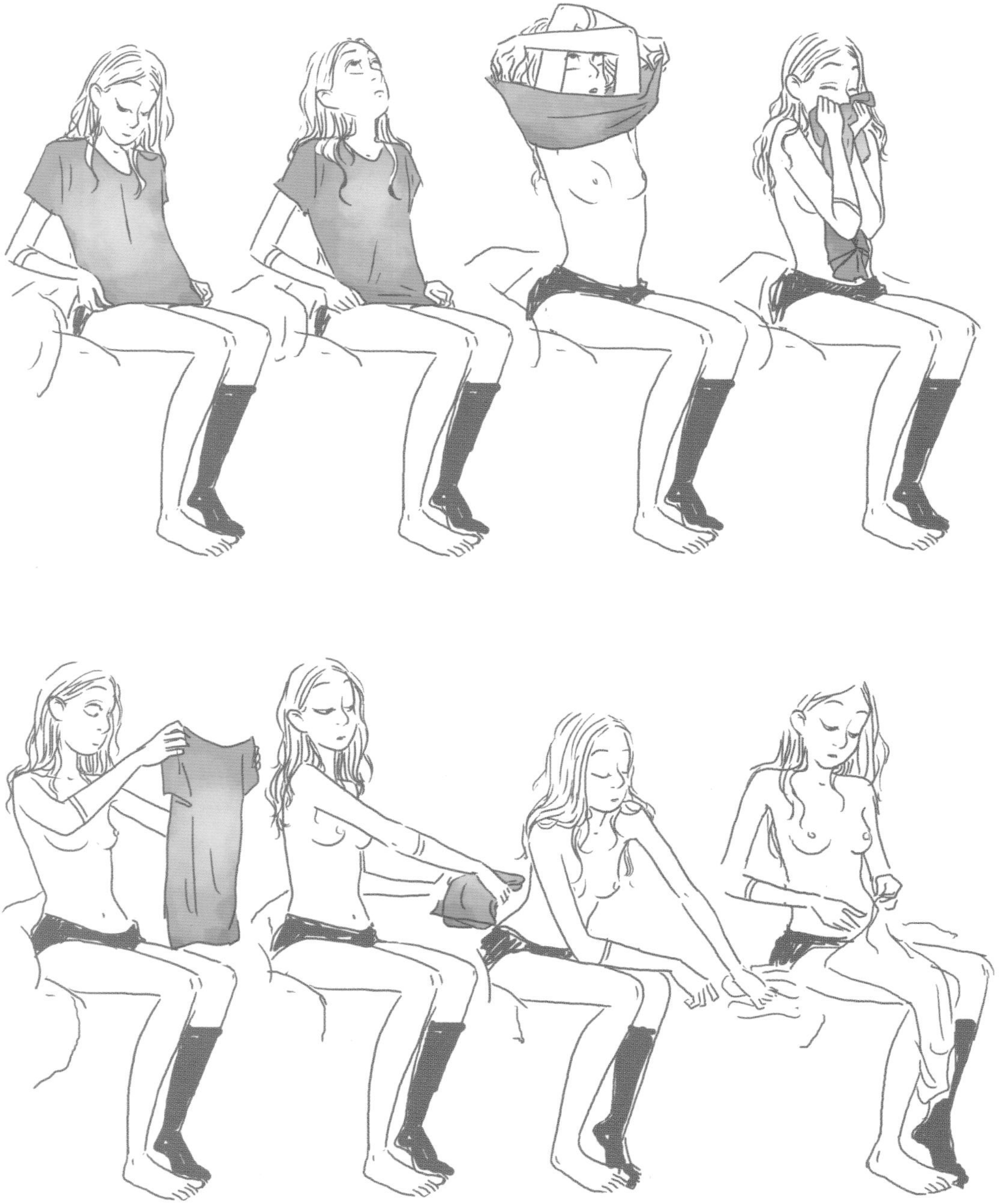

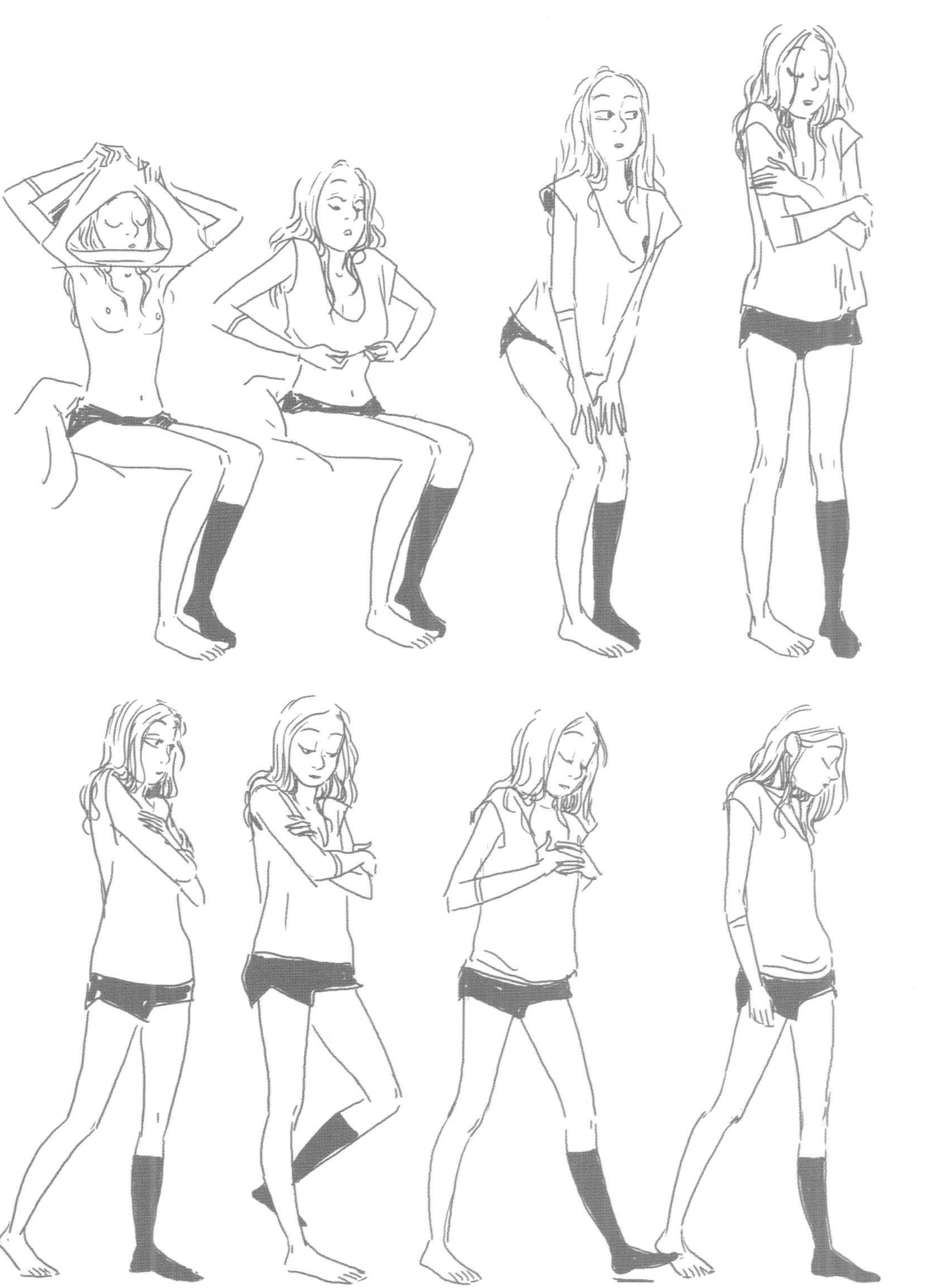

So... what
would you like
to do today?

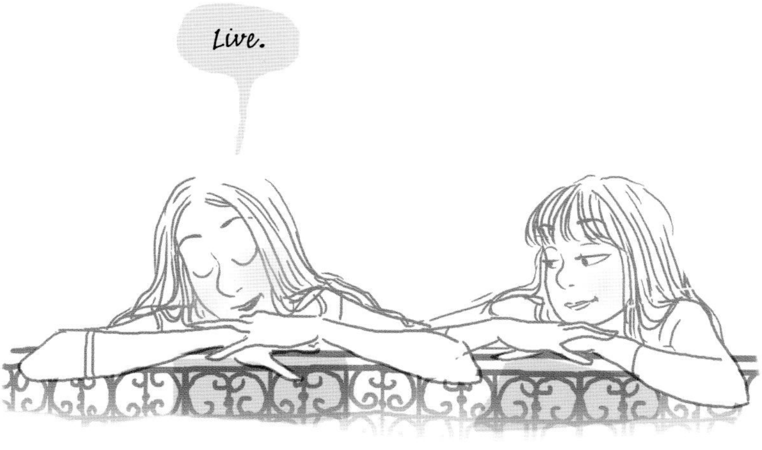
Live.

7. RECOVERY

Planetary Alignment

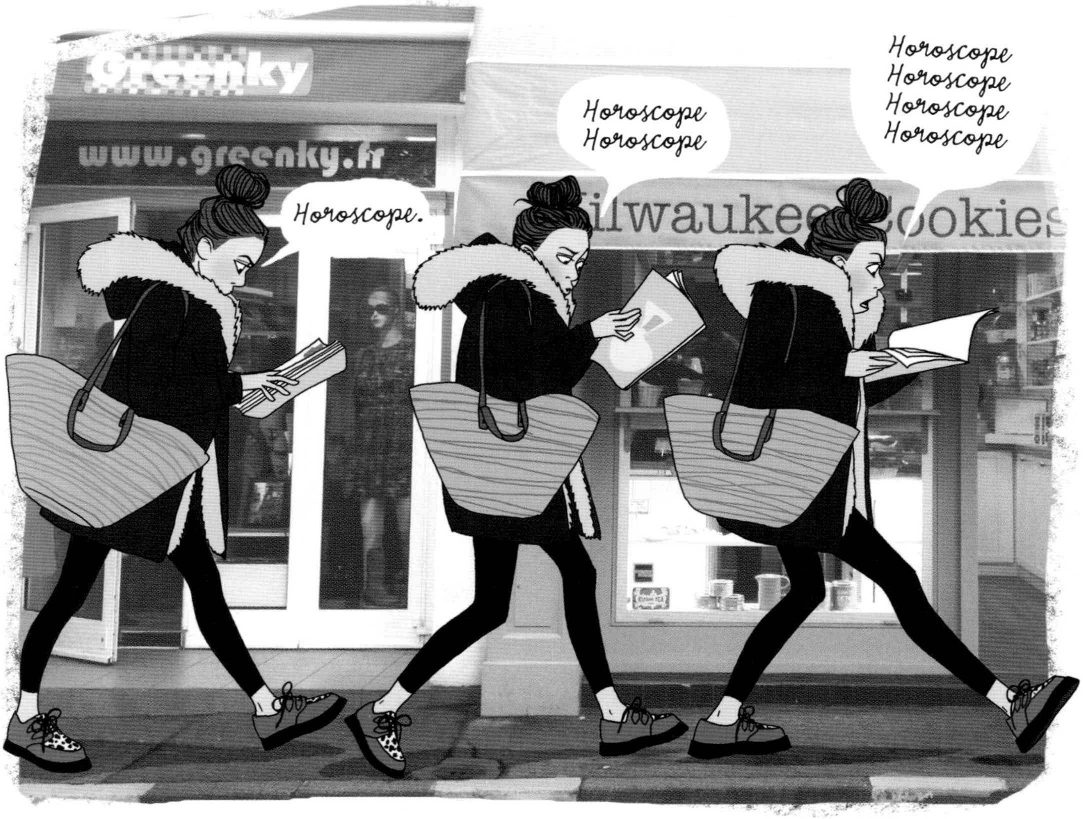
Greenky
www.greenky.fr
Horoscope.
Horoscope
Horoscope
Horoscope
Horoscope
Horoscope
Horoscope

After a breakup, you need psychological support.
That's what horoscopes are for.

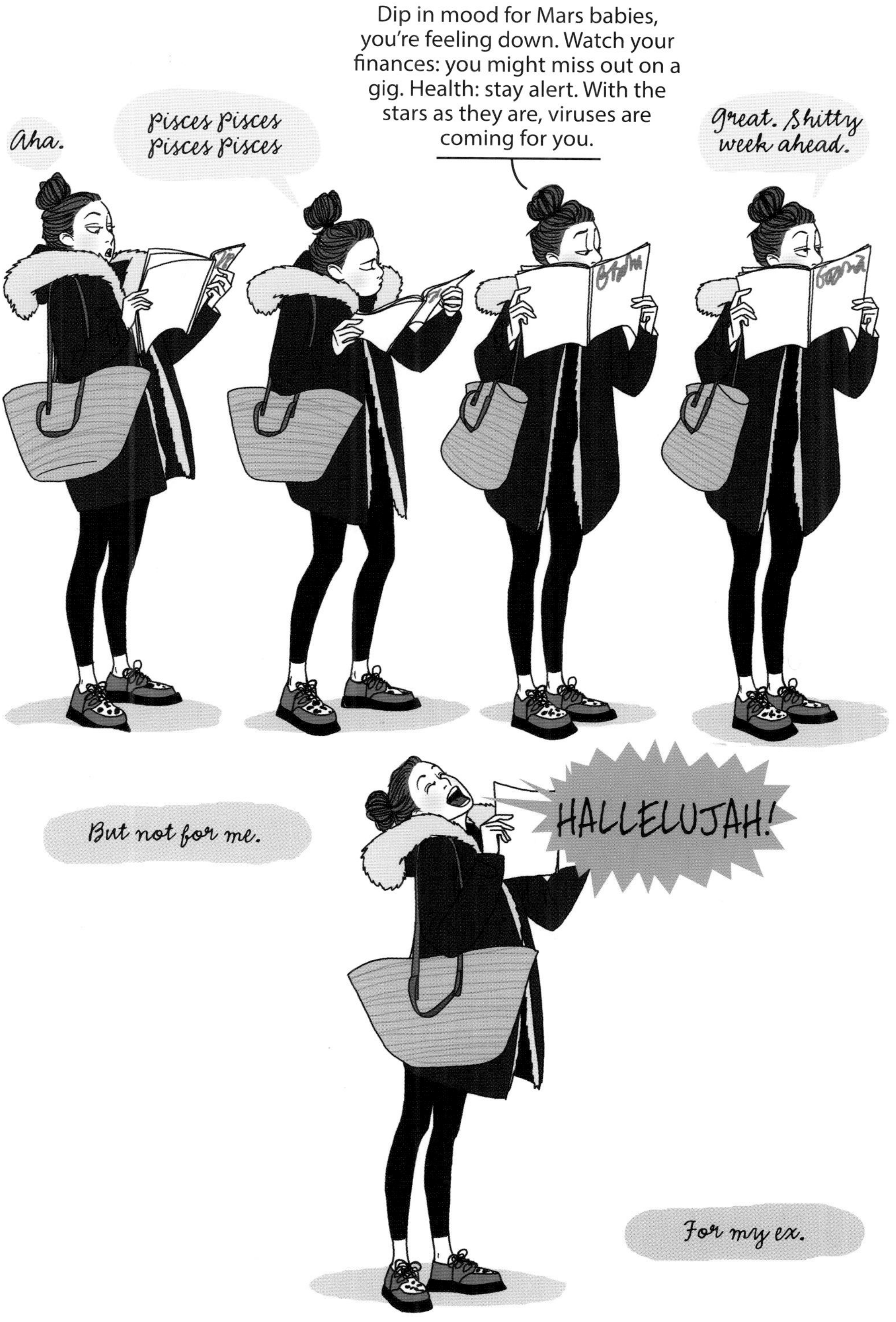
Aha.
Pisces Pisces Pisces Pisces
Dip in mood for Mars babies, you're feeling down. Watch your finances: you might miss out on a gig. Health: stay alert. With the stars as they are, viruses are coming for you.
Great. Shitty week ahead.
But not for me.
HALLELUJAH!
For my ex.

Looking Truth in the Eye

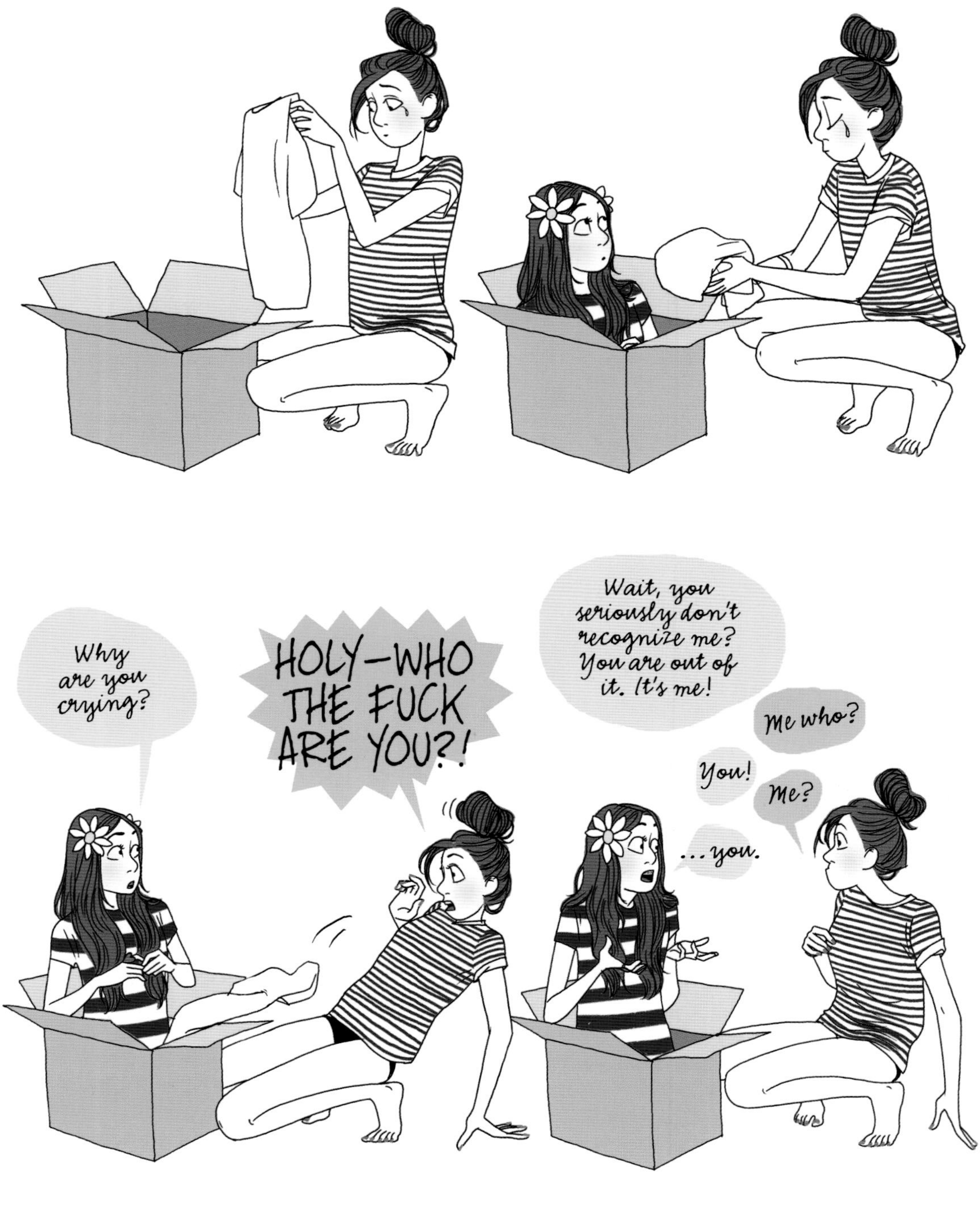

Why are you crying?
HOLY—WHO THE FUCK ARE YOU?!
Wait, you seriously don't recognize me? You are out of it. It's me!
Me who?
You!
Me?
...you.

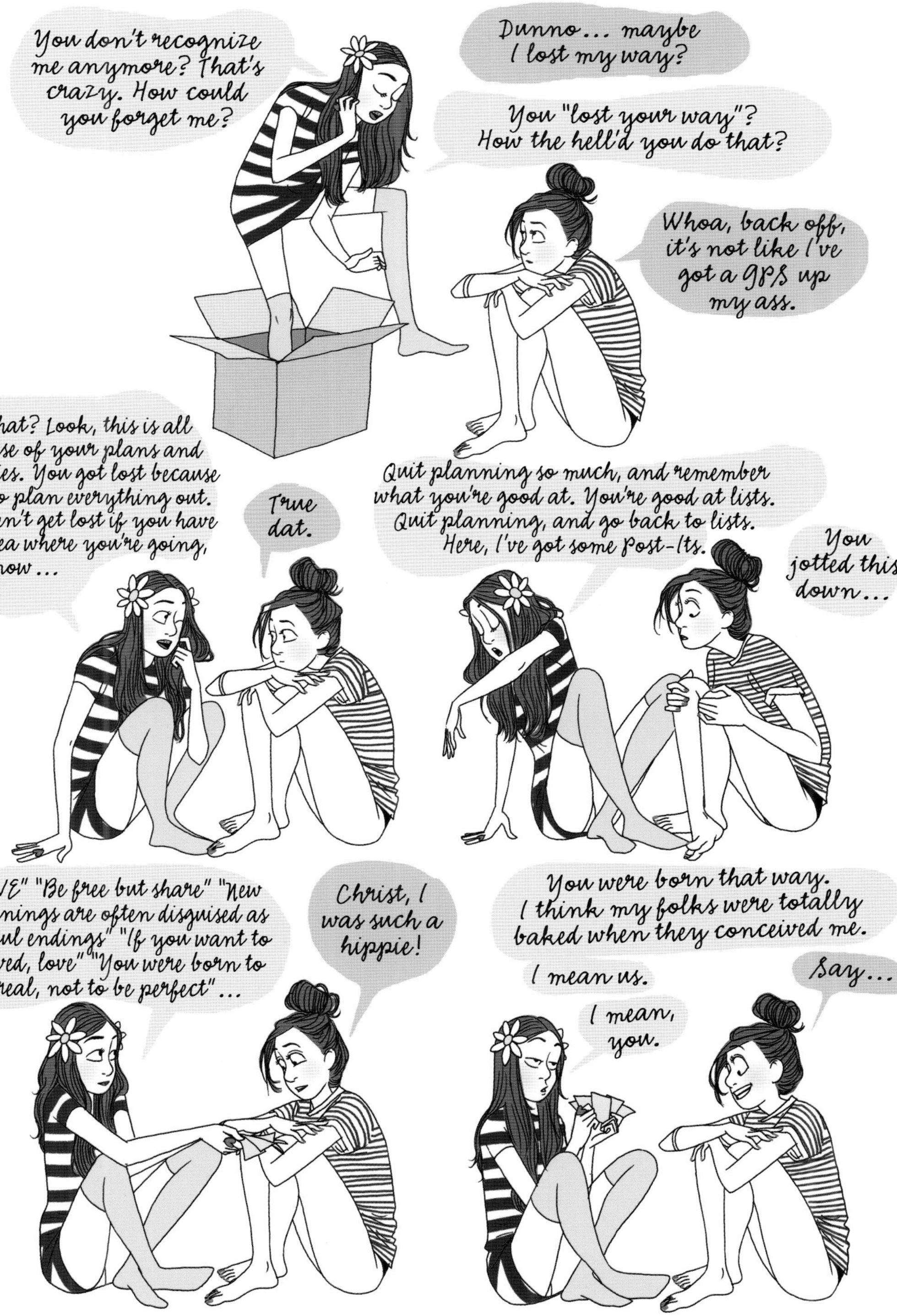
You don't recognize me anymore? That's crazy. How could you forget me?
Dunno... maybe I lost my way?
You "lost your way"? How the hell'd you do that?
Whoa, back off, it's not like I've got a GPS up my ass.
A what? Look, this is all because of your plans and fantasies. You got lost because tried to plan everything out. You can't get lost if you have no idea where you're going, y'know...
True dat.
Quit planning so much, and remember what you're good at. You're good at lists. Quit planning, and go back to lists. Here, I've got some Post-Its.
You jotted this down...
"L<3VE" "Be free but share" "New beginnings are often disguised as painful endings" "If you want to be loved, love" "You were born to be real, not to be perfect"...
Christ, I was such a hippie!
You were born that way. I think my folks were totally baked when they conceived me.
I mean us.
I mean, you.
Say...

Can I have those? They'd be good reminders to help me move on.
NOOOO. Pull your head out of your ass and reconnect with yourself. I'm not giving you a cheat sheet! WORK FOR IT!!
Keep being such a bitch and I foresee a glorious future for you, featuring divorce, stretch marks, and a hemorrhoid flare-up in the middle of a December 6 Jill Scott concert, sweetie...

"When the night has come, and the land is daaaark…"

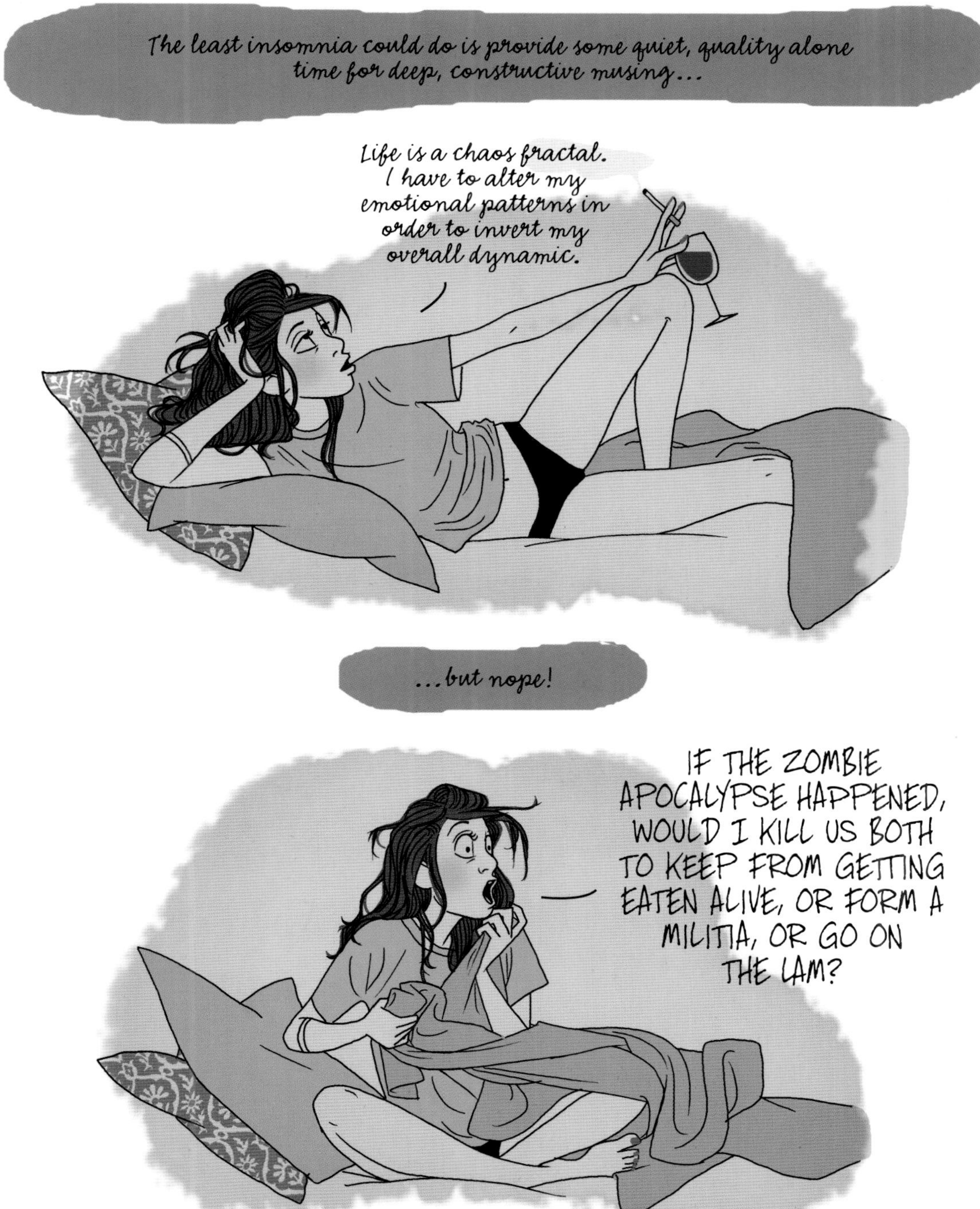

The least insomnia could do is provide some quiet, quality alone time for deep, constructive musing...
Life is a chaos fractal. I have to alter my emotional patterns in order to invert my overall dynamic.
...but nope!
IF THE ZOMBIE APOCALYPSE HAPPENED, WOULD I KILL US BOTH TO KEEP FROM GETTING EATEN ALIVE, OR FORM A MILITIA, OR GO ON THE LAM?

Revelations

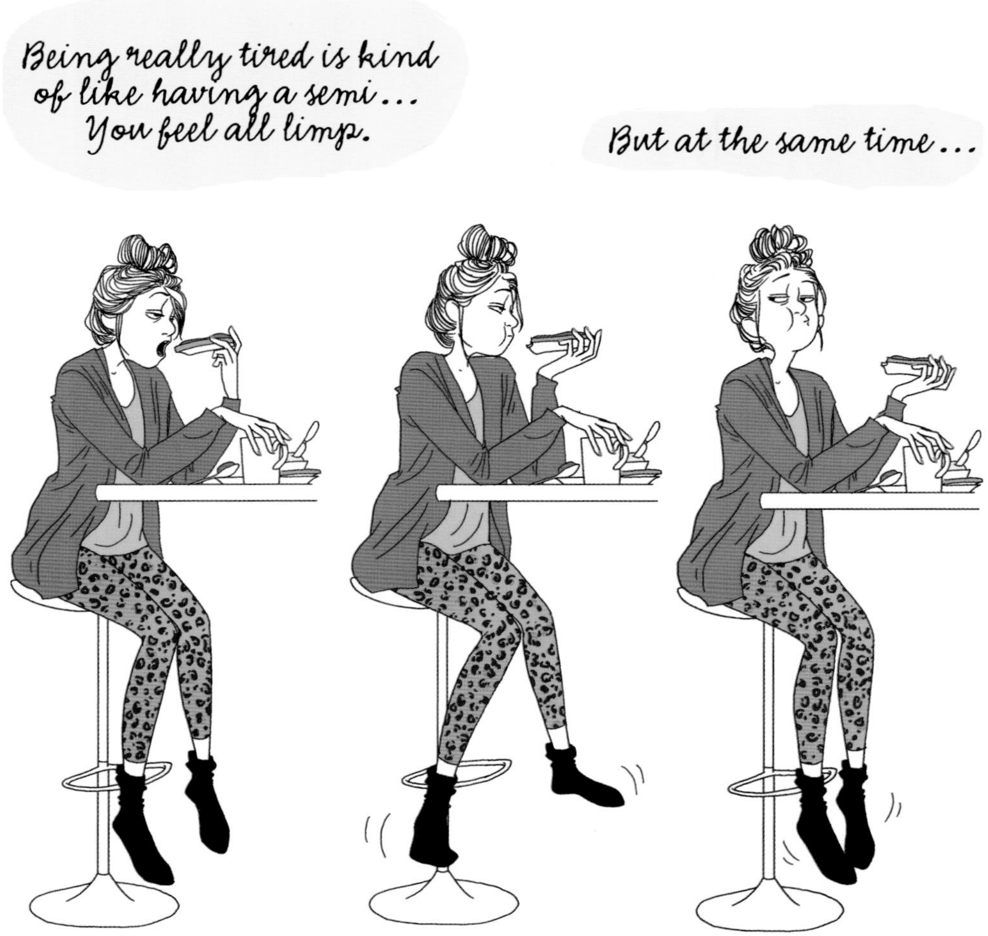
Being really tired is kind of like having a semi... You feel all limp.
But at the same time...

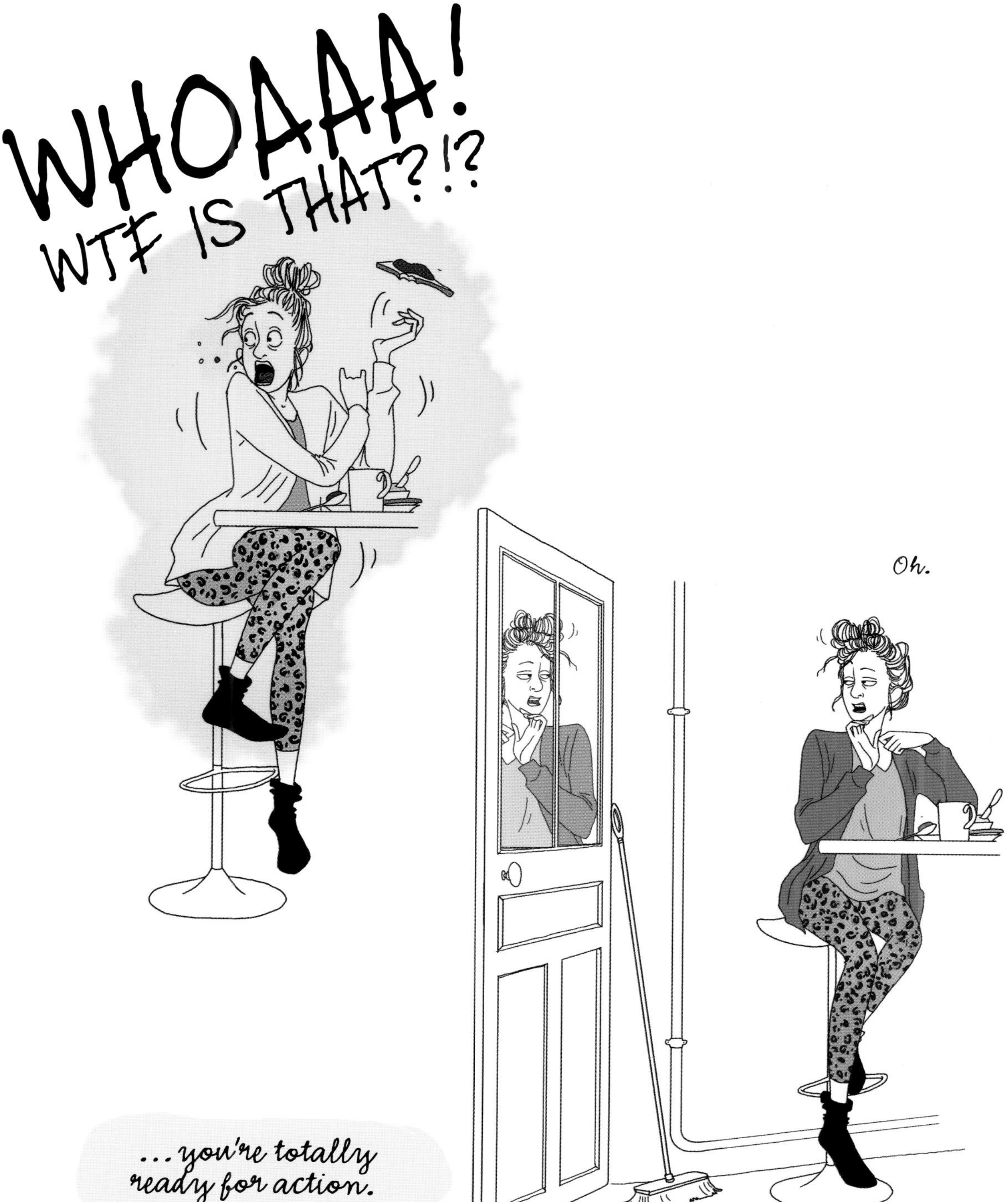
WHOAAA!
WTF IS THAT?!?
Oh.
...you're totally ready for action.

A Brand New Me

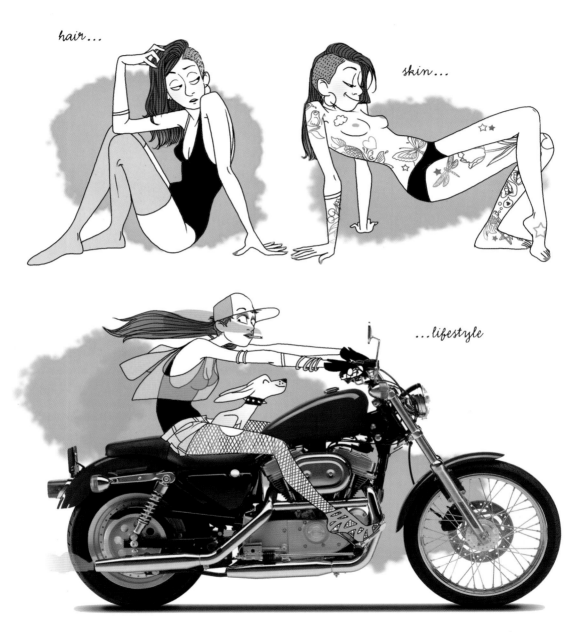

hair...

skin...

...lifestyle

Right when you're about to turn a new leaf, you always get this visceral urge to radically change certain details of your life...

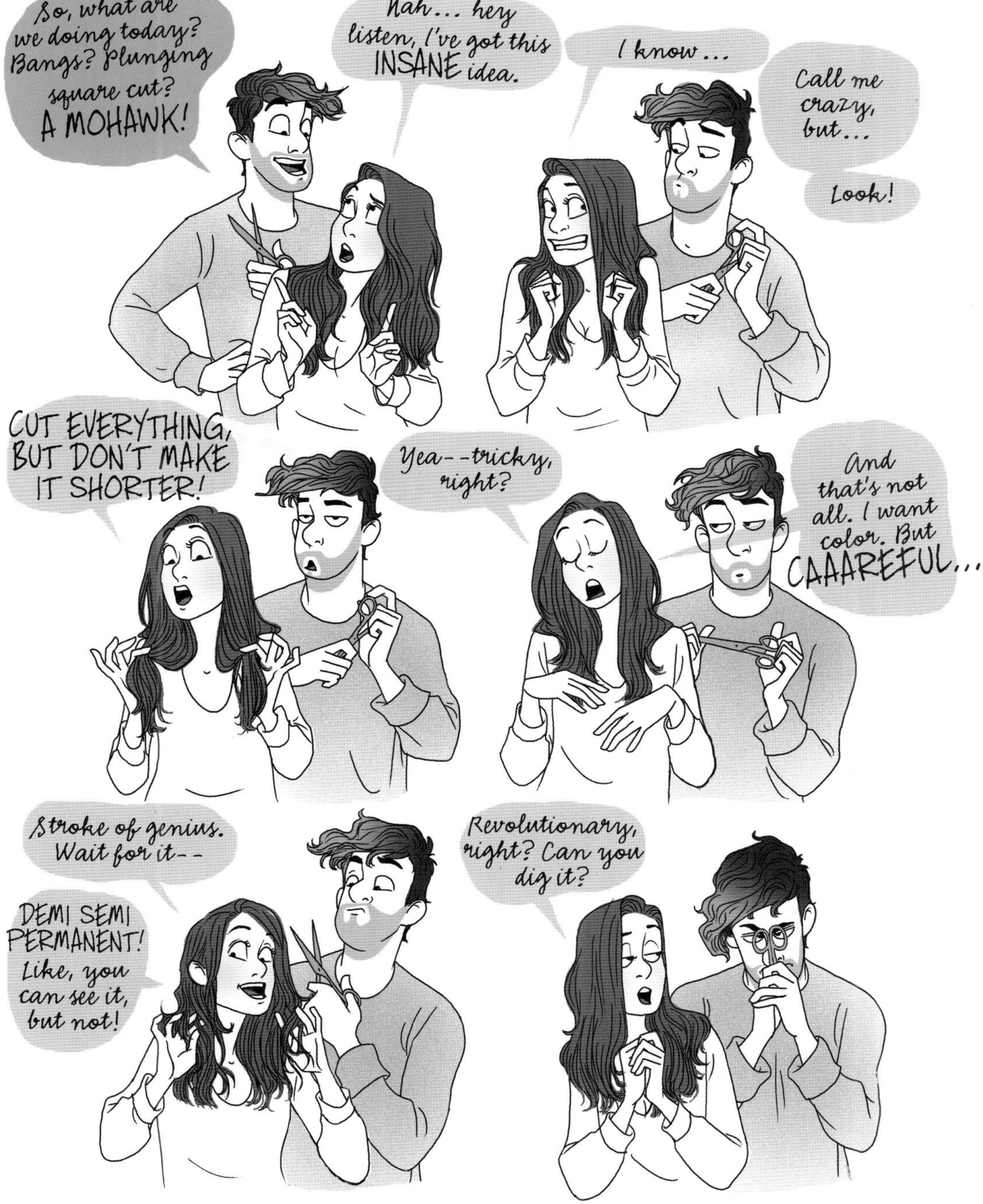
So, what are we doing today? Bangs? Plunging square cut? A MOHAWK!
Nah... hey listen, I've got this INSANE idea.
I know...
Call me crazy, but...
Look!
CUT EVERYTHING, BUT DON'T MAKE IT SHORTER!
Yea--tricky, right?
And that's not all. I want color. But CAAAREFUL...
Stroke of genius. Wait for it--
DEMI SEMI PERMANENT! Like, you can see it, but not!
Revolutionary, right? Can you dig it?

Alas, the world is clearly not always ready for these kinds of radical upheavals.

Awkward

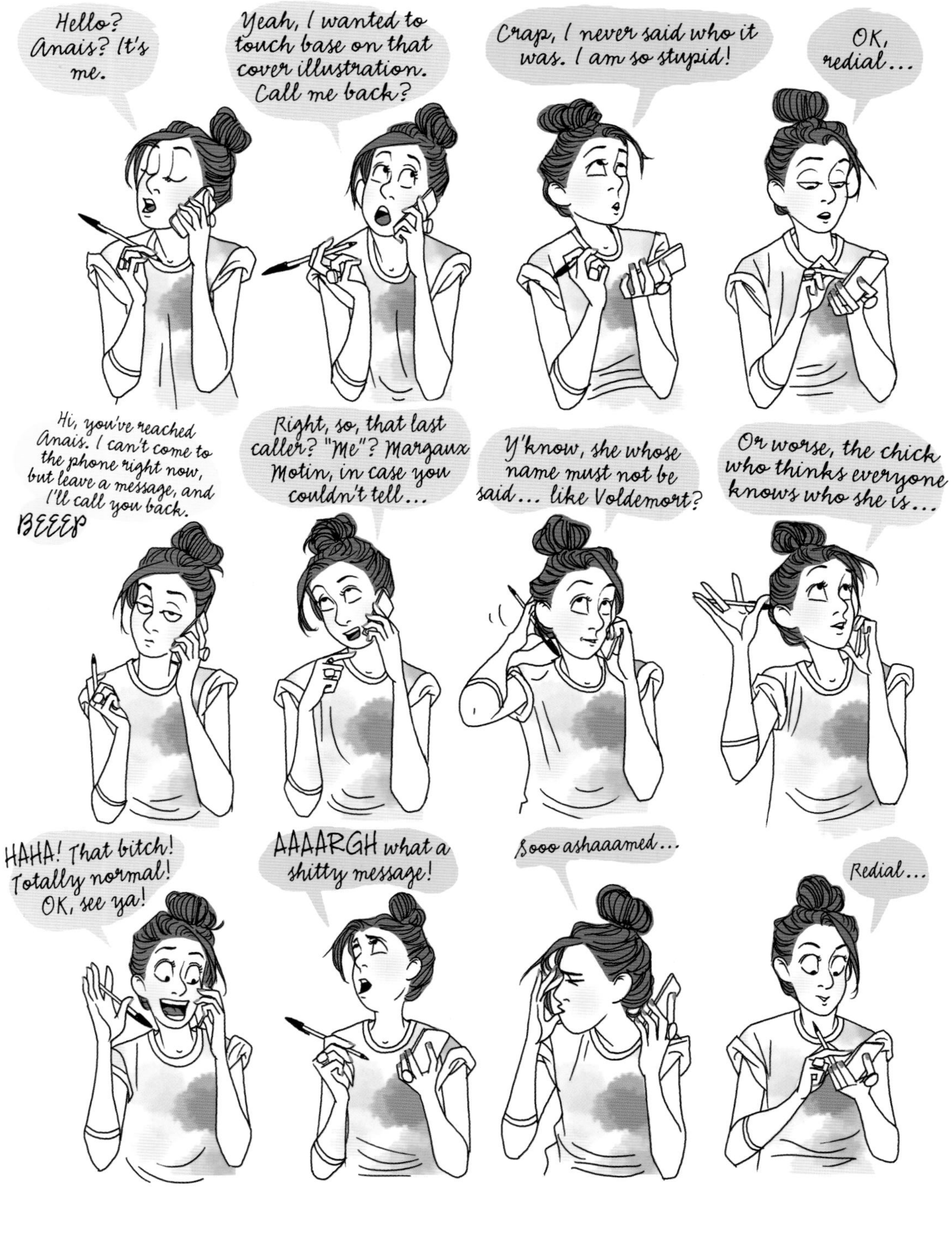
Hello? Anais? It's me.
Yeah, I wanted to touch base on that cover illustration. Call me back?
Crap, I never said who it was. I am so stupid!
OK, redial...
Hi, you've reached Anais. I can't come to the phone right now, but leave a message, and I'll call you back.
BEEEP
Right, so, that last caller? "Me"? Margaux Motin, in case you couldn't tell...
Y'know, she whose name must not be said... like Voldemort?
Or worse, the chick who thinks everyone knows who she is...
HAHA! That bitch! Totally normal! OK, see ya!
AAAARGH what a shitty message!
Sooo ashaaamed...
Redial...

Anais? Hey, it's me again. Look, forget those messages, I totally lost it.

Wasn't thinking straight, on my period...

MY PERIOD?! WHAT THE—?!

Anyway, call me back, OK? MWAH MWAH!!

"MWAH MWAH"? She's a client!

Functionally stunted. Kill me now...

LEAVE ME ALONE! IT'S OVER! I'M NEVER SETTING FOOT OUTSIDE AGAIN! THERE ARE TOO MANY PEOPLE OUT THERE. I NEVER EVER WANT TO SPEAK TO ANOTHER HUMAN BEING AS LONG AS I LIVE. TAKE A GOOD LOOK: FI-NI-TO! VOW OF SILENCE TILL I DIE! OK? OK???

AND SOME PEOPLE WANT ME TO GET A TWITTER ACCOUNT. BUNCH OF PSYCHOS.

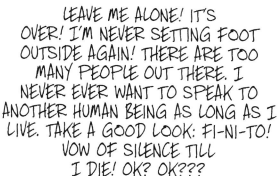

It's a Sabotage

I'm 34 years old. I'm doing a lot of self-work so I can be at peace with myself, start loving myself. I'm taking big strides psychologically, lots of affirmations--pretty heavy, complicated stuff, hand-in-hand with really difficult sessions. I'm giving it my all: time, energy, commitment...

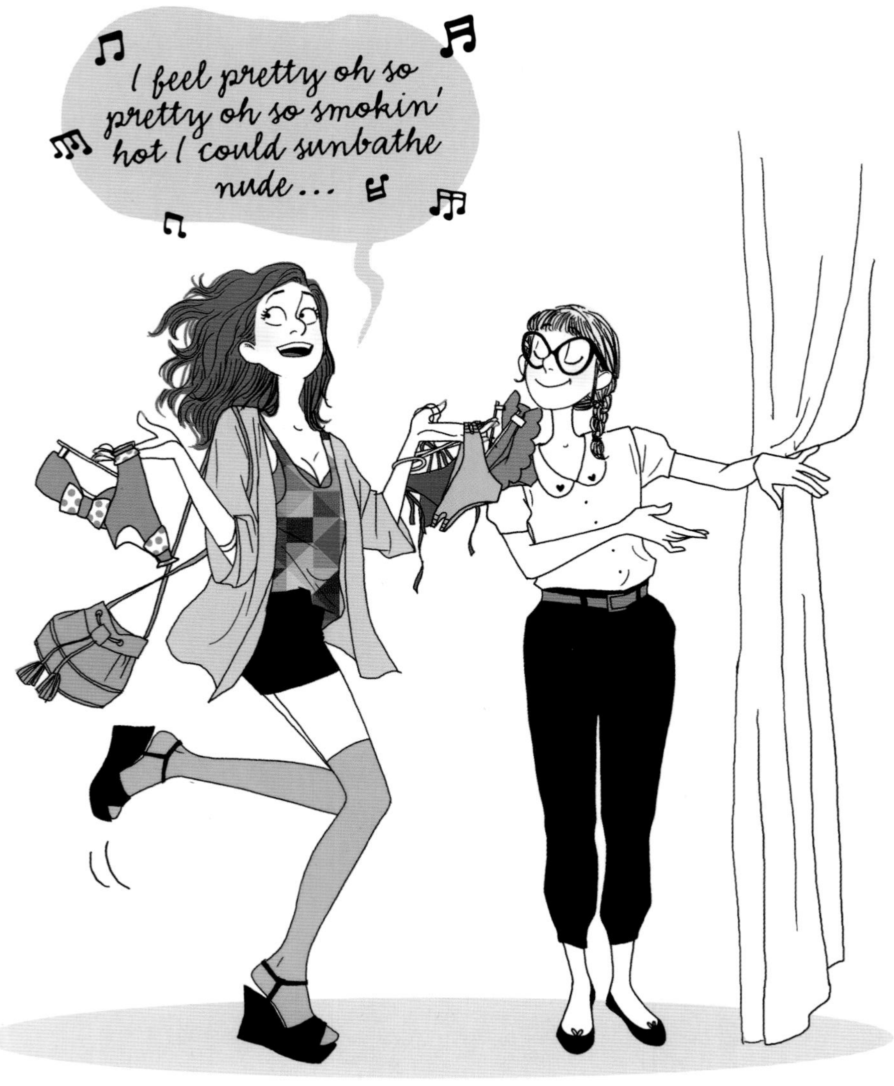
I feel pretty oh so pretty oh so smokin' hot I could sunbathe nude...

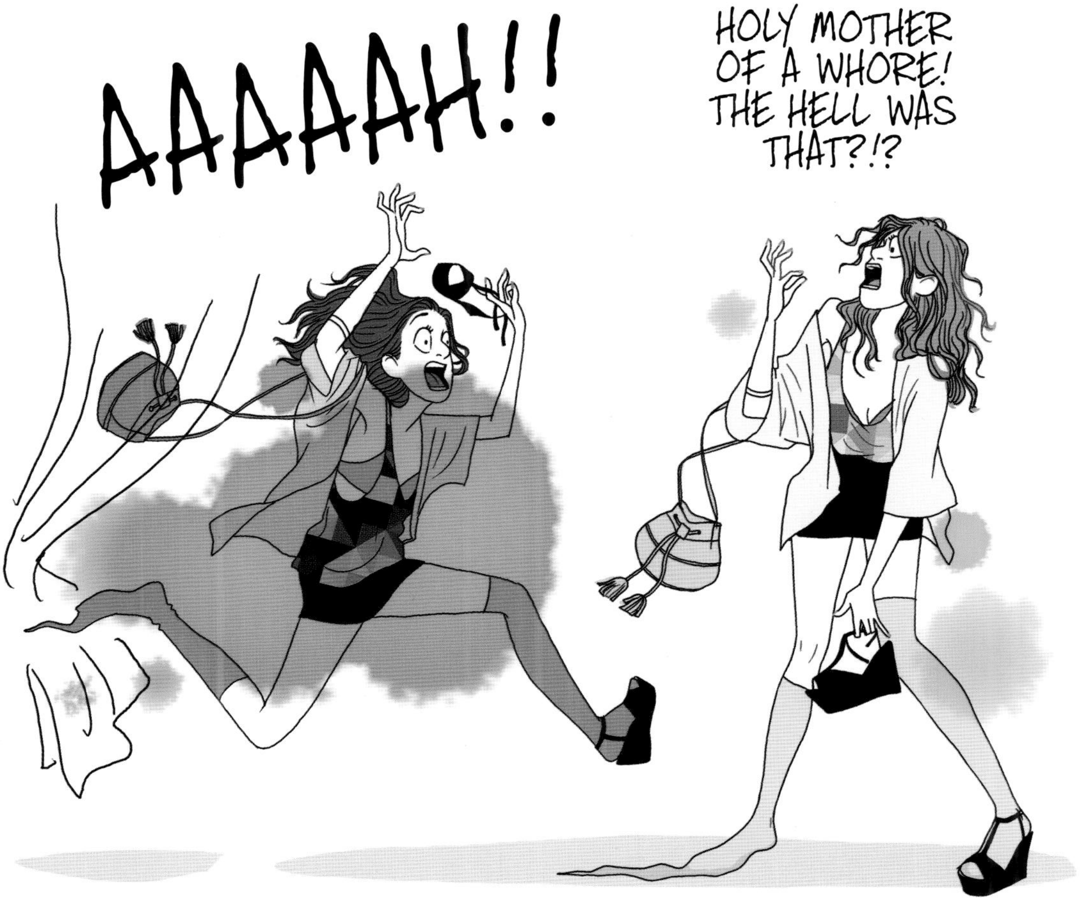
AAAAAH!!
HOLY MOTHER OF A WHORE! THE HELL WAS THAT?!?

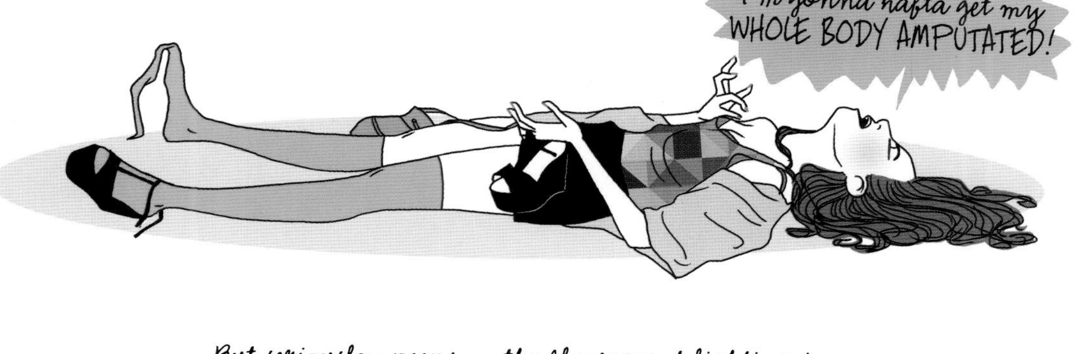
I'm gonna hafta get my WHOLE BODY AMPUTATED!

But seriously, peeps... the fluorescent lighting in changing rooms has got to go. Now.

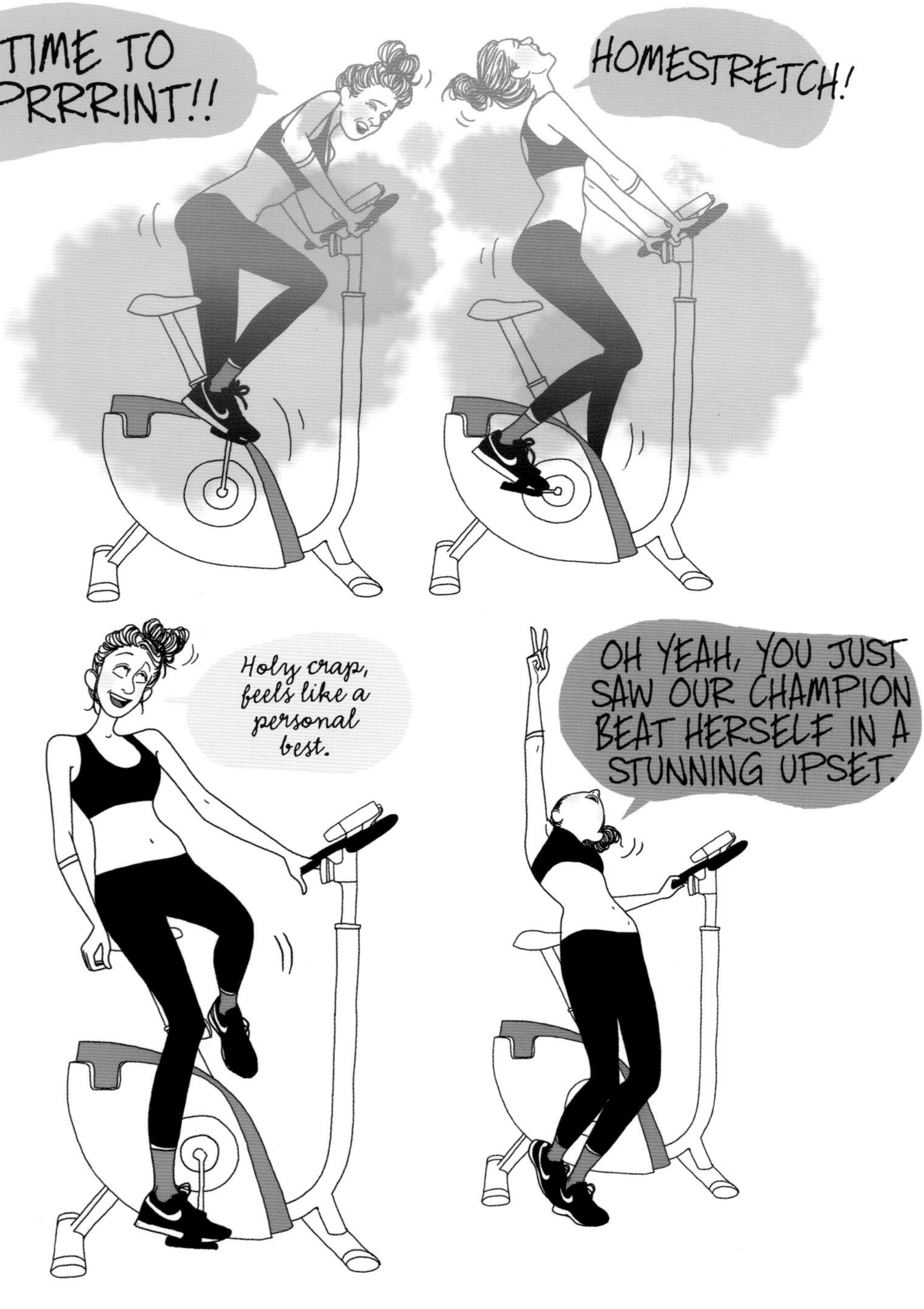
TIME TO SPRRRINT!!
HOMESTRETCH!
Holy crap, feels like a personal best.
OH YEAH, YOU JUST SAW OUR CHAMPION BEAT HERSELF IN A STUNNING UPSET.

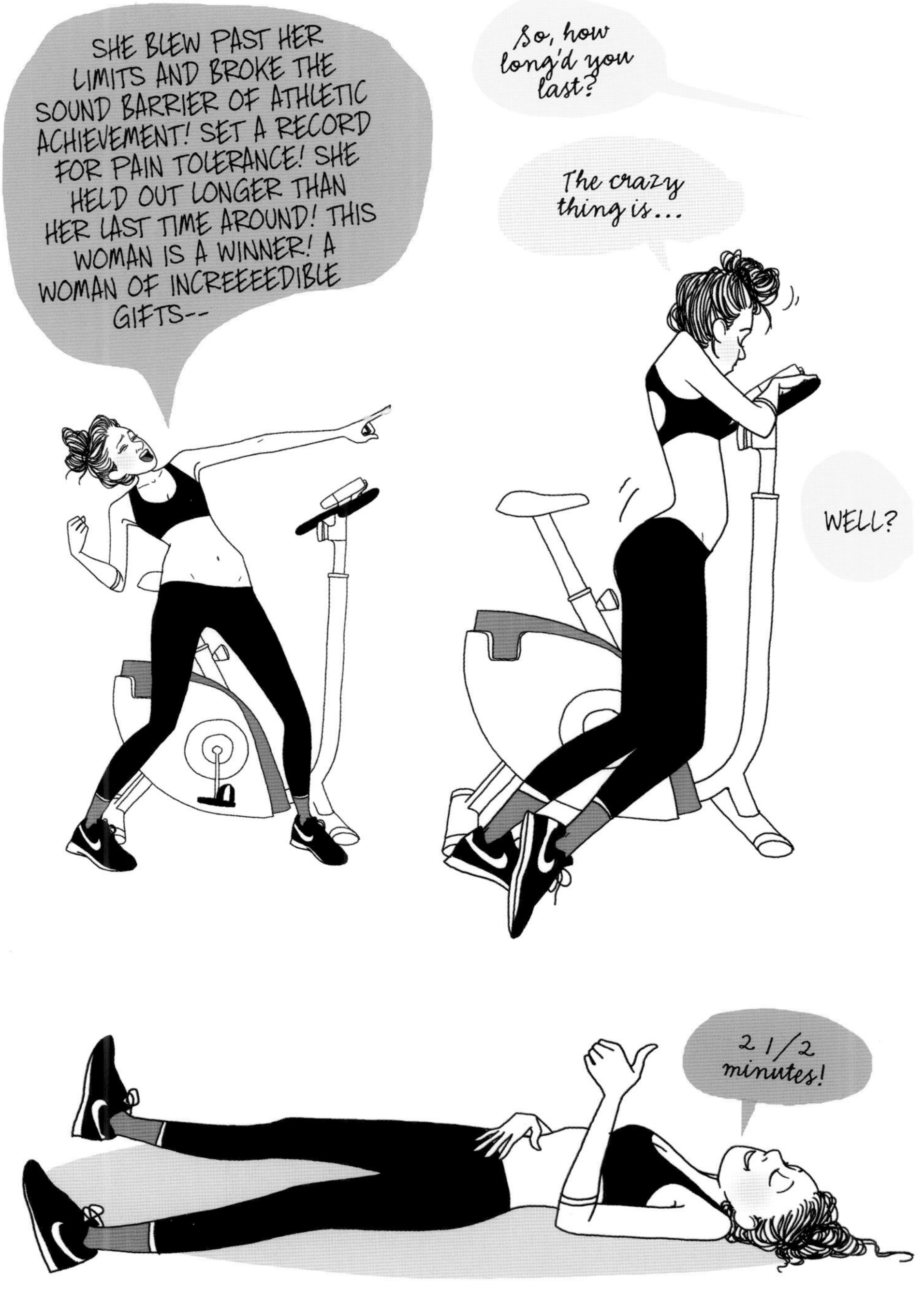
SHE BLEW PAST HER LIMITS AND BROKE THE SOUND BARRIER OF ATHLETIC ACHIEVEMENT! SET A RECORD FOR PAIN TOLERANCE! SHE HELD OUT LONGER THAN HER LAST TIME AROUND! THIS WOMAN IS A WINNER! A WOMAN OF INCREEEEDIBLE GIFTS--
So, how long'd you last?
The crazy thing is...
WELL?
2 1/2 minutes!

THERE ARE NO SMALL VICTORIES...

Good Resolutions

You need new goals when you're putting your life back together.

Careful, though: swimming twice a week, putting on wrinkle cream every night, brushing your teeth for 3 minutes--all too easy.

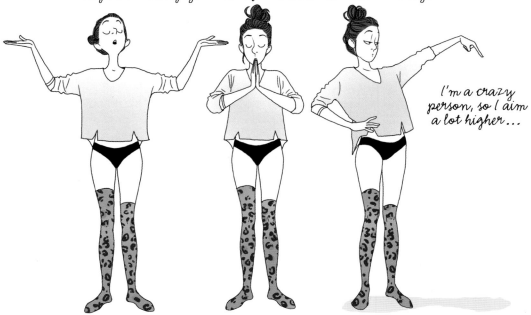

I'm a crazy person, so I aim a lot higher...

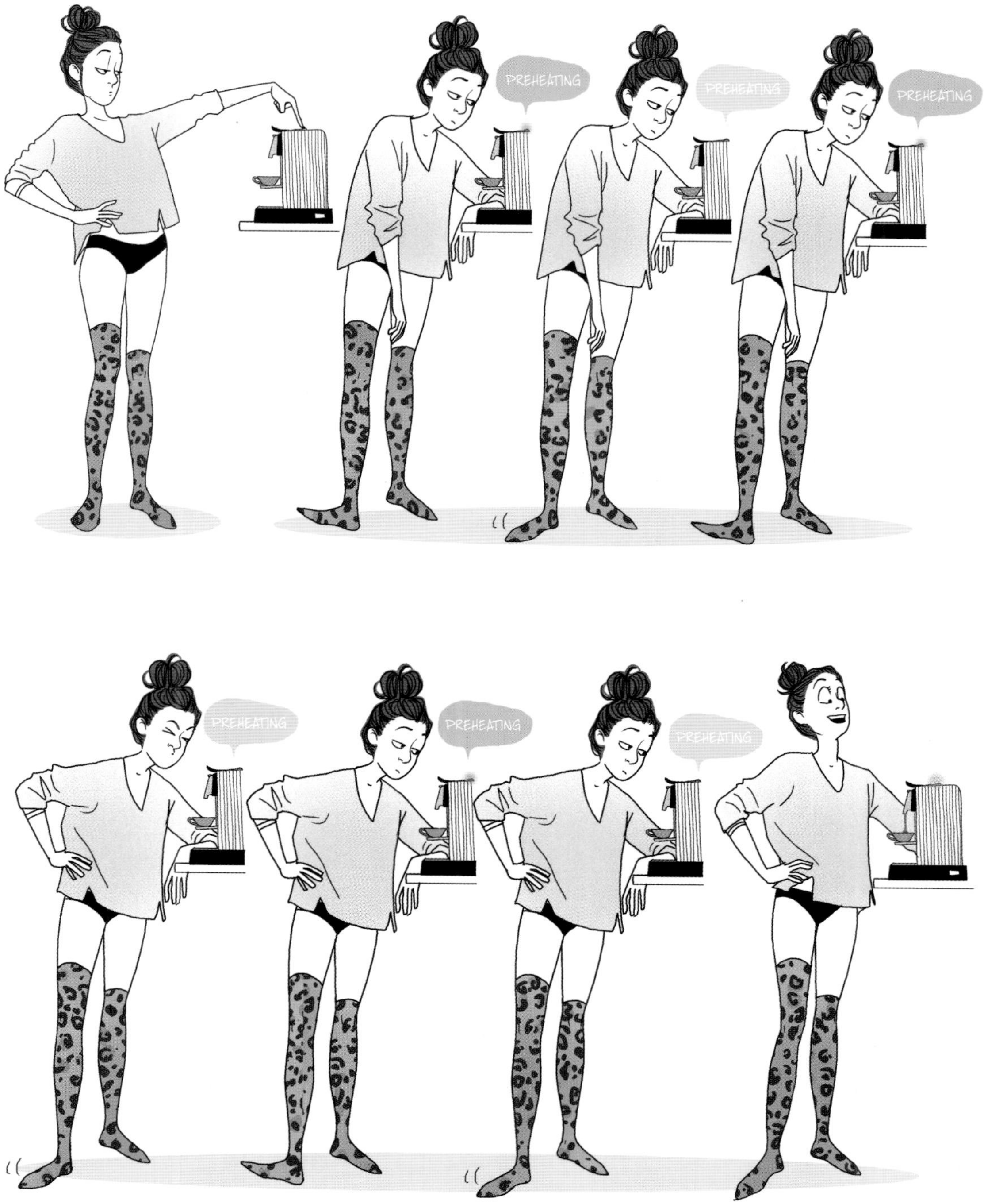
PREHEATING
PREHEATING
PREHEATING
PREHEATING
PREHEATING
PREHEATING

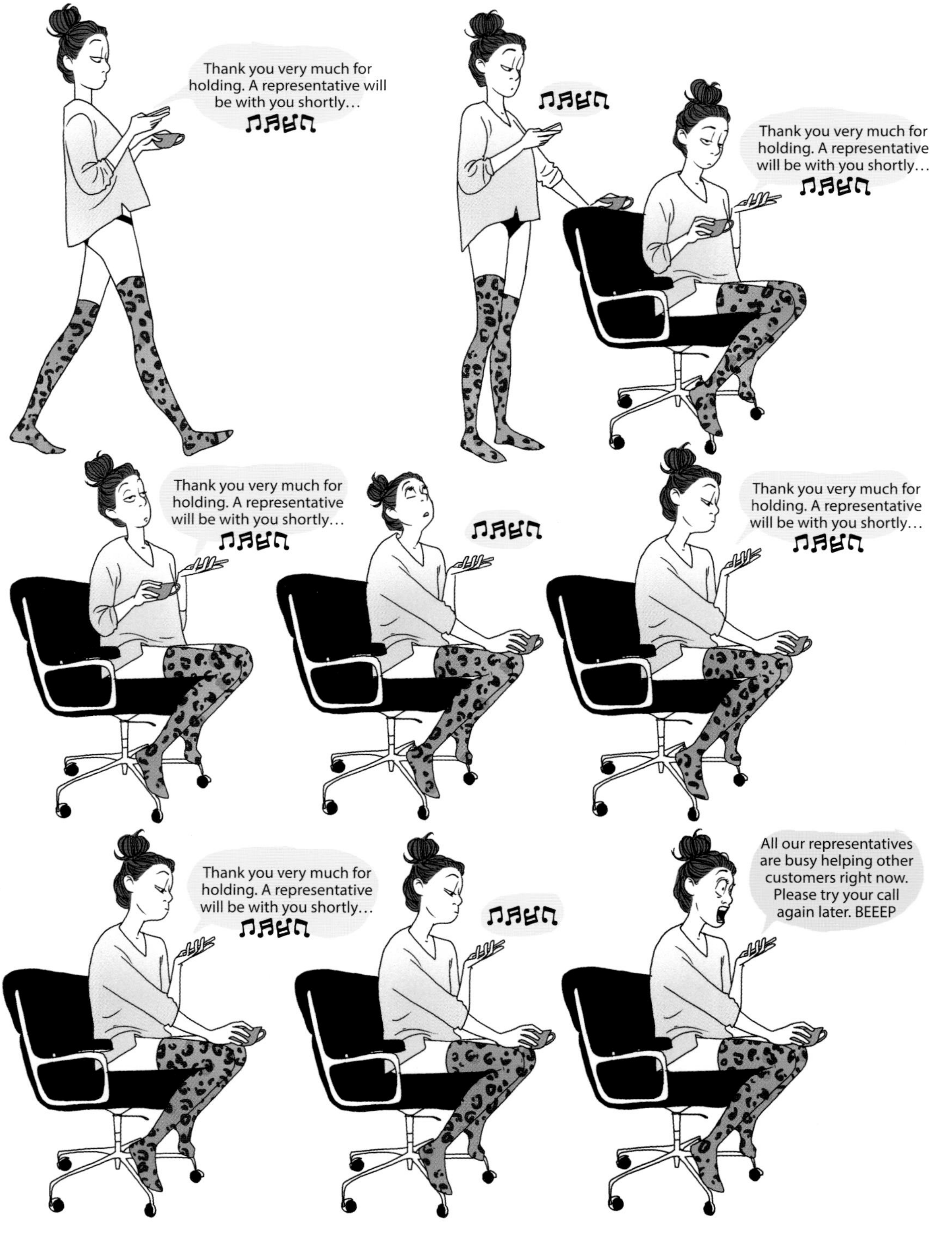
Thank you very much for holding. A representative will be with you shortly...
Thank you very much for holding. A representative will be with you shortly...
Thank you very much for holding. A representative will be with you shortly...
Thank you very much for holding. A representative will be with you shortly...
Thank you very much for holding. A representative will be with you shortly...
All our representatives are busy helping other customers right now. Please try your call again later. BEEEP

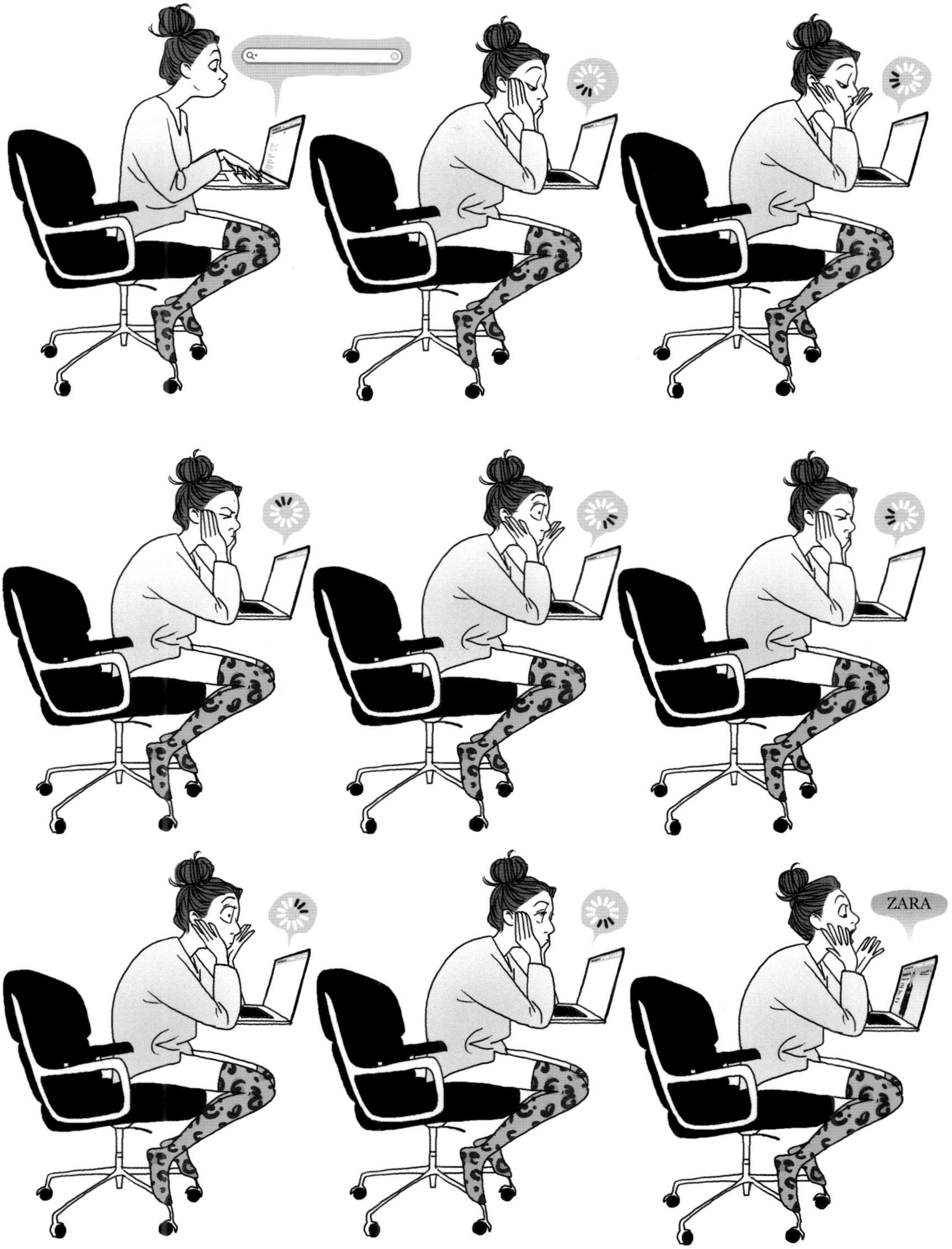
ZARA

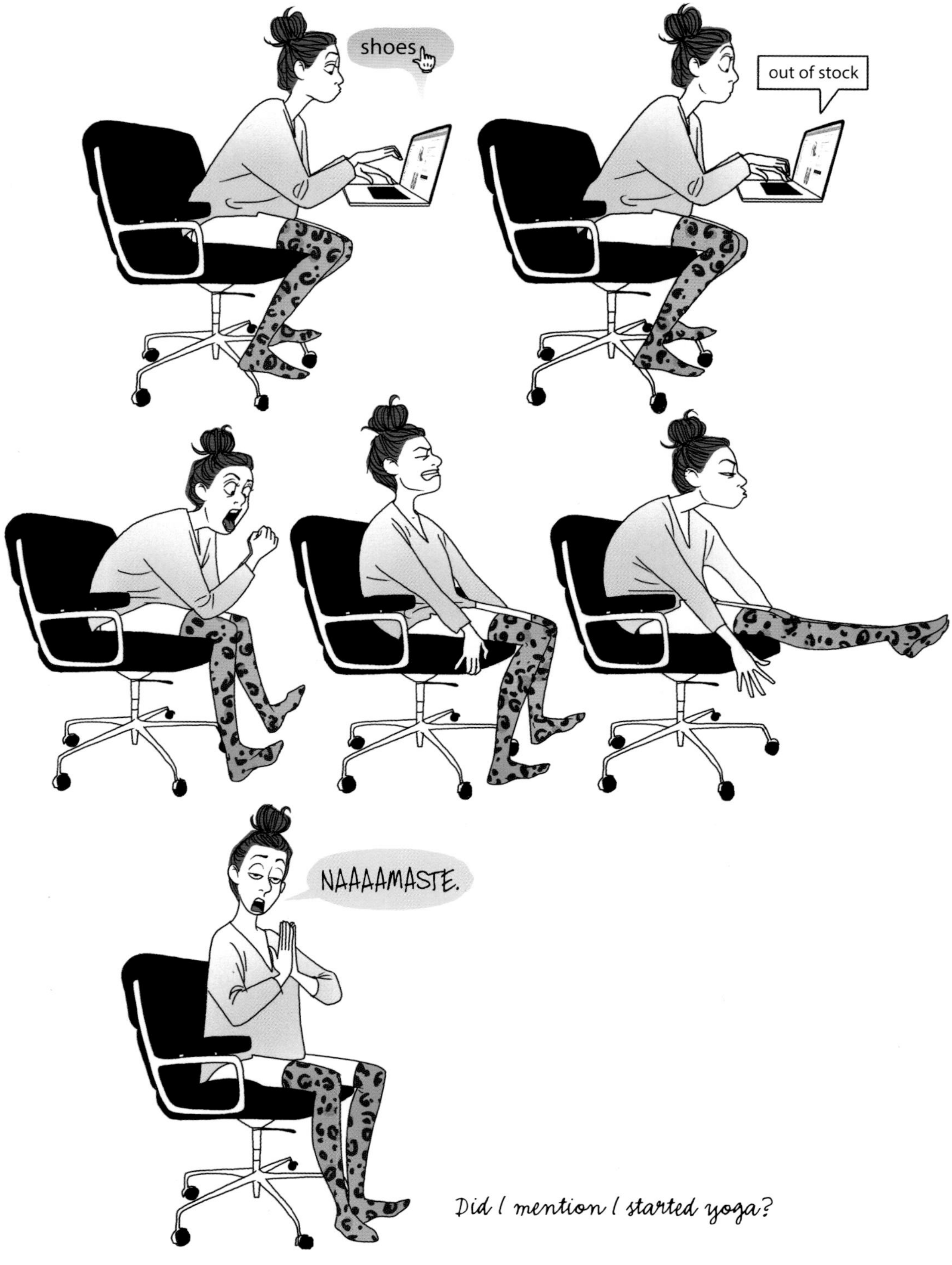
shoes
out of stock
NAAAAMASTE.
Did I mention I started yoga?

"Golden"

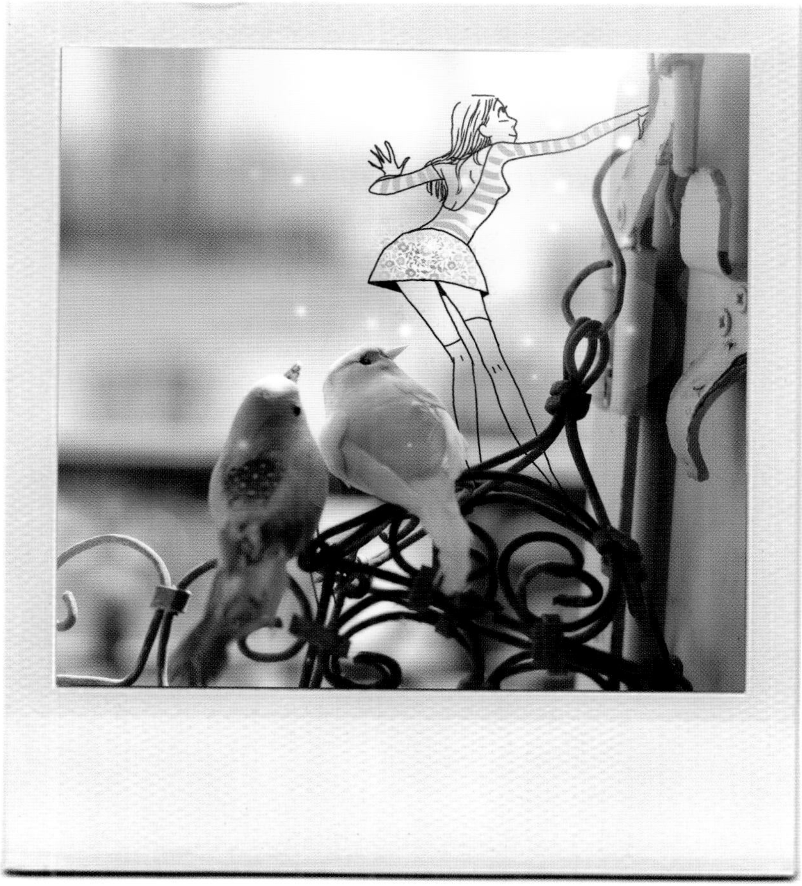

I'm taking my freedom, pulling it off the shelf,
Putting it on my chain, wear it around my neck,
I'm taking my freedom, putting it in my car
Wherever I choose to go, it will take me far
I'm livin' my life like it's golden...

Jill Scott

*Jill Scott "Golden"

To become a Zen master, you have to start simple

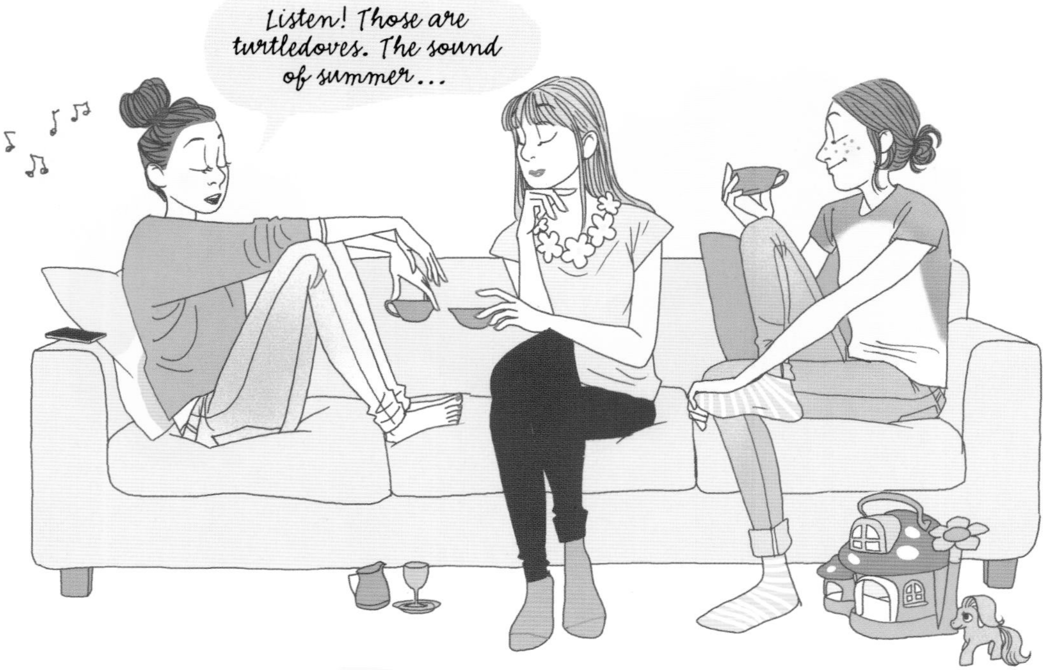
Listen! Those are turtledoves. The sound of summer...

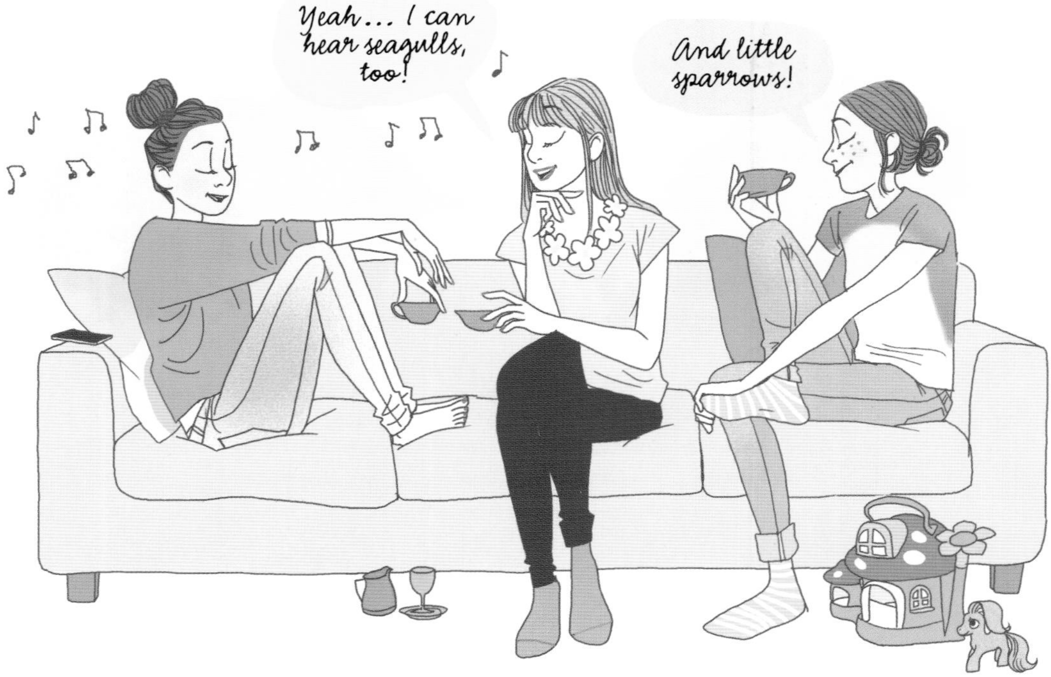
Yeah... I can hear seagulls, too!
And little sparrows!

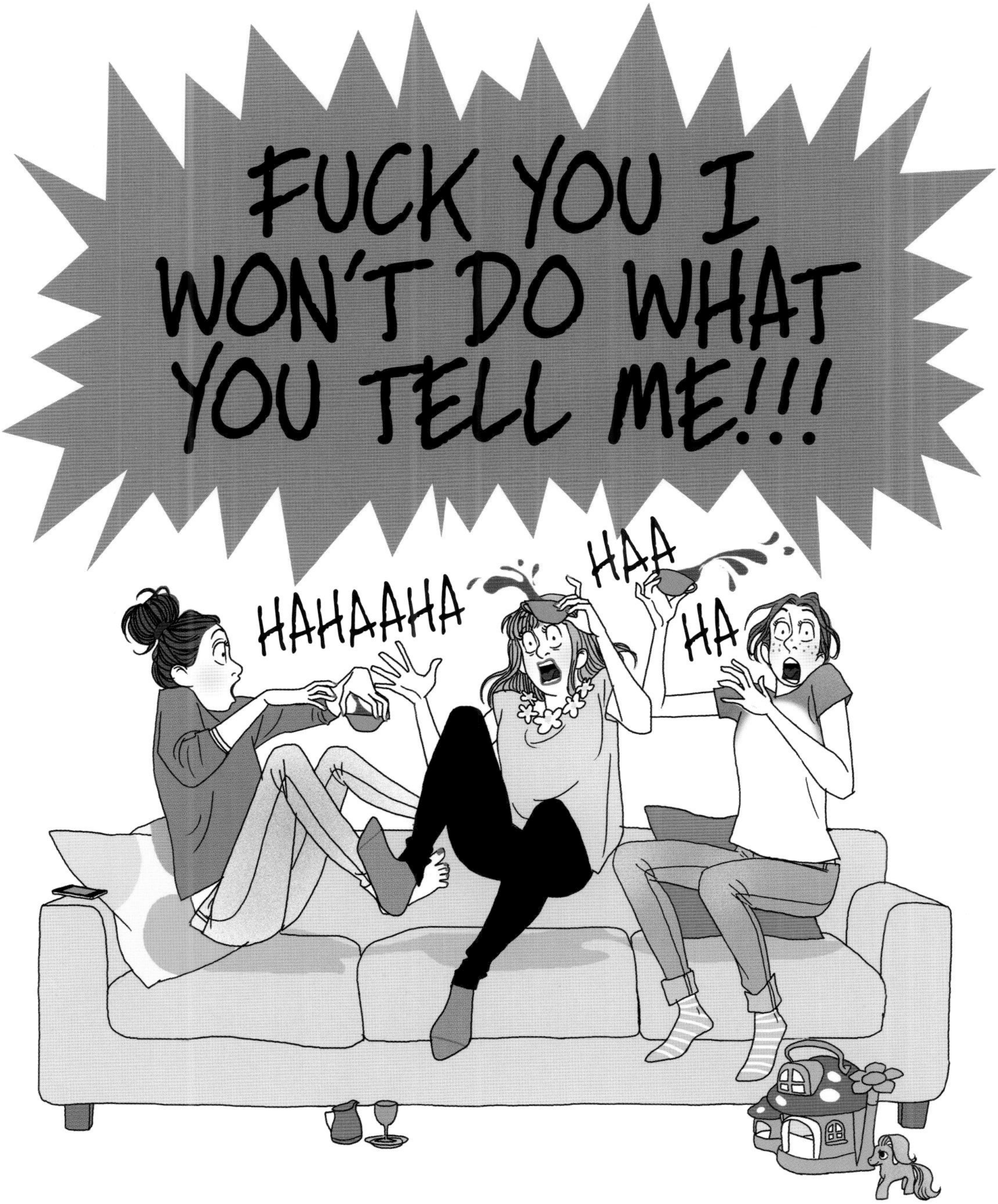
FUCK YOU I WON'T DO WHAT YOU TELL ME!!!
HAHAAHA
HAA
HA

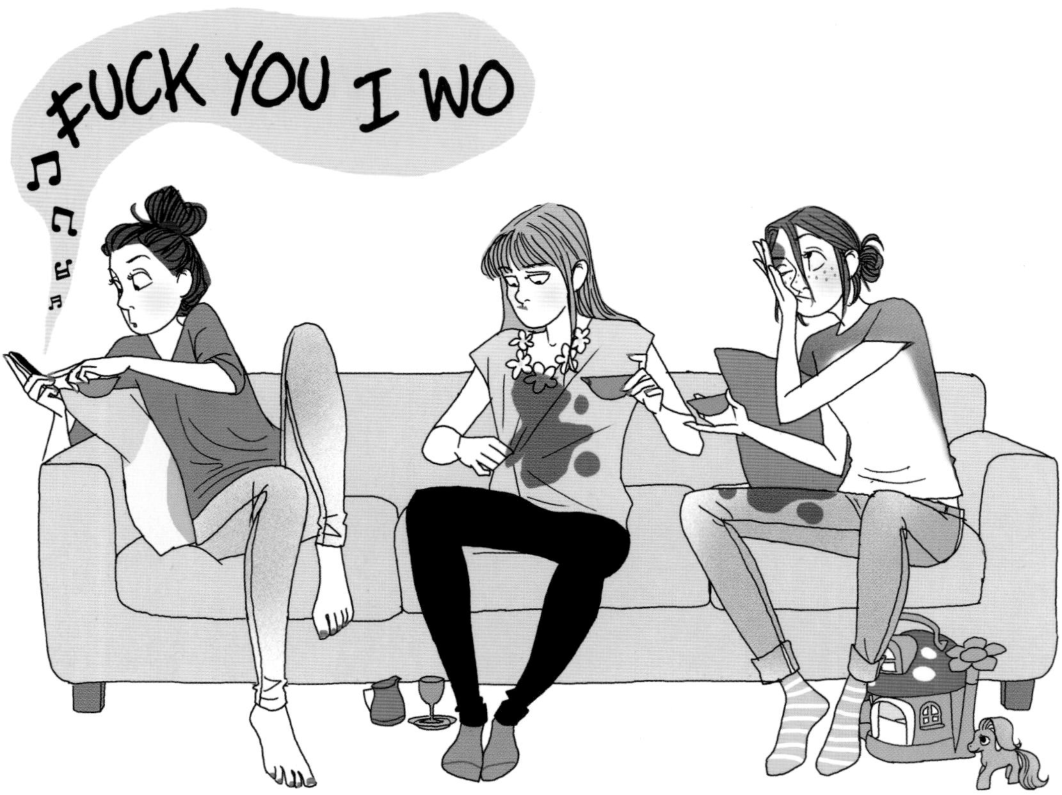
FUCK YOU I WO

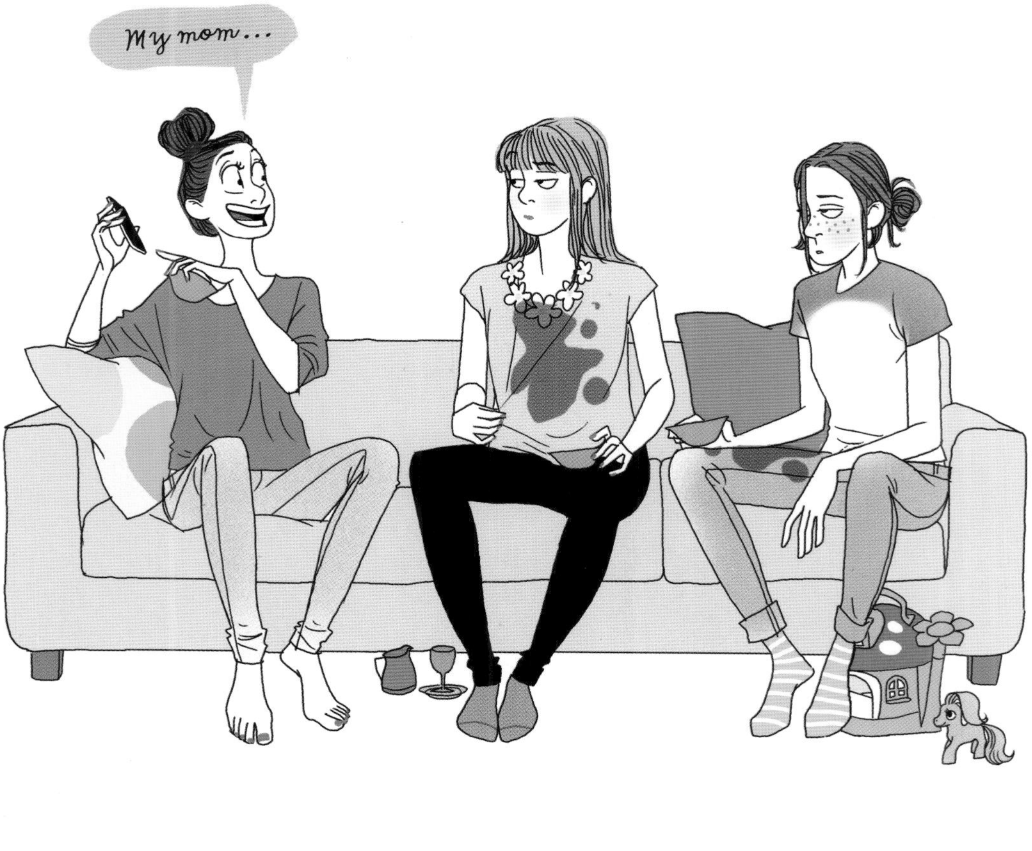
My mom...

CHANGING MY RINGTONES SEEMS LIKE A GOOD PLACE TO START.

The Lord Moves in Mysterious Ways

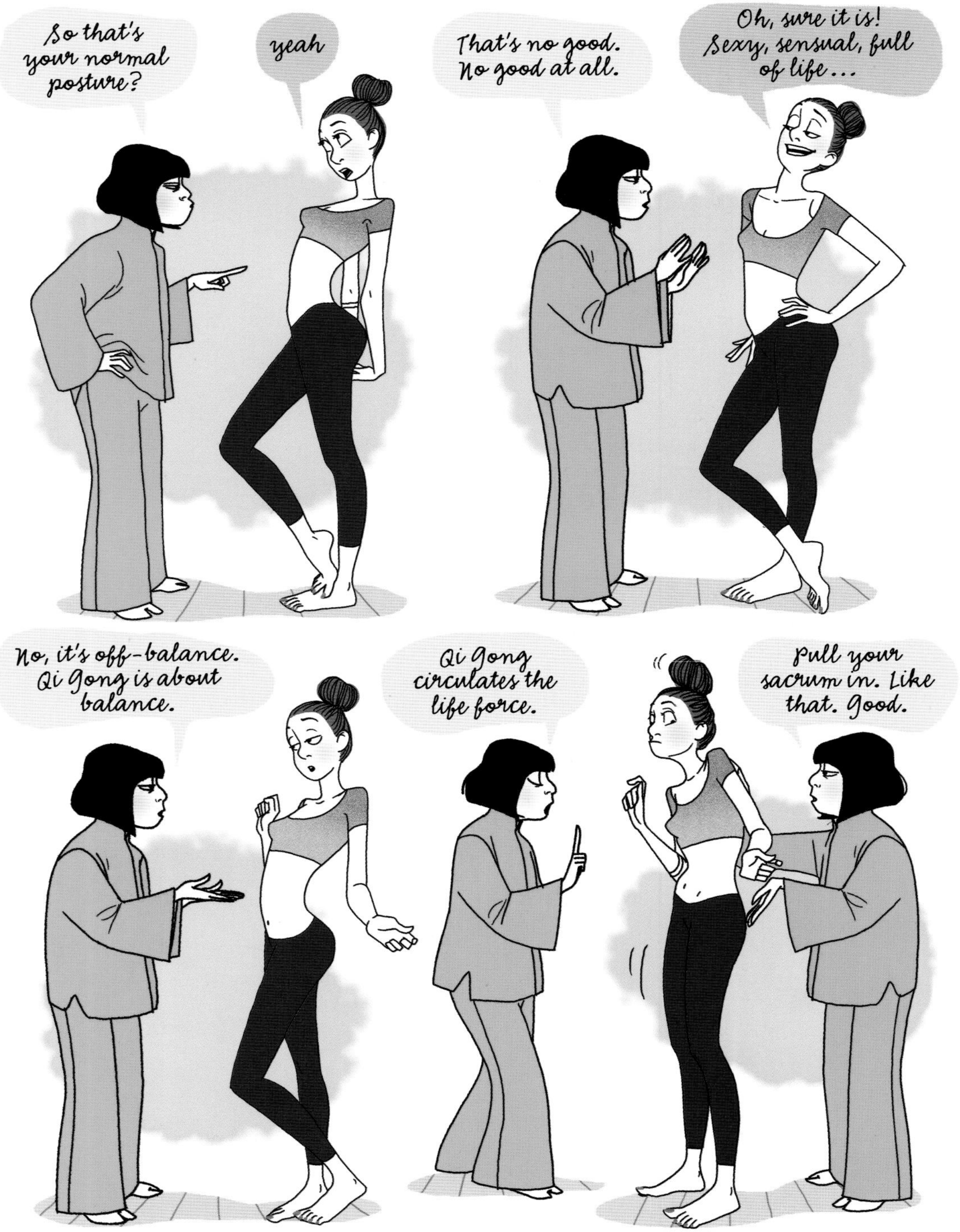
So that's your normal posture?
yeah
That's no good. No good at all.
Oh, sure it is! Sexy, sensual, full of life...
No, it's off-balance. Qi Gong is about balance.
Qi Gong circulates the life force.
Pull your sacrum in. Like that. Good.

Soft knees. Soft knees important for circulation of Qi and feeling grounded. You are reed. Bend, not break.
Arms out to side for breathing, like fish. Lungs free now, very very good.
Good posture = serenity.

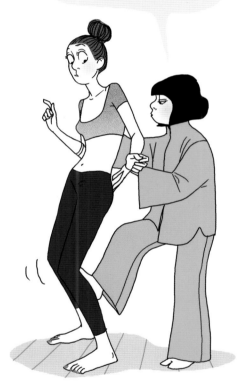

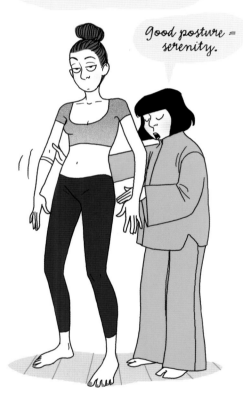

OK, things are circulating, great, I'm breathing through my armpits, sound mind in a sound body...
But seriously, this serene posture stuff, now that I look like a short-haired otter, I've got a question...

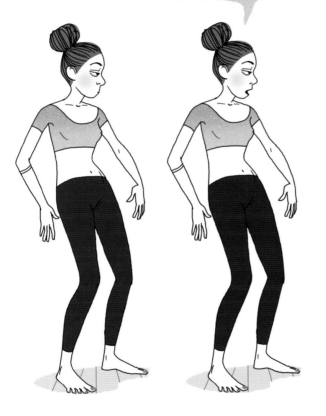

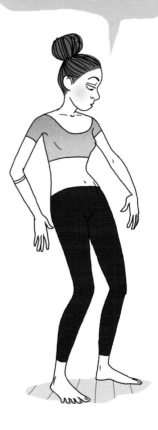

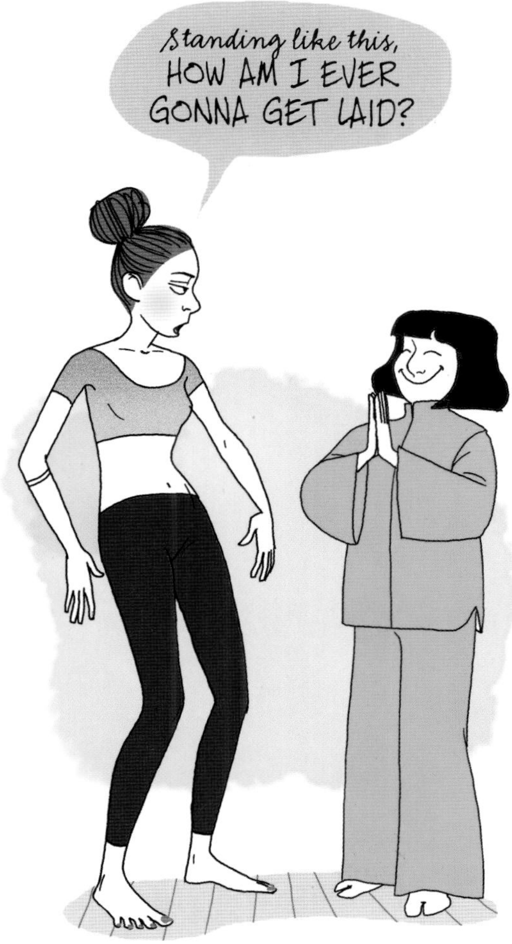
Standing like this, HOW AM I EVER GONNA GET LAID?

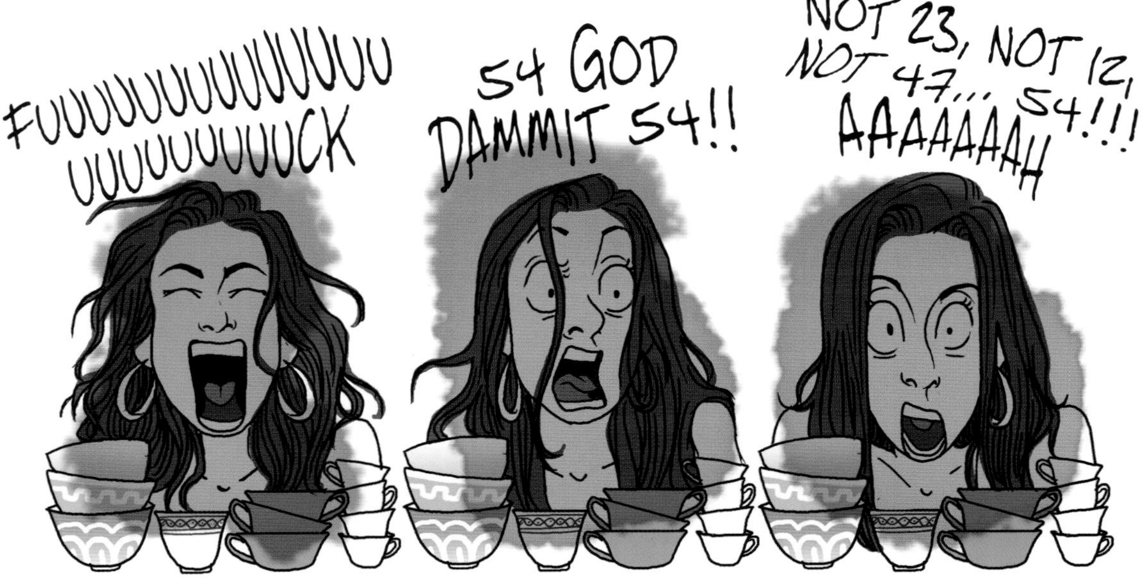
FUUUUUUUUUUUUUUU UUUUUUUUUCK
54 GOD DAMMIT 54!!
NOT 23, NOT 12, NOT 47,... 54!!!
AAAAAAAH

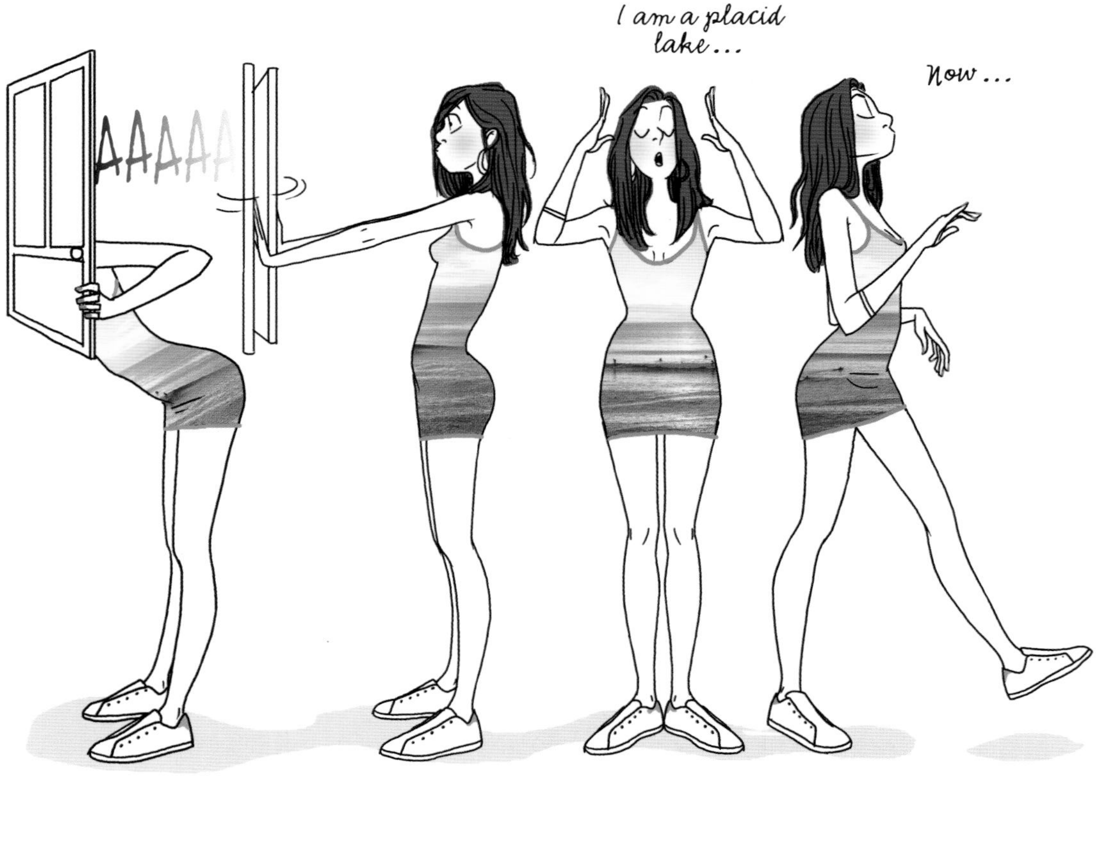
AAAAA
I am a placid lake...
Now...

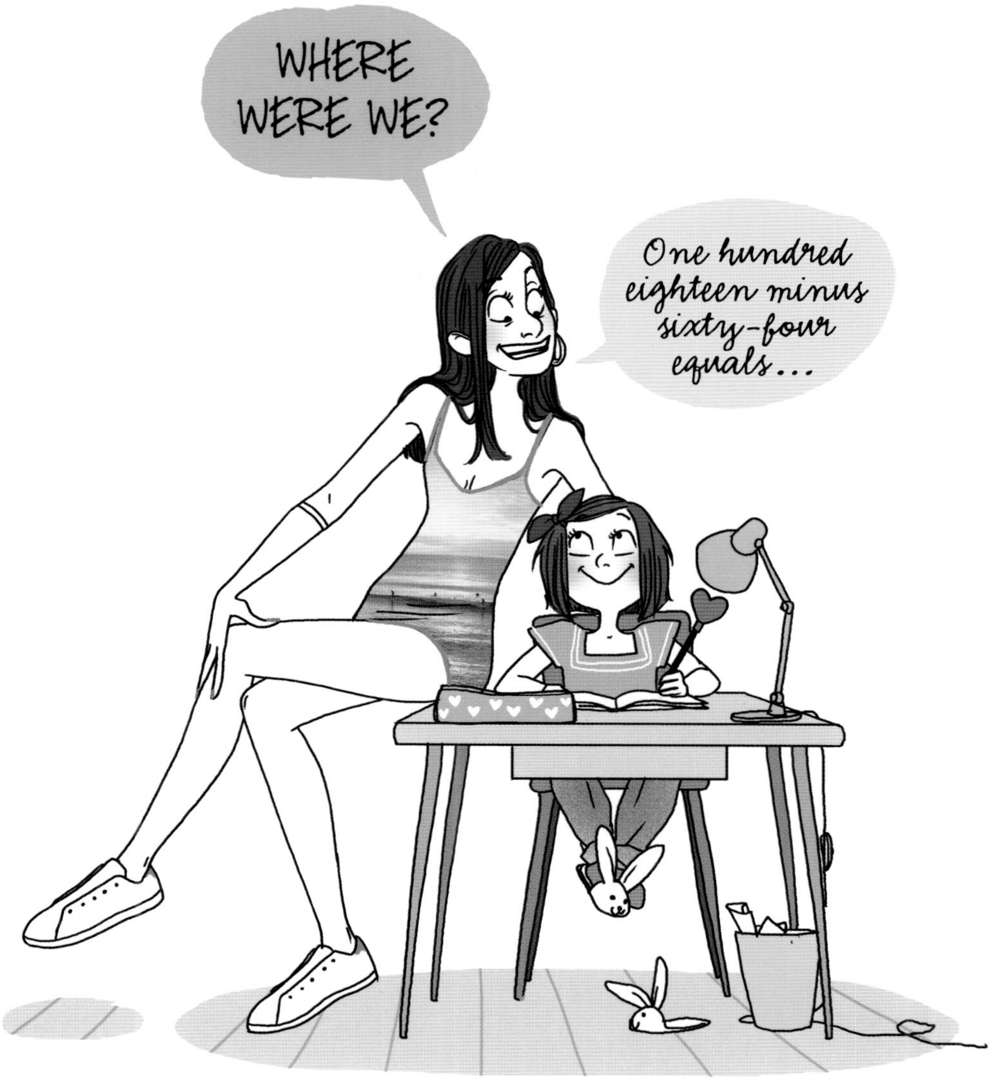
WHERE WERE WE?
One hundred eighteen minus sixty-four equals...

HOMEWORK: A TIME OF CLOSENESS, LOVE, AND SERENITY.

"The World is Blue as an Orange"
[Poem by Paul Éluard]

Qi Gong will help you repair the imbalance of body and mind. Your body will tell you what you need to change.
I feel a weight on my chest. I often have trouble breathing.
Your solar plexus is locked shut. Your shoulder blades are the key to opening it and freeing your emotions. This is the flowering city. A vast garden for you...

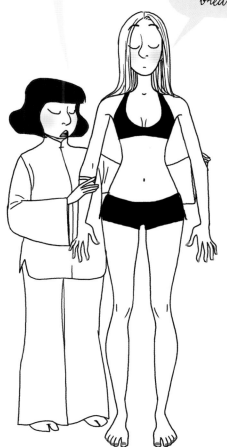

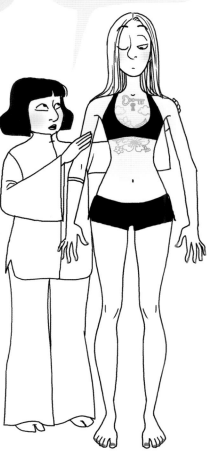

Also open your heart. Child's heart full of laughter. Your inner child lacks room to laugh and play. You must open up inside.
And it hurts a lot here. All knotted up.
This is the butterfly of your femininity and fertility. Spread its wings so you can give birth to yourself.

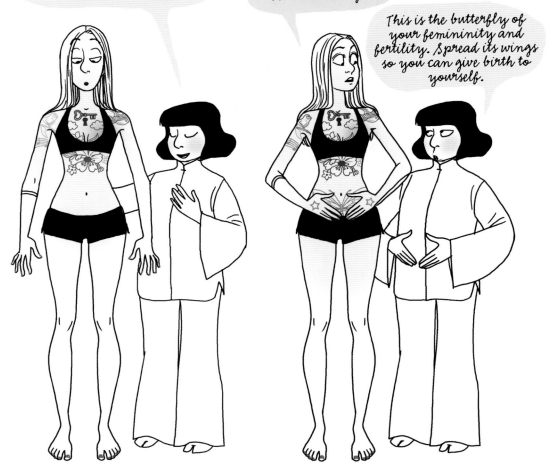

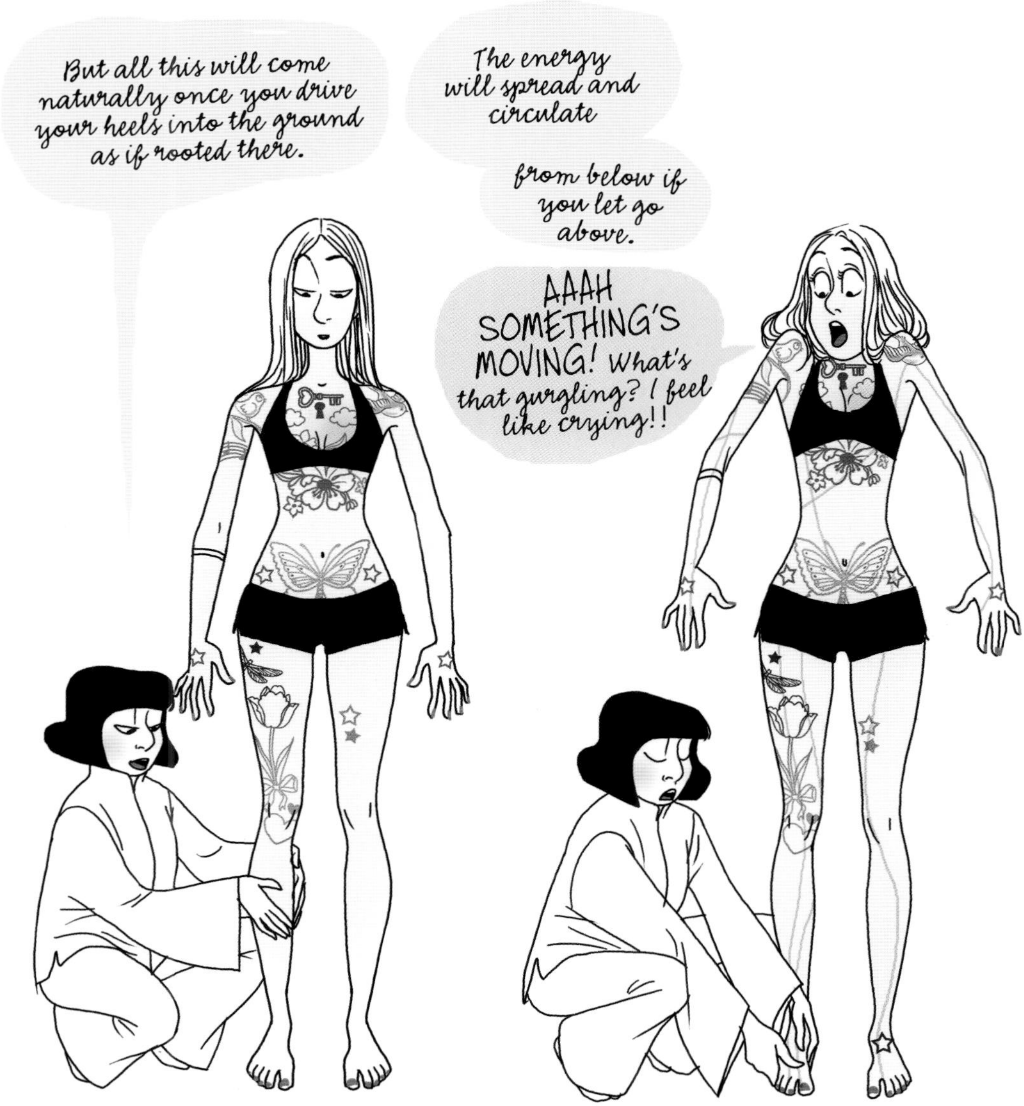

But all this will come naturally once you drive your heels into the ground as if rooted there.
The energy will spread and circulate
from below if you let go above.
AAAH SOMETHING'S MOVING! What's that gurgling? I feel like crying!!

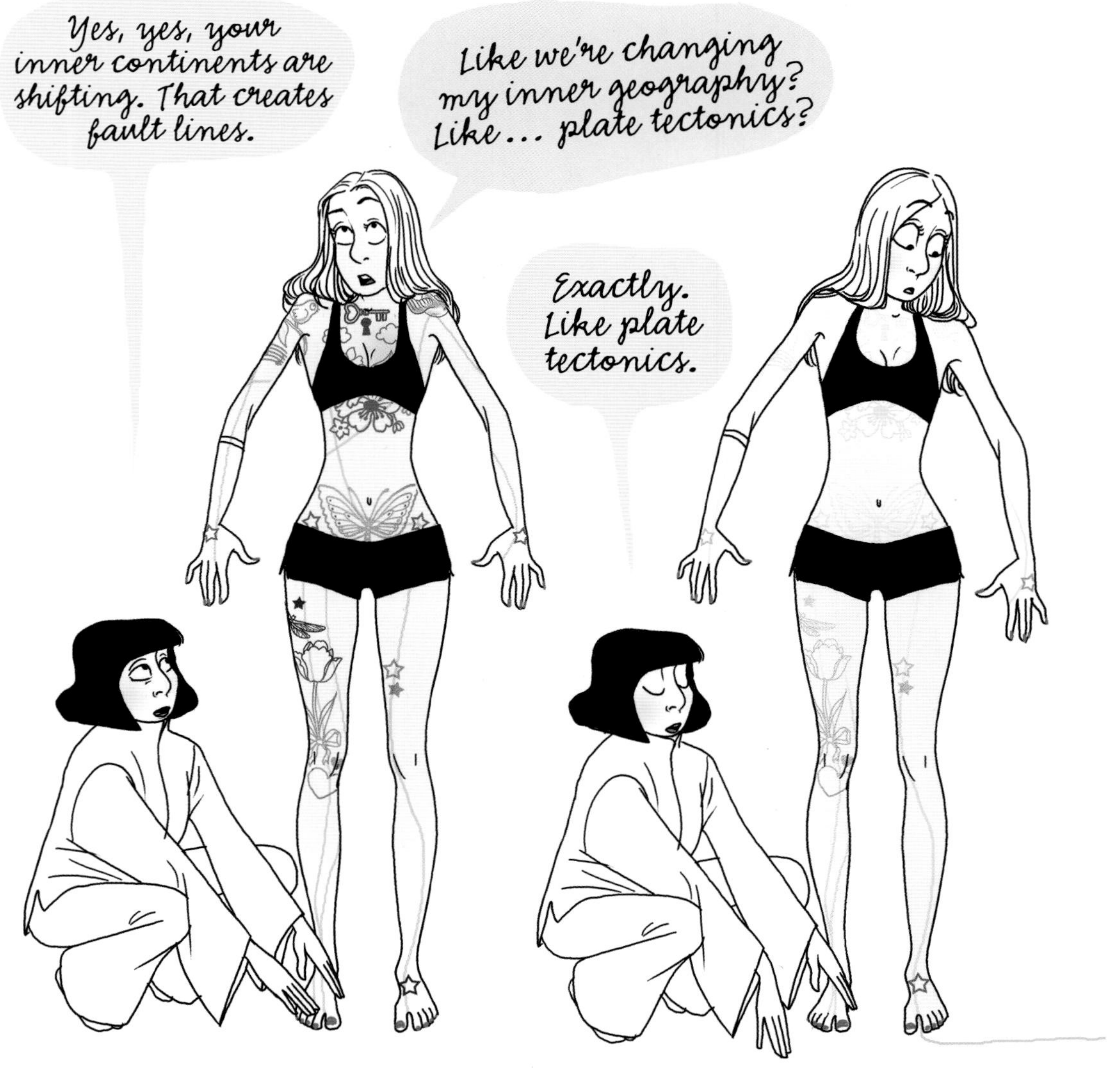
Yes, yes, your inner continents are shifting. That creates fault lines.
Like we're changing my inner geography? Like... plate tectonics?
Exactly. Like plate tectonics.

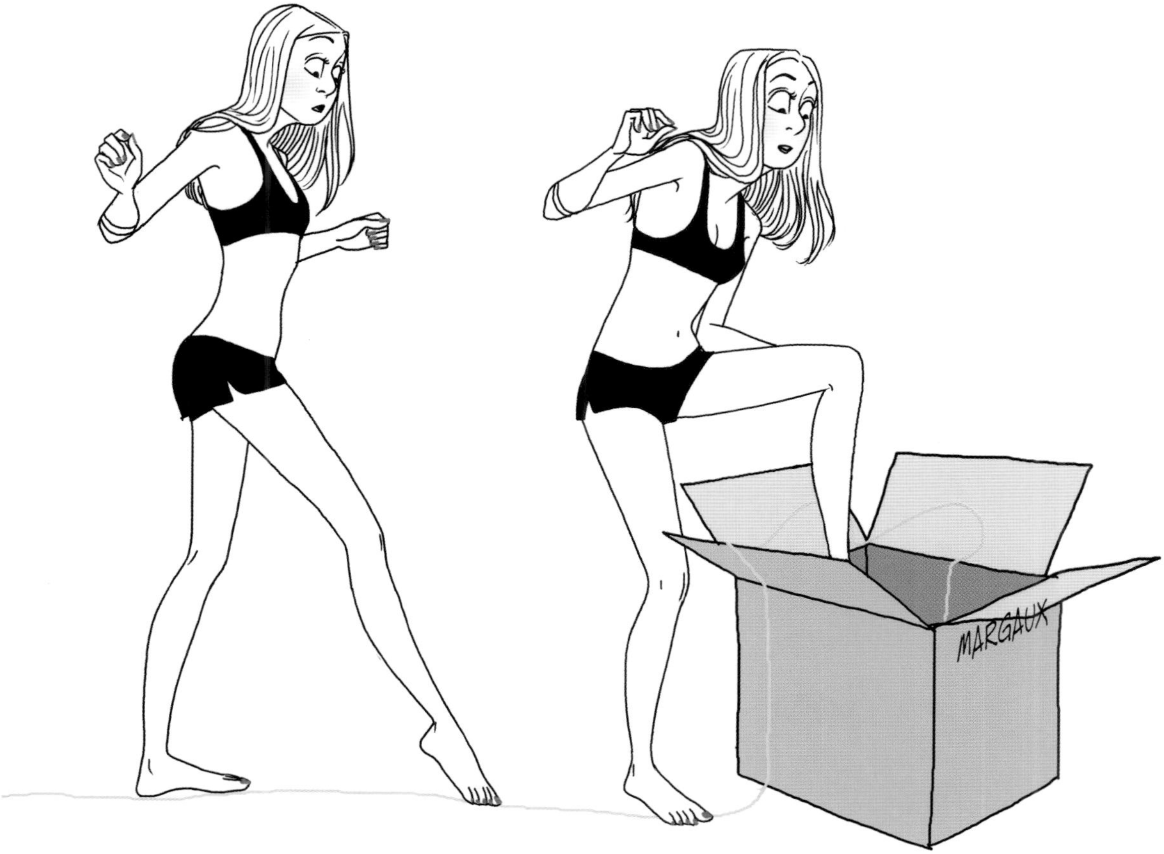
MARGAUX

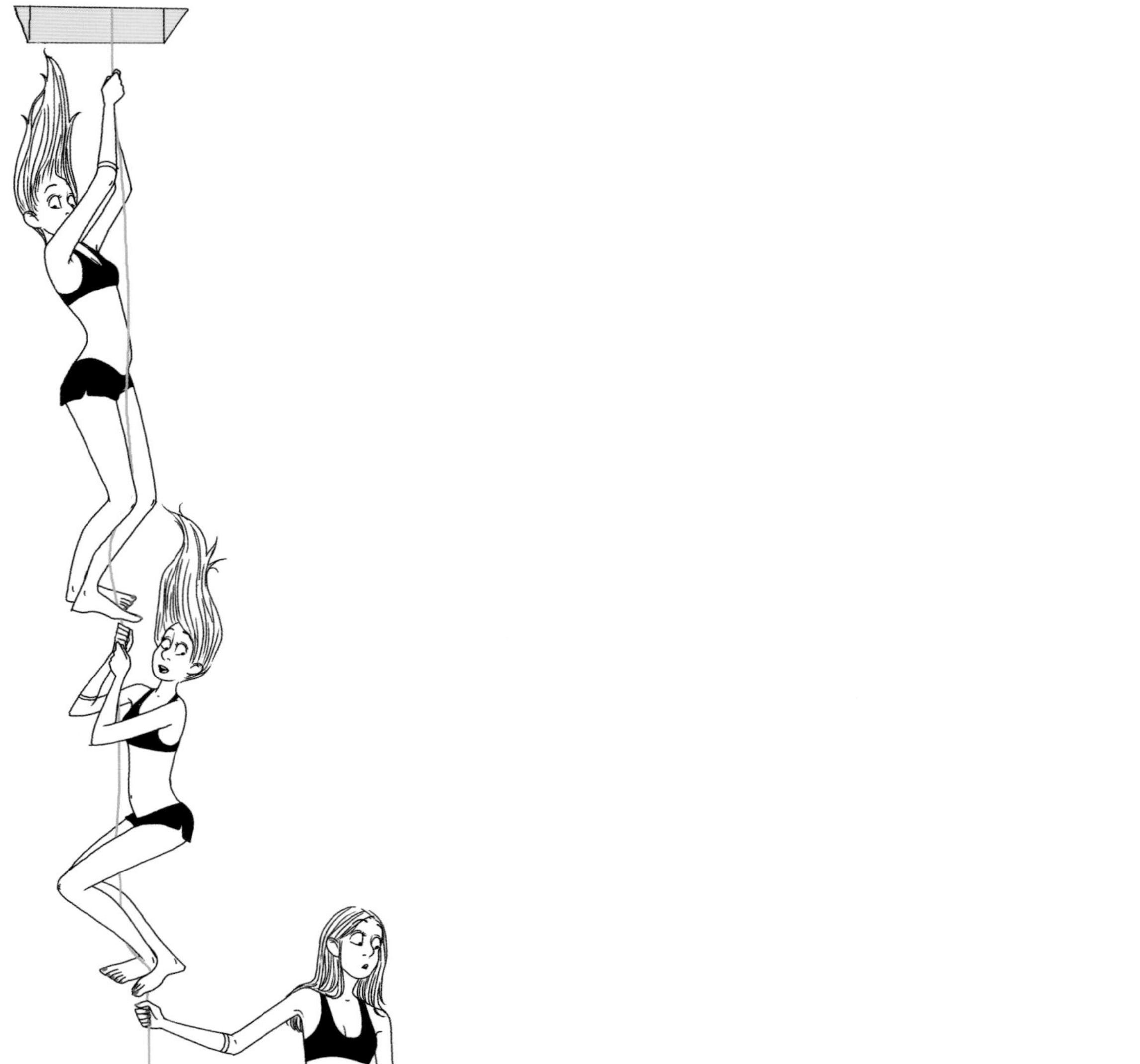

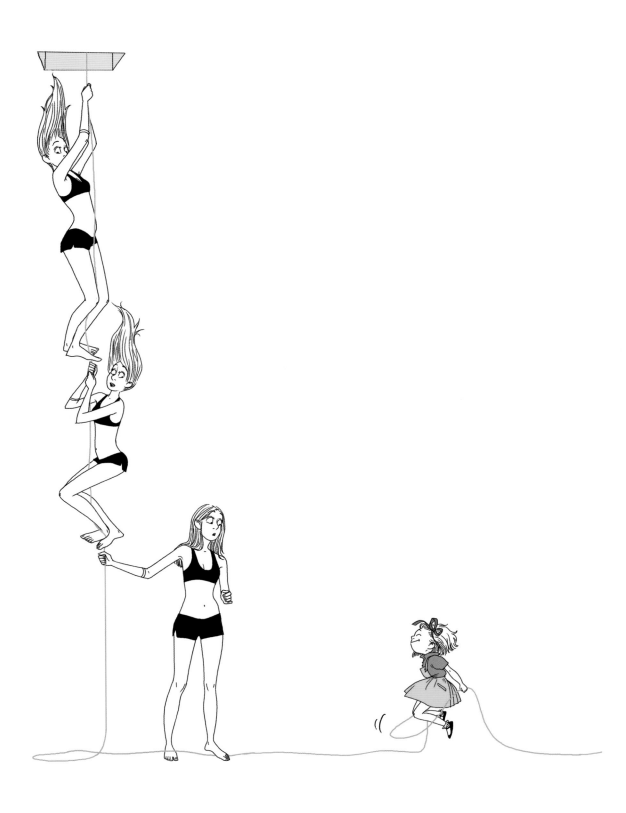

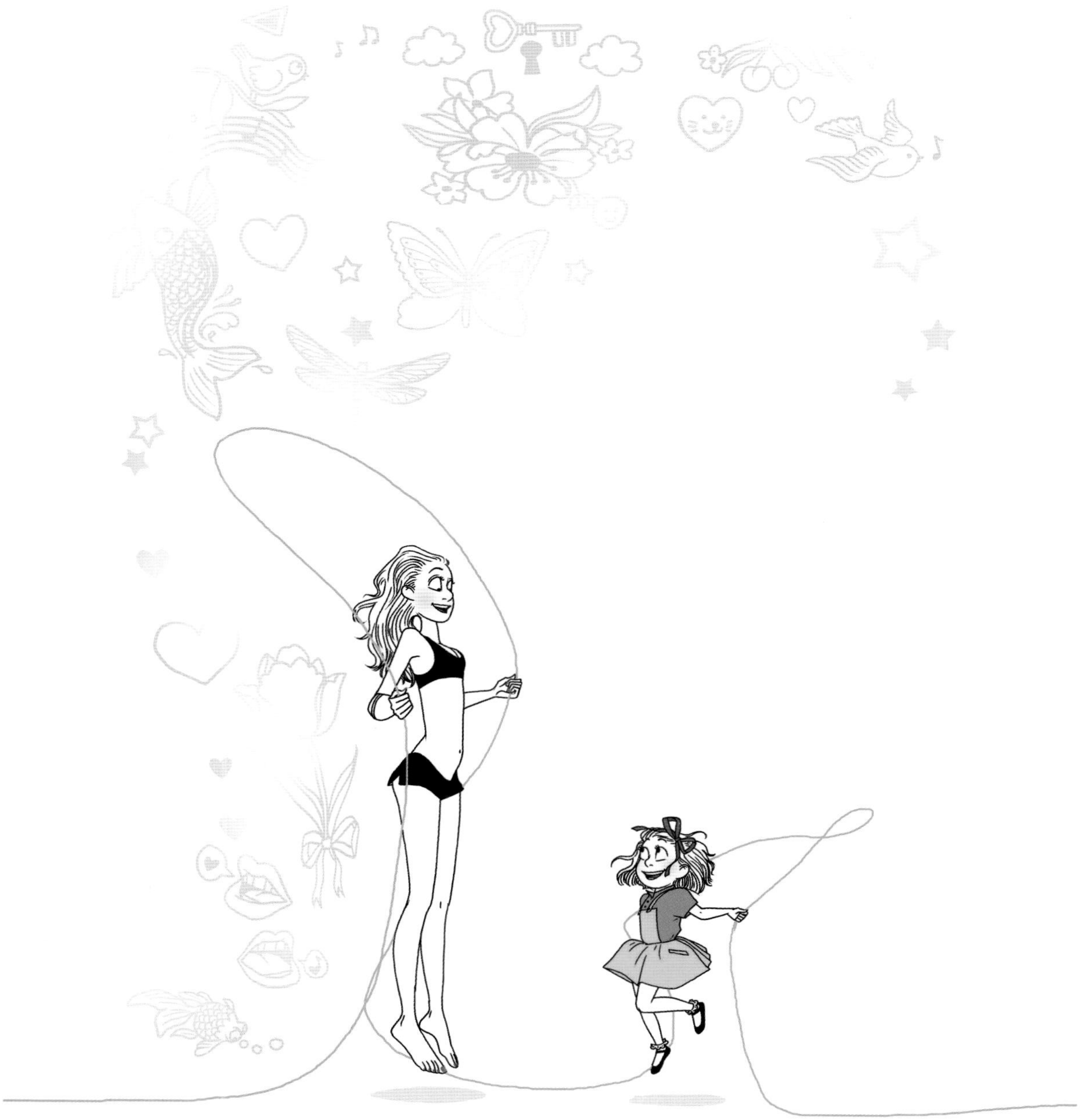

"In every real man a child is hidden that wants to play." ~ F. Nietzsche

Six and a Half Years Old

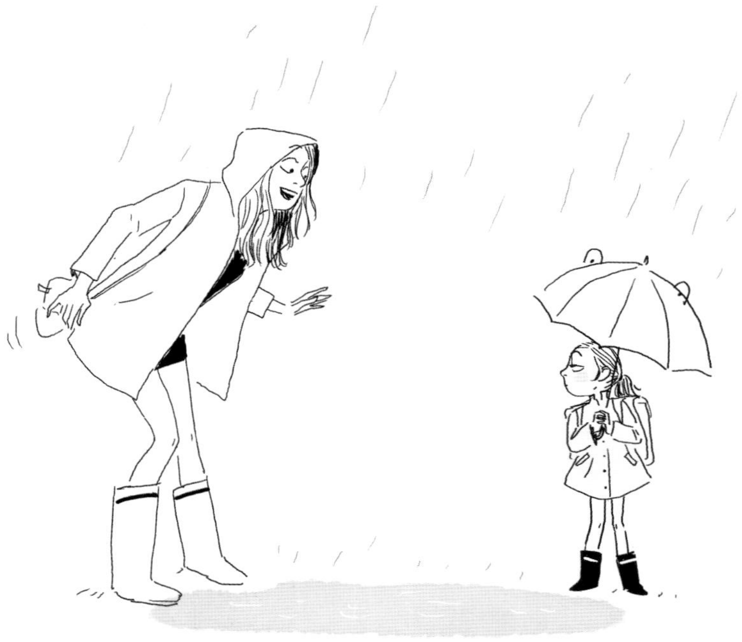

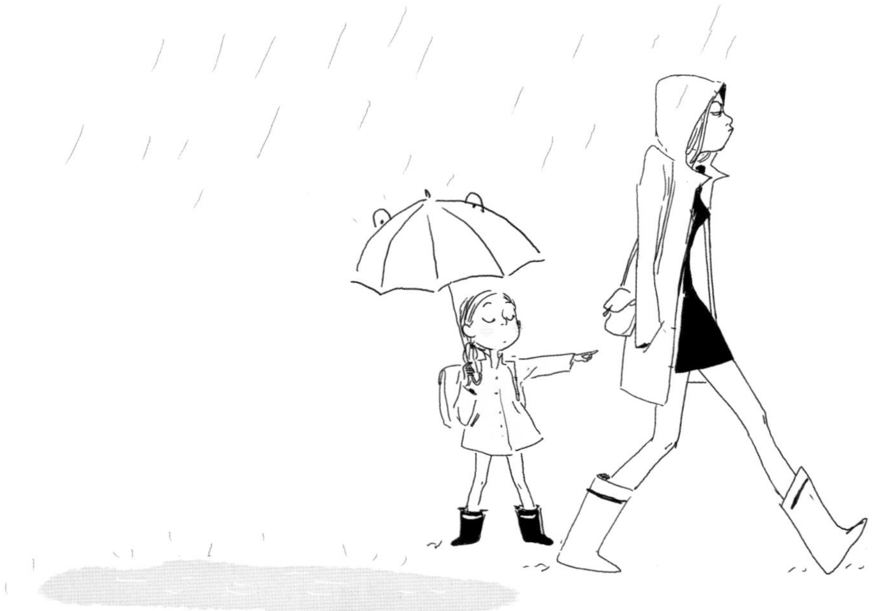

"Hello, you've reached Margaux. I can't come to the phone right now…"

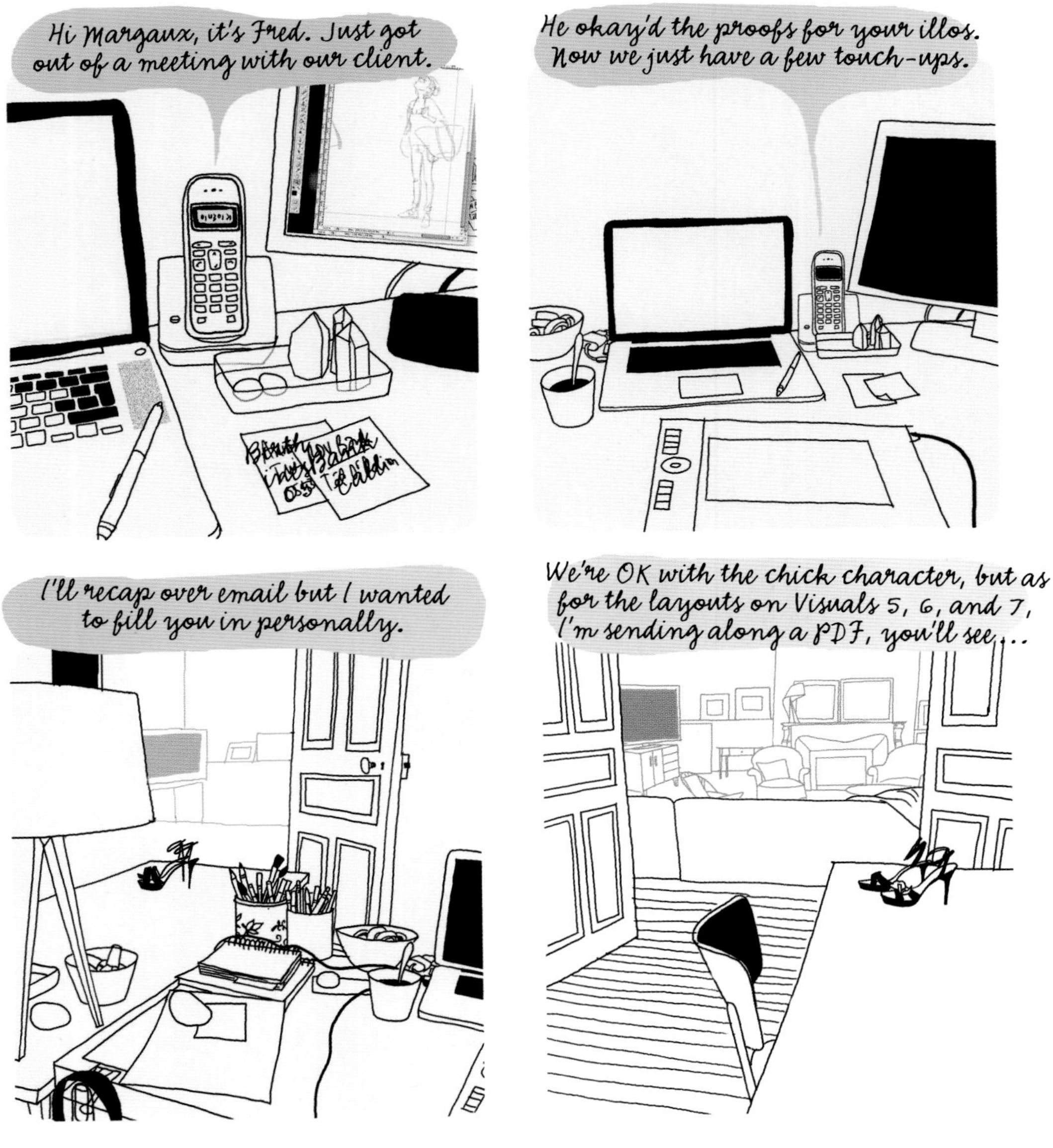

Hi Margaux, it's Fred. Just got out of a meeting with our client.
He okay'd the proofs for your illos. Now we just have a few touch-ups.
I'll recap over email but I wanted to fill you in personally.
We're OK with the chick character, but as for the layouts on Visuals 5, 6, and 7, I'm sending along a PDF, you'll see…

They don't jibe with the poster format, so could you maybe...
...have her sitting down? And for the design of Visual 5, in the office...
We were hoping for a more contemporary décor. Maggie's prepping some images for you, she'll be emailing them in 5...
As for Visuals 1 and 2...

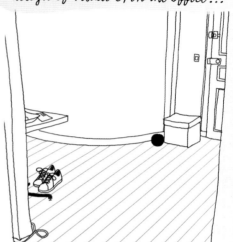

There were some
remarks on her outfit.

Maybe she could be wearing a
bit more? This is coming out in
autumn, y'know, and...

Anyway, that's about it, just sent you
the email recapping everything.

We're running up against the
printer's deadline, so timing wise...

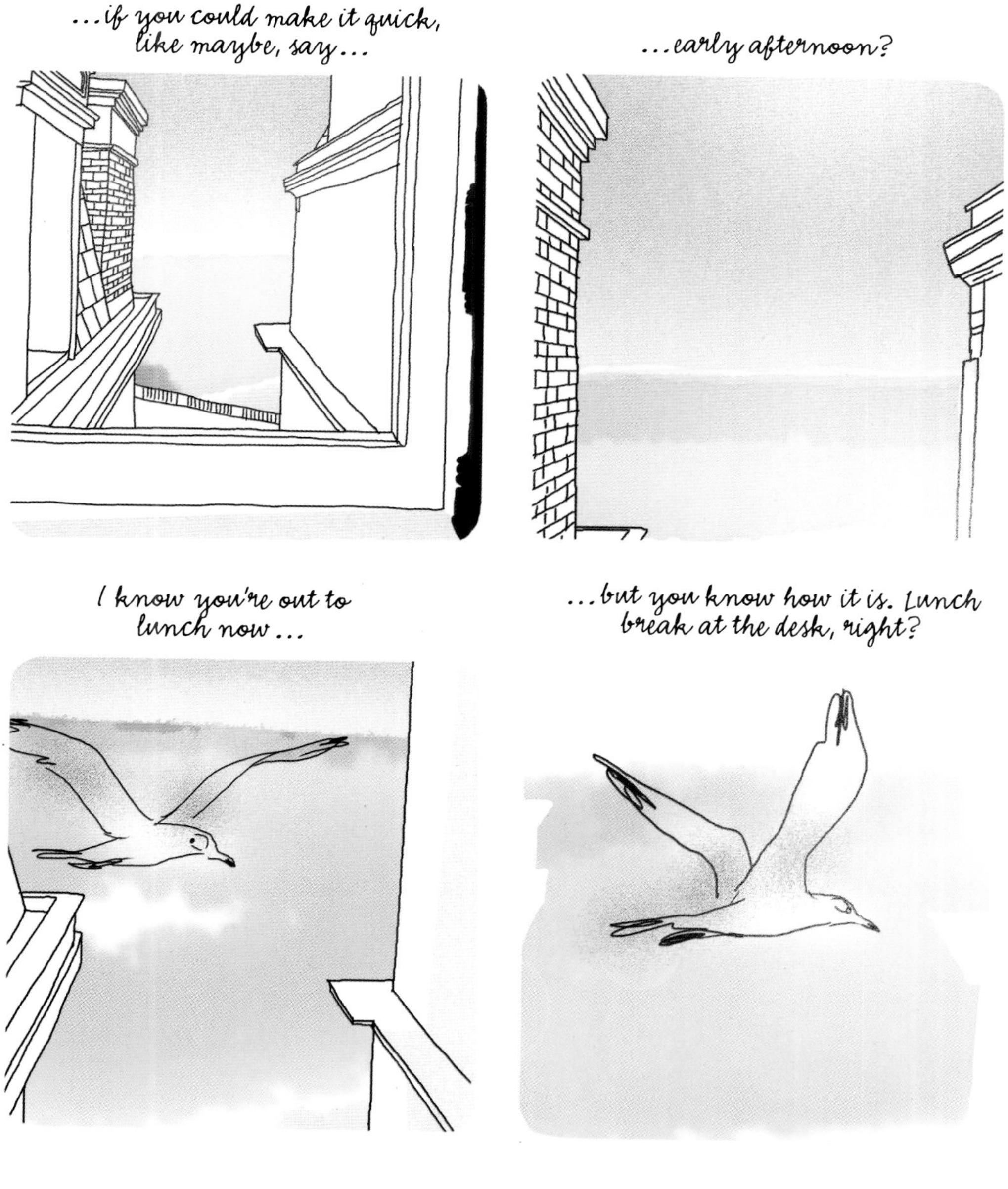
...if you could make it quick, like maybe, say...
...early afternoon?
I know you're out to lunch now...
...but you know how it is. Lunch break at the desk, right?

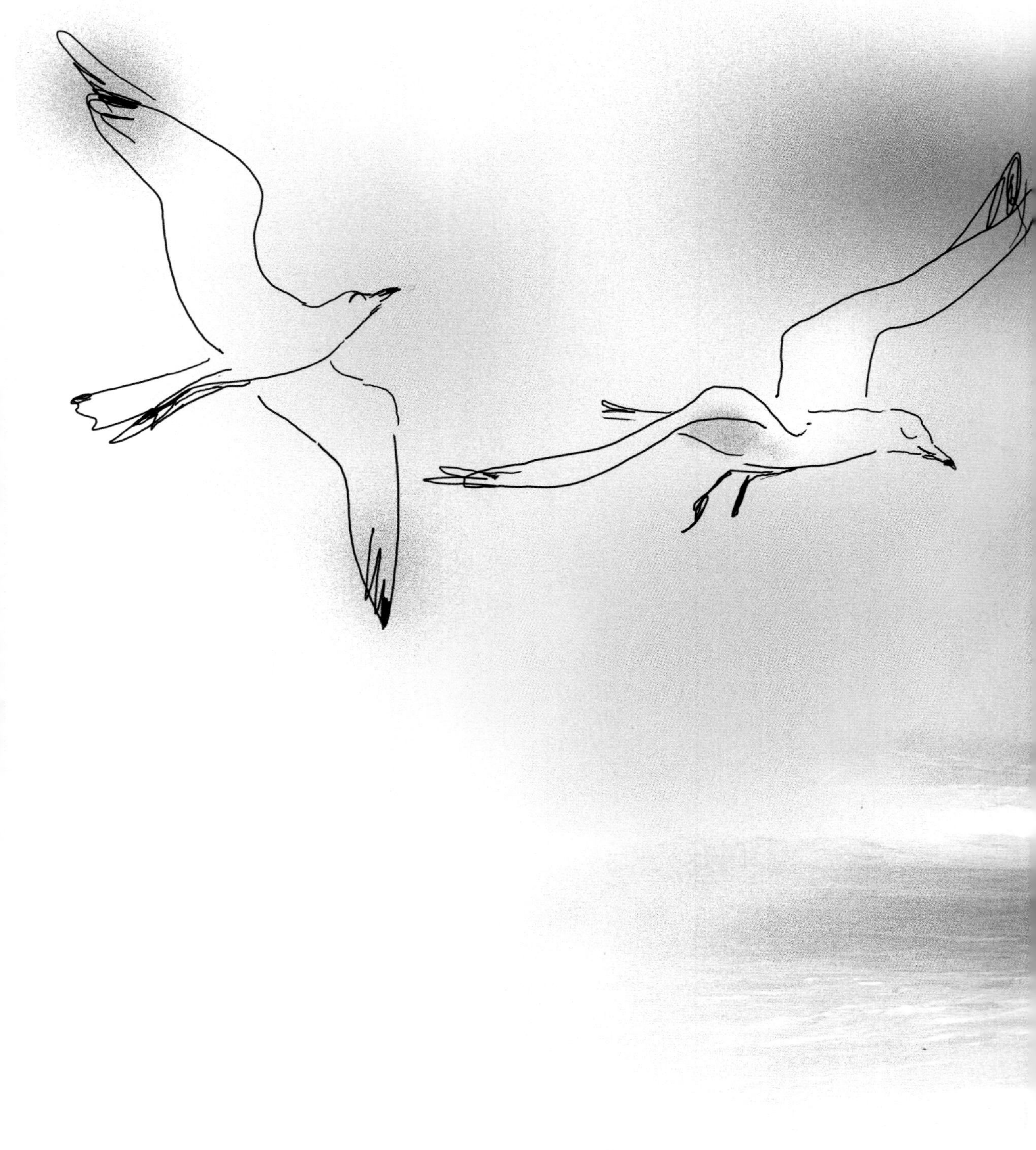

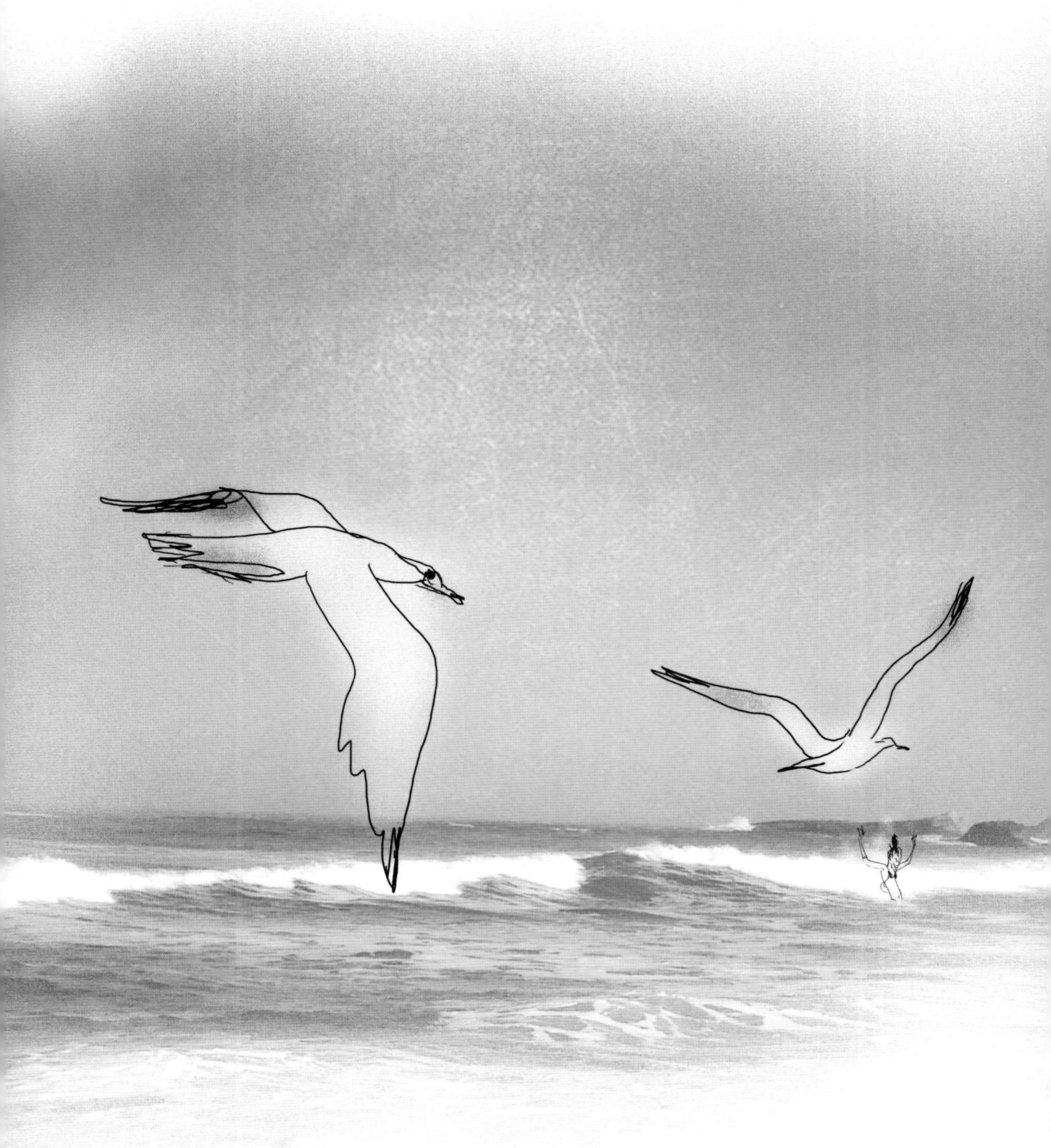

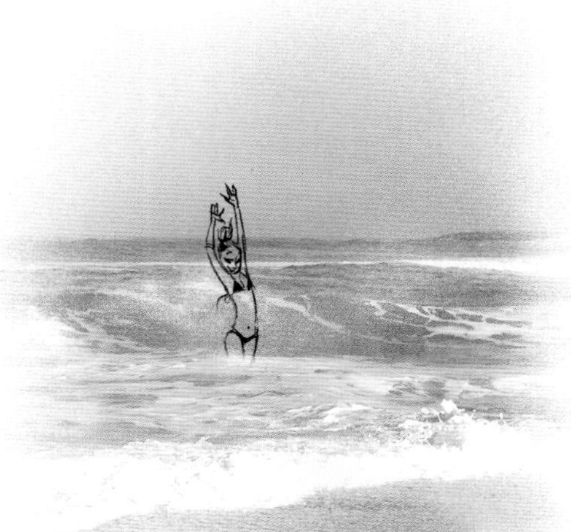

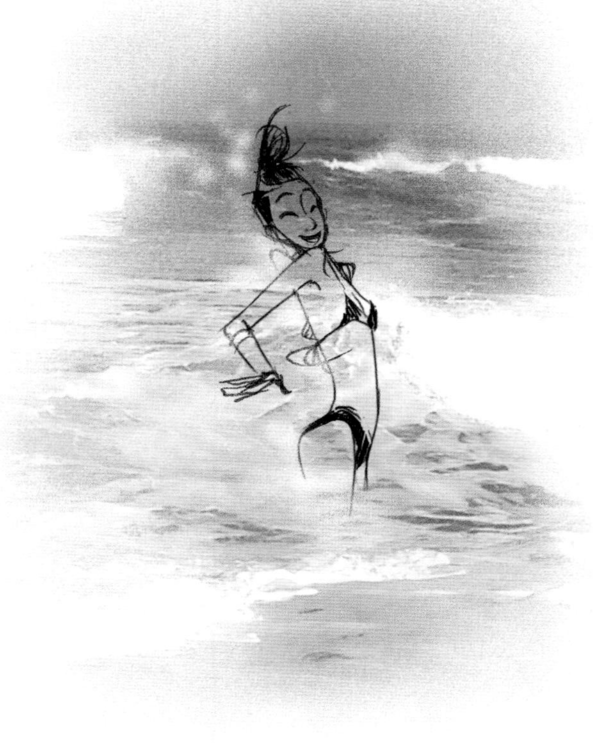

I'm too busy living…

THANKS

to Pumpkin, my sunshine.

The wee Basque fairies for their welcome.
And every good witch of the Southwest for
always lighting the stars along my path.
Thanks to my editor, Anaïs.

Thanks to all my readers, women and men
alike, for making this adventure possible.

And above all…

DIIING
DOONG!
Coming!

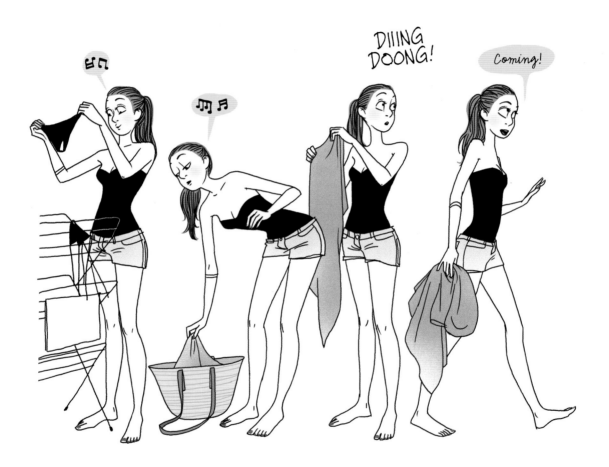

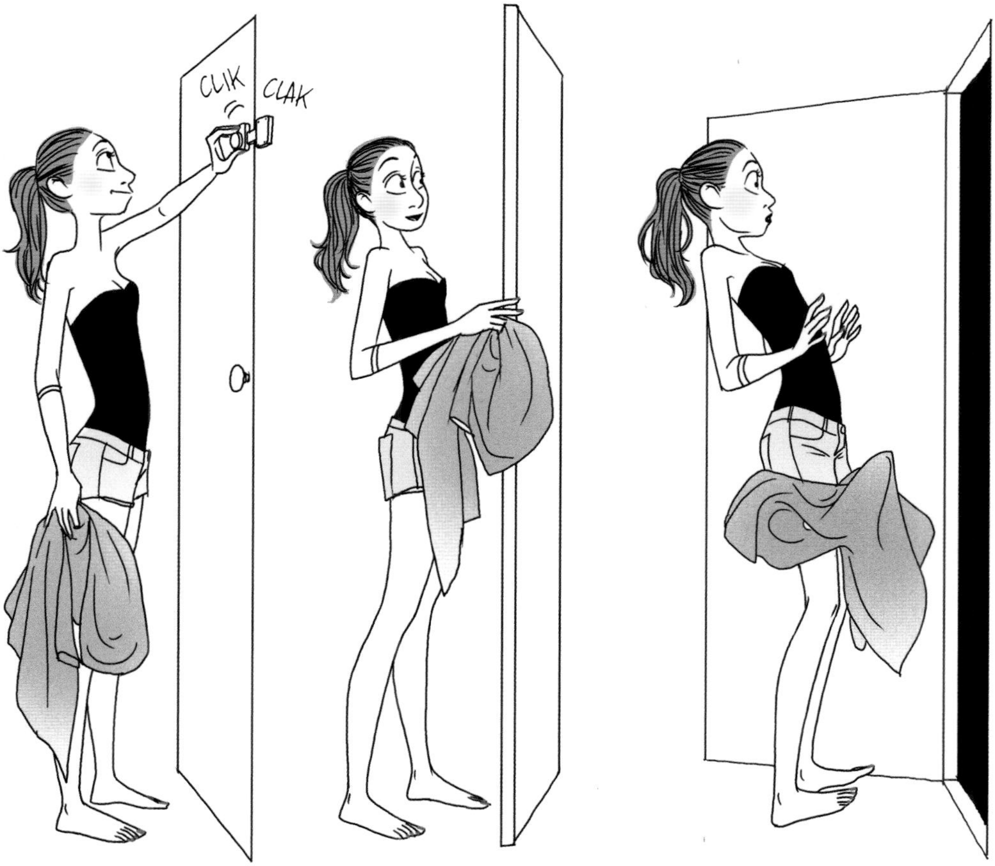
CLIK
CLAK

...thank YOU.

DISCOVER
GROUNDBREAKING TITLES

ASAF HANUKA
THE REALIST

LONG WALK TO VALHALLA
ADAM SMITH MATTHEW FOX

THE MARCH OF THE CRABS
THE CRABBY CONDITION
ARTHUR DE PINS

Jane
ALINE BROSH McKENNA
RAMÓN K. PÉREZ

ROYDEN LEPP
RUST
VOLUME ONE
VISITOR IN THE FIELD

MOUSE GUARD
THE BLACK AXE
DAVID PETERSEN

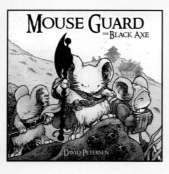

The Realist
Asaf Hanuka
ISBN: 978-1-60886-688-5 | $24.99 US

The Realist: Plug and Play
Asaf Hanuka
ISBN: 978-1-60886-953-4 | $24.99 US

Long Walk to Valhalla
Adam Smith, Matt Fox
ISBN: 978-1-60886-692-2 | $24.99 US

The March of The Crabs
Arthur De Pins
Volume 1: The Crabby Condition
ISBN: 978-1-60886-689-2 | $19.99 US
Volume 2: The Empire of the Crabs
ISBN: 978-1-68415-014-4 | $19.99 US

Jane
Aline Brosh McKenna, Ramón K. Pérez
ISBN: 978-1-60886-981-7 | $24.99 US

Rust
Royden Lepp
Volume 0: The Boy Soldier
ISBN: 978-1-60886-806-3 | $10.99 US
Volume 1: Visitor in the Field
ISBN: 978-1-60886-894-0 | $14.99 US
Volume 2: Secrets of the Cell
ISBN: 978-1-60886-895-7 | $14.99 US

Mouse Guard
David Petersen
Mouse Guard: Fall 1152
ISBN: 978-1-93238-657-8 | $24.95 US
Mouse Guard: Winter 1152
ISBN: 978-1-93238-674-5 | $24.95 US
Mouse Guard: The Black Axe
ISBN: 978-1-93639-306-0 | $24.95 US

The Cloud
K.I. Zachopoulos, Vincenzo Balzano
ISBN: 978-1-60886-725-7 | $24.99 US

Cursed Pirate Girl Coloring Book
Jeremy A. Bastian
ISBN: 978-1-60886-947-3 | $16.99 US

ARCHAIA™

AVAILABLE AT YOUR LOCAL COMICS SHOP AND BOOKSTORE
To find a comics shop in your area, visit www.comicshoplocator.com
WWW.**BOOM-STUDIOS**.COM